IRS Enrolled Agent
Exam Study Guide

The comprehensive guide to passing the IRS Special Enrollment Examination
For testing period May 1, 2016–February 28, 2017

Rain Hughes

Published by Fast Forward Academy, LLC

http://fastforwardacademy.com

(888) 798-PASS (7277)

© 2016 Fast Forward Academy, LLC.

All rights reserved. No part of this publication may be reproduced or distributed in any form or by any means, or stored in a database or retrieval system, without the prior written permission of the publisher.

ISBN-10: 1-938440-44-7

ISBN-13: 978-1-938440-44-1

First Edition – R1

Printed in the United States of America

The information provided in this publication is for educational purposes only, and does not necessarily reflect all laws, rules, or regulations for the tax year covered. This publication is designed to provide accurate and authoritative information concerning the subject matter covered, but it is sold with the understanding that the publisher is not engaged in rendering legal, accounting, or other professional services. If legal advice or other expert assistance is required, the services of a competent professional person should be sought.

To the extent any advice relating to a Federal tax issue is contained in this communication, it was not written or intended to be used, and cannot be used, for the purpose of (a) avoiding any tax related penalties that may be imposed on you or any other person under the Internal Revenue Code, or (b) promoting, marketing or recommending to another person any transaction or matter addressed in this communication.

About Us

Fast Forward Academy, LLC provides companies and individuals around the world with the tools to manage their professional education needs efficiently. Our principal focus is to supply rapid training and streamlined continuing education to professionals in the fields of taxation, securities, and insurance. The name "Fast Forward Academy" reflects the scope of our mission—helping students and professionals accomplish more in less time. To realize this goal, we make every effort to provide the most useful and efficient exam prep material in the marketplace, all designed to help our students *Learn Fast and Pass*.

Online Study Bank

Register online at **fastforwardacademy.com** and gain access to a number of resources that will help you prepare for your exam.

- View your overall performance trend.
- Track your ***study time***, including time per question.
- Focus on areas you need to improve with a complete ***performance*** analysis and ***opportunities filters***.
- The ***session history reports*** track each question, answer, and rationale that you see.

Practice Exams

Using our advanced testing platform, you can create simulated exams for each part of the Special Enrollment Exam (SEE). Once you complete an exam, you can access numerous analytics and reports to measure your performance.

- We Provide Feedback. See how you measure up against the community, and track your progress with detailed analytics. Every answer is tracked to measure your progress.
- Move from question to question as needed—forward, backward, or jump to a specific question.
- An exact timer keeps track of the total test time to measure how fast you answer each question.
- Reports provide performance results, rationale, correct answers, and all the important metrics you need to *Learn Fast and Pass*.
- View your performance and compare yourself to the community for each section of the SEE. This report includes performance details specific to subjects covered on the exam. Areas of weakness are highlighted so you know where to focus your time efficiently.
- View completed exams and dive into specific questions, answers, and rationale.

Preface

The use of the singular male pronoun throughout this text is not intended to suggest any gender bias. It is used to make the text easier to read. In every instance, the word "he" should be understood to refer equally to "he or she." Likewise, all references to singular taxpayers should be understood to refer to plural taxpayers, such as joint filers or married persons filing separately, except where it is specified or clear from the context that only the singular reference is appropriate.

Introduction

Thank you for choosing our *IRS Enrolled Agent Exam Study Guide*. This course, along with our online question bank, will provide you with everything you need to pass the IRS Special Enrollment Exam. We designed our course to save you time, utilizing the experience of Enrolled Agents, CPAs, and former IRS employees. It provides only the *essential* material you need to pass the test and leaves out unnecessary information that would only bog you down. Our course is half the size … on purpose!

Outline Format for Study-Efficiency

The IRS has a "study kit" for the exam that lists 112 separate forms, form instructions, and publications that "provide much of the basic information to assist you in preparing for the examination." There are thousands of pages within these documents, yet not one is designed to help you prepare for the exam. While the information within these publications may appear overwhelming, you do not need to remember it all to pass.

In the field of taxation, there are often exceptions, additional details, or extenuating circumstances that could affect a situation. While this course is comprehensive, it does not include every rule (or variation of a rule) that "could" appear on the exam. This is intentional. Spending time on rules that do not show up on the exam will not help you pass. In this course, we cover the relevant information you must know to pass. If you stray too far from the path, you risk losing focus on the important details needed for success.

The chapters within our study guide contain comprehensive outlines whenever possible. This format helps you better *visualize* and *retain* the important points of each section, resulting in maximum study efficiency and reduced study time.

Understanding the Symbols Used in this Book

A "Key Concept" you should master. This information is very important in your review.

Practical information you might want to remember.

An example to demonstrate a point or concept.

About the IRS Special Enrollment Exam

The EA Exam, officially known as the Special Enrollment Examination (SEE), is a three-part exam administered by Prometric on behalf of the Internal Revenue Service. You will take each part as a separate, 100-question exam. You will have up to 3 1/2 hours to complete each exam, which equates to just over two minutes per question. We suggest that you not study for all three exams at once. Pass one exam, and then move on to the next one. If you are like most people, you will probably study the Individuals (Part 1) exam first. Part 2 is the most challenging of the three exams, so after you pass Part 1, we suggest you take the representation exam next. There is much less content to study, and passing it can give you a boost of confidence going into the last exam. The IRS does not require you to take the tests in any particular order.

Part 1 – Individuals	Percent of Exam
Section 1: Preliminary Work and Taxpayer Data	20%
Section 2: Income and Assets	25%
Section 3: Deductions and Credits	25%
Section 4: Taxation and Advice	17%
Section 5: Specialized Returns for Individuals	13%
TOTAL	**100%**

Part 2 – Businesses	Percent of Exam
Section 1: Business Entities	33%
Section 2: Business Financial Information	46%
Section 3: Specialized Returns and Taxpayers	21%
TOTAL	**100%**

Part 3 – Representation, Practices, and Procedures	Percent of Exam
Section 1: Practices and Procedures	30%
Section 2: Representation before the IRS	28%
Section 3: Specific Types of Representation	22%
Section 4: Completion of the Filing Process	20%
TOTAL	**100%**

A new examination period commences each year on May 1 and continues through the end of February the following year. No testing occurs during March or April. The period that begins on May 1, 2016, will include questions based on the 2015 tax year, as the law exists on Dec 31, 2015. A passing score on each part of the exam is required before the IRS will admit an enrolled agent to practice. Scaled scores are determined by ranking your exam results against others taking the exam, on a scale ranging between 40 and 130. A score of 105 is the minimum required to pass. Test results are available immediately following the exam. Those who pass are informed, but they do not receive a score. Those who fail receive a score and a diagnostic report indicating the areas of weakness. A candidate may re-take each part up to four times during each testing period. Once a candidate passes the first part, he must pass the other two parts of the exam during a two-year window.

How to Register for the IRS Special Enrollment Exam

To schedule an exam, you need a Preparer Tax Identification Number (PTIN). To obtain a PTIN, you must complete a W-12 by mail, fax, or online at www.irs.gov. The PTIN user fee is $50.00. The online method is quickest and provides you with the instantaneous issuance of the PTIN.

Examinations are administered by computer at Prometric testing centers. Currently, the Special Enrollment Examination is given at nearly 300 Prometric testing centers located across the United States and internationally. Test centers are located in most major metropolitan areas. Once you have your PTIN, you may register for your exam online at www.prometric.com/irs.

Question Types

The IRS Special Enrollment Exam contains only multiple-choice questions. Each provides four options from which you choose your answer. Three different multiple-choice formats are used.

Format 1 – Direct question

Which of the following entities are required to file Form 709, U.S. Gift Tax Return?

A. An individual
B. An estate or trust
C. A corporation
D. All of the above

Format 2 – Incomplete sentence

Supplemental wages are compensation paid in addition to an employee's regular wages. They **do not** include payments for the following:

A. Accumulated sick leave
B. Nondeductible moving expenses
C. Vacation pay
D. Travel reimbursements paid at the Federal Government per diem rate

Format 3 – All of the following except

There are five tests that must be met for you to claim an exemption for a dependent. Which of the following is **not** a requirement?

A. Citizen or Resident Test
B. Member of Household or Relationship Test
C. Disability Test
D. Joint Return Test

Table of Contents

About Us v
Online Study Bank v
Practice Exams v
Preface v
Introduction vi
About the IRS Special Enrollment Exam vii

SEE EXAM PART 1 **INDIVIDUALS** 1

CH 1 FILING INFORMATION 1
General Requirements 1
Accounting Periods and Methods 5
Filing Requirements 6
Foreign Account and Asset Reporting 7
Aliens 13
Form 1040 and Schedules 14
Form 1040NR 18
Tax Withholding and Estimated Tax 20
Nonresident Income Taxes and Withholding 21
Filing Status 23
Personal Exemptions and Dependents 25

CH 2 GROSS INCOME 29
Wages, Salaries, and Other Earnings 29
Special Rules for Certain Employees 33
Interest Income 34
Dividends and Other Corporate Distributions 35
Rental Income and Expenses 36
Social Security Benefits 40
Retirement Plans, Pensions, and Annuities 40
Other Income 42

CH 3 DEPRECIATION AND BASIS 45
Depreciation 45
Basis of Property 46

CH 4 GAINS AND LOSSES 53
Disposition or Sale of Property 53
Reporting Gains and Losses 56

CH 5 ITEMS EXCLUDED FROM GROSS INCOME 63
Items Excluded from Gross Income 63
Municipal Bond Interest 64
Gain on Sale of Main Home 65
Discharge of Qualified Principal Residence Indebtedness 67
Employee Achievement Awards 67
Fringe Benefits 67
Housing Allowance for Members of Clergy 69
Military and Government Disability Pensions 70
Education-related Benefits 70
Workers' Compensation 73
Compensation for Sickness or Injury 74
Life Insurance Proceeds 74
Foreign Earned Income Exclusion and Foreign Housing Exclusion 75

CH 6 ADJUSTMENTS TO GROSS INCOME 77
Individual Retirement Arrangements (IRAs) 77
Health Savings Accounts (HSAs) 85
Self-employed Health Insurance 86

Moving Expenses	86
Alimony	88
Education Related Adjustments	89
Other Adjustments to Income	90

CH 7 STANDARD AND ITEMIZED DEDUCTIONS 93
- Standard Deduction 93
- Itemized Deductions 94
- Medical and Dental Expenses 94
- Taxes 96
- Interest Expense 97
- Charitable Contributions 98
- Non-business Casualty and Theft Losses 101
- Miscellaneous Deductions Subject to the 2% Limit 102
- Deductions NOT Subject to the 2% Limit 109
- Nondeductible Expenses 109

CH 8 TAXES AND CREDITS 111
- Tax Calculations 111
- Alternative Minimum Tax 112
- Net Investment Income Tax 113
- Tax on Investment Income of Certain Children 113
- Taxes for Household Employees 114
- Individual Shared Responsibility Payment 115
- Child and Dependent Care Credit (Non-refundable) 116
- Education Credits 117
- Adoption Credit (Non-refundable) 120
- Earned Income Credit (Refundable) 121
- First-time Homebuyer Credit (Refundable, but expired in 2011) 123
- Credit for Elderly or the Disabled (Non-refundable) 124
- Child Tax Credit (Non-refundable) 125
- Foreign Tax Credit (Non-refundable) 126
- Saver's Credit (Non-refundable) 126

CH 9 ESTATE TAX AND GIFT TAX 127
- Overview 127
- Gift Tax Returns (Form 709) 128
- Estate Tax Returns (Form 706) 129

SEE EXAM PART 2 BUSINESSES 133

CH 10 BUSINESS ENTITIES 135
- Business Entity Overview 135
- Employees 136
- Tax Withholding and Reporting 137
- Informational Returns 139
- Accounting Periods 144
- Accounting Methods 145
- Inventory 146
- Uniform Capitalization Rules 150
- Recordkeeping 151

CH 11 BUSINESS TAXATION 153
- Expenses and Deductions 153
- Employee Compensation 161
- General Business Credits 165
- Net Operating Losses 168
- Loss Limitations 169
- Not-for-profit Activities 171

    Employer Provisions in the Affordable Care Act 171
CH 12 BUSINESS PROPERTY 173
    Property Types 173
    Depreciation 174
    Section 179 Deduction 178
    Basis of Property 179
    Like-kind Exchanges 184

CH 13 CORPORATIONS 189
    Businesses Taxed as Corporations 189
    Property Exchanged for Stock 190
    Filing and Paying Income Taxes 192
    Income, Deductions, and Special Provisions 194
    Shareholder Earnings and Profits (E&P) 195
    Distribution and Recognition Requirements 197
    Redemption of Stock 199
    Special Deductions 199
    Figuring Tax 201
    S Corporations 202

CH 14 PARTNERSHIPS 207
    Forming a Partnership 207
    Partnership Return (Form 1065) 209
    Limitations on Losses, Deductions, and Credits 211
    Unrealized Receivables and Inventory 211
    Partnership Distributions to Partners 212
    Transactions between Partnership and Partners 215
    Basis in Partnership 217
    Disposition of Partner's Interest 219

CH 15 RETIREMENT PLANS 221
    Common Terms 221
    SEP IRA 222
    SIMPLE IRA 224
    403(b) Plans 225
    Qualified Plans 226

CH 16 SPECIALIZED RETURNS 235
    The Final Return 235
    Estate Income Tax 237
    Trusts 239
    Farmers 243
    Exempt Organizations 246

SEE EXAM PART 3 REPRESENTATION, PRACTICES, AND PROCEDURES 251

CH 17 PREPARING RETURNS 253
    Return Preparers 253
    Penalties 254
    Taxpayer Supporting Documentation 260
    Applying to Become an Authorized E-File Provider 260
    The E-File Process 262
    Identity Theft 267

CH 18 PRACTICE BEFORE THE IRS 271
    Practice Before the IRS 271
    Preparer Considerations 272
    Enrollment 273
    Continuing Professional Education 274

Duties and Restrictions	275
Sanctions and Penalties	279
Disciplinary Proceedings	280

CH 19 REPRESENTATION BEFORE THE IRS 287

Power of Attorney	287
Audits/Examinations	289
Appeals Conference	293
Penalties and Interest	294
Collection Process	299

CH 20 TAX LAW 305

The Court System	305
Burden of Proof	306
Tax Law and Regulations	306
Legal Reference	307

GLOSSARY 311
APPENDIX 323
INDEX 325

SEE EXAM PART 1
INDIVIDUALS

1 Filing Information

General Requirements · Accounting Periods and Methods · Filing Requirements · Aliens
Tax Withholding and Estimated Tax · Filing Status · Personal Exemptions and Dependents

This chapter summarizes some of the general rules and requirements contained in IRS Publications 17, 519 and 597, and Form 1040, 1040NR and 1040NR-EZ instructions regarding the preparation of U.S. Federal Income Tax Returns.

General Requirements

Social Security Number

Enter a valid *Social Security number* (SSN) for all parties on the return, including each dependent claimed. If no SSN is available, list the *individual taxpayer identification number* (ITIN) or *adoption taxpayer identification number* (ATIN) when applicable. If a child was born and died in the same year and a taxpayer does not have an SSN for the child, he may attach a copy of the child's birth certificate, death certificate, or hospital records instead. The document must show the child was born alive.

Individual Taxpayer Identification Number

An *Individual Taxpayer Identification Number (ITIN)* is a tax processing number issued by the IRS upon receipt of *Form W-7*. The IRS issues ITINs to individuals required to have a U.S. taxpayer identification number who are not eligible for a Social Security Number (SSN) from the Social Security Administration. ITINs issue regardless of immigration status because both resident and nonresident aliens may have a U.S. filing or reporting requirement under the Internal Revenue Code. Individuals must have a filing requirement and file a valid federal income tax return to receive an ITIN, unless an exception applies. Each ITIN is a nine-digit number that always begins with the number nine.

Filing Deadlines

The income tax return is due by the 15th day of the 4th month after the close of the tax year. Usually, this falls on April 15. If the due date falls on a Saturday, Sunday or legal holiday, the due date is delayed until the next business day. The IRS considers a paper return "on time" when it arrives with a proper address and sufficient postage and bears a postmark on or before the due date. A return sent using IRS e-file is on time if the *authorized electronic return transmitter* postmarks the transmission by the due date.

Tax Payments

A non-business taxpayer with tax due from a tax return can pay by check, money order, credit card or debit card. If you're an individual taxpayer, IRS Direct Pay offers you a free, electronic payment method directly from your bank account. Online payments are available at https://www.irs.gov/payments. Checks should be made payable to the "United States Treasury." The IRS instructs taxpayers to write identifying information on the check, including the first SSN used on the return. A payment by mail should include a *Form 1040-V Payment Voucher*, although it is not a requirement.

Installments

A taxpayer may request a monthly installment plan if he is unable to pay the full amount of tax owed. Before applying for any payment agreement, a taxpayer must file all required tax returns. Installment agreements generally provide up to 72 months to pay the tax. In certain circumstances, the payment period could be longer or the amount agreed to could be less than the amount of tax owed. An installment plan is not valid unless accepted by the IRS. However, if a taxpayer owes $10,000 or less and meets certain other criteria, the IRS <u>must</u> accept the request. Those requirements are:

- During the past five tax years, the taxpayer (and spouse if filing jointly) has timely filed all income tax returns and paid any tax due, and has not entered into an installment agreement for payment of income tax.
- The IRS determines that the taxpayer cannot pay the tax owed in full when it is due and the taxpayer gives the IRS any information needed to make that determination.
- The taxpayer agrees to pay the full amount within three years and to comply with the tax laws while the agreement is in effect.

An *installment agreement* generally requires equal monthly payments, and the taxpayer must fully pay all of the tax owed within the time left in the 10-year period during which the IRS can collect the tax. If a taxpayer cannot pay in full by the end of the collection period, but can pay some of the tax owed, he may qualify for a partial payment installment agreement. To request an installment agreement a taxpayer can attach *Form 9465 Installment Agreement Request* to the front of his tax return, or–in cases where the return is already filed–mail it directly to the IRS.

> If the balance due is not more than $50,000, the taxpayer can apply online for a payment agreement instead of filing Form 9465. To do that, go to IRS.gov and enter *Online Payment Agreement* in the search box.

If the IRS approves a request, they send a notice detailing the terms of the agreement and request a fee of $120 ($52 if payments are by electronic funds withdrawal). Lower income taxpayers may qualify to pay a reduced fee of $43. Once approved, a taxpayer may submit a request to modify or terminate the installment agreement. This request will not suspend the statute of limitations on collection. While the IRS considers a request to modify or terminate the installment agreement, the taxpayer must comply with the existing agreement.

If a taxpayer is able to pay the full amount owed within 120 days, he should not request an installment agreement on Form 9465. Instead, he can call or apply online to establish a request to pay in full. A taxpayer who can pay within the 120-day period can avoid paying the fee to set up the agreement.

A taxpayer with outstanding tax liability (including penalties and interest) of $50,000 or less may file Form 9465, or 9465-FS. This is known as a *streamlined installment agreement* because the <u>IRS does not require a financial statement</u> (Form 433-A, Form 433-B, Form 433-D, or Form 433-F) or substantial disclosure of financial information. A liability greater than $50,000 can be considered if the taxpayer pays down the liability to $50,000 or less prior to the agreement being granted. Generally, a taxpayer must pay off the balance due on a streamlined IA within a 72-month period.

If the total amount the taxpayer owes is greater than $25,000 but not more than $50,000, the taxpayer may use a slightly expanded *Form 9465-FS Installment Agreement Request.* This form has an extra page (Part II) with additional information to complete. A taxpayer using Form 9465-FS must agree to a Direct Debit Installment Agreement (DDIA) to qualify for an IA without completing a financial statement (Form 433-F, Collection Information Statement).

The IRS generally may not levy against property:

- While a request for an installment agreement is being considered,
- While an installment agreement is in effect,
- For 30 days after a request for an agreement has been rejected,
- For 30 days after termination of an installment agreement (due to taxpayer default), or
- While the IRS Office of Appeals is evaluating an appeal of the rejection or termination.

However, the IRS may file a Notice of Federal Tax Lien to secure the government's interest against other creditors. Termination of an installment agreement may cause the filing of a Notice of Federal Tax Lien and/or an IRS levy action.

Refund Deposits

A taxpayer who is due a refund due to an overpayment of tax may apply his refund to his estimated tax liability for the following tax year, or request a repayment. The IRS can mail a check; however, the fastest way to receive a refund is through direct deposit. *Form 8888* is necessary when the taxpayer wants the refund to go into more than one account or he wants to buy up to $5,000 in paper series I savings bonds. Otherwise, a taxpayer may enter routing and account information for his financial institution or bank directly on his tax return. The taxpayer can have his refund (or part of it) deposited directly to a traditional IRA, Roth IRA, or SEP-IRA, but not a SIMPLE IRA. He must establish the IRA at a bank or other financial institution before requesting the direct deposit. The IRS can also send a deposit to a TreasuryDirect® online account to buy U.S. Treasury marketable securities and savings bonds.

Filing a Claim for Refund

The normal deadline for filing a claim for refund or credit is three years from date for filing the original return or two years after paying the tax, whichever is later. The IRS treats payments or returns made before the due date—without regard to extensions—as received on the due date.

The return of a taxpayer filed on March 1 is considered filed on the due date of April 15. However, if he had an extension to file (for example, until October 15) but files earlier and the IRS receives it July 1, the return is considered filed on July 1.

If a claim is filed within three years after the date of filing the return, the credit or refund cannot be more than the part of the tax paid within the three-year period—plus any extension of time for filing the return—immediately before the claim was filed. If a claim is filed after the 3-year period, but within two years from the time the tax is paid, the credit or refund cannot be more than the tax paid within the two years immediately before filing the claim.

You made estimated tax payments of $1,000 and got an automatic extension of time from April 15, 2016, to October 15, 2016, to file your 2015 income tax return. When filing your return on that date, you pay an additional $200 tax. Three years later, on October 15, 2019, you file an amended return and claim a refund of $700. Because you filed within 3 years after filing your return, you could get a refund of any tax paid after April 15, 2016.

> The situation is the same as in the prior example, except that you file your return on October 31, 2016, after the extension period ends. You paid an additional $200 on that date. Three years later, on October 27, 2019, you file an amended return and claim a refund of $700. Although you filed your claim within 3 years from the date you filed your original return, the refund is limited to $200. The estimated tax of $1,000 was paid before the 3 years plus the 6-month extension period.

A notable exception to the 3-year rule is an amended return based on a bad debt or worthless security, which a taxpayer generally must file within seven years after the due date of the return for the tax year in which the debt or security became worthless.

A taxpayer generally files *Form 1040X* with the IRS center determined by where he lives at the time. A taxpayer may use Form 1040X to do the following:

- Correct Forms 1040, 1040A, 1040EZ, 1040EZ-T, 1040NR, or 1040NR-EZ
- Make certain elections after the prescribed deadline
- Change amounts previously adjusted by the IRS
- Make a claim for a carryback due to a loss or unused credit

A taxpayer files Form 1040X only after filing the original return, and before the expiration of the deadline. The taxpayer files a separate form for each year or period involved, and includes an explanation of each item of income, deduction, or credit he uses as a basis for the claim. The taxpayer must attach all appropriate forms and schedules to Form 1040X or it will be returned. A taxpayer who files an erroneous refund claim may be subject to a penalty of 20% of the disallowance.

Joint and Several Liability

A married taxpayer is *jointly and severally liable* for the tax and any additions to tax, interest, or penalties that arise because of a joint return, even after divorce. Joint and several liability means that each taxpayer is legally responsible for the entire liability. One spouse may be held responsible for all the tax due, even if the other spouse earned all the income or claimed improper deductions or credits. Relief from joint liability, such as *innocent spouse relief*, is different from an *injured spouse claim*.

Injured Spouse Relief

> Sometimes a liability belongs only to one spouse. A taxpayer is an "*injured spouse*" if he files a joint return and all or part of his share of the refund was, or will be, applied against the separate past-due federal tax, state tax, child support, or federal non-tax debt (such as a student loan) of his spouse with whom he filed the joint return. An injured spouse may be entitled to recoup their share of the refund.

The injured spouse files *Form 8379* with a jointly filed tax return when the joint overpayment was—or is expected to be—applied to a past-due obligation of the other spouse. By filing Form 8379, the injured spouse may be able to get back his or her share of the joint refund. The taxpayer may file form 8379 with a joint return, with an amended return, or by itself at a later time.

> Tom and Lucy expect a refund of $5,000 when they jointly file their tax return. Tom has $60,000 in past-due taxes that he accumulated prior to getting married. To prevent the entire refund from being applied against his past-due obligation, they can file Form 8379, to protect Lucy's share of the refund.

Extensions

A taxpayer may request an *automatic six-month extension* by filing Form 4868 (via paper or electronically) by the due date of the return or by paying all or part of the income tax due using a credit or debit card. For most taxpayers, this extends the due date until October 15.

> Please note that this is NOT an extension of time to pay taxes. The taxpayer must estimate the taxes due and can submit the payment with the extension request.

- **Serving in a Combat Zone** – When individuals serve in a qualified combat zone, the deadline for filing and payment increases by 180 days after the latter of the last day in a qualified combat zone or the last day of a continuous hospitalization related to injury from service. In addition to the 180 days, a service member in a qualified combat zone can receive a deadline extension of up to three and a half months, based on the number of days remaining to file upon entering the combat zone. This period is representative of the time normally allotted for filing taxes (January 1–April 15). If entering the combat zone before the first of the year, the service member may add the entire three and a half months to the 180-day extension.
- **Individuals Outside the United States** – A taxpayer who is a U.S. citizen (or resident) may receive an automatic two-month extension to file a return <u>and pay</u> any federal income tax due if—on the due date of the return—he is in the military or naval service on duty outside the United States and Puerto Rico, or lives and maintains a main place of business outside the United States and Puerto Rico. Interest applies from the due date until paid. The taxpayer must attach a statement to his return explaining which situation applies.

Accounting Periods and Methods

The typical period covered by personal income tax returns is the 12-month period from January 1 through December 31, also known as a *calendar year*. A *fiscal year* is another typical accounting period. A regular fiscal year is a 12-month period that ends on the last day of <u>any</u> month except December. A taxpayer will choose the type of accounting period (tax year) when he files his first income tax return.

Cash Method

Most individual taxpayers use the *cash method*. If this method is used, the taxpayer must report income in the year of *constructive receipt*. Constructive receipt occurs when the income is available for a taxpayer's unrestricted withdrawal. Physical possession is not a requirement. Examples of constructive receipt include the following:

- Garnished wages (considered income received for the year)
- Debt canceled or paid for a taxpayer but not as a gift or loan (gross income to the recipient)
- Income payments paid directly to a third party from property owned by a taxpayer (treated as received by the taxpayer and paid to the third party)
- Income paid in advance (includable in gross income for the year received)
- Checks received and available to the taxpayer without restriction

Exception: Do not report interest on Series E and EE U.S. savings bonds until the final maturity date.

> Jill is a cash basis taxpayer. To earn extra money, she works as a photographer in the month of December. Jill shot a family portrait for the Johnson family on December 15, 2015 and receives a check for her work on that date. The Johnsons dated the check January 2, 2016 and asked Jill not to cash it until that time. Jill does not recognize this income in 2015 because of the restriction on withdrawal.

Accrual Method

Another method is the *accrual method*. When using the accrual method, report income when earned, whether the taxpayer has received it or not. The IRS considers the taxpayer to have earned income when all the events have occurred that fix the right to receive such income and the amount can be determined with reasonable accuracy.

Filing Requirements

Individuals

The *gross income threshold* determines whether the taxpayer must file a return. It is the sum of the standard deduction and personal exemption amounts for each filing status. If gross income is not greater than the gross income threshold, the taxpayer need not file a return. See Table 1-1.

Table 1-1. 2015 Filing Requirements for Most Taxpayers

IF filing status is...	AND at the end of 2015, the taxpayer was ...	THEN file a return if the gross income was at least ...
Single	younger than 65	$10,300
	65 or older	$11,850
Married Filing Jointly	younger than 65 (both spouses)	$20,600
	65 or older (one spouse)	$21,850
	65 or older (both spouses)	$23,100
Married Filing Separately	any age	$4,000
Head of Household	younger than 65	$13,250
	65 or older	$14,800
Qualifying Widow(er) with Dependent Child	younger than 65	$16,600
	65 or older	$17,850

Dependents

Factors such as marital status, age, income, and blindness determine whether a dependent must file a return. Dependents must file individual returns under the circumstances described in Table 1-2. *Earned income* includes salaries, wages, tips, professional fees, taxable scholarships, and fellowship grants. *Unearned income* includes unemployment compensation, taxable Social Security benefits, taxable pensions, annuity income, canceled debt, unearned income from a trust, taxable interest, dividends, and capital gains. *Gross income* is the total of *earned* and *unearned income*.

Table 1-2. 2015 Filing Requirements for Single Dependents

Single dependents – Were you either age 65, older, or blind?

☐ **No.** You must file a return if any of the following apply.
• Your unearned income was more than $1,050.
• Your earned income was more than $6,300.
• Your gross income was more than the larger of:
  - $1,050, or
  - Your earned income (up to $5,950) plus $350.
☐ **Yes.** You must file a return if any of the following apply.
• Your unearned income was more than $2,600 ($4,150 if 65 or older and blind).
• Your earned income was more than $7,850 ($9,400 if 65 or older and blind).
• Your gross income was more than the larger of:
  - $2,600 ($4,150 if 65 or older and blind), or
  - Your earned income (up to $5,950) plus $1,900 ($3,450 if 65 or older and blind).

Certain Children Younger than 19 Years of Age or Full-time Students

Parents can elect to include a child's income on the parent's return (Form 8814) when a child's only income is interest, dividends or capital gain distributions. If making this election, the child does not have to file a return. The child must meet the following conditions to qualify:

- At the end of the year, must be younger than age 19 or a full-time student younger than age 24
- Must have gross income of less than $10,500
- Must be required to file a return unless the election is made
- Must not file a joint return for the year
- Must not have made estimated tax payments for the tax year, and no overpayment from the previous year can apply to the tax year under his name and Social Security number
- Must not have any federal income tax taken out of his income under the backup withholding rules

Additional Filing Requirements

A taxpayer is required to file a return if any of the conditions listed below apply, even if income is less than the amount shown in Table 1-1 or Table 1-2:

- Special taxes are owed, or certain credits must be recaptured
- Net earnings from self-employment are at least $400
- Wages are $108.28 or more from a church or qualified church-controlled organization that is exempt from employer Social Security and Medicare taxes

Foreign Account and Asset Reporting

FATCA Requirements

The *Foreign Account Tax Compliance Act (FATCA)* is a tax law addressing tax non-compliance by U.S. taxpayers with foreign accounts by focusing on reporting by U.S. taxpayers and foreign financial institutions.

In general, federal law requires U.S. citizens and resident aliens to report any worldwide income, including income from foreign trusts and foreign bank and securities accounts. In most cases, affected taxpayers need to complete and attach Schedule B to their tax returns. Part III of Schedule B asks about the existence of foreign accounts, such as bank and securities accounts, and generally requires U.S. citizens to report the country in which each account is located.

In addition, certain taxpayers may also have to complete and attach to their return *Form 8938 Statement of Special Foreign Financial Assets*.

Generally, U.S. citizens, resident aliens and certain nonresident aliens must report specified foreign financial assets on Form 8938 if the aggregate value of those assets exceeds $50,000 on the last day of the tax year or $75,000 at any time during the tax year (higher threshold amounts apply to married individuals filing jointly and individuals living abroad).

The FATCA Form 8938 requirement does not replace or otherwise affect a taxpayer's obligation to file an FBAR Form 114.

FBAR Requirements

FBAR refers to **Form 114, Report of Foreign Bank and Financial Accounts**, that must be filed with the Financial Crimes Enforcement Network (FinCEN), which is a bureau of the Treasury Department. *FinCEN Form 114* is used to report a financial interest in or signature authority over a foreign financial account. The FBAR must be received by the Department of the Treasury on or before June 30th of the year immediately following the calendar year being reported.

A United States person that has a financial interest in or signature authority over foreign financial accounts must file an FBAR if the aggregate value of the foreign financial accounts **exceeds $10,000** at any time during the calendar year.

General FBAR Definitions

- **Financial Account** – A financial account includes, but is not limited to, securities, brokerage, savings, demand, checking, deposit, time deposit, or other account maintained with a financial institution (or other person performing the services of a financial institution). A financial account also includes a commodity futures or options account, an insurance policy with a cash value (such as a whole life insurance policy), an annuity policy with a cash value, and shares in a mutual fund or similar pooled fund (i.e., a fund that is available to the general public with a regular net asset value determination and regular redemptions).

- **Joint Account** – A financial account type listed above owned jointly by two or more persons.

- **Foreign Financial Account** – A foreign financial account is a financial account located outside of the United States. For example, an account maintained with a branch of a United States bank that is physically located outside of the United States is a foreign financial account. An account maintained with a branch of a foreign bank that is physically located in the United States is not a foreign financial account.

- **Financial Interest** – A United States person has a financial interest in a foreign financial account for which:

    1) the United States person is the owner of record or holder of legal title, regardless of whether the account is maintained for the benefit of the United States person or for the benefit of another person; or

    2) the owner of record or holder of legal title is one of the following:

        A) An agent, nominee, attorney, or a person acting in some other capacity on behalf of the United States person with respect to the account;

B) A corporation in which the United States person owns directly or indirectly: (i) more than 50 percent of the total value of shares of stock or (ii) more than 50 percent of the voting power of all shares of stock;

C) A partnership in which the United States person owns directly or indirectly: (i) an interest in more than 50 percent of the partnership's profits (e.g., distributive share of partnership income taking into account any special allocation agreement) or (ii) an interest in more than 50 percent of the partnership capital;

D) A trust of which the United States person: (i) is the trust grantor and (ii) has an ownership interest in the trust for United States federal tax purposes. See 26 U.S.C. sections 671-679 to determine if a grantor has an ownership interest in a trust;

E) A trust in which the United States person has a greater than 50 percent present beneficial interest in the assets or income of the trust for the calendar year; or

F) Any other entity in which the United States person owns directly or indirectly more than 50 percent of the voting power, total value of equity interest or assets, or interest in profits.

- **Person** – A person means an individual (including a minor child) and legal entities including, but not limited to, a limited liability company, corporation, partnership, trust, and estate.

Generally, a child is responsible for filing his or her own FBAR report. If a child cannot file his or her own FBAR for any reason, such as age, the child's parent, guardian, or other legally responsible person must file it for the child. **Signing the child's FBAR** – If the child cannot sign his or her FBAR, a parent or guardian must electronically sign the child's FBAR.

- **Signature Authority** – Signature authority is the authority of an individual (alone or in conjunction with another individual) to control the disposition of assets held in a foreign financial account by direct communication (whether in writing or otherwise) to the bank or other financial institution that maintains the financial account. Certain exceptions apply.

- **United States** – For FBAR purposes, the United States includes the States, the District of Columbia, all United States territories and possessions (e.g., American Samoa, the Commonwealth of the Northern Mariana Islands, the Commonwealth of Puerto Rico, Guam, and the United States Virgin Islands), and the Indian lands as defined in the Indian Gaming Regulatory Act. References to the laws of the United States include the laws of the United States federal government and the laws of all places listed in this definition.

- **United States Person** – United States person means United States citizens (including minor children); United States residents; entities, including but not limited to, corporations, partnerships, or limited liability companies created or organized in the United States or under the laws of the United States; and trusts or estates formed under the laws of the United States.

The federal tax treatment of an entity does not determine whether the entity has an FBAR filing requirement. For example, an entity that is disregarded for purposes of Title 26 of the United States Code must file an FBAR, if otherwise required to do so. Similarly, a trust for which the trust income, deductions, or credits are taken into account by another person for purposes of Title 26 of the United States Code must file an FBAR, if otherwise required to do so.

FBAR Filing Considerations

The FBAR is an annual report and must be filed on or before June 30th of the year following the calendar year being reported. The FBAR must be filed electronically through FinCEN's BSA E-Filing System.

There is no extension of time available for filing an FBAR. Extensions of time to file federal tax returns do NOT extend the time for filing an FBAR.

Persons required to file an FBAR must retain records that contain the name in which each account is maintained, the number or other designation of the account, the name and address of the foreign financial institution that maintains the account, the type of account, and the maximum account value of each account during the reporting period.

The records must be retained for a period of 5 years from June 30th of the year following the calendar year reported and must be available for inspection as provided by law.

An officer or employee who files an FBAR to report signature authority over an employer's foreign financial account is not required to personally retain records regarding these accounts.

Exceptions to FBAR Filing

- **Certain Accounts Jointly Owned by Spouses** – The spouse of an individual who files an FBAR is not required to file a separate FBAR if the following conditions are met: (1) all the financial accounts that the non-filing spouse is required to report are jointly owned with the filing spouse; 2) the filing spouse reports the jointly owned accounts on a timely filed FBAR electronically signed; and (3) the filers have completed and signed *Form 114a, Record of Authorization to Electronically File FBARs* (maintained with the filers' records). Otherwise, both spouses are required to file separate FBARs, and each spouse must report the entire value of the jointly owned accounts.

- **Consolidated FBAR** – If a United States person that is an entity is named in a consolidated FBAR filed by a greater than 50 percent owner, such entity is not required to file a separate FBAR.

- **Correspondent/Nostro Account** – Correspondent or nostro accounts (which are maintained by banks and used solely for bank-to-bank settlements) are not required to be reported.

- **Governmental Entity** – A foreign financial account of any governmental entity of the United States (as defined above) is not required to be reported by any person. For purposes of this form, governmental entity includes a college or university that is an agency of, an instrumentality of, owned by, or operated by a governmental entity. For purposes of this Form 114, governmental entity also includes an employee retirement or welfare benefit plan of a governmental entity.

- **International Financial Institution** – A foreign financial account of any international financial institution (if the United States government is a member) is not required to be reported by any person.

- **IRA Owners and Beneficiaries** – An owner or beneficiary of an IRA is not required to report a foreign financial account held in the IRA.

- **Participants in and Beneficiaries of Tax-Qualified Retirement Plans** – A participant in or beneficiary of a retirement plan described in Internal Revenue Code section 401(a), 403(a), or 403(b) is not required to report a foreign financial account held by or on behalf of the retirement plan.

- **Signature Authority** – An individual who has signature authority over, but no financial interest in, a foreign financial account is not required to report the account in the following situations:

    1) An officer or employee of a bank that is examined by the Office of the Comptroller of the Currency, the Board of Governors of the Federal Reserve System, the Federal Deposit Insurance Corporation, the Office of Thrift Supervision, or the National Credit Union Administration is not required to report signature authority over a foreign financial account owned or maintained by the bank.

2) An officer or employee of a financial institution that is registered with and examined by the Securities and Exchange Commission or Commodity Futures Trading Commission is not required to report signature authority over a foreign financial account owned or maintained by the financial institution.

3) An officer or employee of an Authorized Service Provider is not required to report signature authority over a foreign financial account that is owned or maintained by an investment company that is registered with the Securities and Exchange Commission. Authorized Service Provider means an entity that is registered with and examined by the Securities and Exchange Commission and provides services to an investment company registered under the Investment Company Act of 1940.

4) An officer or employee of an entity that has a class of equity securities listed (or American depository receipts listed) on any United States national securities exchange is not required to report signature authority over a foreign financial account of such entity.

5) An officer or employee of a United States subsidiary is not required to report signature authority over a foreign financial account of the subsidiary if its United States parent has a class of equity securities listed on any United States national securities exchange and the subsidiary is included in a consolidated FBAR report of the United States parent.

6) An officer or employee of an entity that has a class of equity securities registered (or American depository receipts in respect of equity securities registered) under section 12(g) of the Securities Exchange Act is not required to report signature authority over a foreign financial account of such entity.

- **Trust Beneficiaries** – A trust beneficiary with a financial interest described in section (2)(e) of the financial interest definition is not required to report the trust's foreign financial accounts on an FBAR if the trust, trustee of the trust, or agent of the trust: (1) is a United States person and (2) files an FBAR disclosing the trust's foreign financial accounts.
- **United States Military Banking Facility** – A financial account maintained with a financial institution located on a United States military installation is not required to be reported, even if that military installation is outside of the United States.

Table 1-3. FATCA vs. FBAR

	Form 8938, Statement of Specified Foreign Financial Assets	FinCEN Form 114, Report of Foreign Bank and Financial Accounts (FBAR)
Who Must File?	Specified individuals, which include U.S citizens, resident aliens, and certain non-resident aliens that have an interest in specified foreign financial assets and meet the reporting threshold	U.S. persons, which include U.S. citizens, resident aliens, trusts, estates, and domestic entities that have an interest in foreign financial accounts and meet the reporting threshold
Does the United States include U.S. territories?	No	Yes, resident aliens of U.S territories and U.S. territory entities are subject to FBAR reporting
Reporting Threshold (Total Value of Assets)	$50,000 on the last day of the tax year or $75,000 at any time during the tax year (higher threshold amounts apply to married individuals filing jointly and individuals living abroad)	$10,000 at any time during the calendar year
When do you have an interest in an account or asset?	If any income, gains, losses, deductions, credits, gross proceeds, or distributions from holding or disposing of the account or asset are or would be required to be reported, included, or otherwise reflected on your income tax return	Financial interest: you are the owner of record or holder of legal title; the owner of record or holder of legal title is your agent or representative; you have a sufficient interest in the entity that is the owner of record or holder of legal title. Signature authority: you have authority to control the disposition of the assets in the account by direct communication with the financial institution maintaining the account.
What is Reported?	Maximum value of specified foreign financial assets, which include financial accounts with foreign financial institutions and certain other foreign non-account investment assets	Maximum value of financial accounts maintained by a financial institution physically located in a foreign country
When Due?	By due date, including extension, if any, for income tax return	Received by June 30 (no extensions of time granted)
Where to File?	File with income tax return pursuant to instructions for filing the return	File electronically through FinCEN's BSA E-Filing System. The FBAR is not filed with a federal tax return.
Penalties	Up to $10,000 for failure to disclose and an additional $10,000 for each 30 days of non-filing after IRS notice of a failure to disclose, for a potential maximum penalty of $60,000; criminal penalties may also apply	If non-willful, up to $10,000; if willful, up to the greater of $100,000 or 50 percent of account balances; criminal penalties may also apply

Aliens

Resident Alien or Nonresident Alien

Most U.S. source income a nonresident alien receives is subject to withholding with a tax rate of 30%. A nonresident who receives U.S. income must file a return (Form 1040-NR) if additional taxes are due or if conducting a business in the U.S. A nonresident alien who is married to a U.S. citizen or resident at the end of the year can choose tax treatment as a U.S. resident.

> A taxpayer who is not a citizen of the United States must determine if he is a resident alien or a nonresident alien for tax purposes. Resident aliens must file a tax return following the same rules that apply to U.S. citizens. Nonresident aliens must file special forms and adhere to different rules.

Generally, the IRS considers a person a *resident alien* if he meets either the *green card test* or the *substantial presence test*.

- **Green Card Test** – A lawful permanent resident of the United States at any time during 2015 and took no steps to be a resident of a foreign country under an income tax treaty. In most cases, the taxpayer is a lawful permanent resident if issued an alien registration card, also known as a green card.

- **Substantial Presence Test** – You are considered a U.S. resident if you meet the substantial presence test. You meet this test if you were physically present in the United States for at least:

    1) 31 days during 2015, and

    2) 183 days during the 3-year period that includes 2015, 2014, and 2013, counting:

        A) All of the days present in 2015

        B) One-third of the days present in 2014

        C) One-sixth of the days present in 2013

For purposes of the substantial presence test, the term "United States" includes all 50 states and the District of Columbia, territorial waters, and the seabed and subsoil of those submarine areas that are adjacent to U.S. territorial waters and over which the United States has exclusive rights under international law to explore and exploit natural resources. The term does not include U.S. possessions and territories or U.S. airspace.

> Generally, the IRS considers a taxpayer a nonresident alien for the year if he is not a U.S. resident under either of these tests. However, a taxpayer may still qualify as a nonresident alien if he is a resident of a treaty country within the meaning of an income tax treaty between the United States and that country. The complete text of most U.S. tax treaties is available on the IRS website.

Election to be Taxed as a Resident Alien

Generally, a taxpayer cannot file as married filing jointly if either spouse was a nonresident alien at any time during the tax year. However, nonresident aliens married to U.S. citizens or residents can choose to be treated as U.S. residents and file joint returns. A nonresident alien can elect taxation as a U.S. resident for the whole year if <u>all</u> of the following apply:

- He is married.

- His spouse was a U.S. citizen or resident alien on the last day of the tax year.

- He files a joint return for the year of the election using Form 1040, 1040A, or 1040EZ.

The taxpayer must include worldwide income for the whole year on the return, subjecting the entire amount to taxation under U.S. tax laws. The taxpayer must agree to keep the records, books, and other information needed to figure the tax. A taxpayer who made the election in an earlier year can file a joint return or separate return for 2015.

Dual-Status Tax Year

A dual-status year is one in which you change status between nonresident and resident alien. Different U.S. income tax rules apply to each status. Most dual-status years are the years of arrival or departure. Before you arrive in the United States, you are a nonresident alien. After you arrive, you may or may not be a resident, depending on the circumstances. If you become a U.S. resident, you stay a resident until you leave the United States.

Form 1040 and Schedules

A citizen or resident of the United States who is required to file a tax return will use Form 1040 to report information to the IRS. There are three variations: Form 1040EZ, Form 1040A, or Form 1040.

- **Form 1040EZ** – Form 1040EZ is the simplest form to use. The taxpayer must use the tax table to figure tax due, and cannot use Form 1040EZ to report any other tax.
- **Form 1040A** – Those who do not qualify to use Form 1040EZ may be able to use Form 1040A.
- **Form 1040** – All other taxpayers must use Form 1040.

Form 1040EZ

As the name suggests, Form 1040EZ is the easiest to file, but it does not apply to all situations. Only single and joint filers with no dependents are able to use Form 1040EZ. It is a tax return in its most basic form. A taxpayer does not attach any additional schedules to form 1040EZ. In order to file with form 1040EZ the taxpayer must meet all of the following conditions:

- Taxable income must be less than $100,000
- Cannot claim any dependents
- Filing status must be single or married filing jointly. If the taxpayer was a nonresident alien at any time in 2015, their filing status must be married filing jointly
- The taxpayer (and their spouse if married filing a joint return) must be under age 65 and not blind at the end of 2015
- Income is only from wages, salaries, tips, unemployment compensation, Alaska Permanent Fund dividends, taxable scholarship and fellowship grants, and taxable interest of $1,500 or less
- The taxpayer cannot claim any adjustments to income, such as a deduction for IRA contributions or student loan interest
- No credits allowed other than the *earned income credit*
- The taxpayer cannot owe household employment taxes on wages for a household employee
- Cannot claim the additional standard deduction

 Form 1040-EZ is useful only for taxpayers with simple returns. Of the three choices, Form 1040-EZ is the most limited in scope. A taxpayer who can benefit from the Head of Household filing status or claiming dependents should use Form 1040 or Form 1040A.

Form 1040A

A taxpayer of any age or filing status may use Form 1040A. Even if a taxpayer can use Form 1040EZ, using Form 1040A may be beneficial. A common reason to file Form 1040A is to claim the head of household filing status, which usually results in a lower tax than filing with a status of single. While form 1040A applies to a greater number of taxpayers, it is not available to all taxpayers. A taxpayer using Form 1040A must meet all the following conditions:

- Taxable income must be less than $100,000

- In addition to the income available for a 1040EZ filer, those using form 1040A may also have income from the following sources: IRA distributions, pensions and annuities, interest, ordinary dividends, capital gain distributions (but not unrecaptured section 1250 gain, section 1202 gain, or collectibles gain), taxable social security and railroad retirement benefits

- Adjustments to income cannot be for anything other than the following items:
    1) IRA deduction
    2) Student loan interest deduction
    3) Educator expenses
    4) Tuition and fees deduction

- The taxpayer cannot itemize deductions

- Taxes can only come from the following items:
    1) Tax Table
    2) Alternative minimum tax
    3) Recapture of an education credit
    4) Form 8615, Tax for Certain Children Who Have Investment Income of More Than $2,000
    5) Qualified Dividends and Capital Gain Tax Worksheet

- The taxpayer can only claim the following tax credits:
    1) The credit for child and dependent care expenses
    2) The credit for the elderly or the disabled
    3) The child tax credit
    4) The additional child tax credit
    5) The education credits
    6) The retirement savings contributions credit
    7) The earned income credit

- The taxpayer cannot have an alternative minimum tax adjustment on stock acquired from the exercise of an incentive stock option

Form 1040A is more flexible than 1040EZ with respect to sources of income, deductions, credits, and tax; however, it is not without limits. Substantial limitations of Form 1040A include the lack of ability to itemize deductions or report business income. As a result, taxpayers most often use Form 1040.

Form 1040

A taxpayer who cannot use Form 1040EZ or Form 1040A must use Form 1040 to report all types of income, deductions, and credits. The tax calculation is no different from one form to another; however, it is possible that a taxpayer may pay less tax by filing Form 1040 because of the ability to claim itemized deductions, additional adjustments to income, and credits not available on Form 1040A or Form 1040EZ. A taxpayer must use form 1040 if any of the following apply:

- Taxable income is $100,000 or more
- The taxpayer will itemize deductions
- The taxpayer has income that cannot be reported on Form 1040EZ or Form 1040A, including tax-exempt interest from private activity bonds issued after August 7, 1986.
- The taxpayer claims any credits or adjustments to gross income not allowed on Form 1040A.
- The taxpayer has Form W-2 that shows either of the following:
    1) Uncollected employee tax (social security and Medicare tax) on tips or group-term life insurance
    2) Income from Nonqualified deferred compensation plans (box 12 with a code Z)
- The taxpayer received $20 or more in unreported tips in any 1 month
- The taxpayer was a bona fide resident of Puerto Rico and excludes income from Puerto Rico sources
- The taxpayer owes excise tax on insider stock compensation from an expatriated corporation
- The taxpayer has a qualified health savings account funding distribution from their IRA
- The taxpayer is an employee and their employer did not withhold social security and Medicare tax
- It is necessary to file other forms with the return to report certain exclusions, taxes, or transactions
- The taxpayer is a debtor in a bankruptcy case filed after October 16, 2005
- The taxpayer has a net disaster loss attributable to a federally declared disaster
- The taxpayer must recapture the first-time homebuyer credit
- The taxpayer received a refund or credit of certain taxes or net disaster loss claimed as part of their standard deduction

Form 1040 Schedules

A taxpayer may file certain schedules along with Form 1040, and in certain cases Form 1040A. Assemble any schedules and forms behind Form 1040 (or 1040A) in order of the "Attachment Sequence No." shown in the upper right corner of the schedule or form. A taxpayer filing with Form 1040 or 1040A can attach the following schedules to their return:

- **Schedule B, Interest and Ordinary Dividends** – A taxpayer completes this schedule if any of the following conditions apply:
    1) The taxpayer has over $1,500 of taxable interest or ordinary dividends
    2) Receipt of interest from a seller-financed mortgage and the buyer used the property as a personal residence
    3) He has accrued interest from a bond
    4) He reports original issue discount (OID) less than the amount shown on Form 1099-OID
    5) He reduces interest income on a bond by the amount of amortizable bond premium

6) He claims an exclusion of interest from series EE or I U.S. savings bonds issued after 1989

7) He receives interest or ordinary dividends as a nominee

8) He has certain interest in a financial account in a foreign country or a foreign trust

- **Schedule EIC, Earned Income Credit** – A taxpayer with one or more qualifying children can file this schedule to claim the earned income credit.

- **Schedule R, Credit for the Elderly or the Disabled** – A U.S. citizen or resident alien with limited income who is age 65 or older at the end of the year can file this schedule to receive a credit.

The following schedules are <u>only</u> available when using Form 1040 to file a tax return:

- **Schedule A, Itemized Deductions** – When itemized deductions exceed the amount of the standard deduction, a taxpayer attaches Schedule A to Form 1040 in order to claim the higher amount.

- **Schedule C, Net Profit or Loss from Business** – A "self-employed" taxpayer files Schedule C with Form 1040 to report income and deductions resulting from their trade or business. To file this schedule the taxpayer must operate a business as one of the following:

    1) Sole proprietor or disregarded entity (single member LLC treated as a sole proprietor)

    2) Qualified joint venture

    3) Statutory employee

- **Schedule C-EZ, Net Profit from Business** – This is really just a simplified version of Schedule C. It is available if a taxpayer has a small business that does not have a loss. Other requirements for a taxpayer using this schedule include:

    1) Business expenses of $5,000 <u>or</u> less

    2) Must use the cash method of accounting

    3) Cannot have an inventory at any time during the year

    4) Must have only one business as a sole proprietor, qualified joint venture, or statutory employee

    5) Cannot have employees

    6) Cannot deduct expenses for business use of home

    7) Cannot have prior year disallowed passive activity losses from the business

    8) Cannot be required to file form 4562, Depreciation and Amortization for the business

- **Schedule D, Capital Gains and Losses** – A taxpayer uses Schedule D to report the sale or exchange of capital assets. Most property held for personal purposes, pleasure, or investment is a capital asset. Many transactions that, in previous years, would have been reported on Schedule D or D-1 must be reported on *Form 8949* if they occur in 2015. Schedule D-1 is no longer in use as Form 8949 replaces it. A taxpayer must now use Form 8949 to list all capital gain and loss transactions; the subtotals from this form will then be carried over to Schedule D (Form 1040), where gain or loss will be calculated in aggregate. The transactions reportable on this schedule include the following:

    1) Sales, exchanges, or involuntary conversions of capital assets

    2) Capital gain distributions not reported directly on Form 1040

    3) Nonbusiness bad debts

- **Schedule E, Supplemental Income and Loss** – A taxpayer attaches Schedule E to report income or loss from rental real estate, royalties, partnerships, S corporations, estates, trusts, and residual interests in REMICs.

- **Schedule F, Profit or Loss from Farming** – Farmers use Schedule F to figure net profit or loss from regular farming operations. This includes farm products raised for sale or products bought for resale.
- **Schedule J, Income Averaging for Farmers and Fishermen** – Use Schedule J to elect to figure income tax by averaging, over the previous 3 years (base years), all or part of current year taxable income from farming or fishing. This election does not apply when figuring alternative minimum tax.
- **Schedule SE, Self-Employment Tax** – Withholding tax for social security or Medicare does not apply to net earnings from self-employment. A self-employed taxpayer uses Schedule SE to figure the tax due on net earnings from self-employment. The taxpayer uses *Schedule SE* and calculates self-employment tax, which is essentially social security and Medicare tax for the self-employed. A taxpayer must include their share of certain partnership income and guaranteed payments as income from self-employment.

Form 1040NR

Who Must File

In general, a nonresident alien who receives U. S. source income must file a return (Form 1040NR) if additional taxes are due or if conducting a business in the United States. A nonresident alien who is married to a U.S. citizen or resident at the end of the year can choose tax treatment as a U.S. resident.

A taxpayer must file Form 1040NR if any of the following four conditions apply:

- A nonresident alien engaged in a trade or business in the United States during 2015 must file even if he does not receive income from the trade or business, has no U.S. source income, or receives income exempt from U.S. tax. However, a nonresident alien taxpayer with no gross income does not complete the schedules for Form 1040NR. Instead, he should attach a list of the kinds of exclusions claimed and the amount of each.
- A nonresident alien not engaged in a trade or business in the United States during 2015 who received income from U.S. sources reportable on *Schedule NEC, Tax on Income Not Effectively Connected with a U.S. Trade or Business* and not all of the U.S. tax owed was withheld from that income.
- The taxpayer represents a deceased person who would have had to file Form 1040NR.
- The taxpayer represents an estate or trust that has to file Form 1040NR.

A nonresident alien must also file a return if owing any special taxes, including any of the following:

- Alternative minimum tax.
- Additional tax on a qualified plan, including an individual retirement arrangement (IRA), or other tax-favored account. However, if this is the only tax owed, the taxpayer can file Form 5329 by itself.
- Household employment taxes. If this is the only tax owed, the taxpayer can file Schedule H by itself.
- Social security and Medicare tax on tips not reported to the employer or on wages received from an employer who did not withhold these taxes.
- Recapture of first-time homebuyer credit.
- Write-in taxes or recapture taxes, including uncollected social security and Medicare or RRTA tax on tips reported to an employer or on group-term life insurance and additional taxes on HSAs.
- The taxpayer has net earnings from self-employment of at least $400 and is a resident of a country with whom the United States has an international social security agreement.

A nonresident alien does not need to file Form 1040NR in 2015 if:

- The only U.S. trade or business was the performance of personal services; and
    1) Wages were less than $4,000; and
    2) He has no other need to file a return to claim a refund of over withheld taxes, to satisfy additional withholding at source, or to claim income exempt or partly exempt by treaty
- The taxpayer is a nonresident alien student, teacher, or trainee temporarily present in the United States under an "F," "J," "M," or "Q" visa, and has no income that is subject to tax under section 871.
- The taxpayer is a partner in a U.S. partnership that was not engaged in a trade or business in the United States during the tax year and Schedule K-1 (Form 1065) includes only income from U.S. sources that is reportable on Schedule NEC.

Nonresident Filing Status

One key difference between Form 1040NR and Form 1040 is filing status. A taxpayer that is a nonresident alien at any time during the tax year cannot file as head of household. The only filing status available for nonresidents from most countries (except Canada, Mexico and South Korea) is:

- **Single** – The rate schedule for single filers is more favorable than for married filing separately.
- **Married Nonresident Aliens Filing Separately** – A married nonresident aliens who is not married to a US citizen or resident generally must use the tax rate schedule for married filing separate returns when determining the tax on income effectively connected with a US trade or business. The taxpayer normally cannot use the tax rate schedule for single individuals.

Exemptions

Resident aliens can claim personal exemptions and exemptions for dependents in the same way as U.S. citizens. However, nonresident aliens generally can claim only one personal exemption for themselves on their U.S. tax return. A nonresident alien may be able to claim an exemption for a spouse and a dependent if any of the following situations apply:

- **Residents of Mexico or Canada or U.S. nationals** – If a spouse had no gross income for U.S. tax purposes and cannot be claimed as the dependent on another U.S. taxpayer's return. Residents of Mexico, Canada, or nationals of the United States must use the same rules as U.S. citizens to determine who is a dependent and for which dependents exemptions can be claimed.

Deductions

Nonresident aliens (other than those covered by the United States–India Income Tax Treaty) cannot claim the standard deduction. A nonresident alien generally cannot claim deductions related to income that is not connected with his U.S. business activities. A nonresident alien can deduct certain itemized deductions if he receives income effectively connected with his U.S. trade or business. These deductions include state and local income taxes, charitable contributions to U.S. organizations, casualty and theft losses, and miscellaneous deductions. Use Schedule A of Form 1040NR to claim itemized deductions. A taxpayer filing Form 1040NR-EZ can only claim a deduction for state or local income taxes. In order to claim any other itemized deduction, the taxpayer must file Form 1040NR.

Form 1040NR-EZ

A nonresident alien filing *Form 1040NR-EZ* can only claim "Single nonresident alien" or "Married nonresident alien" as the filing status. A nonresident alien can use Form 1040NR-EZ instead of Form 1040NR under the following conditions:

- Cannot be claimed as a dependent on someone else's return.

- Only U.S. income is from wages, salaries, and tips, refunds of state and local income taxes, and/or scholarship or fellowship grants.
- Taxable income is less than $100,000.
- The taxpayer does now owe any other taxes.
- The taxpayer cannot claim the following:
    1) Dependents
    2) Exemption for a spouse
    3) Tax credits
    4) Itemized deductions other than for state and local income taxes
    5) Adjustments to income other than exclusions for scholarship and fellowship grants

Tax Withholding and Estimated Tax

Federal income tax is a "pay-as-you-go" system. Failure to pay or a significant under-estimation of the amount owed may lead to the assessment of penalties and interest. There are two payment methods, withholding and estimated tax.

Withholding

An employer withholds income tax from an employee's pay and deposits with the IRS in the name of the employee. In order to determine the proper amount of withholding, an employee completes *Form W-4, Employee's Withholding Allowance Certificate* indicating the number of personal allowances and provides the form to the employer. A taxpayer may indicate an additional amount of tax to withhold from their pay. An exemption from withholding is possible by writing the word "EXEMPT" on line 7, if the taxpayer can meet both of the following conditions for exemption:

- Last year they had no tax liability, and a right to a refund of all federal income tax withheld, and
- This year they expect a refund of all federal income tax withheld because they expect no tax liability

Individuals may withhold tax on income sources like pensions, bonuses, commissions, and gambling winnings. Recipients of pensions, annuities (including commercial annuities), and certain other deferred compensation will use *Form W-4P, Withholding Certificate for Pension or Annuity Payments* to tell payers the correct amount of federal income tax to withhold, to choose not to have any federal income tax withheld, or to have an additional amount of tax withheld. Like Form W-4, a taxpayer indicates the proper number of personal allowances on the form. The taxpayer can check a box and elect not to withhold. The withholding agent does not send these forms to the IRS unless there is a written request.

Estimated Tax

Income from dividends, interest, capital gains, rent, royalties, and self-employment is not subject to withholding. A taxpayer with income from these sources must make estimated quarterly payments.

An individual with no tax liability in the previous full year is <u>not</u> required to pay estimated tax. Estimated tax liability exists when both of the following conditions exist:

- An individual will owe at least $1,000 in tax, after subtracting withholding and credits
- Withholding and credits will be <u>less</u> than the smaller of one of the following:
  1) 90% of the tax to be shown on this year's tax return
  2) 100% of the tax shown on last year's return (110% if AGI more than $150,000)

Jason earns $130,000, and his tax liability for the current year is $10,000, double what it was the prior year. He can avoid a penalty if his combined payments are at least $5,000 (100% of prior year liability).

The IRS may issue a penalty even if a refund is due when a sufficient amount of tax is unpaid by the due date for each of the periods as indicated in the following table (next business day if on holiday). Non-business taxpayers use Form 1040-ES to make estimated payments to the IRS.

For the period:	Due date:
Jan. 1–Mar. 31 (3 months)	April 15 (fourth month)
Apr. 1–May 31 (2 months)	June 15 (sixth month)
Jun. 1–Aug. 31 (3 months)	September 15 (ninth month)
Sep. 1–Dec. 31 (4 months)	January 15 (first month following tax year)

Margaret sold an investment property in July. She has no other income and did not owe taxes the prior year. She estimates owing $25,000 in taxes because of the transaction. If she is required to pay estimated tax, she must make her fist payment by September 15. However, she had no tax liability in the prior year, and is not required to make estimated payments.

Nonresident Income Taxes and Withholding

NRA Withholding

Aliens must report certain income on a U.S tax return. For *resident aliens*, this includes income from sources both within and outside the United States. For *nonresident aliens (NRA)*, this includes both income *effectively connected* with a trade or business in the United States (graduated tax rates) and income from U.S. sources that is not effectively connected (flat 30% tax rate or lower tax treaty rate).

Generally, a foreign person is subject to U.S. tax on U.S. source income. Most types of U.S. source income received by a foreign person are subject to U.S. tax at a rate of **30%**. A reduced rate, including exemption, may apply if there is a tax treaty between the foreign person's country of residence and the United States. The tax is generally withheld from the payment made to the foreign person.

The term **NRA withholding** refers to withholding required under sections 1441, 1442, and 1443 of the Internal Revenue Code. Generally, NRA withholding describes the withholding regime that requires withholding on a payment of <u>U.S. source income</u>. Payments to foreign persons, including nonresident alien individuals, foreign entities, and governments, may be subject to NRA. Generally, the U.S. person who pays an amount subject to NRA withholding is the person responsible for withholding, also known as the *withholding agent*. The withholding agent is <u>personally liable</u> for any tax required to be withheld.

This liability is independent of the tax liability of the foreign person to whom the payment is made. If the withholding agent fails to withhold and the foreign payee fails to satisfy its U.S. tax liability, then both are liable for tax, as well as interest and any applicable penalties.

Effectively Connected Income (ECI)

Generally, when a foreign person engages in a trade or business in the United States, all income from sources within the United States connected with the conduct of that trade or business is considered to be Effectively Connected Income (ECI). This applies whether or not there is any connection between the income, and the trade or business being carried on in the United States, during the tax year.

Whether a taxpayer is engaged in a trade or business in the United States depends on the nature of his activities. A taxpayer who performs personal services in the United States is usually considered to be engaged in a U.S. trade or business. Certain kinds of investment income are treated as ECI if they pass either of the two following tests:

- **Business Activities Test** –Usually applies when income, gain, or loss comes directly from the active conduct of the trade or business. Under this test, if the conduct of the U.S. trade or business was a material factor in producing the income, the income is effectively connected.

- **Asset Use Test** – The income must be associated with U.S. assets used in, or held for use in, the conduct of a U.S. trade or business.

Source of Income

All profits or losses from U.S. sources that are from the operation of a business in the United States are effectively connected with a trade or business in the United States. For example, profit from the sale in the United States of inventory property purchased either in this country or in a foreign country is effectively connected trade or business income. A share of U.S. source profits or losses of a partnership that is engaged in a trade or business in the United States is also effectively connected with a trade or business in the United States. A nonresident alien (NRA) usually is subject to U.S. income tax only on U.S. source income. The general rules for determining U.S. source income that apply to most nonresident aliens are shown below:

Table 1-4. Summary of Source Rules for Income of Nonresident Aliens

Item of Income:	Factor Determining Source:
Salaries, wages, other compensation	Where services performed
Business income: Personal services	Where services performed
Business income: Sale of inventory -purchased	Where sold
Business income: Sale of inventory -produced	Where produced (Allocation may be necessary §1.863-3(f))
Interest	Residence of payer
Dividends	Whether a U.S. or foreign corporation*
Rents	Location of property
Royalties: Natural resources	Location of property
Royalties: Patents, copyrights, etc.	Where property is used
Sale of real property	Location of property
Sale of personal property	Seller's tax home (Publication 519, for exceptions)
Pensions	Where services were performed that earned the pension
Scholarships - Fellowships	Generally, the residence of the payer
Sale of natural resources	Based on FMV of product at export terminal. §1.863–1(b)
*Exceptions include: a) Dividends paid by a U.S. corporation are foreign source if the corporation elects the Puerto Rico economic activity credit or possessions tax credit. b) Part of a dividend paid by a foreign corporation is U.S. source if at least 25% of the corporation's gross income is effectively connected with a U.S. trade or business for the 3 tax years before the year in which the dividends are declared	

Filing Status

In general, filing status depends on marital status. A person is considered unmarried for the whole year if—on the last day of the tax year—he is unmarried or legally separated from a spouse under a divorce or separate maintenance decree. If a spouse dies during the year, the IRS considers the surviving spouse married for the whole year and allows married filing jointly as the filing status.

For federal tax purposes, individuals of the same sex are considered married if they were lawfully married in a state (or foreign country) whose laws authorize the marriage of two individuals of the same sex, even if the state (or foreign country) in which they now live does not recognize same-sex marriage.

Single (S)

An individual is "single" if, on the last day of the year, he is unmarried or legally separated from a spouse under a final court decree and does not qualify for another status.

Head of Household (HH)

Filing as **head of household** usually results in lower tax rates than those for single or married filing separately. To qualify, a person must be unmarried or **considered unmarried** (file a separate return and spouse did not live in home the last 6 months of the tax year) on the last day of the year and pay more than half the cost of keeping up a home for the year. A *qualifying person* must live with the taxpayer more than half of the year, with the exception of a mother or father. A *qualifying person* must be a **qualifying child** or **qualifying relative** for whom the taxpayer can claim an exemption. A qualifying relative must be a member of the taxpayer's family (not merely a member of the household) in order to be a qualifying person for this status. The taxpayer must pay more than half the cost of maintaining the parent's home (or the cost of a facility), if claiming based on a dependent parent.

Married Filing Jointly (MFJ)

Taxpayers may choose *married filing jointly* as the filing status if they are married and agree to file a joint return. Both are responsible, jointly and individually, for the tax and any interest or penalty due. While different accounting methods are allowable, both must use the same accounting period and are generally required to sign the return. All combined income and allowable expenses must be reported. They may file a joint return even if one spouse has no income or deductions. When a court decree of annulment reverses a marriage, they must amend previous joint returns. If one spouse is a nonresident alien, they must have either a SSN or an ITIN to file a joint return.

Married Filing Separately (MFS)

Married couples can choose *married filing separately* as a status if they want to be responsible only for their respective taxes. They will *usually* pay more total tax on separate returns than when using another filing status. When choosing this filing status, the following special rules apply:

- Cannot take the credit for child and dependent care expenses in most cases, and the limit on income excluded under an employer's dependent care assistance program is $2,500.
- No earned income credit.
- No exclusion or credit for adoption expenses in most cases.
- Cannot take the education credits (Lifetime Learning or American Opportunities), the deduction for student loan interest, or the tuition and fees deduction.
- No exclusion on interest income from U.S. savings bonds when used for education expenses.
- If the taxpayer lived with a spouse at any time during the tax year, the following conditions apply:
    1) Cannot claim the credit for the elderly or the disabled
    2) Must include in income more (up to 85%) of any Social Security the taxpayer received
- The *child tax credit* and *retirement savings contribution credit* reduce at a level of income equal to one-half of the amount allowable to joint filers.
- The deduction limit for a capital loss is $1,500 (instead of $3,000 for joint returns).
- The standard deduction is half that allowed to joint filers. If one spouse itemizes deductions, the other cannot claim the standard deduction.
- The exemption amount for the alternative minimum tax is half that allowed to joint filers.

Qualifying Widow(er) with Dependent Child (QW)

If one spouse dies during the tax year, the survivor can file jointly (MFJ) if he otherwise qualifies for that status. The year of death is the last year to file jointly with a deceased spouse. In certain cases, *qualifying widow(er) with dependent child* is the filing status for <u>two tax years</u> following the year a spouse died. This filing status entitles them to use joint return tax rates and the highest standard deduction amount (if not itemizing deductions). To file as a qualifying widow(er) with dependent child, a taxpayer must meet <u>all</u> of the following tests:

- Must be entitled to file a joint return with his spouse for the year the spouse died
- Must not remarry before the end of the tax year
- Must have a child or stepchild (not a foster child) for whom he can claim an exemption
- A child lived in the person's home all year, except for temporary absences
- The taxpayer and the deceased spouse paid more than half of the cost of maintaining a home

Jane files a joint return the year her husband dies (2015). If her son meets the requirements discussed above, she can choose Qualifying Widow with Dependent Child as her status for 2016 and 2017.

Personal Exemptions and Dependents

There are two types of exemptions: *personal exemptions* and *exemptions for dependents*. While each is worth the same amount **($4,000 for 2015)**, different rules apply. A taxpayer may lose part of the deduction for exemptions if adjusted gross income (AGI) is more than the following:

- $154,950 for a married individual filing a separate return
- $258,250 for a single individual
- $284,050 for a head of household, and
- $309,900 for married individuals filing jointly or a qualifying widow(er).

Reduce the dollar amount of exemptions by 2% for each $2,500, or part of $2,500 ($1,250 if married filing separately), that AGI exceeds the filing status threshhold. If the excess is more than $122,500 ($61,250 if married filing separately), the deduction for exemptions is reduced to zero.

Personal Exemptions

Single taxpayers generally receive one *personal exemption*. If another taxpayer can claim an individual as a dependent, that individual is unable to claim a personal exemption. This is true even if the other taxpayer does not actually claim him as a dependent.

- **Joint return (MFJ)** – An additional exemption is available for a spouse.
- **Separate return (MFS)** – On a separate return, claim an additional exemption for a spouse who has no gross income, does not file a return, and is not the dependent of another taxpayer.
- **Death of spouse** – If a spouse dies and the surviving spouse does not remarry that year, the survivor can claim an exemption for the deceased spouse. An individual without gross income who remarries in the year of a spouse's death can be claimed as an exemption on both the final separate return of a deceased spouse and the separate return of a new spouse. If filing a joint return with a new spouse, the exemption is appropriate <u>only</u> for that return.
- **Divorced or separated spouse** – An exemption for a former spouse is not available in the year a decree of divorce or separate maintenance is final. This rule applies even for those who provide all of a former spouse's support.

Exemptions for Dependents

To claim an exemption for a dependent, a taxpayer must meet <u>all</u> three of the following tests:

- **Dependent Taxpayer Test** – The taxpayer cannot qualify as a dependent of another person.
- **Joint Return Test** – A taxpayer cannot claim a married person who files a joint return as a dependent, unless the married person files the return only as a claim for refund.
- **Citizenship or Resident Test** – A dependent must be a U.S. citizen, U.S. resident alien, U.S. national, or a resident of Canada or Mexico, for some part of the year.

In general, a taxpayer cannot claim a person as a dependent unless he provides more than half of the total annual support and that person is a *qualifying child* or *qualifying relative*.

- **Qualifying Child** – There are additional tests for a child to be a qualifying child:

    1) <u>Relationship Test</u> – The child must be a son, daughter, stepchild, foster child, brother, sister, half-brother, half-sister, stepbrother, stepsister, or a descendant of any of them.

    2) <u>Age Test</u> – To meet this test, a child must be <u>younger</u> than the taxpayer (or spouse if filing jointly) and meet one of the following conditions:

        A) Younger than age 19 at the end of the year

        B) Younger than age 24 at the end of the year and a full-time student

        C) Any age if permanently and totally disabled (does not need to be younger than taxpayer)

    3) <u>Residency Test</u> – Child must live with taxpayer more than half of year. A child who is born or dies during the year qualifies if the home was the child's home the entire time he was alive. A child is considered to live with a taxpayer when at the hospital following birth, or temporary absences due to special circumstances such as illness, education, business, vacation, or military service. If born alive but living for a moment (not stillborn) official documentation must prove live birth.

    4) <u>Support Test</u> – The child cannot provide more than half of his own support.

    <u>Special rule for qualifying child of more than one person</u> – If a child can be a qualifying child of more than one person, the taxpayer taking the exemption must be the person entitled to claim the child as a qualifying child. In most cases, because of the residency test, a child of divorced or separated parents is the qualifying child of the custodial parent. A noncustodial parent may claim the exemption only if the custodial parent agrees in writing (Form 8332).

- **Qualifying Relative** – A qualifying relative can be any age. There are four tests that must be met:

    1) <u>Not a qualifying child test</u> – The child cannot be a qualifying child of any taxpayer.

    2) <u>Support Test</u> – A taxpayer generally must provide more than half of a person's total support during the year. Under a written *multiple support agreement*, if two or more persons together provide more than half of the support, they can agree that one will claim the exemption. The person claiming the dependency exemption must provide more than 10% of the total support for the qualifying individual, and no other person can pay over half of the total support. Each eligible person who pays over 10% of support must provide the taxpayer with a signed statement agreeing not to claim the qualifying individual as a dependent. The taxpayer will file *Form 2120, Multiple Support Declaration* with their tax return attesting to the agreement.

    3) <u>Gross Income Test</u> – The person's gross income for 2015 must be <u>less</u> than **$4,000**.

    4) <u>Member of Household or Relationship Test</u> – To meet this test, a person must meet one of the following conditions:

        A) Live with the taxpayer all year as a member of the household, <u>or</u>

        B) Must be related in one of the following ways:

            (a) A child, stepchild, foster child, or a descendant of any of them (for example, a grandchild). Treat a legally adopted child the same as a child.

            (b) A brother, sister, half-brother, half-sister, stepbrother, or stepsister.

            (c) A father, mother, grandparent, or other direct ancestor, but <u>not</u> foster parent.

(d) A stepfather or stepmother.

(e) A son or daughter of the taxpayer's brother or sister.

(f) A brother or sister of the taxpayer's father or mother.

(g) A son or daughter-in-law, father or mother-in-law, brother or sister-in-law.

A qualifying relative must be related in one of the ways listed above, or live with the taxpayer all year as a member of the household. If the relationship does not violate local law, any person meeting the tests above can be a "qualifying relative," even if not a blood relative. A qualifying relative by virtue of family lineage need not live with the taxpayer.

2 Gross Income

Wage, Salaries, and Other Earnings · Tip Income · Interest Income · Dividends and Other Corporate Distributions · Rental Income and Expenses · Retirement Plans, Pensions and Annuities · Social Security · Other Income

This chapter summarizes the various forms of gross income that a taxpayer must report on a tax return. This information is based on IRS Publications 17, 527, 925, and 4681.

Wages, Salaries, and Other Earnings

Wages

Wages, salaries, and other forms of employee compensation are included in gross income. Generally, the employer reports annual employee compensation to employees on Form W-2, which the employer must provide to the employee by the end of January each year.

Self-employment Income

A self-employed taxpayer reports business income and expenses on Schedule C. The net income or loss is part of gross income on his personal tax return. The IRS defines net earnings from self-employment as the gross income from a trade or business, less business deductions. A partner's distributive share of ordinary income or loss is also self-employment income. A self-employed taxpayer must pay self-employment tax on net earnings from self-employment. A self-employed taxpayer may take a deduction on his personal return for a portion of the employment tax paid. For 2015, the self-employment tax rate is 15.3%. In determining net earnings from self-employment, take account of the deduction for one-half of self-employment tax. The Internal Revenue Code lists income from the following sources as specifically not income from self-employment:

- Income earned as an employee
- Income from rental real estate (unless a real estate dealer)
- Dividends from stocks or bonds (unless a securities dealer)
- Payments to a retired partner that continue after death
- Income received for services as an employee of a state (one example is a notary)

Partnership and S Corporation Income

Generally, certain flow-through entities such as partnerships or S corporations do not pay tax on income. Instead, the entity files an informational return with the IRS and distributes a Schedule K-1 to each partner or shareholder. The income, gains, losses, deductions, and credits pass through to the owners based on their respective shares.

Childcare Providers

When taxpayers provide childcare, regardless of location, the pay received must be included in gross income. Taxpayers who are not employees must include payments for services on Schedule C (Form 1040). The same rules apply for persons babysitting, even if only periodically and/or just for relatives.

Foreign Income

U.S. citizens and resident aliens must report income from sources outside the United States (foreign income) on their tax return unless it is exempt by U.S. law. This applies to earned income (such as wages and tips) as well as unearned income (such as interest, dividends, capital gains, pensions, rents, and royalties). U.S. citizens and resident aliens residing outside the United States may be able to exclude all or part of their foreign source earned income. *See foreign earned income exclusion in Chapter 5.*

Advance Commissions

Under the cash method, a taxpayer receiving advance commissions or other amounts for future services must include these amounts as income in the year received.

Cost-of-living Allowances and Reimbursements

Cost-of-living allowances are generally included in income. However, allowances for a federal civilian or federal court employee stationed in Alaska, Hawaii, or outside the United States are exempt from the rule and are not included as income. Allowances that increase an employee's basic pay as an incentive for taking a less desirable assignment are part of compensation and must be included in income.

Back Pay

Amounts awarded in a settlement or judgment for back pay should be included in income. These include payments made to a person for damages, unpaid life insurance premiums, and unpaid health insurance premiums. Employers should report on Form W-2.

Bonuses and Awards

Bonuses or awards received from an employer are included in income and should appear on Form W-2. If the award is goods or services, include the fair market value in income.

Severance Pay

Severance pay and any payment received due to the cancellation of an employment contract must be included in income amounts. This includes any payment received for accrued leave and monies withheld from severance for outplacement services.

Sick Pay

Pay received from an employer while sick or injured is part of salary or wages. In addition, employees must include in income sick pay benefits received from any of the following payors:

- A welfare fund
- A state sickness or disability fund
- An association of employers or employees
- An insurance company, if the employer paid for the plan

However, if the employee paid the premiums on an accident or health insurance policy, the benefits received under the policy are not taxable.

Disability Income

Generally, employees must report as income any amount received for personal injury or sickness through an accident or health plan when the employer pays plan premiums. If both the employee and employer pay for the plan, the employee must report only the amount received that is due to the employer's payments. However, certain payments may not be taxable to the employee. For example, a taxpayer need not report as income any reimbursement for medical expenses incurred after the plan was established. A taxpayer may need to include reimbursements for medical expenses deducted on a prior return as income in the current year.

Accident or Health Plan

Generally, the value of accident or health plan coverage provided to a taxpayer by an employer is not included in income. Benefits received from the plan may be taxable.

Fringe Benefits

Fringe benefits received in connection with the performance of services are included in income as compensation unless the employee paid fair market value for the benefits or specifically excluded by law. The IRS treats abstaining from the performance of services (for example, under a covenant not to compete) as the performance of services for purposes of these rules.

Group Term Life Insurance

Generally, the cost of up to $50,000 of group term life insurance coverage provided by an employer (or former employer) is not included in income. However, the cost of employer-provided insurance that exceeds the cost of $50,000 of coverage reduced by any amount paid toward the purchase of the insurance must be included in income. If an employer provides more than $50,000 of coverage, the employer must report the amount included in income as part of wages in box 1 of Form W-2. Employer-paid premiums for whole life or permanent insurance are included in the employee's income.

Transportation

For 2015, if an employer provides a qualified transportation fringe benefit, the taxpayer may exclude it from income, up to certain limits. A qualified transportation fringe benefit includes the following:

- Transportation in a commuter highway vehicle between the employee's home and workplace, as well as the following items:

    1) A transit pass – Include the excess more than $250 per month in gross income.

    2) Qualified parking – Include the excess more than $250 a month in gross income.

    3) Qualified bicycle commuting – Up to $20 reimbursement for each month the taxpayer uses a bicycle regularly for a substantial portion of travel between home and place of employment. Can cover expenses incurred during the year for the purchase of a bicycle and bicycle improvements, repair, and storage.

Restricted Property

Generally, the fair market value of property received for services is income in the year the taxpayer receives the property. A taxpayer does not include the value of stock or other property in income if there are certain restrictions that affect its value, e.g., a substantial risk of forfeiture. The taxpayer must report the property as income once it substantially vests (is no longer restricted). A taxpayer can choose to include the value of the property in income in the year the transfer occurs if making a proper *83(b) election* within 30 days of the grant date. The IRS treats restricted stock dividends as compensation and not as dividend income unless the taxpayer has recognized the stock as income. The holding period begins when the taxpayer includes the amount in income. The benefit of the 83(b) election is that future income or gains may receive more preferential dividend and capital gain tax treatment.

Stock Options

- If an employee receives a ***non-statutory stock option*** that has a readily determinable fair market value at the time it is granted, the option is treated similarly to other property received as compensation. Otherwise, the amount of income to include (and the time to include it) depends on the fair market value of the option when the employee does one of the following:

    1) Exercises the option (uses it to buy or sell the stock or other property)

    2) Sells or otherwise disposes of the option

- However, if the option is a ***statutory stock option***, the employee will not have any income until he sells or exchanges the stock. The tax treatment for ISOs is more favorable than that of NSOs. Capital gain tax rates apply to a gain from ISOs if an employee holds the stock more than one year from the date of exercise and more than two years from the option grant date prior to disposing of the stock; otherwise ordinary income rates apply to the gain at the time of sale.

In 2007, MicroMedia grants Doug non-statutory options giving him the right to purchase 1,000 shares of MicroMedia stock for a price of $25 per share. On the grant date, MicroMedia shares traded at $5. Douglas does not recognize income when he receives the options because his exercise price is above the current share price; therefore, there is no readily determinable market value. In 2015, Doug exercises his options when the price of the stock is $95. He receives $70,000 in compensation, which is the difference between what he pays ($25,000) and the value of the stock at exercise ($95,000). MicroMedia should include the compensation on Doug's W-2, and withhold any applicable social security and Medicare tax.

Tip Income

All tips received are income and subject to federal income tax. Include in gross income all tips received directly, charged tips paid by an employer, and any tips received under a tip splitting or tip pooling arrangement. The IRS also considers non-cash tips such as tickets, passes, or other items of value as taxable income, based on their value. To report tip income correctly, employees must:

- Keep a daily tip record
- Report tips to employer by the 10th of the following month if more than $20
- Report all tips on the income tax return

Tip income is subject to social security and Medicare tax. The taxpayer must give his employer a written report of cash and charge tips if he receives $20 or more in tips during a month. A taxpayer uses *Form 4137* to figure the social security and Medicare tax owed on tips he did not report to his employer, including any allocated tips shown on Form(s) W-2 that he must report as income.

A taxpayer may be subject to a 6652(b) penalty equal to 50% of unpaid social security and Medicare taxes due on unreported tips. The penalty amount is in addition to those taxes. The taxpayer can avoid this penalty if there is reasonable cause for not reporting the tips to the employer. To do so, the taxpayer attaches a statement to the tax return explaining the reason for not reporting the tips.

Special Rules for Certain Employees

Clergy

Members of the clergy must include in income any salary and fees received for masses, marriages, baptisms, funerals, etc. Payments to the religious institution are not taxable. Members of religious organizations who give outside earnings to the organization must include the earnings as income and may take a charitable deduction for the amount paid to the organization.

- **Pension** – Pension or retirement pay for a clergy member usually receives normal treatment.
- **Housing** – The rental value of a home (including utilities) or any designated *housing allowance* is excludable from income. The exclusion cannot be more than the reasonable pay for services rendered. Any allowance designated for the cost of utilities is excludable, up to the actual utility cost. The home or allowance must represent compensation for services rendered as an ordained, licensed, or commissioned minister. However, the rental value of the home or the housing allowance must be included as earnings from self-employment (on Schedule SE) if self-employment tax is applicable.

Members of Religious Orders

The treatment of renounced earnings turned over to a religious order by a member under a vow of poverty depends on whether or not the member performed the services specifically for the order.

- **Services performed for the order** – If the member performed services as an agent of the order in the exercise of duties required by the order, the amounts turned over to the order should not be included as income. If the member performed services for another agency of the supervising church or an associated institution, and the order mandated said service, the IRS considers the member to have performed the services as an agent of the order. Any wages a member earns as an agent of an order and turns over to the order are not included as income.
- **Services performed outside the order** – If a member of an order is directed to work outside the order, the services rendered are not an exercise of duties required by the order unless they meet both of the following requirements:
    1) The services are the kind of services that are ordinarily the duties of members of the order.
    2) They are part of the duties that the member must exercise for the religious order as its agent.

Foreign Employer

Special rules apply if the employer is a foreign employer. A U.S. citizen who works in the United States for a foreign government, an international organization, a foreign embassy, or any foreign employer must include salary in income. Employees of an international organization or a foreign government in the United States are exempt from Social Security and Medicare employee taxes. However, such an employee must pay self-employment taxes on earnings from services performed in the United States, even though the employee is not self-employed.

Military Pay

A member of a military service must generally report payments received as a service member as wages for tax purposes, except for retirement pay, which is taxable as a pension.

Interest Income

Taxable Interest

A taxpayer must generally report taxable interest from Form 1099-INT or Schedule K-1 for partnerships and S corporations, estates, and trusts. Taxable interest includes income from various sources such as the following:

- Bank, savings and loan, or credit union accounts
- Certificates of deposit
- U.S. treasury bills, notes, and bonds (exempt from all state and local income taxes)
- Loans made to others
- Gifts more than $10 for opening financial accounts. ($20 if the account is more than $5,000)
- Interest received on tax refunds
- U.S. Savings Bond Interest
    1) Series H and HH – Report semi-annual interest payments in the year received.
    2) Series I, E, and EE – Interest is credited at maturity. Taxpayers who use the cash method of accounting may elect to defer reporting interest until maturity; those using the accrual method must report interest on U.S. savings bonds each year as it accrues. Interest may be tax free if used for qualified education expenses.

> Interest from Series I or EE bonds may be tax free if used to pay for qualified education expenses the same year. This exclusion is known as the Education Savings Bond Program, and is not available when married filing separately. A taxpayer uses Form 8815 to figure the exclusion and attaches the form to Form 1040 or Form 1040A.

Nominees

Generally, if someone receives interest as a nominee for you, that person will give you a Form 1099-INT showing the interest received on your behalf. If you receive a Form 1099-INT that includes amounts belonging to another person, report the full amount shown as interest on Schedule B. Then, below a subtotal of all interest income listed, enter "Nominee Distribution" and the amount that actually belongs to someone else. Subtract that amount from the interest income subtotal. An example of when this occurs is with a joint account with one owner indicated as the tax-reporting holder.

A taxpayer who receives interest as a nominee in 2015 must file a Form 1099-INT for that interest with the IRS with a Form 1096, Annual Summary and Transmittal of U.S. Information Returns, by March 1, 2016 (March 31, 2016, if filing Form 1099-INT electronically). In addition, the taxpayer must furnish the actual owner of the interest with Copy B of Form 1099-INT by January 31, 2016.

In certain circumstances, a shareholder may receive dividends as a nominee on form 1099-DIV. When this occurs, the same rules apply except the taxpayer must submit form 1099-DIV to the actual owner.

Original Issue Discount (OID)

Original issue discount (OID) is a form of interest. Taxpayers include a portion of the discount as income as it accrues over the term of the debt instrument, even if they do not receive any payments from the issuer. A debt instrument generally has OID when the debtor issues the instrument for a price that is less than its stated redemption price at maturity. OID is the difference between the stated redemption price at maturity and the issue price. The IRS presumes that all debt instruments that do not pay interest before maturity are issued at a discount. Zero coupon bonds are one example of these instruments.

The OID accrual rules generally do not apply to short-term obligations (those with a fixed maturity date of one year or less from date of issue). The taxpayer may treat the discount as zero if it is less than one-fourth of 1% (.0025) of the stated redemption price at maturity multiplied by the number of full years from the date of original issue to maturity. This small discount is known as "*de minimis*" OID.

Exceptions to Reporting OID

The OID rules discussed in this chapter do not apply to the following debt instruments:

- Tax-exempt obligations
- U.S. savings bonds
- Short-term debt instruments (with a fixed maturity date one year or less from the date of issue)
- Obligations issued by an individual before March 2, 1984
- Loans between individuals, if <u>all</u> the following are true:
    1) The lender is not in the business of lending money.
    2) All outstanding loans between the same individuals total $10,000 or less.
    3) Avoiding any federal tax is not one of the principal purposes of the loan.

Dividends and Other Corporate Distributions

Ordinary Dividends

Ordinary (taxable) dividends are the most common type of distribution from a corporation. The corporation pays ordinary dividends out of its earnings and profits, and the shareholders must report such payments as ordinary income.

Qualified Dividends

Qualified dividends are subject to the same 0%, 15%, or 20% maximum tax rate that applies to net capital gain. Qualified dividends are subject to the 20% rate if the regular tax rate that would apply is 39.6%. If the regular tax rate that would apply is less than 39.6% but greater than 15%, qualified dividends are subject to the 15% rate. The tax rate is 0% on any amount that otherwise would be taxed at a regular rate of 10% or 15%. To qualify for the maximum rate, the following must be true:

- The dividends must be paid by a U.S. corporation or a qualified foreign corporation.
- The taxpayer must hold the stock for more than 60 days during the 121-day period that begins 60 days before the ex-dividend date. (Include the day the stock was disposed, but not the day acquired. The ex-dividend date is the first date following the declaration of a dividend on which the buyer of a stock will not receive the next dividend payment. Instead, the seller will get the dividend.)

Dividends Used to Buy More Stock

Some corporations have a dividend reinvestment plans that allow for the purchase of more stock in the corporation instead of receiving the dividends in cash. Taxpayers who are members of this type of plan must still report the dividends as income. If the plan allows the purchase of more stock at a price less than its fair market value, the taxpayer must report the fair market value of the additional stock as dividend income on the dividend payment date.

Money Market Funds

A taxpayer reports amounts received from money market funds as dividend income. Money market funds are a type of mutual fund, not to be confused with bank money market accounts that pay interest.

Capital Gain Distributions

Capital gain distributions reflect income paid or credited to the taxpayer's account by mutual funds (or other regulated investment companies) and real estate investment trusts (REITs). A taxpayer must report capital gain distributions as long-term capital gains regardless of how long the taxpayer has owned the shares of the mutual fund or REIT. Some mutual funds and REITs keep their long-term capital gains and pay tax on them.

> Shareholders receive **Form 2439** reflecting their share of undistributed long-term capital gains. Each must treat his share of gain as a distribution, even if not actually received. Report undistributed capital gains as long-term capital gains on Schedule D. A taxpayer can apply for a refund or credit of any payments made by including the amount in the "Payments" section of their tax return, and checking the appropriate box next to "2439."

Non-dividend Distributions

A *non-dividend distribution* (return of capital) is a distribution that is not a payment from the earnings and profits of a corporation. It is a return of an investment in the stock of the company and reduces the basis of the stock. It is not taxable until the taxpayer fully recovers his basis. When stock basis reaches zero, report any additional non-dividend distribution as a capital gain. Whether the taxpayer should report it as a long-term or short-term capital gain depends on his holding period.

Distributions of Stock and Stock Rights

Distributions by a corporation of its own stock or stock rights (also known as "stock options") are generally not taxable, and a holder of such options need not report them on a return. Distributions of stock dividends and stock rights are taxable if any of the following apply:

- Shareholders have the choice to receive cash or other property instead of stock or stock rights.
- The distribution gives cash or other property to some shareholders and an increase in the percentage interest in the corporation's assets or earnings and profits to other shareholders.
- The distribution is in convertible preferred stock, resulting in a change of ownership.
- The distribution is preferred stock for some common shareholders and common stock to others.
- The distribution is on preferred stock.

Rental Income and Expenses

Several factors determine the amount of rental income to include on a taxpayer's return. The IRS allows certain expenses as a deduction against gross rental income, resulting in either a gain or loss from rental activities. Report gross rental income and expenses on Schedule E, and transfer the resulting net gain or allowable loss amount to Form 1040.

Personal Use Property

The IRS treats rental real estate property as a home, if used for personal purposes more than the greater of **14 days or 10% of the total days rented to others.**

- If the taxpayer does <u>not</u> use the property as a home, report all the rental income and deduct all the rental expenses. Deductible rental expenses can be more than gross rental income.
- If the taxpayer uses the property as a home, the rental income and deductions depend on how many days the taxpayer rented the unit at a fair rental price.
    1) If rented **fewer than 15 days** during the year, do <u>not</u> treat that period as rental activity. Do not include any of the rent as income and do not deduct any of the rental expenses.
    2) If rented 15 days or more, include all rental income and allocate expenses between rental and personal use. If resulting in a loss, not all expenses may be deductible.
        A) Personal use is use by owners, family members, or anyone for less than fair value.
        B) Any day that the taxpayer rents the unit at a fair rental price is a day of rental use even if used for personal purposes that day.
        C) Any day that the unit is available but not actually rented is not a day of rental use.

Rental Income

Generally, a taxpayer must include all amounts received as rent in gross income. Rental income is any payment received for the use or occupation of property. In addition to amounts received as normal rent payments, other amounts may be rental income.

- **Advance rent** – Advance rent is any amount received before the period that it covers. Include advance rent as rental income during the year the taxpayer received the income, regardless of the period covered or the method of accounting used.
- **Security deposits** – Do not include a security deposit as income when the taxpayer receives the deposit if the taxpayer is to return the deposit to the tenant at the end of the lease. Include any part of the security deposit the taxpayer keeps because the tenant does not live up to the terms of the lease as income in that year. A taxpayer must treat a security deposit as income (advance rent) when received if the security deposit may be used as a final payment of rent.
- **Expenses paid by tenant** – If a taxpayer's tenant pays any of the taxpayer's expenses, the taxpayer must report the payments as rental income. These payments should be included as income. The taxpayer may deduct certain deductible *rental expenses*.
- **Property or services** – Include the fair market value of the property or services a tenant provides the taxpayer in place of rent as rental income when received. If the tenant provides the services at an agreed upon or specified price, that price is generally considered the fair market value.
- **Rents from personal property** – If renting out personal property, such as equipment or vehicles, the method for reporting income and expenses depends upon whether or not the rental activity is a business conducted for profit. In general, if the primary purpose is income or profit and the taxpayer is regularly involved in the rental activity, it is a business. Report income and expenses on Schedule C. If a rental activity is not a business, report rental income as other income on Form 1040 and include any expenses as an adjustment to gross income.

Rental Expenses

- **Related expenses** – Deductions from rental income include advertising, cleaning and maintenance, utilities, taxes, interest, commissions for the collection of rent, travel, and transportation.
- **Fire and liability insurance** – If the taxpayer pays insurance premiums for more than one year in advance, the part of the premium payment that will apply to a future year is not a deduction until that year. The taxpayer may not deduct the total premium in the year it was paid.

- **Depreciation** – Depreciate rental property when it is ready and available for rent. Depreciation is a method to recover the cost of income producing property through yearly tax deductions. The recovery period for residential real property is 27.5 years. The recovery period for non-residential real property is 39 years. Taxpayers may not depreciate the cost of land.

- **Repairs** – A repair keeps property in good operating condition. It does not materially add to the value of the property or substantially prolong its life. Repainting the property inside or out, fixing gutters or floors, fixing leaks, plastering, and replacing broken windows are examples of repairs. If the taxpayer makes repairs as part of an extensive remodeling or restoration of the property, the whole job is considered an improvement. The taxpayer may deduct the cost of repairs to the rental property. The taxpayer may not deduct the cost of improvements. Instead, the taxpayer may recover the cost of improvements by taking depreciation.

- **Improvements** – An improvement adds to the value of property, prolongs its useful life, or adapts it to new uses. If the taxpayer makes improvements to the property, the taxpayer <u>must capitalize</u> the cost of the improvement. Examples of improvements include putting a recreation room in an unfinished basement, adding a bathroom or bedroom, building a fence, installing new plumbing, wiring, or cabinets, putting on a new roof, and paving a driveway.

> A unit of property with an acquisition cost of $100 or less is generally not required to be capitalized and is treated instead as materials and supplies. All costs to improve eight specified building systems must be treated as capital expenditures. Those systems are HVAC, plumbing, electrical, escalators, elevators, fire protection and alarm, security, and gas distribution.

Additional Considerations

- **Local benefit taxes** – Generally, a taxpayer may not deduct charges for local benefits that increase the value of the property. Examples of these charges include charges for putting in streets, sidewalks, or water and sewer systems. These charges are non-depreciable capital expenditures, and the taxpayer must add them to the basis of the property.

- **Vacant rental property** – If holding property for rental purposes, ordinary and necessary expenses may be deducted (including depreciation) for managing, conserving, or maintaining the property while the property is vacant. Income loss due to a vacancy is not deductible.

- **Uncollected rent** – Cash basis taxpayers do not deduct uncollected rent because it was never considered as income. Under the accrual method, taxpayers report income when earned. If the taxpayer is unable to collect the rent, he may be able to deduct it as a bad business debt.

- **Not rented for profit** – If the taxpayer rents a property but does not rent the property to make a profit, the taxpayer may deduct rental expenses, but only up to the amount of the rental income. The taxpayer cannot deduct losses nor carry them forward to the next year if rental expenses are more than the rental income for the year.

- **Property changed to rental use** – If a property converts to rental use at any time after the beginning of the tax year, taxpayers divide yearly expenses such as taxes and insurance between rental and personal use. Only the portion of expenses relative to the rental use is deductible. The IRS does not permit deductions for depreciation or insurance during periods of personal use.

- **Renting part of property** – If the taxpayer rents part of the property, the taxpayer must divide certain expenses between the part of the property used for rental purposes and the part of the property used for personal purposes; it would be as though two separate pieces of property existed. The taxpayer need not divide expenses that belong only to the rental part of the property. The taxpayer may deduct depreciation on the part of the house used for rental purposes as well as on the furniture and equipment used for rental purposes.

Limits on Rental Losses

The following rules may limit the loss deduction allowed on a rental real estate activity. One must consider these rules in the order shown below:

- **At-risk rules** – Apply these rules first if there is investment in the taxpayer's rental real estate activity for which the taxpayer is not at risk. This applies only if the real property was placed in service after 1986. Generally, the IRS allows any loss from an activity subject to the at-risk rules <u>only</u> to the extent of the total amount that is at risk in the activity at the end of the tax year. A taxpayer is at risk in an activity to the extent of cash and the adjusted basis of other property contributions and certain amounts borrowed for use in the activity. Losses disallowed because of the at-risk limits are deductions from the same activity in the next tax year.

- **Passive activity limits** – Generally, the IRS considers rental real estate activities as passive activities, and a loss is not deductible unless income from another passive activity exists to offset it. The taxpayer may carry any excess *passive activity loss (PAL)* or credit forward to the next tax year. However, a loss may offset ordinary income if under the following two exceptions:

    1) A *real estate professional* may deduct losses against ordinary income, when both of the following conditions exist:

        A) More than <u>half</u> of work is involved in real property trades or businesses in which the taxpayer *materially participates*

        B) More than **750 hours** of material participation in real property trades or businesses.

    2) If rental losses are **less than $25,000**, and the taxpayer or spouse *actively participates* in the rental activity, the passive activity limits may not apply. Active participation is a less stringent standard than material participation. Active participation includes management decisions such as approving tenants, rental terms, approving expenditures, etc. If a taxpayer has modified adjusted gross income (MAGI) more than $100,000, the $25,000 special allowance is limited to 50% of the difference between $150,000 and MAGI. There is no allowance if MAGI is more than $150,000.

Modified adjusted gross income (MAGI) – Adjusted gross income figured without considering:

- The taxable amount of Social Security or equivalent tier 1 railroad retirement benefits
- The deduction allowed for contributions to IRAs or certain other qualified retirement plans
- The exclusion from income of interest from Series EE and I U.S. savings bonds
- The exclusion of amounts received under an employer's adoption assistance program
- Any passive activity income or loss included on Form 8582
- Any rental real estate loss allowed to real estate professionals
- Any overall loss from a publicly traded partnership
- The deductions allowed for self-employment tax, student loan interest, qualified tuition and fees
- The domestic production activities deduction

Pedro and his wife manage the daily activities of his 10-unit apartment building. He collects rent and orders repairs. The loss from this rental activity is $40,000. They also own an oil partnership generating $5,000 in passive income. MAGI is $125,000. They actively participate in the rental activity and can deduct $12,500 (50% of difference between MAGI and $150,000) against ordinary income on a jointly filed return. The remaining $27,500 is passive loss. They can use $5,000 of that loss in the current year against other passive income, and may carry forward the remaining $22,500 into the following year.

Social Security Benefits

Only a portion of Social Security benefits <u>may</u> be included in gross income.

- **Step 1:** Determine provisional income:

    1) **One-half** of Social Security benefits, *plus*

    2) All other income, including tax-exempt interest, *reduced by* all deductions for AGI, except those for tuition and fees, student loan interest or domestic production activities

Compare provisional income to the base amounts for filing status:

Bracket Location	S, HH, QW	MFJ	Taxable SS
Above Upper Base Amount	$34,000 +	$44,000+	85% MAX
Between Base Amounts	$25,000 to $34,000	$32,000 to $44,000	50% MAX
Below Lower Base Amount	0 to $25,000	0 to $32,000	NONE

- **Step 2:** Identify the <u>lowest</u> result from the steps below, and include that in gross income.

    1) Determine the maximum amount of benefits subject to tax as indicated below:

        A) If provisional income is **less than the lower** base amount, **NO** benefits are subject to tax.

        B) If **between** the brackets, a **MAXIMUM of 50%** of benefits is subject to tax.

        C) If it is **more than the upper** base amount, a **MAXIMUM of 85%** of benefits is subject to tax.

    2) Multiply the amount of provisional income between the brackets by 50% and the amount above the upper base amount by 85%, and then add together.

> For exam purposes, the chances are slim that you encounter questions with provisional income falling between the upper and lower base amounts. However, you should understand the level where a taxpayer will not pay any tax on benefits, and the level subjecting 85% of benefits to tax.

Retirement Plans, Pensions, and Annuities

The taxpayer must include distributions other than the taxpayer's cost (basis) from certain retirement plans or annuities in gross income. The IRS treats distributions of basis as a tax-free return of principal. A loss may arise if the entire account is withdrawn and a taxpayer receives less than his cost basis.

Qualified Retirement Plans and IRAs

For *qualified retirement plans (QP)* (401k, 403b, and certain pension plans) and *individual retirement arrangements (IRA)*, basis equals the amount of after-tax contributions remaining within the plan. Contributions that the taxpayer excludes from income do not constitute basis. Distributions from a qualified plan are usually taxable because most recipients have no cost basis. If the taxpayer has a basis, the pro rata portion of each withdrawal that represents basis is not taxed. Withdrawals, other than required distributions, can maintain tax-deferred treatment if transferred into another qualified plan or IRA within 60 days. This is commonly referred to as a *rollover*. Any amount withdrawn and not rolled over within this period is subject to tax. A *conversion* is a distribution from a qualified retirement plan or IRA into a Roth IRA. Conversions are taxed as ordinary distributions.

Annuities

An annuity in a qualified plan or IRA will receive the same tax treatment afforded to those plans. If the annuity is a *non-qualified annuity* (funded with after-tax dollars), individuals do not receive a tax deduction for the investment; therefore, the initial basis is the total of all contributions to the policy. Factors in addition to cost basis may also determine the tax treatment of withdrawals:

- *Annuitization* – The process of converting an annuity into a series of periodic payments.
    1) **Accumulation phase** – Prior to annuitizing, withdrawals are removed earnings first. The IRS treats any amount in excess of basis as ordinary income.
    2) **Distribution phase** – After annuitizing, allocate the periodic payments to income and basis according to an exclusion ratio. The exclusion ratio refers to the basis portion of each payment that is exempt from tax.
        A) Under the Simplified Method, figure the tax-free part of each annuity payment by dividing the cost by the total number of anticipated monthly payments. For an annuity that is payable for the lives of the annuitants, this number is based on the annuitants' ages on the annuity starting date and is determined from a table. For any other annuity, this number is the number of monthly annuity payments under the contract.
- **Exchanges** – During the accumulation phase, a policyholder may exchange an annuity under §1035 for a policy with another provider without recognition of taxes.

> George spends $100,000 for an immediate annuity. The insurance company will pay George $500 each month for the next 20 years. The tax-free portion of each payment is $416.67 ($100,000 / 240).

Qualified Distributions

Withdrawals other than *qualified distributions* may be subject to a 10% additional tax on the distribution. This tax applies to the amount received that the person must include in income. A qualified distribution is a payment that meets one the following criteria:

- Made on or after the date the person reaches age 59.5, (55 and separated from service for QP)
- Made because the taxpayer is disabled
- Made as part of a series of substantially equal periodic payments (rule 72t)
- Made to a beneficiary or to the taxpayer's estate after death
- Used to purchase the taxpayer's first home, up to a $10,000 lifetime limit

Mandatory Distributions

An owner of a tax-deferred retirement plan must begin mandatory *Required Minimum Distributions* from his account for each year starting with the year he reaches age 70.5 *(required beginning date)*. The first distribution is due April 1 following the year he reaches 70.5. All other future required distributions must occur by December 31 of each year. Figure the required minimum distribution for each year by dividing the IRA account balance (as of the close of business on December 31) of the preceding year by the applicable distribution period or life expectancy.

> Once a taxpayer reaches age 70.5 he can no longer contribute to an IRA, and must begin taking annual withdrawals. The RMD rules prevent people from leaving money in retirement accounts indefinitely. Failure to take RMD can result in a penalty equal to 50% of the required distribution amount. A non-qualified annuity is not subject to the age 70.5 restrictions.

Distributions Due to Death

The surviving spouse may elect to treat an inherited IRA or qualified retirement plan as his own by rolling the account into his name. All other beneficiaries must withdraw the entire balance of the retirement account over a specified period, depending on several factors, including age of decedent, age of beneficiary, and the type of beneficiary (i.e., individual, trust, or estate).

> A portion of funds within retirement plans or annuities has never been taxed or has accumulated free of tax. This amount, if withdrawn by the original account owner, would be subject to income tax. If the account owner dies, this amount becomes *income in respect of a decedent* (IRD) and is taxable to the beneficiary of the account upon withdrawal.

Roth IRAs

- No tax deduction on contributions
- Mandatory distributions are not required when attaining age 70.5
- Earnings inside of the Roth IRA are tax deferred, and qualified distributions are tax free when removed. Distributions from a Roth IRA are qualified only if made after the five-year anniversary of establishing and funding the account.

Other Income

A taxpayer must include certain other sources on income on his tax return. If applicable, the taxpayer should list the type and amount of each source on Form 1040, line 21.

Alimony

Payments to a former spouse that meet the criteria of *alimony* are included in the gross income of the recipient. *Property settlements* or payments of court ordered *child support* are not alimony and do not qualify as income or deduction items. For a more detailed discussion of alimony, *see Alimony in Ch. 6.*

Bartering Income

Bartering is an exchange of property or services. The taxpayer must report the fair market value of property or services received in bartering as income. The fair market value should be determined at the time of the exchange.

Canceled Debt

Generally, if a creditor cancels or forgives a debt, the debtor must report the canceled or forgiven amount as income. If the creditor intends the canceled debt as a gift or bequest, the debtor does not have to report it as income. A debt includes any indebtedness for which the taxpayer is liable or which attaches to property held by the taxpayer. Do not consider canceled debt as income in these cases:

- **Bankruptcy** – Debt canceled in a title 11 bankruptcy case.
- **Insolvency** – Immediately before the cancellation, liabilities exceed assets.
- **Certain student loans** – If the creditor canceled the debt due to performance of services.
- **Qualified real property business indebtedness** – Debt used to acquire, construct, or substantially improve new business real property; or to refinance business real property acquired before 1993.
- **Qualified principal residence indebtedness** – Debt incurred in acquiring, constructing, or substantially improving a principal residence and secured by the principal residence. Also includes

any debt resulting from the refinancing of such debt but only to the extent of the prior debt. Cash taken during refinancing is not qualified principal residence indebtedness.

- **Qualified farm indebtedness** – Debt directly related to business of farming, and more than 50% of gross receipts for past three years are from farming.

Unemployment Benefits

The IRS considers the amount of unemployment compensation received to be income. Unemployment compensation generally includes any amount received under an unemployment compensation law of the United States or of a state. The taxpayer should receive a Form 1099-G, Certain Government Payments, showing the amount of unemployment compensation paid.

Gambling Winnings

A taxpayer must report gambling winnings, such as lotteries and raffles, as income. In addition to cash winnings, the fair market value of bonds, cars, houses, and other non-cash prizes must be included as income.

A taxpayer may take gambling losses as an itemized deduction on Schedule A but only to the extent of gambling winnings. The taxpayer may not report a net loss from gambling.

Jury Duty Pay

Compensation for jury duty is included in income on Form 1040. If the taxpayer must give the pay to an employer because the employer continues to pay a salary while serving on the jury, he may deduct the amount turned over to the employer as an adjustment to income.

Court Awards and Damages

To determine if settlement amounts received are income, the taxpayer must consider the item that the settlement replaces. Include the following as ordinary income:

- Interest on any award.
- Compensation for lost wages or lost profits in most cases.
- *Punitive damages* (punishment). It does not matter if related to a physical injury or sickness.
- Amounts received in settlement of pension rights (if the taxpayer did not contribute to plan).
- Damages for one of the following:
    1) Patent or copyright infringement
    2) Breach of contract
    3) Interference with business operations
- Back pay and damages for emotional distress under Title VII of the Civil Rights Act of 1964.
- Attorney fees and costs where the underlying recovery is included in gross income.

Do not include in income *compensatory damages* (compensation) for personal physical injury, physical sickness, or emotional distress.

3 Depreciation and Basis

Depreciation · Basis of Property

This chapter summarizes data from IRS Publications 17, 523, 527, 537, 550, 551 and 946.

Depreciation

There are two basic types of property:

- **Tangible property** – Is physical in nature and includes land, structures, equipment, natural resources, etc. Tangible property is further divided into the following categories:
    1) **Real property** – Real estate including land, houses, buildings, etc.
    2) **Personal property** – Any tangible property other than real property
- **Intangible property** – Does not have a physical presence and includes computer software, patents, goodwill, stocks, and bonds

Expenditures that do not have a useful life beyond one year are *expenses*. A taxpayer may generally deduct expenses in the year he incurs them. Property acquired with a useful life greater than one year or *improvements* that increase the value of the property, lengthen its life, or adapt it to a different use are *capital expenditures*. A capital expenditure is *capitalized* (added to capital), and the cost is systematically *recovered* (written off) each year, in various ways, depending on type of property. The methods for recovering the cost of an asset over its useful life include the following:

- **Depreciation** – For tangible income producing property, other than natural resources
- **Depletion** – For assets that diminish over time such as oil, gas, and other natural resources
- **Amortization** – For intangible assets, such as patents and goodwill

The taxpayer may recover the cost of tangible income producing property through yearly tax deductions by depreciating the property, that is, by deducting some of the cost each year on the tax return. Three basic factors determine how much depreciation the taxpayer may deduct:

- The basis in the property
- The recovery period for the property
- The depreciation method used

A taxpayer cannot simply deduct mortgages, principal payments, or the cost of furniture, fixtures, or equipment as an expense. He may deduct depreciation only on the part of property used for a business or income-producing activity. A taxpayer cannot depreciate personal-use property. Depreciation reduces basis for figuring gain or loss on a later sale or exchange.

What Property Can Be Depreciated

- A taxpayer may depreciate property if it meets all the following requirements:

    1) The taxpayer owns the property.

    2) The taxpayer uses the property in business or income-producing activity (rental property).

    3) The property has a determinable useful life.

    4) The taxpayer expects the property to last more than one year.

Depreciation begins when a taxpayer places property in service for the production of income and ends when either the taxpayer fully recovers the cost, or the property is retired from service, whichever happens first. Property is placed in service in a rental activity when it is ready and available for a specific use in that activity. Even if unused, it is in service when it is ready and available for its specific use.

Repairs and Improvements

If depreciable property is improved, the taxpayer must treat the improvement as separate depreciable property. Improvement means an addition to or partial replacement of property that adds to its value, appreciably lengthens its useful life, or adapts it to a different use. Generally, the taxpayer may deduct the cost of repairing business property in the same way as any other business expense. However, a taxpayer must capitalize a repair or replacement that increases the value of the property, makes it more useful, or lengthens its life.

> A unit of property with an acquisition cost of $100 or less is generally not required to be capitalized and is treated instead as materials and supplies. All costs to improve eight specified building systems must be treated as capital expenditures. Those systems are HVAC, plumbing, electrical, escalators, elevators, fire protection and alarm, security, and gas distribution.

Basis of Property

Cost Basis

Basis is the amount of a taxpayer's investment in a property for tax purposes. A gain or loss is determined by subtracting the adjusted basis from the proceeds of the sale, exchange, or other disposition of property. A taxpayer uses basis to figure deductions for depreciation, amortization, depletion, and casualty losses. If a taxpayer uses property for business (or investment) purposes and for personal purposes, the taxpayer must properly allocate basis based on the property use. Only the basis allocated to business or investment use of the property is depreciable. The basis of property is usually its cost. The cost is the amount paid in cash, debt obligations, other property, or services. A taxpayer's cost basis also includes (but is not limited to) amounts paid for:

- Commissions
- Sales tax, freight, installation, and testing
- Legal and accounting fees (when they must be capitalized)
- Excise taxes, revenue stamps, recording fees, and real estate taxes (if assuming seller's liability)

The original basis in property is adjusted (increased or decreased) by certain events:

- Improvements to a property will increase basis.
- Deductions for depreciation or casualty losses or claiming certain credits will reduce basis.

Real Property

Real property, also called real estate, is land and generally anything built on, growing on, or attached to the land. Certain fees and other expenses are part of the cost basis in the property. If a taxpayer buys buildings and the land on which the buildings stand for a lump sum, the taxpayer should allocate cost basis among the land and the buildings. The taxpayer should allocate cost basis according to the respective fair market value (FMV) of the land and buildings at the time of purchase. The basis of each asset is calculated by multiplying the lump sum by a fraction. The numerator is the FMV of that asset, and the denominator is the FMV of the whole property at the time of purchase.

> Since land is not depreciable, a taxpayer must allocate a portion of the purchase price to land prior to calculating the depreciation deduction. Improvements that increase the value of a structure apply only to the structure and do not increase the basis of the land.

If a taxpayer buys property and assumes an existing mortgage on the property, the basis includes the amount paid for the property plus the amount to be paid on the mortgage. The basis is adjusted by certain settlement costs as described below:

- A taxpayer's basis includes the **settlement fees** and **closing costs** paid for buying the property. A fee for buying property is a cost that the taxpayer must pay even if he buys the property with cash. Do not include fees and costs for getting a loan on the property in the basis.

    1) Taxpayers may add the following settlement fees or closing costs to the basis:

        A) Abstract fees (abstract of title fees)

        B) Charges for installing utility services

        C) Legal fees (fees for the title search and preparation of the sales contract and deed)

        D) Recording fees

        E) Survey fees

        F) Transfer taxes

        G) Owner's title insurance

        H) Any amounts the buyer agrees to pay for the seller, such as back taxes or interest, recording or mortgage fees, cost of improvements or repairs, and sales commissions

    2) Taxpayers may not add the following settlement fees and closing costs to basis:

        A) Casualty insurance premiums.

        B) Rent for occupancy of the property before closing.

        C) Charges for utilities or other services related to the property before closing.

        D) Charges connected with getting a loan, such as points (discount points, loan origination fees), mortgage insurance premiums, loan assumption fees, cost of a credit report, and fees for an appraisal required by a lender.

        E) Fees for refinancing a mortgage. If a taxpayer pays points to get a loan (including a mortgage, second mortgage, line of credit, or a home equity loan), the points may not be added to the basis of the related property. Generally, the taxpayer will deduct points over the term of the loan. Special rules may apply to points taxpayers and sellers pay when they receive mortgages to buy their primary homes. If certain requirements are met, a taxpayer may deduct the points in full for the year in which they are paid. The basis of a home must be reduced by any seller-paid points.

F) Amounts placed in escrow for the future payment of taxes and insurance.

The term "points" is used to describe certain charges paid to obtain a home mortgage. Points are prepaid interest, and may be deductible as home mortgage interest. Special rules apply to points paid on a mortgage to buy a main home. If certain requirements are met, a taxpayer may deduct the points in full for the year in which they are paid. Points paid for refinancing generally can only be deducted over the life of the new mortgage. Points do not increase basis.

Points charged for specific services, such as preparation costs for a mortgage note, appraisal fees or notary fees are not interest and cannot be deducted. Points paid by the seller of a home cannot be deducted as interest on the seller's return, but they are a selling expense which will reduce the amount of gain realized. Points paid by the seller may be deducted by the buyer provided the buyer subtracts the amount from the basis, or cost, of the residence. Points you pay on loans secured by your second home can be deducted only over the life of the loan.

Adjusted Basis

Before figuring gain or loss on a sale, exchange, or other disposition of property or figuring allowable depreciation, depletion, or amortization, a taxpayer must usually make certain adjustments (increases and decreases) to the cost of the property. The result is the adjusted basis.

- **Increase** the basis of any property by all items properly added to a capital account. These include (but are not limited to) the following items:

    1) **Capital improvements** – The costs of improvements having a useful life of more than one year, which increase the value of the property, lengthen its life, or adapt it to a different use. Improvements include the following:

        A) Putting a recreation room in an unfinished basement

        B) Adding another bathroom or bedroom

        C) Building a fence

        D) Installing new plumbing or wiring

        E) Installing a new roof

        F) Paving the driveway

    2) **Assessments for local improvements** – Add property assessments for improvements that increase the value of the property assessed to the basis. Do not deduct these assessments as taxes. Examples include assessments for roads, sidewalks, water connections, and extending utility service to the property.

- **Decrease** the basis of any property by all items that represent a return of capital for the period during which the taxpayer held the property. Examples of items that decrease basis include (but are not limited to) the following items:

    1) **Non-taxable corporate distributions** – Also known as non-dividend distributions. This amount reflects a return of capital and reduces basis.

    2) **Casualty and theft losses** – Decrease the basis of property by any insurance proceeds or other reimbursement and by any deductible loss not covered by insurance. Increase the basis in the property by the amount spent on repairs that restore the property to its pre-casualty condition.

3) **Depreciation and Section 179 deduction** – The basis of a taxpayer's qualifying business property will be decreased by any Section 179 deductions taken and the depreciation deducted, or could have deducted (including any special depreciation allowance), on the taxpayer's returns under the method of depreciation selected.

4) **Easements** – Compensation for granting an easement is generally treated the same as proceeds from the sale of an interest in real property. Reduce basis by the amount received.

5) **Certain Credits** – Basis may be reduced by the amount of certain credits received due to the purchase of the property. Examples include the alternative motor vehicle credit, and the residential energy efficient property credit.

Property Received for Services

If a taxpayer receives property for services rendered, its FMV must be included in income. The amount included in income becomes the basis. If the taxpayer performed the services for a price agreed on beforehand, the IRS will accept that price as the FMV of the property if there is no evidence to the contrary. If the property is subject to certain restrictions, the basis in the property is its FMV when it vests substantially. However, this rule does not apply if the taxpayer makes an election to include in income the FMV of the property at the time the transfer of property occurs, less any amount the taxpayer paid for it. Property is substantially vested when it is transferable or when it is not subject to a substantial risk of forfeiture (the taxpayer does not have a good chance of losing it).

Bargain Purchases

A bargain purchase is a purchase of an item for less than its FMV. If, as compensation for services, a taxpayer buys goods or other property at less than FMV, the difference between the purchase price and the property's FMV must be included in income. The basis in the property is its FMV (the purchase price plus the amount included in income).

Involuntary Conversions

A taxpayer may receive replacement property after an *involuntary conversion*, such as a casualty, theft, or condemnation. The basis of the replacement property is based on the converted property.

- **Similar or related property** – If a taxpayer receives replacement property similar or related in service or use to the converted property, the replacement property's basis is the same as the converted property's basis on the date of the conversion, with the following adjustments:

    1) The basis is decreased by the following:

        A) Any loss recognized on the involuntary conversion

        B) Any money received that the taxpayer does not spend on similar property

    2) The basis is increased by the following:

        A) Any gain recognized on the involuntary conversion

        B) Any cost of acquiring the replacement property

- **Money or property not similar or related** – If a taxpayer receives money or property not similar or related in service or use to the converted property, and he buys replacement property similar or related in service or use to the converted property, the basis of the replacement property will be its cost decreased by the gain not recognized on the conversion.

Bill's dog knocks over a glass of milk destroying his work laptop. His basis in the laptop is $2,000. He receives a $2,500 insurance reimbursement and purchases another laptop for $2,200. Bill realizes a gain of $500. He does not spend $300 of the proceeds on the replacement property, reducing his basis. His adjusted basis in the new laptop is $1,900 ($2,200 cost − $300).

Property Received as a Gift

To establish the basis of property received as a gift, a taxpayer must know the adjusted basis to the *donor* (source of gift), its fair market value (FMV) at the time the donor gifted the property, and any gift tax paid on it. The annual exclusion is $14,000 in 2015 *(see Chapter 9)*. The relationship between the FMV and the donor's basis determines the applicable rule. If a taxpayer receives a gift of property and the donor's adjusted basis determines the basis, the IRS considers the taxpayer's holding period to have started on the same day the donor's holding period started. If the fair market value of the property determines the basis, the holding period starts on the day after the date of the gift.

- **FMV <u>less</u> than donor's adjusted basis** – Basis depends on whether a gain or a loss occurs when the property is disposed of. The following *dual basis rules* prevent taxpayers from shifting unrealized losses to other taxpayers:

    1) The basis for figuring gain is the same as the donor's adjusted basis.
    2) The basis for figuring loss is its FMV when the taxpayer received the gift.

- **FMV <u>equal to or greater</u> than donor's adjusted basis** – Basis is the donor's adjusted basis at the time the taxpayer received the gift.

    1) If the donor paid gift tax on the transfer, basis increases by the part of the gift tax that is due to the net increase in value of the gift. The net increase in value of the gift is the FMV of the gift minus the donor's adjusted basis. Figure the increase by multiplying the gift tax paid by a fraction.

$$Gift\ Tax\ Paid\ x\ \frac{FMV\ at\ time\ of\ gift - Donor's\ basis}{Amount\ of\ gift\ (after\ annual\ exclusion)}$$

Property Transferred from a Spouse

The basis and holding period of property transferred to a taxpayer or transferred in trust for the taxpayer's benefit by the taxpayer's spouse is the same as the spouse's adjusted basis. The same rule applies to a transfer by a taxpayer's former spouse that is incident to divorce. The taxpayer does not recognize any gain or loss on property transferred to a spouse or former spouse incident to divorce. This is true even if receiving cash or other consideration.

Inherited Property

With the exception of 2010 transfers electing modified carryover basis, a gain on inherited property is <u>always</u> long-term. Basis of an inherited capital asset is generally the FMV of the property on the date of death or an alternate valuation date, if elected by the personal representative. A *step-up* in basis occurs when the FMV is greater than the *decedent's* (person who died) basis.

The form of ownership can affect the amount of the step-up:

- *Qualified Joint Interest* – A qualified joint interest is any interest in property held by a husband and wife as *tenants by the entirety* or *tenants with rights of survivorship*. One-half of the value of the property receives a step up in basis to FMV.

- *Joint tenancy with rights of survivorship (JTWROS)* – Joint tenants with rights of survivorship share an equal interest in property. As such, they participate equally in income and deductions. If one owner dies, only the portion included in the decedent's estate receives a step-up in basis. The amount is dependent upon the percentage of total consideration for the property provided by the decedent and whether or not it was a gift. Where the capital contribution was 75%, and the decedent did not gift any portion of the property, 75% of the property receives a step-up in basis.

- *Community Property* – In community property states (Arizona, California, Idaho, Louisiana, Nevada, New Mexico, Texas, Washington, and Wisconsin), the husband and wife each usually own half of the community property. When either spouse dies, the total value of all community property, even the part belonging to the surviving spouse, can receive a step-up in basis, provided the decedent's share is part of their gross estate.

> Larry and his wife Kristina own 5,000 shares of Cocomart stock in a joint account, with rights of survivorship. Their basis in the stock is $75,000. At the time of Kristina's death in November of 2015 the stock had a fair market value of $200,000. Larry's new basis in Cocomart stock is $137,500, which represents ½ of the original basis plus a step-up of ½ the fair market value on the date of death.

Property Changed from Personal to Business or Rental Use

If a taxpayer holds property for personal use and then changes it to business use or uses it to produce rent, the taxpayer may begin to depreciate the property at the time of the change. To do so, calculate the property's basis for depreciation. An example of changing property held for personal use to business or rental use would be renting a former personal residence. The basis for depreciation is the lesser of the following amounts:

- The FMV of the property on the date of the change
- The adjusted basis on the date of the change

If the taxpayer sells the property at a loss, the FMV on date of conversion (with adjustments) is the cost for purposes of determining basis. If the taxpayer sells the property at a profit, the original basis (with adjustments) is used. This rule prevents a taxpayer from shifting nondeductible losses on personal property to deductible losses on business property.

Securities

The rules explained below apply to most investors. Dealers in securities and day-traders may utilize different methods to account for their transactions.

- **Stocks or bonds** – The basis of purchased stocks or bonds is generally the purchase price and any costs of purchase, such as commissions and recording or transfer fees.

    1) **Nontaxable stock dividends or stock splits** – In this situation, a shareholder's percentage of ownership does not change. Allocate the total adjusted basis of all shares *pro rata* to each share. Reduce the basis of existing shares by the amount of basis allocated to the new shares. This rule applies only when the additional stock received is identical to the stock held. For example, if a corporation declares a 2 for 1 split, each shareholder receives 2 shares for each share held. A shareholder with 100 shares at a basis of $10 per share, has a total of 200 shares with a basis of $5 per share after the split. The total basis is unchanged at $1,000.

    2) **Return of capital** – Also known as non-dividend distributions. This amount reflects a return of capital and reduces basis.

    3) **Subsequent Transactions** – If transactions occur at various times in varying quantities and the taxpayer cannot adequately identify the shares sold, the basis used is the basis of the securities acquired first. This is the *first in, first out (FIFO)* method. If adequate identification is possible, the taxpayer may elect to report the specific shares sold, regardless of their order of purchase.

- **Mutual Funds** – The rules for other securities also apply to mutual funds with one addition.
    1) **Subsequent Transactions** – In addition to FIFO or specific identification, a mutual fund may use the *average cost method* to calculate basis. Average cost reflects the average basis of all shares. Accounting for re-invested dividends or capital gains is easier with this method.
- **Options** – Gain or loss from the expiration, *closing transaction* (sale or trade to close position) of an option to buy or sell property, is reported as a capital gain or loss in the year these events occur. Upon expiration, if the option to buy or sell is unexercised, the IRS considers the taxpayer to have sold or traded the option on the date that it expired. The tax treatment of transactions is <u>different</u> if the taxpayer *exercises* the options. The option is <u>not</u> reported separately; instead, the option's cost (or proceeds) modifies the basis (or amount realized) on the underlying stock. A *put option* is the right to sell to the *writer (seller)*, at any time before a specified future date, a stated number of shares at a specified price. Conversely, a *call option* is the right to buy from the writer of the option, at any time before a specified future date, a stated number of shares of stock at a specified price. This adjustment depends on several factors:
    1) **Put buyer** – Reduces the amount realized on the sale of stock by the cost of the put
    2) **Call buyer** – Adds the cost of call to the basis of stock purchased
    3) **Put writer** – Reduces the basis of the stock purchased by the amount received for the put
    4) **Call writer** – Increases the amount realized on sale of stock by the amount received for call

Wash Sales

A taxpayer may not deduct losses from sales of stock or securities in a *wash sale*. A wash sale occurs when the taxpayer sells securities at a loss and, within 30 days before or after the sale, the taxpayer obtains the same securities or rights (options) to acquire identical securities. Do not include the date of sale in the calculation of the 30 days. Add the basis of any disallowed loss to the cost of the new securities. This adjustment postpones the loss deduction until the disposition of the new stock or securities.

Moe buys 1,500 shares of Acme stock on December 7, 2015. He sells the shares on December 31, 2015 at a loss of $3,000. Regretting his decision, he buys 1,000 shares of Acme stock on January 29, 2016. This partial wash sale prevents him from claiming the entire loss. He can deduct only $1,000 of the loss due to the 500 shares he did not replace. The remaining loss of $2,000 increases the basis of the replacement stock. On Form 8949, he should report the entire loss with the appropriate box checked; enter "W" in column (b); enter as a positive number in column (g) the amount of the loss not allowed.

4 Gains and Losses

Disposition or Sale of Property · Reporting Gains and Losses

This chapter summarizes data from IRS Publications 17, 523, 527, 537, 550, 551, and 946.

Disposition or Sale of Property

Worthless Securities

Stocks, stock rights, and bonds (other than those held for sale by a securities dealer) that became completely worthless during the tax year are treated as though they were sold on the <u>last day of the tax year</u>. Worthless securities also include securities abandoned after March 12, 2008. To abandon a security, the taxpayer must permanently surrender and relinquish all rights in the security and receive no consideration in exchange for it. Consider all the facts and circumstances to determine whether the taxpayer should characterize the transaction as abandonment or another type of transaction, such as an actual sale or exchange, contribution to capital, dividend, or gift.

Non-business Bad Debt

A taxpayer who is owed money that he cannot collect is said to have a bad debt. The bad debt may be deductible during the year it becomes worthless. There are two kinds of bad debts—business and non-business. A business bad debt, generally, is one that comes from operating a trade or business and is deductible as a business loss. All other bad debts are non-business bad debts and are deductible as short-term capital losses, if the debt meets the following conditions:

- A debt must be <u>totally worthless</u>.

- The debt must be genuine. A debt is genuine if it arises from a debtor-creditor relationship based on a valid and enforceable obligation to repay a fixed or determinable sum of money.

- There must be an intention at the time of the transaction to make a loan and <u>not a gift</u>. If a taxpayer lends money to an individual with the understanding that the individual does not have to pay it back, it is a gift and not a loan. A taxpayer may not take a bad debt deduction for a gift. There cannot be a bad debt unless there is a true creditor-debtor relationship between the taxpayer and the individual or organization that owes the money.

- There is no genuine debt when minor children borrow from their parents to pay for their basic needs. A taxpayer may not take a bad debt deduction for such a loan.

- To deduct a bad debt, the taxpayer <u>must have a basis</u> in it. The amount must have already been included in income or loaned out in cash. For example, a taxpayer cannot claim a bad debt deduction for unpaid court-ordered child support. A cash method taxpayer (most individuals) generally may not deduct unpaid salaries, wages, rents, fees, interest, dividends, and similar items.

- A taxpayer can only take a bad debt deduction in the year the debt becomes worthless. A taxpayer does not have to wait until a debt is due to determine whether it is worthless. A debt becomes worthless when there is no longer any chance that the debtor will pay the amount owed.

- It is not necessary to go to court if the taxpayer can show that a judgment from the court would be uncollectible. A taxpayer need only show that he has taken reasonable steps to collect the debt. Bankruptcy of the debtor is generally good evidence of the worthlessness of a debt.
- If a taxpayer guarantees a debt that becomes worthless, he may not take a bad debt deduction for payments on the debt unless it can be shown that either the reason for making the guarantee was to protect the investment or that the taxpayer entered the guarantee transaction with a profit motive. If the taxpayer made the guarantee as a favor to friends without any consideration in return, the IRS will treat the payments as a gift and the taxpayer may not take a bad debt deduction.

Sale of Property

Calculate the gain or loss on the sale property by subtracting the adjusted basis from the amount *realized* to get the gain or loss. The amount realized is the selling price minus selling expenses. Selling expenses include commissions, advertising fees, legal fees, and loan charges paid by the seller, such as loan placement fees or "points." A taxpayer may exclude from income a gain up to certain levels on the sale of his *main home* (see Exclusions). A taxpayer may not deduct a loss on the sale of his main home; however, the taxpayer must report the loss on Schedule D even though it is not deductible.

Involuntary Conversion

A taxpayer has had a disposition when property is destroyed or *condemned* and the taxpayer receives another property or money in payment, such as insurance or a condemnation award. The IRS treats this as a sale, and the taxpayer may be able to exclude all or part of any gain from the destruction or condemnation of the main home, as explained above.

Installment Sale

Some sales involve arrangements that provide for part or the entire selling price to be paid in a later year. These sales are *installment sales.* The buyer's obligation to make future payments can be in the form of a deed of trust, note, land contract, mortgage, or other evidence of the buyer's debt. If a sale qualifies as an installment sale, the taxpayer must report the gain under the *installment method* unless the taxpayer elects to report the gain in the current year. If the sale results in a loss, a taxpayer may not use the installment method. The following conditions apply to an installment sale:

- Increase the adjusted basis for installment sale purposes by selling expenses (commissions, attorney fees, and any other expenses paid on the sale) and depreciation recapture.
- If a taxpayer sells property on which a depreciation deduction was claimed or could have been claimed, the taxpayer must report the amount of the deduction (or amount that could have been claimed) as *depreciation recapture* income in the year of sale, whether or not an installment payment was received that year. Report the recapture income in full as ordinary income in the year of sale; report only the gain greater than the recapture income on the installment method.
- Each payment on an installment sale usually consists of three parts—interest income, return of adjusted basis in the property, and gain on the sale.
- The method to determine the amount of gain recognized as installment income is as follows:
    1) **Determine gross profit** – Gross profit is the selling price less the adjusted basis for installment sale purposes. If the property is the taxpayer's main home, subtract any gain that the taxpayer can exclude from the gross profit.
    2) **Gross profit percentage** – A certain percentage of each payment (after subtracting interest) is reported as installment sale income. Calculate this *gross profit percentage* by dividing the gross profit from the sale by the contract price.

3) **Installment sale income recognized** – To arrive at the amount recognized, multiply the payments received each year (less interest) by the gross profit percentage.

Jim and Jean purchased a vacation home in 1997 for $100,000. They sold the property for $500,000 and received a down payment of $200,000. They took a mortgage from the purchaser for the remaining $300,000. Gross profit is $400,000 ($500,000 selling price - $100,000 basis). Determine the gross profit percentage by dividing the gross profit from the sale by the contract price. Gross Profit Percentage is 80% ($400,000 gross profit divided by $500,000 selling price). Jim and Jean must report 80% of each payment (after subtracting interest) as installment sale income.

- In each year that a taxpayer receives an installment payment, the taxpayer must include in income both the interest part and the part that is the taxpayer's gain on the sale. If an installment sale contract does not provide for adequate stated interest (when compared to the *applicable federal rate*), the taxpayer may reclassify part of the stated principal amount of the contract as interest. The taxpayer should not include in income the part that is the return of the basis in the property. Basis is the amount of the investment in the property for installment sale purposes.

- If the taxpayer sells depreciable property to certain *related persons*, the taxpayer may not report the sale using the installment method. Instead, all payments due are considered received in the year of sale. However, the taxpayer may use the installment method in a related party transaction if he derives no significant tax deferral benefit from the sale. The taxpayer must show, to the satisfaction of the IRS, that avoidance of federal income tax was not a principal purpose of the sale.

- If the taxpayer sells property to a related person and, within two years, the related person disposes of the property before the taxpayer receives all payments with respect to the sale, the taxpayer may have a reporting obligation. The taxpayer may have to treat part or all of the amount the related person realizes (or the FMV if the disposed property is not sold or exchanged) from the second disposition as if the taxpayer received it at the time of the second disposition.

- **Disposition of an installment obligation** – A disposition generally includes a sale, exchange, cancellation, bequest, distribution, or transmission of an installment obligation. An installment obligation is the buyer's note, deed of trust, or other evidence that the buyer will make future payments to the taxpayer.

    1) If a taxpayer is using the installment method and the installment obligation is disposed of, generally the taxpayer will have a gain or loss to report. The gain or loss applies to the sale of the property for which the taxpayer received the installment obligation. If the original installment sale produced ordinary income, the disposition of the obligation will result in ordinary income or loss. If the original sale resulted in a capital gain, the disposition of the obligation will result in a capital gain or loss.

    2) **Rules to figure gain or loss** – Use the following rules to figure gain or loss from the disposition of an installment obligation:

        A) If the taxpayer sells or exchanges the obligation, or accepts less than face value in satisfaction of the obligation, the gain or loss is the difference between the basis in the obligation and the amount realized.

        B) If the obligation is disposed of in any other way, the gain or loss is the difference between the basis in the obligation and FMV at the time of the disposition. This rule applies, for example, when the taxpayer gives the installment obligation to someone else or cancels the buyer's debt.

3) Calculate the basis in an installment obligation by multiplying the unpaid balance on the obligation by the gross profit percentage. Subtract that amount from the unpaid balance. The result is the basis in the installment obligation.

In 2001, Sue sold an airplane on the installment method. She needed cash in 2015 so she sold the note for $110,000 when the balance due her was $140,000. Her gross profit percentage was 60%. Of the $140,000 still owed to Sue, $84,000 is profit owed to her on the obligation, and $56,000 is her basis. She receives $110,000 for the note so she has a profit of $54,000.

Like-kind Exchanges

If a taxpayer trades business or investment property for other business or investment property of a *like kind*, the taxpayer does not pay tax on any gain or deduct any loss until the taxpayer sells or disposes of the property received. The taxpayer may realize a partial gain to the extent of cash and the fair market value of any unlike property received. If a taxpayer trades property with a *related party* in a like-kind exchange, if either the taxpayer or the related party disposes of the like property within two years after the trade, both parties must report any gain or loss not recognized on the original trade on the return for the year in which the later disposition occurs.

Related Party

A taxpayer may not deduct a loss on the sale or trade of property, other than a distribution in complete liquidation of a corporation, if the transaction is directly or indirectly between the taxpayer and the following related parties:

- Members of taxpayer's family, which includes only brothers and sisters, half-brothers and half-sisters, spouse, ancestors (parents, grandparents, etc.), and lineal descendants (children, grandchildren, etc.)
- A partnership or corporation with more than 50% directly or indirectly owned by the taxpayer
- A tax-exempt charitable or educational organization controlled by taxpayer or family member

Reporting Gains and Losses

Holding Period

In general, the holding period for investment property begins the day after the day the property is acquired (trade date) or receipt of title and includes the date of disposition, transfer, or sale. Gain or loss is *short-term* on property held one year or less; otherwise, the holding period is *long-term*.

Gain Recognition

- **Amount realized** – The amount *realized* from a sale or trade of property is everything received for the property. This includes the money, the fair market value of any property or services, and debt or other liabilities assumed by the buyer.
- **Realized gains** – The difference between adjusted basis and the amount realized in a sale is the realized gain (or loss) on the transaction.
- **Amount recognized** – The amount of income or loss *recognized* is the amount a taxpayer includes in taxable income for the tax year. Certain transactions such as *like-kind exchanges* and *installment sales* may defer recognition of gain.

Pay careful attention to the language of each exam question. Multiple questions may test your understanding of the difference between realized and recognized gains.

Capital Assets

Generally, a sale or trade of a *capital asset* results in a *capital gain* or loss. A sale or trade of a non-capital asset results in *ordinary gain* or loss. In some situations, part of the gain or loss may be a capital gain or loss and part may be an ordinary gain or loss. Rather than defining capital assets, the Internal Revenue Code provides a list of properties that are not capital assets. Any property a taxpayer holds is a capital asset, except the following non-capital assets:

- Inventory or property held mainly for sale to customers or property that will physically become a part of the merchandise that is for sale to customers

- Accounts or notes receivable acquired in the ordinary course of a trade or business for services rendered or from the sale of property held mainly for sale to customers

- Depreciable property used in the taxpayer's trade or business

- Real property (real estate) used in the taxpayer's trade or business

- A copyright, literary, musical, artistic composition, letter or memorandum, or similar property that meets one of the following criteria:

    1) Created by a taxpayer's personal efforts

    2) Prepared or produced for a taxpayer (as in a letter, memorandum, or similar property)

    3) Acquired under circumstances (for example, by gift), entitling the taxpayer to the basis of the person who created the property or for whom it was prepared or produced

- U.S. government publications that a taxpayer received from the government free or for less than the normal sales price, or that was acquired under circumstances entitling the taxpayer to the basis of someone who received the publications free or for less than the normal sales price

- Certain commodities derivative financial instruments held by commodities derivatives dealers

- Hedging transactions, but only if the transaction is clearly identified as a hedging transaction before the close of the day on which it was acquired, originated, or entered into

- Supplies of a type regularly used in the ordinary course of a taxpayer's trade or business

For the most part, everything owned and used for personal purposes, pleasure, or investment is a capital asset. Some examples include the following:

- Stocks or bonds held in a personal account

- House owned and used by the taxpayer and the taxpayer's family

- Household furnishings

- A car used for pleasure or commuting

- Coin or stamp collections

- Gems and jewelry

Investment Property

Investment property is a capital asset. Any gain or loss from its sale or trade is generally a capital gain or loss, unless a dealer holds them for sale. Examples include gold, silver, stamps, coins, gems, stocks, bonds, etc. The taxpayer recaptures depreciation on investment property when he sells the property.

Personal Use Property

Property held for personal use only is a capital asset. If a taxpayer sells personal use property, he must report the difference between the sale price and the basis in the asset, if positive, as a capital gain. The IRS does not permit a deduction for capital loss on the sale of personal use property.

Capital Gains Rates

If a taxpayer has a taxable gain or a deductible loss from a transaction, it may be either a capital gain or loss or an ordinary gain or loss, depending on the circumstances. Capital gains receive more favorable tax treatment than ordinary gains, to which ordinary income tax rates apply. The tax rates that apply to a *net capital gain* are generally lower than the tax rates that apply to other income. These lower rates are the *maximum capital gain rates*. Long-term capital gains (other than gains on collectibles, small business stock, or un-recaptured 1250 gains) receive special tax treatment and are taxed at a maximum rate of 20%. Short-term capital gains are taxed at the same rates as ordinary income. Report overall capital gains and losses on Schedule D (Schedule D is not necessary if only gains are from distributions).

Table 4-1. What Is the Maximum 2015 Capital Gain Rate?

IF the net capital gain is from ...	THEN the maximum capital gain rate is ...
Gain on collectibles or qualified small business stock	28%
Un-recaptured Section 1250 gain	25%
Other gain and the regular tax rate that would apply is 39.6%	20%
Other gain and the regular tax rate that would apply is 25%, 28%, 33% or 35%	15%
Other gain and the regular tax rate that would apply is 15% or lower	0%

> Long-term capital gains (other than gains on collectibles, small business stock, or un-recaptured §1250 gains) receive special tax treatment and a maximum rate of 20%. Ordinary income tax rates apply to short-term capital gains. Report overall capital gains and losses on Schedule D, unless reporting only capital gain distributions, which are reportable directly on Form 1040 without the use of Schedule D.

Form 8949

Many transactions that, in previous years, would have been reported on Schedule D or D-1 must be reported on *Form 8949* if they occur in 2015. Schedule D-1 is no longer in use as Form 8949 replaces it. A taxpayer must now use Form 8949 to list all capital gain and loss transactions; the subtotals from this form will then be carried over to Schedule D (Form 1040), where gain or loss will be calculated in aggregate. Short-term gains are listed together in part I, while long-term gains are listed in part II. There are three categories for each part of the new form:

(A) Transactions reported on Form 1099-B with basis reported to the IRS

(B) Transactions reported on Form 1099-B but basis not reported to the IRS

(C) Transactions for which you cannot check box A or B

A taxpayer with transactions in multiple categories must complete a separate part of Form 8949, for each of the three categories.

A taxpayer uses Form 8949 to report:

- The sale or exchange of a capital asset not reported on another form or schedule,
- Gains from involuntary conversions (other than from casualty or theft) of capital assets not held for business or profit, and
- Nonbusiness bad debts.

Calculating Net Gains and Losses

Tax rates differ, depending upon the nature of the gain and the type of property involved. Combine gains and losses in each category to arrive at a net gain or loss.

- **Short-term gains and losses** – Sale or trade of investment property held one year or less. Combine the taxpayer's share of short-term capital gain or loss from partnerships, S corporations, fiduciaries, and any short-term capital loss carryover with other short-term capital gains and losses to figure the *net short-term capital gain* (NSTCG) or loss (NSTCL).

- **Long-term gains and losses** – Sale or trade of investment property held more than one year is a long-term capital gain or loss. Combine the taxpayer's share of long-term capital gain or loss from partnerships, S corporations, and fiduciaries, as well as any long-term capital loss carryover with other long-term capital gains and losses, to figure *net long-term capital gain* (NLTCG) or loss (NLTCL).

- **Total net gain or loss** – A taxpayer may calculate total net gain or loss by comparing the net short-term capital gain or loss to the net long-term capital gain or loss. If a taxpayer has a:

    1) **Net gain and a net loss** (NLTCG and NSTCL or NLTCL and NSTCG) – The resulting gain or loss maintains the character of the larger item. Example: If net short-term losses exceed net long-term gains, the character of the resulting net loss is short-term

    2) **Both short and long-term losses** (NLTCL and NSTCL) – Each loss maintains its character, either long or short-term

    3) **Both short and long-term gains** (NLTCG and NSTCG) – Each gain is taxed at the tax rates described in table 4-1

Capital Loss Carryover

If capital losses are more than capital gains, a taxpayer may claim a capital loss deduction. The allowable capital loss deduction, figured on Schedule D, is the lesser of the following:

- $3,000 ($1,500 if taxpayer is married and files a separate return)
- The taxpayer's total net loss, as shown on Schedule D

A taxpayer may use his total net loss to reduce income dollar for dollar, up to the $3,000 limit. If the total net loss exceeds the yearly limit on capital loss deductions, carry the unused part over to the next year and treat it as though it had incurred in that next year. If part of the loss is still unused, the taxpayer may carry the unused part over to later years until none of the loss remains. When calculating the amount of any capital loss carryover to the next year, consider the current year's allowable deduction, whether or not the taxpayer has claimed the allowable deduction. When a taxpayer carries over a loss, it remains long term or short term. Any long-term capital losses carried over to the next tax year will reduce that year's long-term capital gains before it reduces that year's short-term capital gains. In calculating the capital loss carryover, a taxpayer should use the short-term capital losses first, even if the taxpayer incurred those losses after a long-term capital loss. If a taxpayer has not reached the limit on the capital loss deduction after using the short-term capital losses, use the long-term capital losses until the taxpayer has reached the limit.

> Sheila has both long and short- term capital losses in 2015. Her net STCL is $5,000 and a net LTCL is $10,000. She can only deduct $3,000 in the current year and must use her short-term loss first. She carries $2,000 STCL and $10,000 LTCL forward to 2016.

Section 1244 Small Business Stock

> A *small business corporation* may qualify for special treatment under **Section 1244**. If so, any gain on the sale of stock is a capital gain if the stock is a capital asset. A taxpayer may deduct the loss on the sale, trade, or worthlessness of Section 1244 stock as an ordinary loss, rather than as a capital loss. The amount a taxpayer may deduct as an ordinary loss is limited to $50,000 each year. On a joint return the limit is $100,000, even if only one spouse has this type of loss.

- A corporation shall be treated as a small business corporation if the aggregate amount of money and other property received by the corporation for stock, as a contribution to capital, and as paid-in surplus, does not exceed $1,000,000.

- During the 5-year period ending before the date the loss, the corporation must derive more than 50 percent of its aggregate gross receipts from sources other than royalties, rents, dividends, interests, annuities, and sales or exchanges of stocks or securities.

Section 1202 Exclusion

Certain eligible C corporations with gross assets under $50 million may qualify for special treatment under *Section 1202* as *qualified small business stock (QSB)*. A taxpayer selling QSB stock held for more than five years can exclude up to 50% of the eligible gain from income (100% for stock acquired during certain periods in 2010 and thereafter).

> For stock acquired after September 27, 2010, the §1202 exclusion is 100% of eligible gains. Congress made the 100% exclusion permanent in the PATH Act of 2015. The amount of gain eligible for the exclusion is limited to the greater of $10,000,000 or 10 times the adjusted bases of disposed QSB stock.

- Certain corporations do not qualify, such as a REIT, REMIC, RIC, DISC, FASIT, cooperative, or corporation electing treatment as a possessions corporation.

- The C corporation must be an active business using at least 80% of assets in the active conduct of a qualified trade or business. The following trades or businesses do not qualify:

    1) Services performed in the fields of health, law, engineering, architecture, accounting, actuarial science, performing arts, consulting, athletics, financial services, or brokerage services
    2) One whose principal asset is the reputation or skill of one or more employees
    3) Any banking, insurance, financing, leasing, investing, or similar business
    4) Any farming business (including the business of raising or harvesting trees)
    5) Oil or gas operations if percentage depletion can be claimed
    6) Any business of operating a hotel, motel, restaurant, or similar business

Passive Activity Losses

A taxpayer reports capital gains or losses from a passive activity on Form 8582. Passive activities occur when there is income from certain businesses where no material participation occurs. Passive losses are not deductible unless the taxpayer has income from other passive activities to offset them.

5 Items Excluded from Gross Income

Items Excluded from Gross Income · Municipal Bond Interest · Gain on Sale of Main Home · Discharge of Qualified Principal Residence Indebtedness · Employee Achievement Awards · Fringe Benefits · Housing Allowance for Members of Clergy · Military and Government Disability Pensions · Education Related Benefits · Workers' Compensation · Compensation for Sickness and Injury · Life Insurance · Foreign Earned Income Exclusion

This chapter summarizes the items specifically excluded from gross income as outlined in Publications 15B, 17, 54, 547, and 970.

Items Excluded from Gross Income

Certain forms of income are not subject to federal income tax. An *exclusion* item is any income that is specifically not taxed. A few of the major exclusions from income are as follows:

- **Municipal bond interest** – Interest from state and local government bonds is generally excluded.
- **Gain on sale of main home** – Up to $500,000 for qualifying married filers.
- **Discharge of debt due to bankruptcy or insolvency**
- **Discharge of qualified principal residence indebtedness** – Up to $2 million.
- **Social Security benefits** – Up to 85% of benefits may be included in gross income; therefore, exclude a minimum of 15% from gross income (for detailed calculations, see *Chapter 2 Gross Income*).
- **Employee achievement awards** – Up to $1,600 for length of service or safety achievement.
- **Fringe benefits** – Certain employer-provided fringe benefits are specifically excluded.
- **Housing allowance for member of clergy** – A reasonable housing allowance may be excluded.
- **Military and government disability pensions** – Must not be based on years of service.
- **Veterans (VA) benefits** – Does not include any veterans' benefits paid under any law, regulation, or administrative practice administered by the Department of Veterans Affairs (VA) in income.
- **Gifts and inheritances** – Generally, property received as a gift, bequest, or inheritance.
- **Scholarships and fellowships** – Exempt if used for qualified educational expenses.
- **Distributions from Coverdell ESA or 529 Plan** – When taxpayer uses distributions to pay for qualified educational expenses of the designated beneficiary.
- **Interest on Series EE and I savings bonds** – When used for qualified higher education expenses.
- **Workers' compensation** – Payments for occupational sickness or injury under the workers' compensation act.
- **Compensation for sickness or injury** – Compensatory damages from a lawsuit, benefits under a health insurance plan where taxpayer paid the premiums or reimbursements for medical care.

- **Welfare or public assistance** – Exclude unless payment for services or obtained fraudulently.
- **Life insurance proceeds** – Death payouts are generally tax free to beneficiary.
- **Accelerated death benefits** – Exclude payments to the terminally or chronically ill.
- **Casualty insurance** – Exclude insurance settlements received to compensate for damaged or stolen property from income. However, include in income any payments for living expenses that are more than the temporary increase in actual living expenses.
- **Qualified disaster relief payments** – Due to terrorist or military action, federally declared disaster area, or an accident involving a common carrier determined to be catastrophic.
- **Property settlements** – A taxpayer does not recognize any gain on a transfer of property to a spouse due to divorce. However, any gain on later distribution or sale of the property may be taxable.
- **Child support** – Child support payments are excluded.
- **Foster care** – In general, exclude payments received as a provider of foster care.
- **Reimbursements for certain employment-related expenses** – Exclude from the employee's income any ordinary and necessary business expenses related to travel, meals, and entertainment paid by the employee and later reimbursed under an employer's *accountable plan*.
- **Foreign earned income exclusion** – Up to $100,800 of foreign earnings per qualifying person in 2015.

Municipal Bond Interest

Generally, interest on a bond used to finance government operations is not taxable if a state, the District of Columbia, a U.S. possession, or any of their political subdivisions issues the bond for a public purpose. Even if interest is not subject to tax, capital gain or loss may apply when sold. Political subdivisions include:

- Port authorities
- Toll road commissions
- Utility services authorities
- Community redevelopment agencies
- Qualified volunteer fire departments (for certain obligations issued after 1980)

Private Activity Bonds

Not all Municipal bond interest is exempt from federal income tax. Interest on bonds used for most private activities is <u>not</u> exempt from income tax. A bond is generally considered a ***private activity bond*** if the amount of the proceeds to finance loans to persons other than government units is more than 5% of the proceeds or $5 million (whichever is less). This is called the "private loan financing test." If the bond is a private activity bond, but is exempt, it is referred to as a *"qualified bond"* or *"qualified private activity bond."* Private activity bonds are often used to build a sports facility or industrial park, airport, for-profit hospital, etc.

Interest on a bond to finance a bridge is exempt from federal income tax. Interest on a bond to build a new sports arena is taxable. Report both on Form 1040, but exclude exempt interest from income.

Interest listed on the 1099 as private activity bond interest is from qualified private activity bonds. Qualified private activity bond interest is listed separately on the 1099 because it is a tax preference item for AMT. Interest from nonqualified private activity bonds is simply added into the taxable interest on the 1099 and not separately stated. This is likely to appear on the exam (i.e., Which of the following items is a preference or adjustment item for AMT?), with *qualified private activity bond interest* being one of the items on a list.

Gain on Sale of Main Home

A taxpayer who meets certain qualifications may exclude gains on the sale of a principal residence. This is a ***Section 121 exclusion***. Usually, the home in which the taxpayer lives most of the time is the main home. In addition to a house, a main home may also be a condominium, cooperative apartment, houseboat, or mobile home. If a taxpayer uses only part of the property as a main home, these rules apply only to the gain or loss on the sale of that part. A taxpayer may not exclude gain on a home acquired in a like-kind exchange for a period of 5 years.

The taxpayer must own and live in the property as his **main home** for at least <u>two years during the five-year period</u> ending on the date of sale.

Ownership and Use Tests

During the five-year period ending on the date of the sale, the taxpayer must meet the following ownership and use tests in order to claim the exclusion:

- **Ownership test** – Owned the home for at least two years.

- **Use test** – Lived in the home as a main home for at least two years. Occupancy does not have to be consecutive so long as periods of residence total 24 months (730 days). Occupancy does not have to begin on, or end on, the dates of purchase or sale of the property.

    1) Taxpayers with occupancy of less than two years may claim a reduced exclusion if the move is due to unexpected changes in employment, health, or other unforeseen circumstances.

    2) Certain members of the military, intelligence community, or Peace Corps volunteers may suspend the five-year test by up to 10 additional years if on qualified official extended duty.

There is an exception to the use test if a taxpayer becomes physically or mentally unable to care for himself, and he owns and lives in the home as a main home for at least 1 year during the 5-year period before the sale of the home. Under this exception, the taxpayer is considered to live in the home during any time within the 5-year period that he owns the home and lives in a facility (including a nursing home). This exception is for the use test only, as the taxpayer still must meet the 2-out-of-5-year ownership test to claim the exclusion.

Maximum Exclusion

- Taxpayers may exclude up to <u>$250,000</u> of the gain if all of the following are true:

    1) The taxpayer meets the ownership test.

    2) The taxpayer meets the use test.

    3) The taxpayer did not exclude the gain from the sale of another home during the two-year period ending on the date of the sale.

- Taxpayers may exclude up to $500,000 of the gain if all of the following are true:

    1) The taxpayer is married and files a joint return for the year.

    2) Either the taxpayer or spouse meets the ownership test.

    3) Both the taxpayer and spouse meet the use test.

    4) During the two-year period ending on the date of the sale, neither taxpayer nor spouse excluded gain from the sale of another home.

Periods of Nonqualified Use

Generally, the gain from the sale or exchange of a main home will not qualify for the exclusion to the extent that the taxpayer allocates gains to periods of nonqualified use. Nonqualified use is any period after December 31, 2008, during which the taxpayer does not use the property as his main home. Allocate the gain resulting from the sale of the property between qualified and nonqualified use periods based on the amount of time the taxpayer held property for qualified and nonqualified use. Gain from the sale or exchange of a main home allocable to periods of qualified use will continue to qualify for the exclusion for the sale of a main home. Gain from the sale or exchange of property allocable to nonqualified use will not qualify for the exclusion.

- A period of nonqualified use does not include:

    1) Any portion of the five-year period ending on the date of the sale or exchange that is after the last date the taxpayer (or spouse) used the property as a main home

    2) Any period (not to exceed an aggregate period of 10 years) during which taxpayer or spouse is serving on qualified official extended duty for any of the following:

        A) As a member of the uniformed services,

        B) As a member of the Foreign Service of the United States

        C) As an employee of the intelligence community

    3) Any other period of temporary absence (not to exceed an aggregate period of two years) due to change of employment, health conditions, or such other unforeseen circumstances as may be specified by the IRS.

- To figure the portion of the gain that is allocated to the period of nonqualified use, multiply the gain by the following fraction:

$$\frac{\textit{total nonqualified use during period of ownership after } 2008}{\textit{total period of ownership}}$$

Business Use or Rental of Home

A taxpayer may be able to exclude gain from the sale of a home that he has used for business or to produce rental income. However, a taxpayer must meet the ownership and use tests. If a taxpayer is entitled to take depreciation deductions because his main home was used for business purposes or as rental property (even if he did not actually claim them), he may not exclude the part of the gain equal to any depreciation allowed or allowable as a deduction for periods after May 6, 1997. If the taxpayer can show, by adequate records or other evidence, that the depreciation allowed was less than the amount allowable, the amount a taxpayer may not exclude is the amount allowed.

Discharge of Qualified Principal Residence Indebtedness

A taxpayer may be able to exclude from gross income a *discharge of qualified principal residence indebtedness*. This exclusion applies to discharges made after 2006 and before 2017. If a taxpayer chooses to exclude this income, reduce the basis of the principal residence by the amount excluded from the gross income (not less than zero).

- **Principal residence** – The principal residence is the home where the taxpayer ordinarily lives most of the time. There can only be one principal residence at any one time.

- **Qualified principal residence indebtedness** – Debt that the taxpayer incurs while acquiring, constructing, or substantially improving a principal residence, for which the principal residence serves as security. Also includes any debt resulting from the refinancing of such debt but only to the extent of prior debt. Cash taken during refinancing is not qualified principal residence indebtedness.

- **Amount eligible for the exclusion** – The exclusion applies only to debt discharged after 2006 and before 2017. The maximum amount that the taxpayer may treat as qualified principal residence indebtedness is $2 million ($1 million if married filing separately). The taxpayer may not exclude discharge of qualified principal residence indebtedness from gross income if the discharge was for services performed for the lender or because of any other factor not directly related to a decline in the value of the residence or to the taxpayer's financial condition.

Employee Achievement Awards

Generally, if tangible personal property is received (other than cash, a gift certificate, or an equivalent item) as an award for length of service or safety achievement, its value may be excluded from the taxpayer's income. However, the amount the taxpayer may exclude is limited to an employer's cost and cannot be more than $1,600 ($400 for awards that are not qualified plan awards) for all such awards received during the year. The award must be part of a meaningful presentation, under conditions and circumstances that do not create a significant likelihood of it being disguised pay. This exclusion does <u>not</u> apply to the following awards:

- A length-of-service award for less than five years of service or if already received another length-of-service award during the previous 4 years,

- A safety achievement award for managers, administrators, clerical employees, or other professional employees or if more than 10% of eligible employees previously received safety achievement awards during the year.

Fringe Benefits

Fringe benefits received in connection with the performance of services are included in income as compensation unless the employee pays fair market value for the benefits or the law specifically excludes them. The IRS treats abstaining from the performance of services (for example, under a covenant not to compete) as the performance of services for purposes of these rules.

- **Accident or health plan** – Generally, the values of an accident or health plan coverage that an employer provided to a taxpayer are not to be included as income. Benefits received from the plan may be taxable, as explained later under *Sickness and Injury Benefits*.

- **Long-term care coverage** – Contributions by employers to provide coverage for long-term care services generally are not included as income. However, contributions made through a flexible spending or similar arrangement (such as a cafeteria plan) must be included in income. This amount appears as wages in box 1 of Form W-2.

- **Archer MSA contributions** – Employer contributions to an Archer MSA generally are not included as income. The total of these contributions appears in box 12 of Form W-2 with code R. The taxpayer must report this amount on Form 8853, Archer MSAs and Long-Term Care Insurance Contracts. A taxpayer should file Form 8853 with his returns. If a taxpayer does not enjoy employer contributions to his MSA, the taxpayer may make his own contributions.

- **Meals and lodging** – An employee can exclude the value of employer provided meals or lodging from gross income if provided on the employer's premises for the employer's convenience.

- **Health flexible spending arrangement (health FSA)** – If an employer provides a health FSA that qualifies as an accident or health plan, the amount of salary reduction and reimbursements of medical care expenses for the employee and those of the employee's spouse and dependents are not included in income.

- **Health reimbursement arrangement (HRA)** – If the employer provides an HRA that qualifies as an accident or health plan, coverage and reimbursements of medical care expenses and those of a spouse and dependents generally are not included in income.

- **Health savings accounts (HSA)** – Employer contributions are not included in income. Distributions from the HSA that the taxpayer uses to pay qualified medical expenses are not included in income. Distributions not used for qualified medical expenses are included in income and may be subject to early withdrawal penalties.

- **De Minimis (Minimal) benefits** – If an employer provides employees with products or services where the cost of it is so small that it would be unreasonable for the employer to account for it, the value is not included in income. Examples of this would include coffee, doughnuts, etc.

- **Holiday gifts** – If an employer gives employees turkeys, hams, or other items of nominal value at Christmas or other holidays, the value of the gift should not be included in income. However, if the employer gives an employee cash, gift certificates, or similar items that may easily be exchanged for cash, the employee should include the value of that gift as extra salary or wages regardless of the amount involved.

- **Dependent care assistance** – Generally, employees may exclude from income up to $5,000 received from an employer's dependent care assistance program.

- **Adoption assistance** – For 2015, an employee may exclude up to $13,400 of expenses incurred by an employer for qualified adoption expenses in connection with the adoption of an eligible child.

- **Educational assistance** – For tax year 2015, employees may exclude from income up to $5,250 of qualified employer-provided educational assistance (payments of tuition, fees, books, supplies, and equipment for either undergraduate or graduate education). Employees may not exclude expenses for meals, lodging, supplies, tools, or transportation. Exclusion is generally not available for education related to sports, games or hobbies unless it has a relationship to the business of the employer or is otherwise required to obtain a degree.

- **Group-term life Insurance** – Generally, the cost of up to $50,000 of group-term life insurance coverage provided by an employer (or former employer) is not included in income. However, the cost of employer-provided insurance that is more than the cost of $50,000 of coverage reduced by any amount the employee pays toward the purchase of the insurance should be included as income. If a group-term life insurance policy includes permanent benefits, such as a paid-up or cash surrender value, an employee should include the cost of the permanent benefits minus the amount paid for them as income in the form of wages. The exclusion is for term life insurance protection (insurance for a fixed period of time), meeting all of the following conditions:

    1) The insurance must provide a general death benefit

2) The insurance must be provided to a group of employees

3) Is insurance must be under a policy carried by the employer

4) The insurance must provide an amount of insurance to each employee based on a formula that prevents individual selection

- **Retirement planning services** – Qualified retirement planning services that an employer provides to employees are not included in income. Qualified services include retirement planning advice, information about the employer's retirement plan, and information about how the plan may fit into the overall individual retirement income plan. Employees may not exclude the value of any tax preparation, accounting, legal, or brokerage services provided by the employer.

- **Transportation** – Employees may exclude employer-provided qualified transportation fringe benefits from income in 2015, within limits. Qualified transportation fringe benefits include the following:

    1) A *transit pass* or transportation in a commuter highway vehicle (such as a van) between the home and workplace (up to $250/month).

    2) Qualified parking (up to $250/month).

    3) Qualified bicycle commuting – Up to $20 reimbursement for each month the taxpayer uses a bicycle regularly for a substantial portion of travel between home and place of employment. This can include expenses for bicycle purchase, improvements, repair, and storage.

- **No additional cost services** – Employees may exclude the value of certain employer-provided services from income when the services do not cause the employer any substantial additional costs. The employer must offer the services to customers in the ordinary course of the line of business in which the employee performs substantial services. Generally, no-additional-cost services are excess capacity services, such as airline, bus, or train tickets; hotel rooms; or telephone services provided free or at a reduced price to employees working in those lines of business.

- **Athletic facilities** – Employees may exclude the value of using employer-owned athletic facilities if substantially all use is by employees, spouses, and dependent children.

- **Employee discounts** – Employees may exclude discounts on either of the following:

    1) Merchandise up to the employer's gross profit percentage

    2) Services up to 20% of the price charged to non-employees

- **Qualified retirement plan contributions** – Employer contributions to a qualified retirement plan for employee accounts are not included in income at the time contributed. Although not immediately taxed, these contributions are not excluded from income when withdrawals occur from the plan.

    1) **Elective deferrals** – An employee contribution is treated the same as an employer contribution to a qualified plan. An elective deferral, other than a designated Roth contribution, is not included in wages subject to income tax at the time contributed. However, it is included in wages subject to Social Security and Medicare taxes.

Housing Allowance for Members of Clergy

A member of the clergy should not include the rental value of a home (including utilities) or a designated housing allowance provided to the member as part of income. However, the exclusion may not be more than the reasonable pay for services. If the member pays for the utilities, he may exclude any allowance designated for utility cost, up to the actual cost. The home or allowance must represent compensation for services rendered as an ordained, licensed, or commissioned minister. If the taxpayer is subject to the self-employment tax, he must include the rental value of the home or the housing allowance as earnings from self-employment on Schedule SE (Form 1040).

Military and Government Disability Pensions

Service-connected Disability

Taxpayers may exclude from income amounts received as a pension, annuity, or similar allowance for personal injury or sickness resulting from active service in one of the following government services:

- The armed forces of any country
- The National Oceanic and Atmospheric Administration
- The public health service
- The foreign service

Conditions for Exclusion

Disability payments should not be included in income if *any* of the following conditions apply:

- The taxpayer is entitled to receive a disability payment before September 25, 1975.
- The taxpayer was a member of a listed government service or its reserve component, or was under a binding written commitment to become a member, on September 24, 1975.
- The taxpayer receives the disability payments for a combat-related injury or sickness that meets one of the following criteria:
    1) Results directly from armed conflict
    2) Takes place while engaged in extra-hazardous service
    3) Occurs under conditions simulating war, including training exercises such as maneuvers
    4) Is caused by an instrumentality of war
- The taxpayer would be entitled to receive disability compensation from the Department of Veterans Affairs (VA) upon the filing of an application. Exclusion under this condition is equal to the amount the taxpayer would be entitled to receive from the VA.

Pension Based on Years of Service

Generally, if a taxpayer receives a disability pension based on years of service, the pension must be included in income. However, if the pension qualifies for exclusion for a service-connected disability as listed above, the part of the pension based on a percentage of disability should not be included as income. The rest of the pension should be included in income.

Education-related Benefits

Scholarships and Fellowships

A candidate for a degree may exclude amounts received as a qualified scholarship or fellowship. A qualified scholarship or fellowship is any amount received that is for one of the following:

- Tuition and fees to enroll at or attend an educational institution
- Any fees, books, supplies, and equipment required for courses at the educational institution.

Amounts used for <u>room and board do not qualify</u> for the exclusion. A taxpayer must include in income the part of any scholarship or fellowship that represents payment for past, present, or future teaching, research, or other services. This applies even if all candidates for a degree must perform the services to receive the degree. Scholarship prizes won in a contest are not scholarships or fellowships if a taxpayer does not <u>have to use the prizes</u> for educational purposes. Include these amounts as income on Form 1040, whether or not the taxpayer used them for educational purposes.

Education Savings Bond Program

Under the Education Savings Bond Program, a taxpayer may exclude all or part of the interest received on the redemption of qualified U.S. savings bonds during the year if the taxpayer uses that interest to pay for qualified higher educational expenses during the same year. Taxpayers will not qualify for this exclusion if their filing status is married filing separately.

- **Qualified U.S. savings bonds** – A qualified U.S. savings bond is a series EE bond issued after 1989 or a series I bond. The bond must be in the taxpayer's name (sole owner) or jointly held with a spouse. The taxpayer must be at least 24 years old before the bond's issue date. The issue date of a bond may be earlier than the date the taxpayer purchased the bond because the issue date assigned to a bond is the first day of the month in which it is purchased.

- **Qualified expenses** – Qualified higher educational expenses are tuition and fees required for a taxpayer and dependents (for whom an exemption is claimed) to attend an eligible educational institution. Qualified expenses include any contribution made to a qualified tuition program or to a Coverdell education savings account.

    1) Qualified expenses <u>do not include</u> expenses for <u>room and board</u> or for courses involving sports, games, or hobbies that are not part of a degree or certificate-granting program.

- **Eligible educational institutions** – These institutions include most public, private, and nonprofit universities, colleges, and vocational schools that are accredited and are eligible to participate in student aid programs run by the Department of Education.

- **Reduction for certain benefits** – A taxpayer must reduce his qualified higher-educational expenses by all of the following tax-free benefits:

    1) Tax-free part of scholarships and fellowships

    2) Expenses used to figure the tax-free portion of distributions from a Coverdell ESA

    3) Expenses used to figure the tax-free part of distributions from a qualified tuition program

    4) Any tax-free payments (other than gifts or inheritances) received for educational expenses:

        A) Veterans' educational assistance benefits

        B) Qualified tuition reductions

        C) Employer-provided educational assistance

    5) Any expense used for the American Opportunity and Lifetime Learning credits

- **Amount excludable** – If the total proceeds (interest and principal) from the qualified U.S. savings bonds redeemed during the year are not more than the adjusted qualified higher educational expenses for the year, the taxpayer may exclude all of the interest. If the proceeds are more than the expenses, the taxpayer may exclude only part of the interest. To determine the amount to exclude from income, divide the qualified expenses by the total bond proceeds. Multiply this percentage by the amount of bond interest to arrive at the amount excluded from income. The remainder of the interest is included in income.

- **Modified adjusted gross income limit** – The interest exclusion is limited if 2015 modified adjusted gross income (MAGI) is as follows:
    1) $77,200 to $92,200 for taxpayers filing single or head of household
    2) $115,750 to $145,750 for married taxpayers filing jointly or for a qualifying widow(er) with dependent child

Qualified Education Expenses

For purposes of the *Coverdell ESA* and *qualified tuition programs (QTP)*, qualified education expenses are the amounts paid for tuition, fees, books, supplies, and equipment required for enrollment or attendance at an eligible educational institution. They also include the reasonable costs of room and board for a designated beneficiary who is at least a half-time student. The cost of room and board qualifies only to the extent that it is not more than the greater of the following two amounts:

- The allowance for room and board, as determined by the eligible educational institution, that was included in the cost of attendance (for federal financial aid purposes) for a particular academic period and living arrangement of the student
- The actual amount charged if the student is residing in housing owned or operated by the eligible educational institution

Adjust qualified education expenses to take into account certain credits, such as the *American Opportunity credit* or *Lifetime Learning credit*, and any other tax-free benefits received to pay for expenses. If a designated beneficiary receives distributions from both a QTP and a Coverdell ESA in the same year, and the total of these distributions is more than the beneficiary's adjusted qualified higher education expenses, allocate the expenses between the distributions. For purposes of this allocation, disregard any qualified elementary and secondary education expenses.

> Qualified education expenses include the cost of room and board for ESAs and QTPs, but not for other purposes such as the education credits, education savings bond program, scholarships and fellowships.

Coverdell Educational Savings Account (ESA)

A Coverdell ESA is a trust or custodial account created or organized in the United States only for paying the qualified education expenses of the designated beneficiary of the account. While there is no tax deduction for contributions, earnings are tax deferred. Exclude distributions from a Coverdell ESA from income up to the amount of qualified education expenses for the year, adjusted for other benefits received. The expenses may be qualified higher education expenses or qualified elementary and secondary education expenses.

- The account must be a designated Coverdell ESA when the taxpayer created the account.
- Account documents must be in writing and must satisfy the following requirements:
    1) The trustee or custodian must be a bank or an entity approved by the IRS.
    2) The trustee or custodian may only accept contributions that meet the following conditions:
        A) The contribution is in cash.
        B) The contribution is made before the beneficiary (other than a special needs beneficiary) reaches age 18.
        C) Contributions for the year (not including rollovers) may not be more than $2,000.
    3) The taxpayer cannot invest the money in the account in life insurance contracts.

4) The taxpayer cannot combine the money in the account with other property except in a common trust fund or common investment fund.

   A) The account balance must be distributed within 30 days after the earlier of the following:

      (a) The beneficiary reaches age 30, unless a special needs beneficiary

      (b) The beneficiary's death

- If modified adjusted gross income (MAGI) is between $95,000 and $110,000 (between $190,000 and $220,000 if filing a joint return), then the $2,000 contribution limit for each designated beneficiary is gradually reduced. If MAGI is $110,000 or more ($220,000 or more if filing a joint return), the taxpayer cannot contribute to anyone's Coverdell ESA.

- Calculate the reduced contribution amount by multiplying $2,000 by a fraction. The numerator (top number) is the MAGI minus $95,000 ($190,000 if filing a joint return). The denominator (bottom number) is $15,000 ($30,000 if filing a joint return). Subtract the result from $2,000. The taxpayer may contribute this amount for each beneficiary.

Qualified Tuition Programs (QTPs)

A qualified tuition program (also known as a *529 program*) is a program set up to allow the taxpayer to either prepay or contribute to an account established for paying a student's qualified higher education expenses at an eligible educational institution. A state, a state agency, an instrumentality of a state, or an eligible educational institution can establish and maintain a QTP.

- The part of a distribution representing the amount paid or contributed to a QTP is not included in income. This is a return of the investment in the program.

- The beneficiary generally does not include earnings distributed from a QTP in income if the total distribution is less than or equal to adjusted qualified higher education expenses. Income is reported to the recipient on Form 1099Q. The beneficiary is the recipient when distributions are made either directly to the beneficiary or to an eligible educational institution for his benefit. Consequently, taxable distributions constitute income to the beneficiary when paid either directly to the beneficiary or to an eligible educational institution for his benefit. Otherwise, the account owner is the recipient.

- The designated beneficiary is generally the student (or future student) for whom the QTP is intended to provide benefits. The taxpayer can change the designated beneficiary.

- Contributions to a QTP on behalf of any beneficiary cannot be more than the amount necessary to provide for the qualified education expenses of the beneficiary.

- There are no income restrictions on the individual contributors.

An ESA and a QTP are similar in that neither offers a tax deduction for contributions to the plan, earnings accumulate free of tax until withdrawn, and withdrawals are excluded from income if used for qualified education expenses. A QTP is different from an ESA in the following ways: the beneficiary of a QTP can be any age and can even change, QTP does not have age-based distribution requirements, contributions can be far more than allowed in an ESA, and there are no income restricitions.

Workers' Compensation

An amount received as workers' compensation for an occupational sickness or injury is fully exempt from tax if paid under a workers' compensation act or similar statute. The exemption also applies to the victim's survivors. The exemption does not apply to retirement plan benefits received based on age, length of service, or prior contributions to the plan, even if an occupational sickness or injury caused retirement. If a taxpayer returns to work after qualifying for workers' compensation, salary payments received for performing light duties are taxable as wages.

Compensation for Sickness or Injury

Many other amounts taxpayers receive as compensation for sickness or injury are not taxable. These include the following amounts:

- Compensatory (not punitive) damages received from a lawsuit for physical injury or physical sickness, whether paid in a lump sum or in periodic payments.
- Benefits under an accident or health insurance policy on which either a taxpayer paid the premiums or the taxpayer's employer paid the premiums and those premiums were included in income.
- Disability benefits received for loss of income or earning capacity because of injuries under a no-fault car insurance policy.
- Compensation for permanent loss (or loss of use) of a part or function of the body, or for permanent disfigurement. This compensation must be based only on the injury and not on the period of absence from work. These benefits are not taxable, even if an employer pays for the accident and health plan that provides these benefits.
- A reimbursement for medical care is generally not taxable. However, it may reduce the medical expense deduction.

Life Insurance Proceeds

Life insurance proceeds paid because of the death of the insured person are <u>not taxable</u> unless the taxpayer sold the policy to another for a price (*see Viatical Settlements*). This is true even if the taxpayer received proceeds under an accident or health insurance policy or an endowment contract.

- If the taxpayer receives death benefits paid in a *lump sum* or other than at regular intervals, include in income only the benefits that are more than the amount payable at the time of the death.
- If the taxpayer receives payment of life insurance proceeds in installments, exclude part of each installment from income. To determine the excluded part, divide the amount held by the insurance company (generally the total lump sum payable at the death of the insured person) by the number of installments to be paid. Include anything more than this excluded part in income as interest.
    1) If the spouse of the taxpayer died before October 23, 1986, and the taxpayer receives payment in installments of insurance proceeds because of the death, the taxpayer may exclude up to $1,000 a year of the interest included in the installments, even if the taxpayer remarries.
- *Endowment contract proceeds* – An endowment contract is a policy under which the taxpayer receives a specified amount of money on a certain date. If the taxpayer dies before that date, the money goes to the designated beneficiary. Endowment proceeds paid in a lump sum at maturity are taxable only if the proceeds are more than the cost of the policy. To determine the cost, take any amount previously received under the contract (and excluded from income) and subtract that from the total premiums (or other consideration) paid for the contract. Include the part of the lump sum payment that is more than the cost in income.
- *Accelerated death benefits* – Exclude certain amounts paid as accelerated death benefits under a life insurance contract or viatical settlement before the insured's death if the insured is terminally or chronically ill.

1) **Exclusion for terminal illness** – Accelerated death benefits are fully excludable if the insured is a terminally ill individual, certified by a physician as having an illness or condition reasonably expected to result in death within 24 months from the date of the certification.

2) **Exclusion for chronic illness** – If the insured is a chronically ill individual, who is not terminally ill, accelerated death benefits paid based on costs incurred for qualified long-term care services are fully excludable. Accelerated death benefits paid on a *per diem* or other periodic basis are excludable up to a limit.

3) **Viatical settlement** – This is the sale or assignment of any part of the death benefit under a life insurance contract to a *viatical settlement provider* in the business of buying insurance contracts on the lives of insured individuals who are terminally or chronically ill.

Foreign Earned Income Exclusion and Foreign Housing Exclusion

A U.S. citizen or resident alien of the United States who lives abroad pays taxes on his worldwide income. However, he may qualify to exclude some or all of his foreign earnings from income. For tax year 2015, the exclusion cannot be more than the smaller of the following:

- $100,800 ($201,600 MFJ and both meet the requirements)
- Foreign earned income for the tax year minus the amount of foreign housing exclusion

The taxpayer may exclude or deduct certain foreign housing amounts, limited to the lesser of the foreign housing costs paid for with employer-provided amounts or the amount of foreign earned income. For purposes of determining the foreign housing exclusion or deduction, a taxpayer cannot consider housing expenses that exceed a certain limit. The limit on housing expenses is generally 30% of the maximum foreign earned income exclusion, but it may vary depending upon the location in which you incur housing expenses. A calendar year taxpayer with $100,800 or less of foreign earned income in a 12-month period can use *Form 2555-EZ* to claim the earned income exclusion. A taxpayer with self-employment income, business or moving expenses, or those claiming the foreign housing exclusion or deduction must use *Form 2555*.

To claim the *foreign earned income exclusion*, the *foreign housing exclusion*, or the *foreign housing deduction* (deduction only available if the taxpayer is self-employed), a taxpayer must meet all three of the following requirements:

- The *tax home* must be in a foreign country. A tax home is the place where a taxpayer permanently or indefinitely engages to work as an employee or self-employed individual. The tax home is not in a foreign country for any period in which the taxpayer's abode is in the United States. An abode is one's home, habitation, residence, domicile, or place of dwelling.

- The *taxpayer* must have foreign earned income.

- The taxpayer must meet <u>one</u> of the following tests:

    1) **Bona Fide Residence Test** – A taxpayer does not automatically acquire bona fide resident status merely by living in a foreign country for one year. The length of stay and the nature of the job are additional factors that determine whether a taxpayer meets the test. A taxpayer who travels to a foreign country to work on a particular construction job for a specified period-of-time ordinarily is not a bona fide resident of that country even if working there for more than one tax year. To be a bona fide resident a taxpayer must be:

        A) A U.S. citizen who is a bona fide resident of a foreign country or countries for an uninterrupted period that includes an entire tax year, or

B) A U.S. resident alien who is a citizen or national of a country with which the United States has an income tax treaty in effect and who is a bona fide resident of a foreign country or countries for an uninterrupted period that includes an entire tax year

2) **Physical Presence Test** – A U.S. citizen or a U.S. resident alien physically present in a foreign country or countries for at least 330 full days during any period of 12 consecutive months. The physical presence test is based only on how long the taxpayer is in a foreign country. This test does not depend on the kind of residence established, intentions about returning, or the nature and purpose of the stay abroad.

There is a differece between the *Physical Presence Test* and the *Substantial Presence Test* used to determine U.S. residency status. Aside from the number of days required, the former measures time in a foreign country while the latter measures time in the United States.

6 Adjustments to Gross Income

Individual Retirement Arrangements (IRAs) · Health Account Deductions · Moving Expenses · Self-employed Health Insurance · Self-employed SEP, SIMPLE, and Qualified Plans · Alimony · Education-related Adjustments · Miscellaneous Adjustments

This chapter summarizes adjustments to gross income referenced in Publications 17, 521, 590, and 969.

Individual Retirement Arrangements (IRAs)

An **individual retirement account** is a trust or custodial account set up in the United States for the exclusive benefit of a taxpayer or his beneficiaries. A taxpayer creates this account with a written document. The document must show that the account meets all of the following requirements:

- The trustee or custodian must be a bank, a federally insured credit union, a savings and loan association, or an entity approved by the IRS to act as trustee or custodian.
- The trustee or custodian generally should not accept contributions of more than the deductible amount for the year. However, rollover contributions and employer contributions to a simplified employee pension (SEP) can be more than this amount.
- Contributions, except for rollover contributions, must be in cash.
- The taxpayer must have a non-forfeitable right to the amount at all times.
- The account holder cannot use money in the account to buy a life insurance policy.
- The account holder cannot combine assets with other property, except in a common trust or investment fund.
- Distributions must begin by April 1 of the year after the taxpayer reaches age 70.5.

Traditional IRAs

A traditional IRA (sometimes called an ordinary or regular IRA) is any IRA that is not a Roth IRA or a SIMPLE IRA. A traditional IRA can be an individual retirement account or annuity. It can be part of either a simplified employee pension (SEP) or an employer or employee association trust account. Two advantages of a traditional IRA are as follows:

- Contributions may be tax deductible, depending on the circumstances
- Amounts in the IRA, including earnings and gains, are not taxed until distributed

Taxpayers can set up and contribute to a traditional IRA only if the following conditions exist:

- Taxpayer or spouse received **taxable compensation** during the year
- Taxpayer is younger than age 70.5 at the end of the year

Individuals can have a traditional IRA even if covered by another retirement plan. Contributions may not be deductible if the taxpayer (or spouse) is covered by an employer retirement plan. If both a taxpayer and a spouse have compensation and are younger than age 70.5, each can set up an IRA; however, they cannot participate in the same IRA. If filing a joint return, only one spouse needs to have compensation.

- **Compensation** – Generally, compensation is the amount earned from working. Compensation includes wages, salaries, tips, professional fees, bonuses, and other amounts individuals receive for providing personal services. For IRA purposes, compensation includes amounts considered taxable alimony and nontaxable combat pay. For the *self-employed* (a sole proprietor or a partner), compensation is the *net earnings* (do not consider a net loss) from a trade or business (provided the personal services are a material income-producing factor) reduced by the total of the following:

    1) The deduction for contributions made on the taxpayer's behalf to retirement plans
    2) The deduction allowed for the employer-equivalent portion of self-employment taxes

- Compensation does NOT include any of the following:

    1) Earnings and profits from property, such as rental, interest, and dividend income
    2) Pension or annuity income
    3) Deferred compensation received (compensation payments postponed from a past year)
    4) Income from a partnership if taxpayer does not provide services that are a material income-producing factor
    5) Amounts excluded from income (other than combat pay), such as foreign earned income

Contribution Deadlines

A taxpayer can make contributions to a traditional IRA at any time during the year or by the due date for filing the return for that year, not including extensions. For most taxpayers, this is April 15.

Jim makes a contribution to his IRA on February 3, 2016. Jim can apply his contribution to 2015 or 2016. He can apply the contribution to the 2015 tax year since it is made before the due date of his 2015 tax return. He can apply the contribution to 2016, the actual year of deposit.

General Limit on IRA Contributions

For 2015, an individual taxpayer's maximum contribution to a traditional IRA is the smaller of the following:

- $5,500 ($6,500 if 50 or older, due to a $1,000 catch-up contribution)
- 100% of taxable compensation for the year

Spousal IRA Limit

If filing a joint return with a spouse, the IRA contribution for the person with the lowest compensation cannot exceed:

- $5,500 ($6,500 if 50 or older)
- The total compensation includible in the gross income of both spouses for the year, reduced by the following two amounts:

    1) The other spouse's IRA contribution for the year to a traditional IRA
    2) Any contribution for the year to a Roth IRA on behalf of the other spouse

The total combined contributions that a taxpayer can make for the year to both IRAs can be as much as $11,000 ($12,000 if one is 50 or older, or $13,000 if both are 50 or older).

Tax on Excess Contributions

Contributions above the allowed limits are *excess contributions*. If the taxpayer does not withdraw excess contributions by the due date of the return (including extensions), a taxpayer is subject to a 6% tax and must pay the 6% tax each year on excess amounts that remain in the traditional IRA.

Deduction Limits

Generally, the deduction is the lesser of the following:

- The actual contributions to a traditional IRA for the year
- The general limit on contributions (or the spousal IRA contribution limit, if it applies)

The deduction may be limited if an employer retirement plan covers either spouse at any time during the year for which contributions are made. The deduction limitation does not affect the amount that the taxpayer can contribute.

Table 6-1. Effect of MAGI on Deduction if Taxpayer Is Covered by a Retirement Plan at Work – 2015

IF your filing status is	AND your modified AGI is	THEN you can take
single or head of household	$61,000 or less	a full deduction
	between $61,000 – $71,000	a partial deduction
	$71,000 or more	no deduction
married filing jointly or qualifying widow(er)	$98,000 or less	a full deduction
	between $98,000 – $118,000	a partial deduction
	$118,000 or more	no deduction
married filing separately	less than $10,000	a partial deduction
	$10,000 or more	no deduction

Table 6-2. Effect of MAGI on Deduction if Taxpayer Is **NOT** Covered by a Retirement Plan at Work – 2015

IF your filing status is	AND your modified AGI is	THEN you can take
single, head of household, or qualifying widow(er)	any amount	a full deduction
married filing jointly or **separately** and spouse is not covered by a plan at work	any amount	a full deduction
married filing jointly and spouse is covered by a plan at work	$183,000 or less	a full deduction
	between $183,000 – $193,000	a partial deduction
	$193,000 or more	no deduction
married filing separately with a spouse who is covered by a plan at work	less than $10,000	a partial deduction
	$10,000 or more	no deduction

The deduction amount is decreased (phased out) when income rises above a certain amount, and it is eliminated altogether when it reaches a higher amount. These amounts vary depending on filing status. To determine if the deduction is subject to phase-out, compare modified adjusted gross income (MAGI) to the base amounts.

- When MAGI is <u>less than</u> the <u>lower base amount</u>, taxpayers receive a <u>full deduction</u>.
- If MAGI is <u>more than</u> the <u>upper base amount</u>, the IRS does not allow <u>any deduction</u>.
- If MAGI is <u>between</u> the base amounts, a <u>partial deduction</u> amount is determined by subtracting MAGI from the upper base amount and multiplying it by a percentage, according to filing status:

    1) **Married Filing Jointly/Qualifying Widow(er) and you are covered by an employer plan** – The total IRA deduction is 27.5% (32.5% if 50 or older) of the difference between MAGI and the upper base amount.

2) **All others** – The total IRA deduction is 55% (65% if 50 or older) of the difference between MAGI and the upper base amount.

Nondeductible Contributions

Although the deduction for IRA contributions may be reduced or eliminated, contributions can be made up to the general limit or, if it applies, the spousal IRA limit. The difference between the total permitted contributions and the IRA deduction is a *nondeductible contribution*. A nondeductible contribution increases the basis of the IRA and is not taxable when withdrawn.

> To designate contributions as nondeductible, a taxpayer must file **Form 8606**, even if not required to file a tax return for the year. If a taxpayer does not report nondeductible contributions, the IRS treats all contributions to a traditional IRA as deductible contributions—meaning distributions will be taxed!

A traditional IRA consisting only of deductible contributions and earnings does not have a basis. If the IRA has a basis resulting from nondeductible contributions, distributions consist partly of nondeductible contributions (basis) and partly of deductible contributions, earnings, and gains (if any). Until the entire basis has been distributed, each distribution is partly nontaxable and partly taxable. To determine the nontaxable percentage of the distribution, divide the basis at the beginning of year (*plus* contributions for the tax year) by the total value of all IRAs at the end of the year (*plus* distributions in the tax year).

> Jim makes a $6,000 nondeductible contribution in 2015 to his IRA and properly files Form 8606. His prior year deductible contributions to the account total $15,000. The balance in his IRA at the end of 2015 is $50,000. Jim withdraws $10,000 during 2015. The nontaxable portion is $1,000, reflecting 10% of the distribution amount. $6,000 /($50,000+$10,000) = 10%

Age 59.5 Rule

> Generally, a taxpayer younger than age 59.5 pays a 10% additional tax on the distribution of any assets from a traditional IRA. The tax applies to the part of the distribution the taxpayer must include in gross income, and is in addition to any regular income tax due.

Exceptions to this rule include the following:

- The taxpayer has unreimbursed medical expenses that are more than 10% of AGI (7.5% if age 65).
- The distributions are not more than the cost of medical insurance for certain unemployed taxpayers.
- The taxpayer is disabled.
- The taxpayer is the beneficiary of a deceased IRA owner.
- The taxpayer receives distributions as an annuity, or series of substantially equal periodic payments.
- The distributions are not more than the taxpayer's qualified higher education expenses
- The distribution is to buy, build, or rebuild a first home:
    1) Up to $10,000 for qualified acquisition costs if used within 120 days of distribution.
    2) $10,000 for each spouse if both are *first-time homebuyers*. A first-time homebuyer cannot own a main home during the two-year period ending on the date of acquisition of the home.
    3) Must be used on qualified acquisition costs for the main home of a taxpayer, spouse, child, grandchild, parent, or other ancestor.
- The distribution is due to an IRS levy of the qualified plan.

- The distribution is a qualified reservist distribution.
- The amount is rolled into another retirement plan within 60 days.

Age 70.5 Rule

Money cannot remain in a traditional IRA indefinitely, and eventually a taxpayer must take a *required minimum distribution (RMD)*.

> April 1 of the year following the year in which the taxpayer reaches age 70.5 is referred to as the **required beginning date**. The taxpayer must withdraw the RMD for any year after the year attaining age 70.5 by December 31 of that later year. If distributions are less than the RMD for the year, taxpayers may have to pay a 50% excise tax on the amount not distributed as required.

Figure the RMD for each year by dividing the IRA account balance as of the close of business on December 31 of the preceding year by the applicable distribution period or life expectancy. To calculate the divisor, compare the taxpayer's age at the end of the year to the corresponding number in the *Uniform Lifetime Table*, or the *Joint Lifetime Table* if a spouse is more than 10 years younger.

> The penalty may be waived if the account owner establishes that the shortfall in distributions was due to reasonable error and that reasonable steps are being taken to remedy the shortfall. In order to qualify for this relief, the taxpayer must file **Form 5329** and attach a letter of explanation.

Qualified Charitable Distribution

A qualified charitable distribution (QCD) is a nontaxable distribution made directly by the trustee of an IRA (other than a SEP or SIMPLE IRA) to an organization eligible to receive tax-deductible contributions. The taxpayer must have been at least age 70.5 when making the distribution. The taxpayer must keep the same type of acknowledgement of the contribution that he would need to claim a deduction for a charitable contribution. Total QCDs for the year cannot be more than $100,000 ($200,000 if MFJ). The amount of the QCD is limited to the amount of the distribution that would otherwise be included in income. If the IRA includes nondeductible contributions, the distribution is first considered to be paid out of otherwise taxable income. The *PATH Act of 2015* made this deduction permanent.

Inherited IRAs

Beneficiaries must begin withdrawals from a traditional IRA by December 31 of the year following the IRA owner's death. For non-spouse *designated beneficiaries* (not a trust or estate), these required distributions must occur under one of the following methods:

- **Lump sum** – Distribute entire account immediately.
- **Life expectancy** – Use the divisor from the *Single Life Table*, minus one each year.
- **Five-year deferral** – The IRS does not allow this method when an IRA owner is beyond the *required beginning date* at the time of death. A beneficiary who is an individual may be required to take the entire account by the end of the fifth year following the year of the owner's death. If this rule applies, no distribution is required for any year before that fifth year.

A taxpayer who inherits an IRA from a deceased spouse can elect to treat the IRA as his own and move the account into his own name, or begin withdrawals as described previously.

Prohibited Transactions

Generally, a prohibited transaction is any improper use of a traditional IRA account or annuity by a taxpayer, a beneficiary, or any disqualified person. Disqualified persons include the fiduciary and members of a taxpayer's family (spouse, ancestor, lineal descendant, and any spouse of a lineal descendant). The following are examples of prohibited transactions with a traditional IRA:

- Borrowing money from it
- Selling property to it
- Receiving unreasonable compensation for managing it
- Using it as security for a loan
- Buying property for personal use (present or future) with IRA funds

Generally, if there is a prohibited transaction in connection with a traditional IRA account at any time during the year, the account stops being an IRA as of the first day of that year. At that time, the entire account balance is considered a distribution, and the taxpayer may need to pay a 10% penalty if under age 59.5. If someone other than the owner or beneficiary of a traditional IRA engages in a prohibited transaction, that person may be liable for certain taxes. There is a 15% tax on the amount of the prohibited transaction and a 100% additional tax if not corrected.

Roth IRAs

> The deductions mentioned in this chapter are adjustments to gross income, otherwise known as "above the line" deductions. A taxpayer subtracts above the line deductions from total income to arrive at AGI. Roth IRAs contributions or distributions usually do not impact the return of a taxpayer. A Roth IRA contribution is never deductible and is not an adjustment to gross income. The Roth IRA rules appearing below are there to help you absorb its differences and similarities to a traditional IRA.

Regardless of age, individuals may be able to establish and make nondeductible contributions to a Roth IRA retirement plan. The taxpayer must designate the account as a Roth IRA when establishing the IRA. A Roth IRA is an individual retirement plan that is subject to the rules that apply to a traditional IRA, with the following exceptions:

- Contributions to a Roth IRA are not tax deductible. Do not report them on the tax return.
- Can contribute after age 70.5, and amounts can remain in the account until taxpayer dies (no RMD).
- Certain *qualified distributions* may be tax-free. A qualified distribution meets the following requirements:
    1) Made after the five-year period beginning with the first year a contribution was made
    2) Meets one of the following criteria:
        A) Made on or after the date the taxpayer reaches age 59.5
        B) Made because the taxpayer is disabled
        C) Made to a beneficiary or to estate after death
        D) Meets the requirements listed for a first-time homebuyer ($10,000 lifetime)

If a taxpayer contributes to both Roth IRAs and traditional IRAs, the limit for Roth IRAs generally is the same as the limit would be if contributions were made only to Roth IRAs. However, it is reduced by all contributions for the year to all IRAs other than Roth IRAs. Employer contributions under a SEP or SIMPLE IRA plan do not affect this limit. The contribution limit is the lesser of the following:

- $5,500 ($6,500 if age 50 or older) minus all contributions (other than employer contributions under a SEP or SIMPLE IRA plan) for the year to all IRAs other than Roth IRAs

- Taxable compensation minus all contributions (other than employer contributions under a SEP or SIMPLE IRA plan) for the year to all IRAs other than Roth IRAs. If modified AGI is above a certain amount, the contribution limit is reduced as indicated below:

    1) Modified AGI minus the following:

        A) $183,000 if filing a joint return (MFJ) or qualifying widow(er) (QW)

        B) $-0- if married filing a separate return (MFS) and the taxpayer lived with his spouse at any time during the year

        C) $116,000 for all other individuals

    2) Divide the result by $15,000 ($10,000 if filing status is MFJ, MFS, or QW)

    3) Multiply the resulting percentage by the maximum contribution limit (before reductions)

    4) Subtract the result and all contributions (other than employer contributions to a SEP or SIMPLE IRA plan) for the year to all IRAs other than Roth IRAs from the maximum contribution limit. The result is the reduced Roth IRA contribution limit.

A 6% excise tax applies to any excess contribution to a Roth IRA. For purposes of determining excess contributions, any contribution that is withdrawn on or before the due date (including extensions) for filing the tax return for the year is treated as an amount not contributed. This treatment only applies if any earnings on the contributions are also withdrawn. The earnings are considered earned and received in the year the excess contribution was made.

Sam is 40 years old files jointly with his spouse. He contributes $5,500 to his Roth IRA on July 1, 2015, which grows to $7,000 and his MAGI for 2015 is $190,000. He does not contribute to any other retirement plans. He has excess income of $7,000 ($190,000 - $183,000) and must reduce his contribution and any earnings by 70% ($7,000 / $10,000). He must remove $4,900 from the account by the due date for his return or he is liable for the 6% excise tax.

Table 6-3. Effect of MAGI on Roth IRA Contributions – 2015

IF your filing status is	AND your modified AGI is	THEN you can make
married filing jointly or qualifying widow(er)	$183,000 or less	a full contribution
	between $183,000 – $193,000	a partial contribution
	$193,000 or more	no contribution
married filing separately and live with spouse	$0	a full contribution
	between $0 – $10,000	a partial contribution
	$10,000 or more	no contribution
All others	$116,000 or less	a full contribution
	between $116,000 – $131,000	a partial contribution
	$131,000 or more	no contribution

Roth Conversions

A taxpayer can withdraw all or part of the assets from a traditional IRA and reinvest them (within 60 days) in a Roth IRA. The amount that the taxpayer withdraws and timely contributes (converts) to the

Roth IRA is called a conversion contribution. If properly (and timely) rolled over, the 10% additional tax on early distributions will not apply. The taxpayer must roll over into the Roth IRA the same property received from the traditional IRA. The taxpayer can roll over part of the withdrawal into a Roth IRA and keep the rest of it. The amount kept will generally be taxable (except for the part that is a return of nondeductible contributions) and may be subject to the 10% additional tax on early distributions.

The IRS treats the converted amount as a taxable distribution in the year of the conversion. A taxpayer recognizes the entire amount of a 2015 conversion (other than basis) in income. A taxpayer may convert a traditional IRA or Simple IRA into a Roth IRA, regardless of filing status or income.

Distributions from a Roth IRA

If a taxpayer receives a distribution that is not a qualified distribution, he may have to pay the 10% additional tax on early distributions. The 5-year period used for determining whether the 10% early distribution tax applies to a distribution from a conversion or rollover contribution is separately determined for each conversion and rollover, and is not necessarily the same as the 5-year period used for determining whether a distribution is a qualified distribution.

> For example, if a calendar-year taxpayer makes a conversion contribution on February 25, 2016, and makes a regular contribution for 2015 on the same date, the 5-year period for the conversion begins January 1, 2016, while the 5-year period for the regular contribution begins on January 1, 2015.

- **Ordering Rules** – If a distribution from the Roth IRA is not a qualified distribution, part of it may be taxable. There is a set order in which contributions (including conversion contributions and rollover contributions from qualified retirement plans) and earnings are considered to be distributed from the Roth IRA. For these purposes, disregard the withdrawal of excess contributions and the earnings on them. Order the distributions as follows:

    1) Regular contributions
    2) Conversion and rollover contributions, on a first-in, first-out basis (generally, total conversions and rollovers from the earliest year first). Take these conversion and rollover contributions into account as follows:
        A) Taxable portion (the amount required to be included in gross income because of the conversion or rollover) first, and then the
        B) Nontaxable portion
    3) Earnings on contributions

Designated Roth Accounts

Designated Roth accounts are separate accounts under 401(k), 403(b), or 457(b) plans that accept elective deferrals that are referred to as Roth contributions. A taxpayer includes these elective deferrals in income, but qualified distributions from these accounts are not included in income. Designated Roth accounts are not IRAs and should not be confused with Roth IRAs. Contributions, up to their respective limits, can be made to Roth IRAs and designated Roth accounts according to a taxpayer's eligibility to participate. A contribution to one does not impact eligibility to contribute to the other.

Health Savings Accounts (HSAs)

A taxpayer establishes a health savings account (HSA) with a qualified trustee to pay or reimburse certain medical expenses. The maximum contribution to an HSA depends on the type of *high deductible health plan (HDHP)* coverage, age, the date the taxpayer became an eligible individual, and the date a taxpayer ceases to be an *eligible individual*. For 2015, taxpayers who have self-only HDHP coverage can contribute up to $3,350. For family HDHP coverage, the maximum contribution is up to $6,650. An additional $1,000 catch-up contribution is available if age 55 or older. The benefits of an HSA are as follows:

- The taxpayer receives a tax deduction for contributions that he or someone other than an employer made to the HSA even if not itemizing deductions on Form 1040.

- A taxpayer may exclude employer contributions to an HSA from gross income.

- The contributions remain in the HSA account from year to year until used.

- The interest or other earnings on the assets in the account accumulate tax-free.

- Distributions may be tax-free if used to pay for *qualified medical expenses* (costs that would generally qualify for the medical and dental expenses deduction). However, the additional tax on distributions not used for qualified medical expenses is **20%**

- An HSA is "portable" so it stays with the taxpayer if he changes employers or leaves the work force.

To qualify for an HSA, an individual must meet all the following requirements:

- Must be covered under a high deductible health plan (HDHP) on the first day of the month:

    1) Under the last-month rule, individuals are eligible for the entire year if covered on the first day of the last month of the tax year (December 1 for most taxpayers).

- Must not have other health coverage

- Must not be enrolled in Medicare

- Must not be claimed as a dependent on someone else's tax return

If a taxpayer meets these requirements, he is an eligible individual even if his spouse has non-HDHP family coverage, provided the spouse's coverage does not cover the taxpayer.

An HDHP has the following features:

- A higher annual deductible than typical health plans.

- A maximum limit on the sum of the annual deductible and out-of-pocket medical expenses that the taxpayer must pay for covered expenses. Out-of-pocket expenses include copayments and other amounts, but do not include premiums.

Table 6-4. HDHP Requirements

Type of Coverage	Minimum Annual Deductible		Maximum Annual Deductible and Other Out-of-pocket Expenses	
	2014	2015	2014	2015
Self-only	$1,250	$1,300	$6,350	$6,450
Family	$2,500	$2,600	$12,700	$12,900

Self-employed Health Insurance

A self-employed taxpayer may make an adjustment on his personal income tax return for the amount of medical, dental, and qualified long-term care insurance premiums (limited) that he pays on behalf of himself, his spouse, his dependents, and his child who was under age 27 at the end of 2015, even if the child was not a dependent. For this purpose, a taxpayer is considered self-employed if he is a general partner (or a limited partner receiving guaranteed payments) or if he receives wages from an S corporation in which he is more than a 2% shareholder. The deduction cannot be more than the earned income from the business. The taxpayer must establish the plan under the business. A taxpayer establishes a plan under a business if the policy is in the name of the following:

- A self-employed individual who files Schedule C, or his trade or business
- A partnership or S corporation
- Partners, if the partnership reimburses the partner for premiums paid, and the amount of the reimbursement is included in the partner's income on the K-1 as a guaranteed payment
- More than 2% shareholders, if S corporation reimburses them for the premiums paid, and the amount of the reimbursement is included in the shareholder's wages on Form W-2

A taxpayer cannot deduct payments for medical insurance for any month in which he was eligible to participate in a health plan subsidized by his employer, his spouse's employer, or an employer of his dependent or child under age 27 at the end of the year.

Moving Expenses

> To qualify as an adjustment to gross income, moving expenses must closely relate–both in time and in place– to the start of work at a new job location.

The taxpayer must meet the specific requirements of the *Distance Test* and the *Time Test*:

- **Closely related in time** – Expenses incurred within one year from the date first reporting to work at a new location relate closely in time to the start of work. It is not necessary for a person to arrange to work before moving, as long as he actually goes to work in that location.
- **Closely related in place** – The distance from the new home to the new job location is not more than the distance from the former home to the new job location. If the move does not meet this requirement, an individual may still deduct moving expenses if he meets one of the following:
   1) Is required to live in the new home as a condition of employment
   2) Spends less time or money commuting from the new home to the new job location
- **Distance test** – The new main job location must be at least 50 miles farther from the taxpayer's former home than the old main job location. For example, if the old job was 3 miles away from the former home, the new job location must be at least 53 miles away.
- **Time test** – The requirements for the time test will vary depending on employment. If married filing jointly, only one spouse must satisfy this test. Weeks worked cannot be combined to satisfy that test.

1) **For employees** – Work full time in the same general area for at least 39 weeks during the first 12 months after arriving in the area of the new job location.

   A) Taxpayer does not need to work for the same employer for all 39 weeks.

   B) Do not have to work 39 weeks in a row.

2) **For self-employed person** – Work full time for at least 39 weeks during the first 12 months and for a total of at least 78 weeks during the first 24 months

A taxpayer who expects to meet the requirements may deduct moving expenses even if the taxpayer does not satisfy the time test by the due date of the return. If a taxpayer fails to meet the time test requirements, he must report the moving expense deduction as other income on Form 1040 for the year he cannot meet the test, or amend the prior return, figuring tax without the moving expense deduction.

Deductible Moving Expenses

Taxpayers may deduct the reasonable expenses of the following:

- Moving household goods and personal effects, including the following:

  1) The cost of packing, crating, and transporting household goods and personal effects

  2) Storing and insuring household goods and personal effects within any period of 30 consecutive days after moving the items from the former home (includes in-transit or foreign-move storage)

- Traveling to a new home, consisting of:

  1) Transportation and lodging for the taxpayer and household members. This includes expenses for the day of arrival. There is no deduction for meals.

  2) If traveling by car, a taxpayer may deduct actual expenses such as gasoline or oil if he keeps an accurate record of each expense. There is no deduction for certain automobile expenses such as general repairs, general maintenance, insurance, or depreciation. An alternative is to use the 2015 standard mileage rate of 23 cents per mile. Taxpayers can deduct parking fees and tolls regardless of the method used.

Nondeductible Expenses

A taxpayer cannot deduct the following items as moving expenses:

- Meals while traveling
- Any part of the purchase price of a new home
- Car tags
- Driver's license
- Expenses of buying or selling a home (including closing costs, mortgage fees, and points)
- Expenses of entering into or breaking a lease
- Home improvements to help sell a home
- Loss on the sale of a home
- Losses from disposing of memberships in clubs
- Mortgage penalties
- Pre-move house hunting expenses
- Real estate taxes

- Refitting of carpet and draperies
- Return trips to a former residence
- Security deposits (including any given up due to the move)
- Storage charges except those incurred in transit and for foreign moves

Alimony

Alimony is a payment to (or for) a spouse or former spouse under a divorce or separation instrument. It does not include voluntary payments made by the taxpayer that are not under a divorce or separation instrument. Alimony is deductible by the taxpayer and must be included in the spouse's or former spouse's income. Not all payments under a divorce or separation instrument are alimony. Alimony does not include the following items:

- Child support
- Noncash property settlements
- Payments that are a spouse's part of community income
- Payments to maintain the payer's property
- Use of the payer's property

Mortgage payments on a house owned by the taxpayer do not qualify as alimony, even if the ex-spouse lives there. If the mortgage payments are on a house totally owned by the ex-spouse 100% could be alimony.

A payment to or for a spouse under a divorce or separation instrument is alimony if the spouses do not file a joint return with each other and all the following requirements are met:

- The payment is in cash (checks and money orders).
- The instrument cannot designate the payment as not alimony.
- The spouses are not members of the same household at the time the taxpayer makes the payments.
- There is no liability to make any payment (cash or property) <u>after</u> the death of the recipient spouse.
- The payment is not treated as child support.

Cash payments, checks, or money orders to a third party on behalf of a spouse under the terms of a divorce or separation instrument can be alimony, if they otherwise qualify. These include payments for a spouse's medical expenses, housing costs (rent, utilities, etc.), premiums for insurance on your life to the extent your spouse owns the policy, taxes, tuition, etc. The payments are treated as received by the spouse and then paid to the third party. In addition, cash payments made to a third party at the written request of a taxpayer's spouse may qualify as alimony if they meet all of the following requirements:

- The payments are in lieu of payments of alimony directly to the spouse.
- The written request states that both spouses intend to treat the payments as alimony.
- The taxpayer receives the written request from a spouse before filing the return.

If a divorce or separation instrument requires a taxpayer to pay mortgage payments for a home jointly owned with a spouse or former spouse, <u>one-half of the payments are alimony</u>.

Recapture Rule

The recapture provision prevents a taxpayer from disguising nondeductible property settlements as deductible alimony. If alimony payments decrease or terminate during the first three calendar years, the taxpayer may have to include in the third year part of the alimony payments previously deducted from income as alimony received on Form 1040. The receiving spouse can deduct part of the alimony payments he previously included in income as an adjustment to gross income. A taxpayer is subject to the recapture rule in the third year if one of the following conditions exists:

- Alimony paid in the third year (Y_3) decreases by more than $15,000 from the second year (Y_2).
- The average alimony paid in Y_2 and Y_3 decreases by more than $15,000 from Y_1.

Calculate recapture in each of the first two years:

- Recapture amount for second year $(R_2) = (Y_2 - Y_3) - \$15{,}000$
- Recapture amount for first year $(R_1) = Y_1 - \frac{(Y_2 + Y_3 - R_2)}{2} - \$15{,}000$

The calculation for a decrease in alimony does not include the following amounts:

- Payments made under a temporary support order
- Payments required over a period of at least three calendar years that vary because they are a percentage of income from a business or property, or from compensation for employment
- Payments that decrease because of the death of either spouse or the remarriage of the spouse receiving the payments before the end of the third year

Child Support

A payment that is ***specifically designated as child support*** or treated as specifically designated as child support under a divorce or separation instrument is not alimony. Child support payments are not deductible by the payer and are not taxable to the recipient. The IRS will treat a payment as child support to the extent that the payment declines under either of the following conditions:

- On the happening of a contingency relating to a child, such as becoming employed, dying, leaving the household, leaving school, married, or reaching a specified age or income level
- At a time that can be clearly associated with the contingency

Education Related Adjustments

Educator Expenses

An *eligible educator* may deduct up to $250 of *qualified expenses* as an adjustment to gross income, rather than as a miscellaneous itemized deduction. If filing jointly and both are eligible educators, the maximum deduction is $500. Neither spouse can deduct more than $250 of qualified expenses.

- **Eligible educator** – An eligible educator is a kindergarten through grade 12 teacher, instructor, counselor, principal, or aide who worked in a school for at least 900 hours during a school year.
- **Qualified expenses** – Qualified expenses include ordinary and necessary expenses paid in connection with books, supplies, equipment (including computer equipment, software, and services), and other materials used in the classroom. Qualified expenses do not include costs for home schooling or nonathletic supplies for courses in health or physical education.

Student Loan Interest Deduction

Individuals may deduct up to $2,500 of the interest paid on a *qualified student loan* used for higher education. The loan cannot be from a related person or a qualified employer plan and must be for qualified educational expenses that are as follows:

- For the taxpayer, a spouse, or a dependent at time of the loan, who is enrolled at least <u>half time</u> in a program leading to a degree, certificate, or other recognized educational credential
- Paid or incurred within a reasonable period of time before or after obtaining the loan
- For education provided during an academic period for an eligible student.

Generally, the deduction is available if all of the following apply:

- The taxpayer paid interest on a qualified student loan.
- Filing status is not married filing separately.
- Modified adjusted gross income (MAGI) is less than $80,000 ($160,000 MFJ) for 2015.
- The taxpayer and spouse, if filing jointly, cannot be claimed as a dependent on another return.

Tuition and Fees Deduction

A taxpayer may deduct up to $4,000 of qualified education expenses paid during the year. A taxpayer may be able to take a credit for education expenses instead of a deduction, but not both. An individual can choose the one providing the lower tax. A taxpayer cannot claim a deduction for qualified education expenses paid with certain tax-free funds. He must reduce the qualified education expenses by the amount of any tax-free educational assistance and refunds received.

- Generally, a taxpayer can claim the deduction if <u>all</u> three of the following requirements are met:
    1) He paid qualified education expenses of higher education.
    2) He paid the education expenses for an eligible student.
    3) The eligible student is the taxpayer, his spouse, or a dependent for which he claims an exemption on his tax return.
- A taxpayer cannot claim the tuition and fees deduction if any of the following apply:
    1) Filing status is married filing separately.
    2) Another person can claim an exemption for the taxpayer as a dependent on his tax return, regardless if actually claimed.
    3) Modified adjusted gross income (MAGI) for 2015 is more than $80,000 ($160,000 MFJ).
    4) The taxpayer is a nonresident alien for any part of the year and did not elect treatment as a resident alien for tax purposes.
    5) The taxpayer or anyone else claims an American Opportunity or Lifetime Learning credit for the student for whom the taxpayer paid the qualified education expenses.

Other Adjustments to Income

Deductible Part of Self-employment Taxes

Self-employed taxpayers, other than S corporation shareholders, may deduct 50% of self-employment taxes reported on schedule SE.

Penalty on Early Withdrawal of Savings

The penalty levied upon an early withdrawal of savings is an adjustment to (reduction) gross income.

Domestic Production Activities

Domestic production activities deduction (DPAD) is a deduction under Section 199 directly from income. For 2015, the deduction is equal to **9%** of the lesser of *qualified production activities income (QPAI)* or taxable income (AGI for individual taxpayers and shareholders of pass through entities) determined without regard to the deduction. If a taxpayer builds, manufactures, or produces goods in the United States, he may be engaged in domestic production activities. Qualified production activities include the following:

- Construction of real property performed in the United States (US)
- Engineering or architectural services performed in the US for construction of real property in the US.
- Any lease, rental, license, sale, exchange, or other disposition of the following:
    1) Tangible personal property, computer software, and sound recordings the taxpayer manufactured, produced, grew, or extracted in whole or in significant part within the US.
    2) Any qualified film the taxpayer produced
    3) Electricity, natural gas, or potable water produced in the United States
- The deduction does not apply to income derived from:
    1) The sale of food and beverages prepared at a retail establishment
    2) Property leased, licensed, or rented for use by any related person
    3) The transmission or distribution of electricity, natural gas, or potable water
    4) The lease, rental, license, sale, exchange, or other disposition of land

What is QPAI?

Section 199(c)(1) defines QPAI for any taxable year as an amount equal to the excess of domestic production gross receipts over the sum of: (a) the cost of goods sold (CGS) allocable to such receipts; (b) other deductions, expenses, or losses directly allocable to such receipts; and (c) a ratable portion of deductions, expenses, and losses not directly allocable to such receipts or another class of income.

What are the Limits?

The deduction is limited to 50% of the W-2 wages paid by the employer during the year. This is in addition to the QPAI and net income (or AGI) limitations.

How to Claim the Deduction

Use Form 8903 to claim the deduction. A corporation claims the deduction at the entity level. The deduction for the qualified production activities of a partnership or S corporation is taken at the partner or shareholder level. For simplification purposes, the partnership or S corporation can calculate the QPAI at the entity level and report pertinent information to the shareholder on Schedule K-1. Each partner or shareholder must compute its deduction separately using form 8903.

7 Standard and Itemized Deductions

Standard Deduction · Itemized Deductions · Medical and Dental Expenses · Taxes · Interest Expense · Charitable Contributions · Casualty and Theft Losses · Employee Business Expenses · Work-related Education · Miscellaneous Deductions · Limit on Itemized Deductions.

This chapter summarizes information contained in Pub 17 Chapters 21 through 29, and Pub 529.

Standard Deduction

The standard deduction reduces the amount of income subject to tax. A taxpayer benefits from the standard deduction if it is more than the allowable *itemized deductions*.

The following taxpayers are not eligible for the standard deduction:

- Married filing a separate return (MFS), <u>and</u> the other spouse itemizes deductions.
- Tax return is for a **short tax year** because of a change in annual accounting period.
- **Nonresident** or **dual-status alien** during the year. A dual-status alien is both a nonresident and resident alien during the year. A nonresident alien who is married to a U.S. citizen or resident alien at the end of the year can choose tax treatment as a U.S. resident and as such may claim the standard deduction.

Standard Deduction Amount

The 2015 standard deduction amount depends on filing status:

- $6,300 if filing as single (S) or married filing separately (MFS)
- $9,250 if filing as head of household (HH)
- $12,600 if filing as married filing jointly (MFJ) or qualifying widow(er) (QW)

The standard deduction is higher for taxpayers who are **65 or older** at the end of the year **and/or blind** (less than 20/200 vision). This extra deduction applies to both the taxpayer AND to a spouse if married. Increase the standard deduction by the following for <u>each</u> occurrence of the conditions above.

- $1,250 if MFJ, MFS or QW
- $1,550 if S or HOH

A blind taxpayer and spouse who is not blind, both age 66, may add $3,750 ($1,250 x 3) to the basic standard deduction of $12,600 for a total deduction of $16,350.

Standard Deduction for Dependents

The standard deduction for a dependent cannot exceed the regular standard deduction, based on filing status. The basic standard deduction for an individual for whom an exemption can be claimed on another person's tax return (dependent) is generally limited to the greater of:

- $1,050
- The individual's earned income for the year, plus $350

Itemized Deductions

A taxpayer with deductions that surpass the standard deduction amount, or one who does not qualify for the standard deduction, may wish to itemize on *Schedule A* (Form 1040) if it provides a greater benefit. Common deductions include medical expenses, certain taxes, interest expense, charitable contributions, and certain miscellaneous deductions.

A taxpayer must use Form 1040, as Forms 1040A and 1040EZ do not allow for itemized deductions.

Phase-out of Itemized Deductions

In 2015, certain taxpayers are once again subject to a limit on itemized deductions. The limit applies if gross income is more than:

- $258,250 if single
- $284,050 if head of household
- $309,900 if married filing jointly or qualifying widow(er)
- $154,950 if married filing separately)

The taxpayer must reduce itemized deductions by the smaller of:

- 3% of amount AGI exceeds the applicable income threshold, or
- 80% of total itemized deductions after subtracting certain deductions (medical, investment interest, casualty, theft, or gambling losses)

Medical and Dental Expenses

Medical expenses are the costs of diagnosis, cure, mitigation, treatment, or prevention of disease, and the costs for treatments affecting any part or function of the body. They include the costs of equipment, supplies, and diagnostic devices needed for these purposes. Medical expenses also include dental care, and the cost of insurance. Employees who contribute through payroll deductions towards their medical insurance premiums –or any other benefits–cannot claim a deduction on their personal tax returns for amounts not included in wages, as doing so would provide a double benefit.

- Medical expenses must be primarily to alleviate or prevent a physical or mental defect or illness.
    1) Do not include expenses for procedures that are purely cosmetic or those that are merely beneficial to general health, such as vitamins or a vacation.
- Include only the expenses paid this tax year, regardless of when the services were provided.

- A taxpayer can generally deduct medical expenses paid for himself, and someone who was a spouse or dependent when the services are provided <u>or</u> when the taxpayer paid for them.

- Only the amount of medical and dental expenses that **<u>is more than 10%</u>** of AGI is deductible (7.5% if either spouse is age 65 or older).

Employees who contribute through payroll deductions towards their medical insurance premiums —or any other benefits—cannot claim a deduction on their personal tax returns for amounts not included in wages, as doing so would provide a double benefit.

Deductible Medical Expenses

- **Medical insurance premiums,** (including Medicare parts B and D) for policies that cover:
    1) Hospitalization, surgical services, X-rays
    2) Prescription drugs and insulin
    3) Dental care
    4) Replacement of lost or damaged contact lenses
    5) Long-term care (limited)

An employee may not deduct the cost of insurance premium payments made with pre-tax income that is not included in his wages on Form W-2 (box 1). Certain self-employed taxpayers or S corporation shareholders with a qualifying plan established under the business may benefit more by deducting the cost of insurance as an adjustment to gross income.

- **Meals and lodging**
    1) Include the cost of meals and lodging <u>at a hospital</u> or similar institution if a principal reason for being there is to get medical care.
    2) The cost of such lodging not provided in a hospital or similar institution while away from home if <u>all</u> of the following requirements are met:
        A) The lodging is primarily for and essential to medical care.
        B) A doctor in a licensed hospital or in a medical care facility related to, or the equivalent of, a licensed hospital provided the services.
        C) The lodging is not lavish or extravagant under the circumstances.
        D) There is no significant element of personal pleasure, recreation, or vacation in the travel away from home.
        E) The deduction for lodging cannot be more than $50 for each night for each person. Also, include lodging for a person traveling with the person receiving the medical care. For example, if a parent is traveling with a sick child, up to $100 per night can be included as a medical expense for lodging. Meals are not included.

- **Nursing home** – Costs of medical care in nursing home, home for the aged, or similar institution.

- **Transportation** – Amounts paid for transportation primarily for, and essential to, medical care:
    1) Bus, taxi, train, or plane fares, or ambulance service
    2) Transportation expenses of a parent who must go with a child who needs medical care

3) Transportation expenses of a nurse or other person who can give injections, medications, or other treatment required by a patient who is traveling to get medical care and is unable to travel alone

4) Transportation expenses for regular visits to see a mentally ill dependent, if the medical provider recommended these visits as a part of treatment

- **Car expenses** – Out-of-pocket expenses, such as the cost of gas and oil, when using a car for medical reasons. Individuals <u>cannot</u> include depreciation, insurance, general repair, or maintenance expenses. If preferred, the taxpayer may use the 2015 standard mileage rate of <u>23 cents per mile</u> instead of actual expenses incurred.

Taxes

Deductible Taxes

A taxpayer receives a deduction for taxes <u>he</u> is legally liable to pay:

- State and local income taxes, if applicable, <u>or</u> general sales taxes, but not both.
- Foreign income taxes paid. Generally, one may take either a deduction or a credit for income taxes imposed by a foreign country or a U.S. possession.
- Real estate taxes on real property levied for the general public welfare. Deduct only the taxes that are based on the *assessed value* of the real property and charged uniformly against all property under the jurisdiction of the taxing authority.
    1) If property was bought or sold during the year, divide the current real estate taxes between buyer and seller according to the number of days owned, pro-rata. The seller pays the taxes up to, but not including, the date of sale.
    2) If mortgage payments include taxes placed in escrow, no tax is deductible until paid by the mortgage servicing company.
- Personal property taxes that meet the following criteria:
    1) Based only on the value of the personal property
    2) Charged on a yearly basis, even if they are collected more or less than once a year

Nondeductible Taxes

- Real estate items individuals generally <u>cannot</u> deduct include the following:
    1) Special assessments for local benefits that increase the property value, such as sidewalks or sewer
    2) Itemized fixed charge assessments for services. Service charges used to maintain or improve services (such as trash collection or police and fire protection) are deductible as real estate taxes if the following conditions exist:
        A) Fees or charges are imposed at a like rate against all property in the taxing jurisdiction.
        B) The funds collected are not earmarked; and are part of general revenue funds.
        C) Funds used to maintain or improve services are not limited to or determined by the amount of these fees or charges collected.
    3) Transfer taxes (or stamp taxes)
    4) Rent increases due to higher real estate taxes
    5) Homeowners' association charges

- Employment taxes, including Social Security and Medicare
- Estate, inheritance, legacy, or succession taxes
- Federal income taxes
- Fines and penalties
- Gift taxes
- License fees
- Per capita taxes

Interest Expense

Home Mortgage Interest

A taxpayer may deduct interest paid on *home acquisition debt* to buy, build, or improve a *qualified home* (main home or second home). To receive a full deduction, the mortgages must total $1 million or less. Interest on *home equity debt* (mortgages taken other than to buy, build, or improve a home) is also deductible, but only on amounts of up to $100,000.

Mortgage interest is deductible if all the following conditions exist:

- File Form 1040 and itemize deductions on Schedule A.
- The taxpayer is legally liable for the loan.
- There is a true debtor-creditor relationship between the taxpayer and the lender.
- The taxpayer has an ownership interest in the qualified home that secures the mortgage.

Points

The term "points" describes certain charges paid, or treated as paid, by a borrower to obtain a home mortgage. In general, taxpayers amortize points (deduct ratably over the life of the mortgage). A taxpayer may fully deduct points in the year paid if the following conditions exist:

- The taxpayer must use the loan proceeds to buy, build or improve a <u>main home</u>. Amortize points on a second home, or to refinance an existing loan, over the life of the loan.
- Paying points is an established business practice in the area where the loan was made.
- The points paid were not more than the points generally charged in that area.
- The taxpayer uses the cash method of accounting.
- The points are not in place of amounts that ordinarily are stated separately on the settlement statement, such as appraisal fees, inspection fees, title fees, attorney fees, and property taxes.
- The points are not financed into the mortgage amount.
- The points were computed as a percentage of the principal amount of the mortgage.
- The amount clearly appears on the settlement statement as points charged for the mortgage.

Lamont purchased a new home to use as his primary residence. He pays $5,000 in points to improve the rate on his 15-year loan. On Schedule A, he deducts the points as interest in the year paid. If this were an investment property, he would amortize the points over a period of 15 years.

Mortgage Insurance Premiums

Treat the amount paid during the year for *qualified mortgage insurance* as home mortgage interest. This deduction begins to phase out when AGI exceeds $100,000.

Investment Interest

Interest on loans to buy property held for investment is *investment interest*.

> The deduction for investment interest is <u>limited</u> to the taxpayer's **net investment income**. If the taxpayer does not use the deduction, he may carry it forward into the next year. Interest incurred to produce tax-exempt income is <u>not</u> deductible.

An individual, estate, or trust must use *Form 4952* to claim a deduction for investment interest expenses. Form 4952 is not necessary if a taxpayer meets both the following conditions:

- Income from interest and ordinary dividends (minus any qualified dividends) exceeds the amount of investment interest expenses
- The taxpayer does not have any other deductible investment expenses or carryover of disallowed prior year investment interest expense.

Charitable Contributions

Deductions for contributions to a *qualified organization* are generally limited to 50% of adjusted gross income, but in some cases, 20% and 30% limits may apply. Qualified organizations include:

- Churches, association of churches, temples, synagogues, mosques, and other religious organizations
- Most nonprofit charitable organizations such as the Red Cross and the United Way
- Most nonprofit educational organizations (Boy and Girl Scouts of America, colleges and museums)
- Nonprofit hospitals and medical research organizations
- Utility company emergency energy programs, if the utility company is an agent for a charitable organization that assists individuals with emergency energy needs
- Nonprofit volunteer fire companies
- Public parks and recreation facilities
- Civil defense organizations

Nondeductible Contributions

- Contributions to **specific individuals**, including the following:
    1) Contributions to fraternal societies for paying medical or burial expenses of deceased members
    2) Contributions to individuals who are needy or worthy
    3) Payments to a member of the clergy that the member may spend as he wishes
    4) Expenses paid for another person who provided services to a qualified organization
    5) Payments to a hospital for a specific patient's care or for services for a specific patient
- Contributions to nonqualified organizations:
    1) Groups that are run for a profit

2) Certain state bar associations

3) Chambers of commerce and other business leagues or organizations

4) Civic leagues and associations

5) Country clubs and other social clubs

6) Foreign organizations except certain Canadian, Israeli, or Mexican charitable organizations

7) Homeowners' associations

8) Labor unions

9) Political organizations and candidates

Contributions of Property

A taxpayer claiming a deduction for noncash gifts of more than $500 must file Form 8283. The deductible amount for capital gain property is generally the fair market value of the property at the time of the contribution. The deduction for ordinary income property is limited to the gifts fair market value minus the amount that would be ordinary income or short-term capital gain if the taxpayer sold the property for its fair market value. Ordinary income property includes short-term gain property, inventory, works of art created by the taxpayer, property subject to depreciation recapture, etc.

Donated clothing or household items must be in good used condition or better in order to qualify for a deduction. A good measure of value might be the price that buyers of these used items actually pay in consignment or thrift shops. However, a taxpayer may take a deduction for items in poorer condition if the deduction is more than $500 and the taxpayer includes a qualified appraisal with the return. The IRS requires an appraisal for any single item or group of related items with a value exceeding $5,000.

A taxpayer looking to deduct more than $500 resulting from a donation of a qualified vehicle must attach a copy of the contemporaneous written acknowledgment. In general, a contemporaneous acknowledgement must be issued within 30 days of the contribution or later sale. The organization receiving property may use Copy B of Form 1098-C as the acknowledgment. The deduction is limited to the smaller of the vehicle's FMV on the date of the contribution or the gross proceeds received from a later sale of the vehicle. An acceptable measure of the FMV of a donated vehicle is an amount not in excess of the price listed in a used vehicle-pricing guide for a private party sale of a similar vehicle.

Limits on Charitable Deductions

If a taxpayer receives a benefit because of a contribution to a qualified organization, reduce the charitable deduction by the FMV of the benefit received. The deduction for charitable contributions is also limited to 50% of adjusted gross income. This limit applies to the total of all charitable contributions made during the year.

> The charitable contribution deduction is limited to 50% of adjusted gross income. This limit applies to the total of all charitable contributions made during the year. If a taxpayer makes gifts of appreciated property or gifts to certain types of organizations, those gifts may be limited to a lesser amount.

- **50% limit organizations** – The following is a partial list of the types of organizations that are 50% limit organizations:

    1) Churches and conventions or associations of churches

    2) Educational organizations with a regular faculty and curriculum that normally have a regularly enrolled student body attending classes on site

    3) Hospitals and certain medical research organizations associated with these hospitals

4) Publicly-supported charities

- **30% limit** – A 30% limit applies to the following gifts:

    1) Gifts to all qualified organizations other than 50% limit organizations. This includes gifts to veterans' organizations, fraternal societies, nonprofit cemeteries, and certain private non-operating foundations.

    2) Gifts for the use of any organization.

- Limit for capital gain property:

    1) A **special 30% limit** applies to gifts of capital gain property to 50% limit organizations. However, the special 30% limit does not apply when using cost in place of FMV as the amount of the gift. Instead, only the 50% limit applies.

        A) This special 30% limit for capital gain property is separate from the other 30% limit. Therefore, the deduction of a contribution subject to one 30% limit does not reduce the amount taxpayers can deduct for contributions subject to the other 30% limit. However, the total cannot be more than 50% of adjusted gross income.

    2) A **20% limit** applies to all gifts of capital gain property to or for the use of qualified organizations (other than gifts of capital gain property to 50% limit organizations).

Your adjusted gross income is $50,000. During the year, you gave capital gain property with a fair market value of $15,000 to a 50% limit organization. You do not choose to reduce the property's fair market value by its appreciation in value. You also gave $10,000 cash to a qualified organization that is not a 50% limit organization. The $15,000 gift of property is subject to the special 30% limit. The $10,000 cash gift is subject to the other 30% limit. Both gifts are fully deductible because neither is more than the 30% limit that applies ($15,000 in each case) and together they are not more than the 50% limit ($25,000).

Records for Cash Contributions

Cash contributions include those paid by cash, check, electronic funds transfer, credit card, or payroll deduction. To claim a cash contribution, taxpayers must have one of the following:

- Bank records (canceled check or statement)
- A receipt (or other written communication) from the qualified organization showing the name of the organization, the date of the contribution, and the amount of the contribution
- Payroll deduction records

To deduct a cash contribution of **$250 or more**, the taxpayer must receive an acknowledgment of the contribution from the qualified organization or have certain payroll deduction records.

Out-of-pocket Expenses in Giving Services

The value of taxpayer-provided services given to a qualified organization is not deductible; however, costs (automobile or travel expenses, etc.) associated with providing the services may be. The standard mileage rate is <u>14 cents</u> per mile for charitable miles driven in 2015.

A taxpayer cannot deduct personal expenses for sightseeing, fishing parties, theater tickets, nightclubs, or expenses for family members. To receive a deduction, the expenses must be as follows:

- Unreimbursed

- Directly connected with the services
- Expenses incurred only because of the services provided
- Not personal, living, or family expenses

Conventions

If a taxpayer is a chosen representative attending a convention of a qualified charitable organization, he may deduct actual unreimbursed expenses for travel and transportation, including a reasonable amount for meals and lodging, while away from home overnight in connection with the convention. Expenses are not deductible if attending as a member of the organization rather than as a chosen representative.

Non-business Casualty and Theft Losses

A casualty is the damage, destruction, or loss of property resulting from an identifiable event that is sudden, unexpected, or unusual. Deductible casualty losses include the following:

- Car accidents or shipwrecks
- Earthquakes, fires, floods, or volcanic eruptions
- Storms, including hurricanes and tornadoes
- Terrorist attacks
- Vandalism
- Government-ordered demolition or relocation of a home because of a disaster
- Mine cave-ins
- Sonic booms
- Damage from corrosive drywall

A casualty loss is not deductible if the cause of the damage or destruction is as follows:

- Accidentally breaking articles such as glassware or china under normal conditions
- A family pet
- A fire if the taxpayer willfully set it or paid someone else to set it
- A car accident if the taxpayer's willful negligence or willful act caused it
- Progressive deterioration:
    1) The steady weakening of a building due to normal wind and weather conditions.
    2) The deterioration and damage to a water heater that bursts. However, the rust and water damage to rugs caused by the bursting of a water heater does qualify as a casualty.
    3) Losses of property caused by droughts, other than business or investment property.
    4) Termite or moth damage.
    5) Damage to trees or other plants by a fungus, disease, insects, worms, or similar pests.

Gain or Loss

The loss is the smaller of the adjusted basis in the property before the casualty or theft, or the decrease in FMV of the property because of the casualty or theft, minus any insurance or other reimbursement.

- If the result is a gain, the taxpayer may elect to account for it is as a capital gain on schedule D, or postpone reporting the gain (must acquire related replacement property within two tax years).
- If the result is a loss, the deduction may be limited. There are two limits on the deductible amount for casualty or theft loss on personal use property:
    1) For 2015, reduce each casualty or theft loss by $100 ($100 rule).
    2) The total of all casualty or theft losses is further reduced by 10% of AGI (10% rule).

Taxpayers generally must deduct a casualty loss in the year it occurs. However, if there is a casualty loss from a federally declared disaster, a taxpayer may deduct that loss on his return or amended return for the tax year immediately <u>preceding</u> the tax year of the disaster. If an individual makes this choice, treat the loss as having occurred in the preceding year. Claiming the loss on the previous year's return may result in a lower tax for that year, often producing or increasing a cash refund.

Miscellaneous Deductions Subject to the 2% Limit

A non-business taxpayer may deduct certain expenses as *miscellaneous itemized deductions* when they exceed 2% of adjusted gross income. Calculate the deductible amount by subtracting 2% of AGI from the total of these expenses. Generally, the 2% limit applies after any other deduction limit. There are three categories of deductions that are subject to the 2% limit:

- Unreimbursed employee expenses
- Tax preparation fees
- Other expenses

Unreimbursed Employee Expenses

Unreimbursed employee expenses are deductible provided they meet <u>all</u> the following conditions:

- Paid or incurred during the taxpayer's tax year
- For carrying on the taxpayer's trade or business of being an employee
- Ordinary and necessary – An expense is ordinary if it is common and accepted in the taxpayer's trade, business, or profession. An expense is necessary if it is appropriate and helpful to the business. An expense does not have to be required to be considered necessary.

Individuals may be able to deduct the following items as unreimbursed employee expenses:

- **Business bad debt** – Losses from a debt created or acquired in a trade or business are deductible. Any other worthless debt is a business bad debt only if there is a very close relationship between the debt and the taxpayer's trade or business when the debt becomes worthless.

A taxpayer makes a bona fide loan to the corporation he works for. The company fails to pay him back. The taxpayer had to make the loan in order to keep his job. He has a business bad debt as an employee.

- **Business liability insurance** – Insurance premiums paid for protection against personal liability for wrongful acts on the job are deductible.
- **Damages for breach of employment contract** – Damages paid to a former employer are deductible if the damages are attributable to the pay received from that employer.

- **Depreciation on computers** – Individuals may claim a depreciation deduction for a computer used at work as an employee if its use meets both the following conditions:
    1) For the convenience of the employer
    2) Required as a condition of employment
- **Dues to chambers of commerce and professional societies** – Deduct dues paid to professional organizations (such as bar associations and medical associations) and to chambers of commerce and similar organizations, if membership helps taxpayer carry out his job duties. Dues related to lobbying and political activities may not be deductible. Similar organizations include the following:
    1) Boards of trade
    2) Business leagues
    3) Civic or public service organizations
    4) Real estate boards
    5) Trade associations
- **Educator expenses** – *Eligible educators* may deduct up to $250 of qualified expenses paid in 2015 as an adjustment to gross income on Form 1040 rather than as a miscellaneous itemized deduction. If filing jointly and both are eligible educators, the maximum deduction is $500. However, neither spouse can deduct more than $250 of his qualified expenses. Eligible educators may deduct qualified expenses not taken as an adjustment to gross income as an itemized deduction subject to the 2% limit.
    1) **Eligible educator** – A kindergarten through grade 12 teacher, instructor, counselor, principal, or aide in a school for at least 900 hours during a school year
    2) **Qualified expenses** – Ordinary and necessary expenses paid in connection with books, supplies, equipment (including computer equipment, software, and services), and other materials used in the classroom
- **Home office** – Deduct a part of the operating expenses and depreciation of the home if the taxpayer uses that part of the home regularly and exclusively for one of the following:
    1) As a principal place of business for any trade or business
    2) As a place to meet or deal with patients, clients, or customers
    3) In connection with a trade or business, if a separate structure not attached to the home
- **Job search expenses** – Deduct expenses connected with looking for a new job, even if not hired. Examples of these are employment and outplacement agency fees, and the cost of preparing and mailing copies of a résumé. A taxpayer cannot deduct these expenses if one of the following is true:
    1) He is looking for a job in a new occupation.
    2) There was a substantial break between the ending of the last job and looking for a new one.
    3) He is looking for a job for the first time.
- **Legal fees** – Deduct legal fees related to doing or keeping a job.
- **Licenses and regulatory fees** – Deduct amounts paid to state or local governments for licenses and regulatory fees for the taxpayer's trade, business, or profession.
- **Occupational taxes** – A taxpayer may deduct an occupational tax charged at a flat rate by a locality for the privilege of working or conducting a business in the locality.

- **Repayment of income aid payment** – An "income aid payment" is one that the taxpayer received under an employer's plan to aid employees who lose their jobs because of lack of work. If the taxpayer repays an aid payment included as income in an earlier year, he can deduct the repayment.

- **Research expenses of a college professor** – A college professor may deduct research expenses, including travel expenses, for teaching, lecturing, or writing and publishing on subjects that relate directly to teaching duties. There can be no expectation of profit apart from salary.

- **Rural mail carriers' vehicle expenses** – Expenses while performing services as a rural mail carrier

- **Tools used in work** – Generally, employees can deduct amounts spent for tools used in work if the tools wore out and the taxpayer threw them away within one year from the date of purchase. He can depreciate the cost of tools that have a useful life substantially beyond the tax year.

- **Gift expenses** – Taxpayers can deduct **up to $25** for business gifts given to each person during a tax year. The IRS considers a gift to a member of a customer's family an indirect gift to the customer, unless a bona fide business relationship exists with the family member. The following items do <u>not</u> count toward the $25 limit:

    1) Identical, widely distributed items costing $4 or less with the taxpayer's name imprinted

    2) Signs, racks, and promotional materials to display on the business premises of the recipient

- **Union dues and expenses** – Deduct dues and initiation fees for union membership and assessments for benefit payments to unemployed union members. Any part of the payment for sick, accident, or death benefits is not deductible. Contributions to a pension fund are not deductible. Amounts related to certain lobbying and political activities may not be deductible.

- **Work clothes and uniforms** – The cost and upkeep of work clothes is deductible if the following two requirements are met:

    1) The taxpayer is required to wear them as a condition of employment.

    2) The clothes are not suitable for everyday wear.

A judge required to purchase a robe may deduct his cost and dry cleaning expenses since the robe is not suitable for wear outside of his work. An attorney required to wear suits cannot deduct the cost.

- **Military uniforms** – Individuals generally cannot deduct the cost of uniforms if on full-time active duty in the armed forces. However, an armed forces reservist may deduct the unreimbursed cost of uniforms if military regulations restrict him from wearing it except while on duty.

- **Qualifying work-related education** – A deduction is unavailable if the education is necessary to meet the minimum requirements of the present trade or business, or is part of a program of study that will qualify the taxpayer for a <u>new</u> trade or business. The IRS does not allow a deduction for the cost of travel that in itself constitutes a form of education. For example, a French teacher who travels to France to maintain general familiarity with the French language and culture cannot deduct the cost of the trip as an educational expense. For the costs (tuition, books, supplies, laboratory fees, and similar items) of work-related education to qualify as a business expenses, <u>at least one</u> of the following two tests must be met:

    1) An employer or the law requires the education to maintain present salary, status, or job. The required education must serve a bona fide business purpose of the employer.

    2) The education maintains or improves skills needed in the taxpayer's present work.

Unreimbursed Employee Meals and Entertainment Expenses

> Generally, entertainment expenses (including entertainment-related meals) are deductible only if they **directly relate** to the active conduct of the taxpayer's trade or business. However, the expense only needs to be **associated** with the active conduct of the taxpayer's trade or business if it directly precedes or follows a substantial and bona fide business-related discussion. Only **50%** of business-related meal and entertainment expenses are deductible (**80%** of meals if consumed during any period subject to the Department of Transportation's "hours of service" limits). These limits apply before considering the 2% of adjusted gross income limit. To deduct an entertainment-related meal, the taxpayer or his employees must be present when provided.

A taxpayer may deduct entertainment expenses only if they are both ordinary and necessary and meet <u>one</u> of the following tests:

- **Directly related test** – Taxpayers must show that the following conditions exist:
  1) The main purpose of the combined business and entertainment is the active conduct of business. Business is generally not considered the main purpose when on hunting or fishing trips, or on yachts or other pleasure boats.
  2) Taxpayers engaged in business with the person during the entertainment period and had more than a general expectation of getting income or some other specific business benefit at some future time.

- **Associated test** – If the taxpayer's expenses do not meet the directly related test, they may meet the associated test. The taxpayer must show that the entertainment is as follows:
  1) Associated with the active conduct of his trade or business
  2) Directly before or after a substantial business discussion

Expenses a taxpayer may <u>not</u> deduct include the following:

- **Lavish or extravagant entertainment** – Expenses that are reasonable considering the facts and circumstances will not be disallowed simply because they are more than a fixed dollar amount or take place at deluxe restaurants, hotels, nightclubs, or resorts.

- **If a taxpayer rents a private luxury box** for <u>more</u> than one event at the same sports arena, the taxpayer generally may not deduct more than the price of a non-luxury box seat ticket.

- **Membership dues** (including initiation fees) for any club organized for business, pleasure, recreation, or other social purpose.

- **Cost for the use of an entertainment facility** or any property he owns, rents, or uses for entertainment. Examples include a yacht, hunting lodge, fishing camp, swimming pool, tennis court, bowling alley, car, airplane, apartment, hotel suite, or home in a vacation resort.

Unreimbursed Employee Travel Expenses

Employee travel expenses are those incurred while traveling away from home for an employer. An employee can deduct travel expenses paid or incurred in connection with a temporary work assignment (lasting one year or less). Generally, expenses paid or incurred in connection with an indefinite work assignment are <u>not</u> deductible. Travel expenses may include the following:

- The cost of getting to and from the business destination (air, rail, bus, car, etc.)
- Meals and lodging while away from home
- Taxi fares

- Baggage charges
- Cleaning and laundry expenses

An individual is traveling away from home if duties require the individual to be away from the general area of the individual's *tax home* for a period substantially longer than an ordinary day's work, requiring sleep or rest to meet the demands of work while away. Generally, a tax home is the entire city or general area where the main place of business or work is located, regardless of where the individual maintains the family home.

> A person lives with family in Florida but works in Boston where that person stays in a hotel and eats in restaurants. That person returns to Florida every weekend. The taxpayer may not deduct any of the travel, meals, or lodging in Boston because that is the taxpayer's tax home. The travel on weekends to family home in Florida is not for work, so these expenses are also not deductible.

If a person regularly works in more than one place, the person's tax home is the general area where main place of business or work is located. Deductible travel expenses while away from home include, but are not limited to, the costs of the following:

- Travel by airplane, train, bus, or car between home and business destination.
- Using personal car while at a business destination.
- Fares for taxis or other transportation between an airport or train station and a hotel, a hotel and a work location, and from one customer to another or from a place of business to another.
- Meals and lodging.
- Tips paid for services related to any of these expenses.
- Dry cleaning and laundry.
- Business calls while on business trip. This includes business communications by fax machine or other communication devices.
- Other similar ordinary and necessary expenses related to business travel. These expenses might include transportation to and from a business meal, public stenographer's fees, computer rental fees, and operating and maintaining a house trailer.

A taxpayer may deduct **50% of meals** when traveling if it is necessary for the taxpayer to stop for substantial sleep or rest while traveling away from home on business. The taxpayer may not deduct meals that are lavish or extravagant. Expenses are not lavish or extravagant if reasonable based on the facts and circumstances.

- Travel in the United States:
    1) Taxpayers may deduct all travel expenses if the trip was entirely business related.
    2) If the trip was primarily for business, and while at the business destination, the taxpayer extended his stay for a vacation, made a personal side trip, or had other personal activities, the taxpayer may deduct business-related travel expenses.
    3) If the trip was primarily for personal reasons, such as a vacation, the entire cost of the trip is a nondeductible personal expense. However, a taxpayer may deduct any expenses he had while at a destination directly related to business.
- Travel outside the United States:
    1) If a taxpayer travels outside the United States and spends the entire time on business activities, he may deduct all of the travel expenses:

A) Even if he did not spend the entire time on business activities, the trip is considered entirely for business if the taxpayer meets any of the following exceptions:

   (a) Did not have substantial control over arranging the trip

   (b) Taxpayer was outside the United States for a week or less, combining business and non-business activities

   (c) The taxpayer spent less than 25% of the total time the taxpayer was outside the United States on non-business activities

   (d) The taxpayer can establish that a personal vacation was not a major consideration, even if the taxpayer has substantial control over arranging the trip

2) If the trip is primarily for business but the taxpayer spends some time on other activities, he generally may not deduct all of the travel expenses. The taxpayer may deduct only the business portion of the cost of getting to and from the destination. Individuals must allocate the costs between business and other activities to determine the deductible amount.

3) If the trip is primarily for vacation or for investment purposes, the entire cost of the trip is a non-deductible personal expense. If a taxpayer spends some time attending brief professional seminars or a continuing education program, the taxpayer may deduct registration fees and other expenses directly related to business.

Travel expenses to attend a convention are deductible so long as conference attendance benefits the taxpayer's trade or business. If the convention is for investment, political, social, or other purposes unrelated to the taxpayer's trade or business, he cannot deduct the expenses.

- A taxpayer cannot deduct the travel expenses for his family.

- A taxpayer may deduct expenses of up to $2,000 per year for attending conventions on a *cruise ship* that directly relate to his trade or business. The taxpayer must attach a statement of agenda and attendance by the taxpayer and an officer of the organization sponsoring the trip to the tax return.

Unreimbursed Employee Local Transportation and Lodging

Transportation expenses do not include expenses while traveling away from home overnight. Those expenses are travel expenses. Transportation expenses include the ordinary and necessary costs of all of the following:

- Getting from one workplace to another within the area of an individual's tax home

- Visiting clients or customers

- Going to a business meeting away from a regular workplace

- Getting from home to a temporary (lasting 1 year or less) workplace

   1) Deduct the expenses of the daily round-trip transportation between the taxpayer's home and the temporary location, regardless of distance.

   2) Driving from home to a permanent (more than 1 year) location is not deductible.

Transportation expenses include the cost of transportation by air, rail, bus, and taxi, and the cost of using a taxpayer's vehicle. A deduction for *car expenses* is available if using the taxpayer's vehicle.

- **Business and personal use** – If the taxpayer uses the vehicle for business and personal purposes, divide the expenses between business and personal use based on the miles driven for each purpose. Only the business use portion is deductible. Taxpayers may deduct all business-related parking fees and tolls, regardless of method used.

- Use one of the two following methods to figure deductible car expenses:
  1) **Standard mileage rate** – For 2015, the rate is <u>57.5 cents per mile</u> on business miles driven. To qualify, the taxpayer must use this method for the first year placing the vehicle in service. A taxpayer may not use the business standard mileage rate for a vehicle after using any depreciation method other than straight-line, or after claiming a Section 179 deduction for that vehicle. The taxpayer cannot claim the business standard mileage rate for more than four vehicles used simultaneously. A taxpayer may use the business standard mileage rate for vehicles used for hire, such as taxicabs.
  2) **Actual car expenses** – Depreciation, garage rent, gas, insurance, lease payments, licenses, oil, parking fees, registration fees, repairs, tires, and tolls are deductible expenses.
- In general, commuting between a residence and normal place of business is not deductible.
  1) *Work at two places in a day* – When working at two places in a day, whether or not for the same employer, the expenses of traveling from one workplace to the other are deductible.
  2) *Temporary work location* – Deduct expenses incurred in traveling between the taxpayer's home and a temporary work location if at least one of the following applies:
     A) The work location is outside the area where the taxpayer lives and normally works.
     B) At least one regular work location exists (not in home) for the same trade or business.
  3) *Home office* – Expenses incurred in traveling between home and a workplace if the home is the taxpayer's principal place of business for the same trade or business.

If an employer provides or requires a taxpayer to obtain *lodging* while <u>not</u> traveling away from home, the taxpayer can deduct the cost of the lodging if it meets all the following criteria:

- It is on a temporary basis.
- It is necessary for the taxpayer to be available for a business meeting or employer function.
- The costs are ordinary and necessary, but not lavish or extravagant.

If the employer provides the lodging or reimburses the cost of the lodging, deduct the cost only if the value is included in the taxpayer's gross income as wages on Form W-2.

Tax Preparation Fees

Deduct tax preparation fees in the year paid. These fees include the cost of tax software programs, tax publications, and electronic filing.

Other Expenses

"Other Expenses" include certain miscellaneous itemized deductions subject to the 2% of adjusted gross income limit. A taxpayer may deduct expenses paid for the following:

- To produce or collect income that must be included in gross income
- To manage, conserve, or maintain property held for producing such income
- To determine, contest, pay, or claim a refund of any tax

These other expenses include the following items:

- Appraisal fees for a casualty loss or charitable contribution
- Casualty and theft losses from property used in performing services as an employee
- Clerical help and office rent in caring for investments

- Depreciation on home computers used for investments
- Excess deductions (including administrative expenses) allowed a beneficiary on termination of an estate or trust
- Fees to collect interest and dividends
- Hobby expenses, but generally <u>not</u> more than hobby income
- Indirect miscellaneous deductions of pass-through entities
- Investment fees and expenses
- Legal fees <u>related to</u> producing or collecting taxable income or getting tax advice
- Loss on deposits in an insolvent or bankrupt financial institution
- Loss on traditional IRAs or Roth IRAs, when all amounts have been distributed
- Repayments of income
- Repayments of Social Security benefits
- Safe deposit box rental
- Service charges on dividend reinvestment plans
- Tax advice fees
- Trustee's fees for IRA, if separately billed and paid

Deductions NOT Subject to the 2% Limit

The items listed below are miscellaneous itemized deductions that are not subject to the 2% limit:

- Amortizable premium on taxable bonds
- Casualty and theft losses from income-producing property
- Federal estate tax on income in respect of a decedent
- Gambling losses <u>up to</u> the amount of gambling winnings
- Impairment-related work expenses of persons with disabilities
- Loss from other activities from Schedule K-1 (Form 1065-B), box 2
- Losses from Ponzi-type investment schemes
- Repayments of more than $3,000 under a claim of right
- Unrecovered investment in an annuity

Nondeductible Expenses

A deduction is <u>not</u> available for the following expenses:

- Adoption expenses (may claim credit)
- Broker's commissions that paid in connection with IRA
- Burial or funeral expenses, including the cost of a cemetery lot
- Campaign expenses
- Capital expenses

- Check-writing fees
- Club dues and health spa expenses
- Commuting expenses
- Fees and licenses, such as car licenses, marriage licenses, and dog tags
- Fines and penalties, such as parking tickets
- Hobby losses (but see *Hobby expenses,* earlier)
- Home repairs, insurance, and rent
- Home security system
- Illegal bribes and kickbacks
- Investment-related seminars
- Life insurance premiums
- Lobbying expenses
- Losses from the sale of taxpayer's home, furniture, personal car, etc.
- Lost or misplaced cash or property
- Lunches with co-workers or meals while working late
- Medical expenses as business expenses
- Personal disability insurance premiums
- Personal legal expenses
- Personal, living, or family expenses
- Political contributions
- Professional accreditation fees
- Professional reputation, expenses to improve
- Relief fund contributions
- Residential telephone line
- Stockholders' meeting, expenses of attending
- Tax-exempt income, expenses of earning or collecting
- The value of wages never received or lost vacation time
- Travel expenses for another individual
- Voluntary unemployment benefit fund contributions
- Wristwatches

8 Taxes and Credits

Tax Calculations · Alternative Minimum Tax · Tax on Investment Income of Certain Children · Child and Dependent Care Credit · Education Credits · Earned Income Credit · Credit for Elderly or the Disabled · Child Tax Credit · Other Credits

This chapter summarizes Publications 17, 501, 503, 596, 926, 970, and 972.

Tax Calculations

Calculate income tax as a percentage of *taxable income*. Tax rates vary according to the amount of taxable income. U.S. income tax is a *progressive tax*, whereby rates increase as taxable income increases. The IRS has established *tax brackets* at various income levels. Taxable income within each bracket is taxed at the corresponding tax rate. The *marginal tax rate* is the rate at which the last dollar of income is taxed. After income tax and any *alternative minimum tax (AMT)*, subtract any *non-refundable tax credits* and add any other taxes owed. Non-refundable credits only reduce tax. The taxpayer does not receive a refund of any excess. The result is the taxpayer's *total tax.* Compare the total tax with total payments (including refundable credits) to determine whether a refund or additional tax is due. The IRS treats *refundable credits* the same as payments of tax. If the total of these credits, withheld federal income tax, and estimated tax payments is more than the total tax, the taxpayer can receive a refund of the excess. Most taxpayers use either the Tax Table or the Tax Computation Worksheet to figure their income taxes. However, there are special methods if income includes any of the following items:

- A net capital gain
- Qualified dividends taxed at the same rates as a net capital gain
- Lump-sum distributions
- Farming or fishing income
- Investment income more than $2,100 for certain children
- Parents' election to report child's interest and dividends
- Foreign earned income exclusion or the housing exclusion

After income tax and any AMT (discussed later), determine any *tax credits*. Subtract the tax credits and determine if any other taxes are due. These taxes include, but are not limited to the following:

- Additional taxes on qualified retirement plans and IRAs
- Household employment taxes
- Social Security and Medicare tax on wages and tips
- Uncollected Social Security and Medicare taxes on tips

Alternative Minimum Tax

Taxpayers with income or expenses that receive special treatment under the regular tax system may be subject to an additional tax known as the *alternative minimum tax* (AMT). Figure AMT separately, after eliminating certain deductions and credits, to arrive at *alternative minimum taxable income (AMTI)*. AMT liability exists if taxable income for regular tax purposes, combined with *adjustments* and *tax preference items*, is more than the 2015 *AMT exemption* amount as follows:

- $83,400 if filing status is MFJ or QW
- $53,600 if filing status is single or HOH
- $41,700 if filing status is MFS

The exemption amounts above reduce by 25% of AMTI in excess of the following:

- $158,900 if filing status is MFJ or QW
- $119,200 if filing status is single or HOH
- $79,450 if filing status is MFS

The exemption reduces AMTI; apply a flat tax rate of 26% (up to $185,400, 28% thereafter) to arrive at the *tentative minimum tax*. If the tentative minimum tax exceeds normal income tax liability, the excess is the AMT amount to include on the return.

Adjustments and Tax Preference Items

AMT is caused by two types of adjustments and preferences—deferral items and exclusion items. Deferral items (for example, depreciation) generally do not cause a permanent difference in taxable income over time. Exclusion items (for example, the standard deduction) do cause a permanent difference. The <u>more common</u> adjustments and tax preference items include the following:

- **Adjustments** – The first step to determine AMTI is adjusting the taxpayer's taxable income:
  1) Add the amount claimed for personal or dependency exemptions.
  2) Add the amount claimed for the standard deduction, <u>or</u> itemized deductions for state and local taxes, certain interest (not eligible mortgage on main home), most miscellaneous deductions, and part of medical expenses not greater than 10% of AGI.
  3) Subtract any refund of state and local taxes included in gross income.

- **Preference Items** – The tax code provides preferential treatment to certain income and deduction items. Under AMT rules, these items do not receive special treatment, thus increasing tax liability for an individual who would otherwise pay less tax. Add the following items to arrive at AMTI:
  1) Tax exempt interest from specified <u>private activity</u> municipal bonds
  2) The excess of accelerated depreciation claimed when compared to a hypothetical straight-line amount on property placed in service before 1987
  3) Addition of certain income from incentive stock options
  4) Change in certain passive activity loss deductions
  5) Depletion that is more than the adjusted basis (not applicable to independent producers)
  6) Deduction for excess intangible drilling costs not amortized over a 60-month period
  7) Difference between the gain or loss on the sale of property reported for regular tax purposes and the gain or loss reported for AMT purposes

Credit for Prior Year's Minimum Tax

A taxpayer with AMT liability in the current year may recapture that amount in future years in the form of a credit. This non-refundable credit can offset future tax liability only to the extent prior AMT tax paid was due to deferral items. The credit cannot reduce tax below the *tentative minimum tax* for the year. The refundable portion of the credit for prior year minimum tax has expired.

Net Investment Income Tax

The Net Investment Income Tax (NIIT) is imposed by section 1411 of the Internal Revenue Code. The NIIT applies at a rate of 3.8% to certain net investment income of individuals, estates and trusts that have income above the statutory threshold amounts. Individuals, estates, and trusts will use Form 8960 to compute their Net Investment Income Tax.

A taxpayer with Net Investment Income will owe the tax if modified adjusted gross income exceeds one of the following thresholds:

Filing Status	Threshold Amount
Married filing jointly	$250,000
Married filing separately	$125,000
Single	$200,000
Head of household (with qualifying person)	$200,000
Qualifying widow(er) with dependent child	$250,000

Net Investment Income

In general, investment income includes, but is not limited to: interest, dividends, capital gains, rental and royalty income, non-qualified annuities, income from businesses involved in trading of financial instruments or commodities and businesses that are passive activities to the taxpayer (within the meaning of section 469). The taxpayer may reduce investment income by certain expenses properly allocable to the income.

For purposes of the Net Investment Income Tax (NIIT), net investment income does not include distributions from a qualified retirement plan (for example, 401(a), 403(a), 403(b), 457(b) plans, and IRAs). However, these distributions are taken into account when determining the modified adjusted gross income threshold. Distributions from a nonqualified retirement plan are included in net investment income.

The Net Investment Income Tax does not apply to any amount of gain that is excluded from gross income for regular income tax purposes. The pre-existing statutory exclusion in section 121 exempts the first $250,000 ($500,000 in the case of a married couple) of gain recognized on the sale of a principal residence from gross income for regular income tax purposes and, thus, from the NIIT.

Tax on Investment Income of Certain Children

> When a child has more than $2,100 in income from interest, dividends, or other investments, part of that income may be taxed at the parent's tax rate instead of the child's tax rate. If the child's interest and dividend income (including capital gain distributions) is less than $10,500, the parent may elect to include that income on the parent's return rather than file a return for the child.

The parent can make that election on *Form 8814* only if all the following conditions are met:

- The child was under age 19 (or under age 24 if a full-time student) at the end of the year.

- The child had income only from interest and dividends (including capital gain distributions and Alaska Permanent Fund dividends).
- The child's gross income was less than $10,500.
- The child is required to file a return unless the parent makes this election.
- The child does not file a joint return for the year.
- There is no estimated tax payment or prior year overpayment applied to this year under the child's name and Social Security number.
- No federal income tax was withheld from the child's income.
- The taxpayer cannot file Form 1040A or Form 1040EZ.

Taxes for Household Employees

A taxpayer has a household employee if he hires someone to do household work and that worker is his *employee*. The worker is an employee if the taxpayer controls the work performed and how the worker performs the duties. If the worker controls how duties are performed, he is considered *self-employed*.

While popularly referred to as a "Nanny Tax," other household employees are also subject to these rules. Other examples of workers who do household work are babysitters, cleaning people, drivers, domestic workers, private nurses, yard workers, etc.

> A worker who performs childcare services in his home generally is not an employee of the taxpayer. If an agency provides the worker and controls the work performed and how duties are performed, the worker is not an employee of the taxpayer. Other individuals specifically excluded are the taxpayer's parents (unless caring for the taxpayers child under age 18 and the taxpayer is divorced or widowed), spouse, child under age 21, or anyone under age 18 whose principal occupation is not household employment (for example, a student).

Withholding

A taxpayer is not responsible for withholding federal income tax for household employees unless the employee asks and he agrees; however, he must withhold and pay the following taxes when applicable:

- **Social Security and Medicare taxes** – If a household employee is paid cash wages of $1,900 or more in 2015, the employer must pay 7.65% of wages. The employer may either pay or withhold the employee share, which in 2015 is 7.65%. An employer is required to withhold an additional 0.9% Medicare tax from wages paid to an employee in excess of $200,000 in a calendar year.

- **Federal unemployment** – If the combined cash wages of all household employees is $1,000 or more in any calendar quarter, the employer must pay FUTA tax. The 2015 FUTA tax rate is 6.0%. The tax applies to the first $7,000 in wages paid to each employee during the year. The $7,000 is the federal wage base. The state wage base may be different. Wages more than $7,000 a year per employee are not taxed. The employer may also owe state unemployment tax. Generally, the employer takes a credit against FUTA tax for amounts paid into state unemployment funds. The credit may be as much as 5.4% of FUTA taxable wages. If entitled to the maximum 5.4% credit, the FUTA tax rate after credit is 0.6%. Only the employer pays FUTA tax; it is not withheld from the employee's wages.

Reporting

A taxpayer with a household employee files **Schedule H** to report the tax with his personal tax return by the due date plus extensions. In general, the amount of tax attributed to household employees increases the tax due on the taxpayer's personal return (1040). A household employer needs an employer identification number (EIN), and must provide a W-2 no later than January 31 to all household employees with cash wages of $1,900 or more, or withheld taxes.

Individual Shared Responsibility Payment

The individual shared responsibility provision of the Affordable Care Act requires everyone on the individual income tax return to have qualifying health care coverage for each month of the year or have a coverage exemption. Otherwise, the IRS may require the taxpayer to make an *individual shared responsibility payment*.

> The payment amount for 2015 is the greater of 2 percent of the household income above the taxpayer's filing threshold, or $325 per adult plus $162.50 per child (limited to a family maximum of $975). This payment payment amount is capped at the cost of the national average premium for a bronze level health plan available through the Marketplace.

Depending upon the circumstances, the Health Insurance Marketplace, health coverage providers, and certain employers may provide information forms to the taxpayer and the IRS.

- **Form 1095-A, Health Insurance Marketplace Statement** – The Health Insurance Marketplace sends this form to individuals who enrolled in coverage there, with information about the coverage, who was covered, and when. The deadline for the Marketplace to provide Form 1095-A is February 1, 2016

- **Form 1095-B, Health Coverage** – Health insurance providers send this new form to individuals they cover, with information about who was covered and when. The deadline for coverage providers to provide Form 1095-B is March 31, 2016.

- **Form 1095-C, Employer-Provided Health Insurance Offer and Coverage** – Certain employers send this new form to certain employees, with information about what coverage the employer offered. The deadline for employers to provide Form 1095-C is March 31, 2016.

> Some taxpayers may not receive a Form 1095-B or Form 1095-C by the time they are ready to file their tax return. It is not necessary to wait for Forms 1095-B or 1095-C in order to file. Taxpayers may instead rely on other information about their health coverage to prepare their returns. These new forms should not be attached to the income tax return.

Health Coverage Exemptions

A taxpayer can claim most exemptions using Form 8965, Health Coverage Exemptions, when filing his income tax return. This form is required if the taxpayer or dependent qualifies for a coverage exemption on the tax return. The taxpayer does not need to call the IRS to qualify for the coverage exemption in advance.

> A taxpayer who is not required to file a federal income tax return for a year because gross income is below the return filing threshold is automatically exempt from the shared responsibility provision for that year and does not need to take any further action to secure an exemption. It is not necessary to to file a return solely to report coverage or to claim a coverage exemption.

Certain exemptions must be granted by the Health Insurance Marketplace in advance. This includes exemptions for certain hardship situations and for members of certain religious sects. A taxpayer that can claim the coverage exemption on his tax return does not need to apply for a Marketplace-granted exemption. If the Marketplace grants a coverage exemption, they send a unique *Exemption Certificate Number (ECN)*. The taxpayer enters the ECN on Form 8965 when claiming a coverage exemption.

Child and Dependent Care Credit (Non-refundable)

To qualify for this credit, a taxpayer must meet all the following tests:

- The taxpayer cannot file Form 1040EZ.
- The filing status must be single, head of household, qualifying widow(er) with dependent child, or married filing jointly. Married couples must file a joint return, unless an exception exists.
- The care must be for one or more *qualifying person(s)*.
- The taxpayer (and spouse if married) must have earned income during the year.
- The taxpayer must pay the expenses so taxpayer (and spouse if married) can work or look for work.
- Payments cannot go to the following individuals:
  1) A spouse
  2) Person who is a dependent of taxpayer, or the taxpayer's child if under age 19 at the end of the year (even if not a dependent)
  3) The parent of the qualifying person if the qualifying person is the taxpayer's child (under age 13)
- Taxpayer must identify the care provider on the tax return (name, address, TIN).
- If a taxpayer excludes dependent care benefits provided by a dependent care benefits plan, the total exclusion must be less than the dollar limit for qualifying expenses (generally, $3,000 if one qualifying person was cared for or $6,000 if two or more qualifying persons were cared for).

Qualifying Person Test

For purposes of the *child and dependent care credit*, a qualifying person is:

- A dependent who was **under age 13** when the care was provided
- An individual living with a taxpayer for more than half of a year who is physically or mentally unable to care for himself, if he is:
  1) A spouse
  2) A dependent
  3) Would have been a dependent except for one of the following:
     A) He received gross income of $4,000 or more
     B) He filed a joint return
     C) Another person could claim the taxpayer or the taxpayer's spouse as a dependent

In determining whether a person is a qualifying person, treat a person who is born or dies as living with the taxpayer for the entire year if he lived in the taxpayer's home the entire time he was alive.

A qualifying person for this credit must meet different requirements than a qualifying person for purposes of a dependency exemption or the EIC. All three are important topics on the exam.

Joint Return Test

Generally, married couples must file a joint return to take the credit. However, those legally separated or living apart from a spouse may be able to file a separate return and still take the credit. Only the custodial parent can claim the credit. A married taxpayer living apart from a spouse is not considered married, and he can take the credit if all the following apply:

- Taxpayer files a separate return.
- Taxpayer's home is the home of a qualifying person for more than half the year.
- Taxpayer paid more than half of the cost of keeping up a home for the year.
- Spouse did not live in the taxpayer's home for the last six months of the year.

How to Figure the Credit

The credit is a percentage of *work-related expenses,* which allow the taxpayer to work or look for work. The expenses to figure the credit on **Form 2441** cannot be more than any one of the following:

- $3,000 if one qualifying person, or $6,000 if more than one qualifying person
- Taxpayer's earned income for the year if single at the end of the year
- If married at end of year, the smaller of taxpayer or a spouse's earned income for the year

A spouse who is a full-time student or incapable of self-care is treated as having earned income of at least $250/m if there is one qualifying person in the taxpayer's home, or at least $500 for two or more.

To determine the credit amount, multiply work-related expenses (after applying the earned income and dollar limits) by a percentage (based on AGI). The applicable percentage begins at 35% for taxpayers with AGI less than $15,000 and decreases by 1% for each $2,000 increase in AGI. Taxpayers with AGI more than $43,000 receive the minimum percentage of 20%. The maximum amount of this credit is $1,050 (35% of $3,000) for one qualifying person or $2,100 (35% of $6,000) for more than one.

Education Credits

For 2015, there are two tax credits available to persons who pay expenses for higher (postsecondary) education. They are as follows:

- The Lifetime Learning credit
- The American Opportunity credit

Generally, a taxpayer may claim a credit if he meets all of the following three requirements:

- He pays *qualified education expenses* of higher education.
- He pays the education expenses for an *eligible student.*
- The student is the taxpayer, a spouse, or a dependent (must claim an exemption).

A taxpayer cannot claim a credit if any of the following applies:

- Filing status is married filing separately (MFS).
- Someone else claims a dependency exemption for the taxpayer on his tax return.
- Modified adjusted gross income (MAGI) is above the phase-out limit.

- Taxpayer (or spouse) is a nonresident alien for any part of the year and did not elect to be treated as a resident alien for tax purposes.
- The taxpayer claims another education credit or tuition and fees deduction for same student in the same year.

A taxpayer cannot claim multiple credits for the same student in the same year. The American opportunity credit will always be greater than or equal to the lifetime learning credit for any student who is eligible for both credits. If a taxpayer claims the *American Opportunity credit* for a child on his 2015 tax return, he cannot, for that same child, also claim the Lifetime Learning credit for 2015. A taxpayer who is eligible for more than one credit can choose to claim either credit, but not both. A taxpayer with education expenses for more than one student in the same year can choose to take the credits on a per-student, per-year basis.

For example, a taxpayer can claim the *American Opportunity credit* for one student and the *Lifetime Learning credit* for another student in the same year. A taxpayer can claim both the *American Opportunity credit* and the *Lifetime Learning credit*—but not for the same student.

Qualified Education Expenses

Expenses paid or deemed paid by a dependent are considered paid by the taxpayer. Someone other than the taxpayer, spouse, or dependent (such as a relative or former spouse) may make a payment directly to an eligible educational institution to pay for an eligible student's qualified education expenses. In this case, treat the student as receiving the payment from the other person and, in turn, paying the institution. If the taxpayer claims an exemption on his tax return for the student, he is considered to have paid the expenses. For purposes of the education credits, consider only *qualified education expenses* in determining the credit amount. Qualified education expenses must be <u>required</u> for enrollment or attendance at an *eligible educational institution* and include tuition and required enrollment fees. Expenses include amounts paid to the institution for course-related books, supplies, and equipment.

- Only certain expenses for course-related books, supplies, and equipment qualify:

    1) **American Opportunity credit** – Qualified education expenses include amounts spent on books, supplies, and equipment needed for a course of study, whether or not the taxpayer purchases materials from the educational institution as a condition of enrollment or attendance.

    2) **Lifetime Learning credit** – Qualified education expenses include **only** amounts for books, supplies, and equipment <u>required to be paid</u> to the institution as a condition of enrollment or attendance.

- Qualified education expenses **do not** include amounts paid for:

    1) Room and board, insurance, medical expenses (including student health fees), transportation, or other similar personal, living, or family expenses

    2) Any course or other education involving sports, games, or hobbies, or any noncredit course, unless such course or other education is part of the student's degree program or (for the Lifetime Learning credit only) helps the student acquire or improve job skills

    3) Nonacademic fees, such as student activity fees, athletic fees, insurance expenses, or other expenses unrelated to the academic course of instruction

Expenses paid or deemed paid by a dependent are considered paid by the taxpayer. Someone other than the taxpayer, spouse, or dependent (such as a relative or former spouse) may make a payment directly to an eligible educational institution to pay for an eligible student's qualified education expenses. In this case, treat the student as receiving the payment from the other person and, in turn, paying the institution. If the taxpayer claims an exemption on his tax return for the student, he is considered to have paid the expenses.

American Opportunity Credit (Partially Refundable)

The American Opportunity credit replaces the Hope credit. Students must attend at least half time for one academic period.

- The credit is available for the first **four years** of postsecondary education, and **40% of the credit is refundable** for most taxpayers.

- The maximum credit per student is $2,500 (100% of first $2,000 and 25% of the next $2,000).

- The threshold before the reduction of the credit is <u>more</u> than that for the Lifetime Learning credit. The phase out begins if MAGI is between $80,000 and $90,000 ($160,000 and $180,000 MFJ). A taxpayer cannot claim a credit if MAGI is $90,000 or more ($180,000 MFJ).

Lifetime Learning Credit (Non-refundable)

A Lifetime Learning credit of up to $2,000 is available for *qualified education expenses* paid for students enrolled in *eligible educational institutions*. The amount of the Lifetime Learning credit is 20% of the first $10,000 of qualified education expenses paid for all eligible students. Differences from other credits include the following:

- Student does not need to pursue a degree or other credentials

- Available for unlimited number of years

- Used for courses to acquire or improve job skills and all years of postsecondary education

- No half-year requirement for eligible students, available for one or more courses

- Felony drug conviction rule does not apply

The amount of the Lifetime Learning credit phases out (gradually declines) if modified adjusted gross income (MAGI) is between $55,000 and $65,000 ($110,000 and $130,000 MFJ). No credits are available when (MAGI) exceeds $65,000 ($130,000 MFJ).

Table 8-1. 2015 Education Credits

	American Opportunity Credit	Lifetime Learning Credit
Maximum credit	$2,500 credit per **eligible student**	$2,000 credit per **return**
Limit on (MAGI)	$180,000 MFJ, $90,000 S, HH, or QW	$130,000 if MFJ, $65,000 if S, HH, or QW
Refundable	40% refundable	Non-refundable credit limited to the amount of tax liability.
Availability	Available **ONLY** for the first **4 years**.	Available **ALL years AND** for courses to acquire or improve job skills
Number of tax years' credit available	Available **ONLY** for **4** tax years per eligible student	Available for an **UNLIMITED** number of years
Type of degree required	Student must be pursuing an undergraduate degree or other recognized education credential	Student does not need to be pursuing a degree or other recognized education credential
Number of courses	Student enrolled at least half time for at least one academic period beginning in the tax year	Available for one or more courses
Felony drug conviction	No felony drug convictions on student's records	Felony drug convictions permitted
Qualified expenses	Books, supplies, and equipment **do not** need to be purchased from the institution in order to qualify.	Tuition and required enrollment fees, including required amounts paid to the institution for course-related books, supplies, and equipment.

Adoption Credit (Non-refundable)

A credit is available for *qualified expenses* paid to adopt an *eligible child* (under age 18 or with special needs). For 2015, the maximum adoption credit is $13,400 per child (minus any qualified adoption expenses claimed for the same child in a prior year). The full credit may be allowed for the adoption of a child with special needs even if there are no qualified expenses. For 2015, the adoption credit phases out ratably for taxpayers with MAGI between $201,010 and $241,010. Because the adoption credit is not refundable in 2015, a taxpayer may carry forward any unused credit amounts to future tax years.

- **Qualified adoption expenses** are reasonable and necessary expenses directly related to, and whose principal purpose is for, the legal adoption of an eligible child. These expenses include the following:

    1) Adoption fees

    2) Court costs

    3) Attorney fees

    4) Travel expenses (including meals and lodging) while away from home

    5) Re-adoption expenses to adopt a foreign child

- **Nonqualified expenses** are expenses that meet the following criteria:

    1) Expenses that violate state or federal law

    2) Expenses for carrying out any surrogate parenting arrangement

    3) Expenses for the adoption of spouse's child

    4) Expenses for which the taxpayer received funds under any federal, state, or local program

    5) Expenses allowed as a credit or deduction under any other federal income tax rule

6) Expenses paid or reimbursed by employer or any other person or organization

7) Expenses paid before 1997

When to Claim the Credit

If the eligible child is a U.S. citizen or resident, a taxpayer may claim the adoption credit even if the adoption never became final. A taxpayer may claim expenses paid prior to finalization in the year following the year of payment. Expenses paid in the year the adoption becomes final are included in that year. A taxpayer may claim expenses paid after the adoption becomes final in the year of payment. If the eligible child is not a U.S. citizen or resident, a taxpayer cannot take the adoption credit or exclusion unless the adoption becomes final.

Substantiation Requirements

Taxpayers must now include a copy of one or more adoption-related documents and *Form 8839* along with their return to claim the credit.

- **Domestic or foreign adoption finalized in the United States** – copy of an adoption order or decree.

- **Domestic adoptions that are not final** – include an adoption taxpayer identification number, obtained for the child, or provide a copy of one of the following documents:

    1) A home study completed by an authorized placement agency

    2) A placement agreement with an authorized placement agency

    3) A document signed by a hospital official authorizing the release of a newborn child from the hospital to the taxpayer for legal adoption

    4) A court document ordering or approving the placement of the child for legal adoption

    5) An original affidavit or notarized statement, from an adoption attorney, government official, or other person, stating that he (a) placed or is placing a child with the taxpayer for legal adoption or (b) is facilitating the adoption process for the taxpayer in an official capacity

- **Adoptions of special needs children** – a copy of the state determination of special needs.

Earned Income Credit (Refundable)

The *earned income tax credit (EITC)* is a tax credit for certain people who work and have *earned income* under $53,267. For 2015, the maximum credit is 40% (45% if three or more children) of the first $13,870 of earned income. The EITC is a refundable credit. A taxpayer looking to claim the credit must file a return. Earned income includes all of the following:

- Wages, salaries, and tips
- Union strike benefits
- Long-term disability benefits received prior to minimum retirement age
- Net earnings from self-employment
- Non-taxable combat pay (only if elected and included in taxable income)

Earned Income does not include:

- Interest and dividends
- Pensions

- Social Security or unemployment benefits
- Alimony or child support

Who May Claim the EITC?

To claim the EITC, taxpayers must meet all of the following rules:

- Investment income must be $3,400 or less for the year.
- If married, the taxpayers cannot file separately; they must file a joint return (MFJ).
- Taxpayer(s) and all qualifying children must have a valid Social Security number.
- Taxpayer must be a U.S. citizen or a nonresident alien married to a U.S. citizen or resident alien and filing a joint return.
- Taxpayer cannot file Form 2555 related to foreign-earned income.
- Taxpayer cannot be the *qualifying child* of another person.
- Taxpayer must have earned income; however, earned income and AGI cannot be more than:
    1) $47,747 ($53,267 MFJ) with three or more qualifying children
    2) $44,454 ($49,974 MFJ) with two qualifying children
    3) $39,131 ($44,651 MFJ) with one qualifying child
    4) $14,820 ($20,330 MFJ) with no qualifying children

Taxpayers with no qualifying children must meet the following criteria:

- Be age 25 but younger than 65 at the end of the year
- Live in the United States for more than half of the year
- Not qualify as a dependent of another person

Taxpayers with a qualifying child must meet the *relationship*, *age*, and *residency tests*:

- **Relationship Test** – To be a qualifying child, a child must fall into one of the following categories:
    1) Son, daughter, stepchild, foster child, adopted child, or a descendant of any of them (for example, a grandchild)
    2) Brother, sister, half-brother, half-sister, stepbrother, stepsister, or a descendant of any of them (for example, a niece or nephew)
- **Age Test** – A qualifying child must be as follows:
    1) Younger than the taxpayer or taxpayer's spouse if filing a joint return, and
        A) Under age 19 at the end of the year, or
        B) A full-time (five months or more) student under age 24 at the end of the year
    2) Permanently and totally disabled at any time during the year, regardless of age
- **Residency Test** – Child must have lived with taxpayer in the U.S. for more than half of the tax year.

Sometimes a child meets the rules to be a qualifying child of more than one person. However, only one person can treat that child as a qualifying child and claim the EITC using that child. Taxpayers can choose which person will claim the EITC. If the taxpayers do not reach an agreement and more than one person claims the EITC using the same child, the tiebreaker rule applies, and the parent with whom the child lived the longest during the year receives the credit. If the child lived with each parent the same amount of time, the parent with the higher AGI receives the credit.

Paid preparers of federal income tax returns or claims for refund involving the earned income credit <u>must</u> meet the due diligence requirements in determining if the taxpayer is eligible for, and the amount of, the EITC. Failure to do so in 2015 could result in a **$500** penalty for each failure. See IRC section 6695(g). A tax preparer can use *Form 8867* to document due diligence.

Disallowance of the EITC

Certain errors may cause the IRS to deny a taxpayer the EITC. If the denial is because of taxpayer error due to reckless or intentional disregard of the rules, the taxpayer cannot claim the EIC for the next two years. If the error is due to fraud, the taxpayer cannot claim the EITC for the next 10 years. A taxpayer who wants (and meets the requirements) to claim the EITC must attach *Form 8862* to his return if the EITC was reduced or disallowed for any reason other than a math or clerical error for a year after 1996.

A taxpayer can claim the EITC without filing Form 8862 if he meets all the EITC eligibility requirements and either of the following applies:

- After the EIC was reduced or disallowed in an earlier year:
    1) The taxpayer filed Form 8862 (or other documents) and the EIC was then allowed, and
    2) EITC was not reduced or disallowed again for any reason other than a math or clerical error.
- The taxpayer is taking the EITC without a qualifying child and the only reason the EITC was disallowed in the earlier year was that a child listed on Schedule EIC was not his qualifying child.

First-time Homebuyer Credit (Refundable, but expired in 2011)

To qualify as a first-time homebuyer, a taxpayer (and spouse, if married) cannot own any other main home during the three-year period ending on the date of purchase. Certain first-time homebuyers who bought a home in the United States may claim a refundable credit that is the <u>smaller</u> of **$8,000** ($4,000 MFS), or **10% of the purchase price**. The credit begins to phase-out when MAGI is more than $125,000 ($225,000 MFJ). <u>The first-time homebuyer credit has expired</u>. A taxpayer cannot claim the credit on a 2015 return. This topic is only covered because of the recapture provisions.

Repayment

In general, a taxpayer must repay the credit if he disposes of the home or the home stops being his main home within the <u>36-month period</u> beginning on the purchase date. This includes if he sells the home; converts it to business or rental property; the home is destroyed, condemned, or disposed of under threat of condemnation; or the lender forecloses on the mortgage. The taxpayer can repay the credit by including it as additional tax on the return for the year the home stops being his main home. The following are exceptions to the repayment rule:

- If the sale is not to a related party, the repayment is limited to the amount of gain on the sale. When figuring the gain, reduce the adjusted basis of the home by the amount of the credit.
- If a home is destroyed, condemned, or disposed of under threat of condemnation, and the taxpayer acquires a new main home within two years of the event, he does not have to repay the credit.

- If, as part of a divorce settlement, the taxpayer transfers the home to a spouse or former spouse, the spouse who receives the home is responsible for repaying the credit if required.
- If the taxpayer dies, repayment of the credit is not required. For joint filers, the surviving spouse must repay his or her half of the credit if required.
- In some cases, there is an exception for members of the uniformed services or Foreign Service and for intelligence community employees.

Home Purchased in 2008

For homes purchased in 2008, a different credit was available that generally requires taxpayers begin repaying it on their 2010 return. In addition, taxpayers generally must repay any credit they claimed for a home they bought in 2008 if during the repayment period they sold the home, or the home stopped being their main. If the taxpayer dies, any remaining annual installments are not due. If a spouse dies (files a joint return), the IRS requires the survivor to continue payments for his or her half of the credit.

Credit for Elderly or the Disabled (Non-refundable)

To take the credit for the elderly or the disabled, taxpayers must meet all of the following:

- Must be a qualified individual:

    1) A U.S. citizen or resident alien age 65 or older at the end of the year, or

    2) Younger than age 65 at the end of the year and all of the following statements are true:

        A) Retired on permanent and total disability (expected to result in death or last 12 months or more)

        B) Received taxable disability income in the tax year

        C) On January 1 of the tax year, had not reached mandatory retirement age

- Income no more than certain limits
- Cannot file 1040EZ

An individual is considered to be age 65 on the day before his 65th birthday. If the taxpayer is younger than age 65, he must maintain records containing a statement of permanent and total disability on the date he retired, certified by a physician or the Dept. of Veterans Affairs (VA).

Table 8-2. 2015 Credit for Elderly or Disabled

IF filing status is . . .	AGI Phase-out Begins	THEN, you CANNOT take the credit if . . .	
		AGI is equal to or more than . . .	OR the total of nontaxable Social Security and pension(s) is equal to or more than the BASE AMOUNT
single, head of household, or qualifying widow(er)	$7,500	$17,500	$5,000
married filing a joint return and both spouses qualify	$10,000	$25,000	$7,500
married filing a joint return and only one spouse qualifies	$10,000	$20,000	$5,000
married filing a separate return*	$5,000	$12,500	$3,750

*Married taxpayers must file jointly to claim the credit if living together at any time during the year.

Income Limits

The credit is 15% of the applicable base amount (see table 8-2) reduced by excess AGI and any nontaxable Social Security or other nontaxable pensions received. Nontaxable benefits reduce the base amount dollar for dollar while excess AGI (above the AGI limit) reduces the base amount by $1 for every $2 excess. Due to these reductions, only taxpayers with modest income will qualify for this credit.

Example: A married couple files a joint return, and only one spouse qualifies for the credit. They received $11,500 in taxable IRA distributions and $4,000 in nontaxable Social Security benefits.

- Subtract $4,000 of nontaxable Social Security benefits from the base amount of $5,000.
- Determine excess AGI ($11,500 AGI minus $10,000 threshold equals $1,500 excess AGI).
- Reduce the remaining base amount by $750 (one-half of the excess AGI).
- Multiply the resulting base amount of $250 ($5,000 minus $4,000 minus $750) by 15% to arrive at the credit of $37.50.

Child Tax Credit (Non-refundable)

For each *qualifying child*, a maximum non-refundable *child tax credit* of $1,000 is available, subject to certain income limits. A qualifying child for purposes of the child tax credit is a child who meets the following criteria:

- Is the taxpayer's son, daughter, stepchild, foster child, adopted child, brother, sister, stepbrother, stepsister, or a descendant of any of them (a grandchild, niece, or nephew)
- Was younger than age 17 at the end of the tax year <u>and</u> younger than the taxpayer (and spouse)
- Did not provide more than half of his own support for the year
- Lived with the taxpayer for more than half of the year
- Is claimed as a dependent on the return
- Is a U.S. citizen, a U.S. national, or a resident of the United States

Treat a person who was born or died as having lived with the taxpayer for the entire tax year if the taxpayer's home was the person's home the entire time he was alive. Temporary absences for special circumstances, such as school, vacation, business, medical care, military service, or detention in a juvenile facility, count as time the child lived with the taxpayer.

Limits on the Credit

This credit reduces (phases-out) when *modified adjusted gross income (MAGI)* (AGI plus foreign income that was excluded from AGI) is above the amount shown below the following:

- Married filing jointly – $110,000
- Single, head of household, or qualifying widow(er) – $75,000
- Married filing separately – $55,000

Round income above these levels up to the nearest thousand and multiply by 5% ($50 per $1,000). Subtract the result from the maximum child tax credit. This credit is <u>not</u> refundable and <u>cannot</u> be more than the amount of tax due.

The "child tax credit" is not refundable. If a taxpayer cannot claim the full amount of the child tax credit, a <u>refundable</u> ***additional child tax credit*** may be available. For 2015, the portion refundable as the additional child tax credit is up to 15% of earned income (including tax-free combat pay) that exceeds $3,000. To claim this credit, the taxpayer must attach **Form 8812** to his tax return. Beginning in 2015, a taxpayer filing Form 2555 or 2555-EZ (both relating to foreign earned income), cannot claim the additional child tax credit.

Foreign Tax Credit (Non-refundable)

If a taxpayer paid income tax to a foreign country, he can choose to take a credit against his U.S. income tax or an itemized deduction. He cannot take a credit (or deduction) for foreign income taxes paid on income he excludes from U.S. tax under any of the following:

- Foreign earned income exclusion
- Foreign housing exclusion
- Income from Puerto Rico exempt from U.S. tax
- Possession exclusion

The taxpayer must file Form 1116 to take the credit <u>unless</u> all of the following apply:

- All of the foreign source income is passive income, which generally includes interest and dividends.
- The taxpayer reported all of his foreign source income and the foreign tax paid on it on a qualified payee statement, which includes Form 1099-INT and Form 1099-DIV.
- The total of creditable foreign taxes was not more than $300 ($600 if married filing jointly).
- The taxpayer elects this procedure for the tax year.

Saver's Credit (Non-refundable)

A taxpayer may claim the saver's credit (formerly Retirement Savings Contributions Credit) for qualified contributions or deferrals made to certain retirement plans. The credit amount begins at 50% of the taxpayer's contributions to the plan and is reduced depending on income levels and filing status. The maximum credit is $1,000 ($2,000 MFJ).

- A taxpayer may <u>not</u> take the credit if one of the following is true:
    1) Year 2015 AGI is more than $30,500 ($45,750 HH, $61,000 MFJ).
    2) Someone else claimed the taxpayer as a dependent.
    3) The taxpayer is younger than age 17.
    4) The taxpayer is a student.

9 Estate Tax and Gift Tax

Estate Tax · Gift Tax · Generation Skipping Transfer Tax

This chapter summarizes IRS Publication 950 and the instructions of Form 706 Estate Tax & 709 Gift Tax.

Overview

The tax code imposes additional federal taxes on certain transfers of property (including money). Property transferred or given away during a lifetime may be subject to *gift tax*. Property owned at death (*estate*) may be subject to *estate tax*, and the gross income of the estate may be subject to *income tax*. Lifetime gifts or *bequests* (gifts after death from taxpayer's estate) also may become subject to an additional *generation-skipping transfer (GST)* tax. This occurs when the gifts or bequests are to a person, such as a grandchild, who is more than one generation younger than the taxpayer is. The GST tax rate is 40% for 2015.

Most gifts are <u>not</u> subject to the gift tax, and most estates are <u>not</u> subject to the estate tax. For example, there is usually no tax on transfers to a spouse or to a charity. The gift tax usually does not apply until the value of the gifts to that person exceeds the *annual exclusion* for the year. Even if tax applies to gifts or the estate, it may be eliminated by the *unified credit*.

Unified Credit (Applicable Exclusion Amount)

The *unified credit* reduces or eliminates <u>both</u> the *gift tax* and the *estate tax*. During the life of the taxpayer, the unified credit offsets gift tax due. Any unified credit used against gift tax reduces the amount of credit that the taxpayer can use in a later year. The total amount used during life against gift tax reduces the credit available to use against the estate tax. The sunset provision within the *Economic Growth and Tax Relief Reconciliation Act of 2001 (EGTRRA)* repeals the estate tax in 2010; however, it was to reappear in 2011 with applicable exclusions reverting to substantially lower levels (same as 2002). The *2010 Tax Relief Act* revives the estate tax for those dying after 2009.

For estates of decedents dying in 2015 the top estate tax rate is 40%. There is a $5.43 million *applicable exclusion* amount in 2015, and beneficiaries receive a stepped-up basis. The unified credit for taxable gifts is $2,117,800, exempting $5.43 million from tax in 2015. The unified credit for estate tax increases during the same period.

The following table shows the unified credit and applicable exclusion amount for the calendar years in which a gift is made or a *decedent* dies.

Table 9-1. Unified Credit for Gift & Estate Tax Purposes:

Year	Unified Credit	Applicable Exclusion Amount
2014	$2,081,800	$5,340,000
2015	$2,117,800	$5,430,000

Exemption Portability

The *2010 Tax Relief Act* has a new twist that allows the executor of a deceased spouse's estate to transfer any unused exclusion to the surviving spouse. The exclusion becomes available to the surviving spouse and is in addition to any applicable exclusion to which the survivor is entitled. In the past, only effective estate planning could preserve this benefit.

> There is a catch—the executor of the estate of the deceased spouse must file an estate tax return on which such amount is computed, and make an election on the return. Such election, once made, shall be irrevocable. The portability rule applies to those dying after December 31, 2010.

Gift Tax Returns (Form 709)

The gift tax applies to transfers by gift of property. A gift is made when taxpayers give property (including money), or the use of (or income from) property, without expecting to receive something of at least equal value in return. The IRS may also consider property sold at less than full value or interest-free or reduced-interest loans to be gifts. The general rule is that any gift is a taxable gift. However, there are many exceptions to this rule. Generally, the following gifts are not taxable gifts:

- Gifts, excluding gifts of future interests, that are not more than the annual exclusion for the year
- Tuition or medical expenses paid directly to a medical or educational institution for anyone
- Gifts subject to the *marital deduction* (to a spouse)
- Gifts to a political organization for its use
- Gifts to charities

Annual Exclusion

A separate *annual exclusion* applies each year to each person to whom a gift is made. The gift tax annual exclusion is subject to cost-of-living increases.

> For 2015, a taxpayer generally can give a gift valued at up to **$14,000** each, to any number of people, and none of the gifts will be taxable.

A taxpayer cannot exclude gifts of *future interests* under an annual exclusion provision. A gift of a future interest is a gift that is limited so that its use, possession, or enjoyment will begin at some point in the future.

> Married taxpayers can each give gifts valued at up to $14,000 to the same person in 2015 without making a taxable gift. If one spouse gives more than the $14,000 exclusion to a person in 2015, the spouses can treat the gift as made one-half by each spouse. This is *gift splitting*. Both must consent to split the gift and all other gifts for the year. In 2015, gift splitting allows married couples to give up to $28,000 to a person without making a taxable gift. Taxpayers who wish to split gifts must file a *gift tax return (Form 709)*. Each spouse must file a separate Form 709, as a joint form does not exist.

Generation Skipping Transfer Tax

A taxpayer must report on Form 709 the GST tax imposed on *inter vivos* direct skips. An inter vivos direct skip is a transfer made during the donor's lifetime that is subject to the gift tax, of an interest in property, and made to a skip person.

Like the gift tax, each individual taxpayer has a lifetime GST exemption to exclude a certain amount of assets from the tax. For 2015, the effective GST exemption is $5.43 million, on lifetime transfers or distributions (directly or in trust) to grandchildren.

Filing a Gift Tax Return (Form 709)

A gift tax return is generally due the year following a taxable gift, at the same time as the federal return. Extensions for the federal return automatically extend the time to file the gift tax return. For 2015, the top tax rate on taxable gifts is 40%. The taxpayer also reports GST tax on form 709.

- Generally, a taxpayer <u>must</u> file a gift tax return on Form 709 if any of the following apply:

    1) Gifts to a person (other than a spouse) are more than the annual exclusion for the year.

    2) The taxpayer and his spouse are splitting a gift.

    3) The taxpayer makes the gift to someone (other than a spouse) of a *future interest* that the recipient cannot actually possess, enjoy, or receive income from until sometime in the future.

    4) The taxpayer gave his spouse an interest in property that some future event will end.

- A taxpayer does <u>not</u> have to file a gift tax return to report gifts to (or for the use of) political organizations and gifts made by paying someone's tuition or medical expenses. He also does not need to report the following deductible gifts made to charities:

    1) The taxpayer's entire interest in property, if no other interest has been transferred for less than adequate consideration or for other than a charitable use

    2) A qualified conservation contribution (perpetual restriction on the use of real property)

Estate Tax Returns (Form 706)

A ***taxable estate*** in excess of the *applicable exclusion* ($5.43 million for 2015) may be subject to the estate tax. The taxable estate is the ***gross estate*** less allowable deductions. The ***executor*** of a decedent's estate uses ***Form 706*** to figure the estate tax. This tax is levied on the entire taxable estate and not just on the share received by a particular beneficiary. Form 706 also calculates the *generation-skipping transfer (GST)* tax on ***direct skips*** (transfers of property included in the decedent's gross estate to persons more than one generation younger). For transfers to unrelated persons, a direct skip occurs if the recipient is more than 37.5 years younger than the decedent.

Gross Estate

The gross estate includes the ***fair market value (FMV)*** of all property in which the taxpayer <u>had an interest</u> at the time of death (or an ***alternate valuation date***, if elected).

The gross estate also includes the following:

- The value of property transferred before death where the decedent held a ***retained life estate***
- Certain property transferred before death where the decedent held a ***reversionary interest***
- Property transferred before death where the transfer was ***revocable***
- Transfers taking effect at death
- Life insurance proceeds payable to the estate or, if taxpayer owned the policy
- Certain gifts made within three years of death regarding the above-mentioned property

- The value of certain annuities payable to taxpayer's estate or heirs
- The includible portion of joint estates with right of survivorship
- The includible portion of tenancies by the entirety
- Property over which the decedent possessed a general power of appointment
- Qualified terminable interest property (QTIP)
- Dower or curtesy (or statutory estate) of the surviving spouse
- Community property to the extent of the decedent's interest as defined by applicable law

Alternate Valuation Date

The alternate valuation date is **six months** from the date of death. Any property not sold within that time is valued at the FMV on the alternate valuation date. If the executor elects the alternate valuation date, any property sold within six months is valued at the disposition price.

The executor can make this election <u>only</u> if it reduces both the gross estate and estate tax due.

Taxable Estate

The allowable deductions from the gross estate used in determining the *taxable estate* include:

- Funeral expenses paid out of the estate
- Debts owed at the time of death and other claims against the estate
- Administrative expenses such as court costs, executor fees, and professional fees
- The *marital deduction* (generally, the value of the property that passes to the surviving spouse)
    1) The marital deduction is generally not allowed if the surviving spouse is not a U.S. citizen unless passing to such a surviving spouse in a *qualified domestic trust (QDOT)*.
- The *charitable deduction* (generally, the value of the property that passes from the estate to a qualifying charity for exclusively charitable purposes).
- The state death tax deduction (generally any estate, inheritance, legacy, or succession taxes paid as the result of the decedent's death to any state or the District of Columbia).

Applying the Unified Credit to Estate Tax

The *tentative tax base* includes the taxable estate plus taxable gifts made after 1976. Apply estate tax rates to determine the *tentative estate tax*. The following credits reduce the tax:

- The unified credit
- Credit for foreign death taxes paid
- Credit for federal gift taxes on pre-1977 gifts
- **Credit for tax on prior transfers** – If decedent's estate includes property received from a person who died within 10 years before or two years after the decedent received the gift, the decedent's estate may receive a credit for estate taxes previously paid on the property.

If the combined credits are more than the tentative estate tax, there is no estate tax liability. Otherwise, deduct the credits from the tentative estate tax to arrive at *net estate tax due*.

Filing an Estate Tax Return

An estate tax return, **Form 706**, must be filed for decedents who were citizens or residents of the United States at the time of death and the gross estate, plus any adjusted taxable gifts (post-1976 gifts), is more than the filing requirement for the year of death (same as the applicable exclusion amount). For 2015, a return is not necessary if the taxable estate is less than $5.43 million.

> The executor must file Form 706 to report estate and/or GST tax **within nine months** after the date of the decedent's death, plus extensions.

Under certain circumstances, the IRS may grant an extension of time to pay (up to 10 years) if the executor can show reasonable cause. In addition, estates with gross income more than **$600** or a beneficiary who is a nonresident alien must file a U.S. Income Tax Return for Estates and Trusts **(Form 1041)**.

SEE EXAM PART 2
BUSINESSES

10 Business Entities

Business Entity Overview · Employees · Tax Withholding and Reporting · Accounting Periods · Accounting Methods Inventory Uniform Capitalization Rules · Recordkeeping

This chapter summarizes information from the IRS Publications 15, 15-A, 538, and 583.

Business Entity Overview

- **Sole Proprietor** – An unincorporated business that is owned by one individual.
    1) The business does not exist separately from the owner.
    2) The owner personally accepts the risks of business to the extent of all the owner's assets, whether the owner uses them in the business or uses them personally.
    3) The owner includes business income and expenses on his personal tax return (Schedule C).

- **Partnership** – A relationship between two or more people who join to carry on a business.
    1) Each partner contributes money, property, labor, or skill, and shares in business profits and losses. Partners, other than limited partners, are personally liable for company debts.
    2) Partners can be individuals, corporations, trusts, estates, or other partnerships.
    3) Partnerships must file an annual information return to report operational income, deductions, gains, losses, etc., but do not pay income tax. Instead, any profits or losses "pass through" to its partners. Partners include their respective shares of the partnership items on their tax returns.

- **Qualified Joint Venture** – An unincorporated business jointly owned by a married couple is generally classified as a partnership for federal tax purposes. Previously, married individuals in a business together were considered partners and required to file an annual Form 1065 Partnership Return.
    1) For tax years after 2006, a *qualified joint venture*, whose only members are a husband and a wife filing a joint return, can elect <u>not</u> to be treated as a partnership for federal tax purposes. Each spouse is treated as a sole proprietor and files the appropriate form, such as Schedule C.
    2) A qualified joint venture conducts a trade or business where all the following exist:
        A) The only members of the joint venture are a husband and wife who file a joint return.
        B) Both spouses materially participate in the trade or business (mere joint ownership of property is not enough).
        C) Both spouses elect not to be treated as a partnership.
        D) The business is co-owned by both spouses (and not in the name of a state law entity, such as a partnership or LLC).

- **Corporation** – A person or group of people incorporated by charter from the Secretary of State.
    1) This includes associations, joint stock companies, insurance companies, and trusts and partnerships that operate as associations or corporations.

2) The profit is <u>taxed to the corporation</u> when earned <u>and</u> then is <u>taxed to the shareholders</u> when distributed as dividends. Shareholders cannot deduct any loss of the corporation.

3) An eligible domestic corporation can avoid **double taxation** by electing treatment as an **S corporation**. Generally, an S corporation is exempt from federal income tax other than tax on certain capital gains and passive income. On their tax returns, the S corporation's shareholders include their shares of the corporation's separately stated items of income, deduction, loss, and credit, and their shares of non-separately stated income or loss.

- **Limited Liability Company** – A limited liability company (LLC) is an entity formed under <u>state law</u> by filing articles of organization as an LLC.

    1) LLC members are <u>not</u> personally liable for its debts.

    2) An LLC may elect classification for federal income tax purposes (not legal) as a partnership, a corporation, or a *disregarded entity* (not separate) from its owner.

    3) Unless otherwise elected, the IRS treats a multi-member LLC as a <u>partnership</u> for tax purposes. The LLC may elect an alternative treatment no more than two months and 15 days after the beginning of the tax year the election is to take effect, or anytime in the preceding tax year.

        A) **Form 2553** – The LLC may elect treatment as an <u>SCORP</u> by filing Form 2553.

        B) **Form 8832** – The LLC may elect treatment as a <u>corporation</u> by filing Form 8832.

> **60-month limitation rule** – Once an eligible entity makes an election to <u>change</u> its classification, the entity generally cannot change (without IRS permission) its classification by election again during the 60 months after the effective date. The 60-month limitation does not apply if a <u>newly formed</u> eligible entity made the previous election and the election was effective on the date of formation.

- **Trust** – A trust (excluding a grantor trust) is a separate legal entity for federal tax purposes. A taxpayer may create a trust while alive or upon death by means of a will.

- **Estate** – An estate comes into being upon the death of an individual.

    1) A decedent's estate is a separate legal entity for federal tax purposes.

    2) An estate consists of real and/or personal property of the deceased person.

Employer Identification Number (EIN)

A business must obtain an *employer identification number (EIN)* by filing *Form SS4* if the business meets one of the following conditions:

- Has one or more employees
- Files returns for employment or excise taxes
- Maintains a qualified retirement plan
- Operates as a corporation, partnership, is a non-profit, estate, or trust (not grantor trust)

Employees

Who Are Employees?

Before an employer can know how to treat payments made to workers for services, the employer must first know the business relationship that exists between the employer and worker. The person performing the services may be one of the following:

- **Independent contractor** – People such as lawyers, contractors, subcontractors, and auctioneers who follow an independent trade, business, or profession in which they offer their services to the public, are typically <u>not</u> employees.

> An individual is usually an independent contractor if the employer, the person for whom the individual performs the services, has the right to control or direct only the <u>result</u> of the work and <u>not</u> the <u>means</u> and <u>methods</u> of accomplishing the result.

- **Common-law employees** – Under common-law rules, anyone who performs services for a person is an employee of that person if the employer has the right to control <u>what</u> will be done and <u>how</u> it will be done. This is true even when an employer gives the employee freedom of action. What matters is the <u>right to control</u> the details of how the employee performs the services.

    1) It does not matter whether the individual is employed full time or part time.

    2) An *officer* of a corporation is generally an employee; however, an officer who performs no services or only minor services, and neither receives nor is entitled to receive any pay, is not considered an employee.

    3) A corporate *director* is not an employee with respect to services performed as a director.

    4) Employers generally must withhold and pay income, Social Security, and Medicare taxes on wages paid to common-law employees.

- **Statutory employees** – If someone who works for an individual is not an employee under the common law rules discussed above, the employer must not withhold federal income tax from the employee's pay, unless backup withholding applies. Although the following persons may not be common law employees, they may be considered employees by statute for Social Security, Medicare, and FUTA tax purposes under certain conditions.

    1) A commission (or agent) driver who delivers beverages (not milk), food, laundry, or dry cleaning.

    2) A full-time life insurance sales agent who sells primarily for one life insurance company.

    3) A home worker who works by guidelines of the person for whom the work is done, with materials furnished by and returned to that person or to someone that person designates.

    4) A full-time traveling or city salesperson that works on an individual's behalf and turns in orders to the latter from wholesalers, retailers, contractors, or operators of hotels, restaurants, or other similar establishments. The goods sold must be merchandise for resale or supplies for use in the buyer's business operation. The work performed must be the salesperson's principal business activity.

- **Statutory nonemployees** – Direct sellers, qualified real estate agents, and certain companion sitters are, by law, considered nonemployees. They are treated generally as self-employed for all federal tax purposes, including income and employment taxes.

Tax Withholding and Reporting

Self-employment Tax

Self-employment tax (SE tax) is a Social Security and Medicare tax primarily for individuals who work for themselves. Payments of SE tax contribute to coverage under the Social Security system. Social Security coverage provides the taxpayer with retirement benefits, disability benefits, survivor benefits, and hospital insurance (Medicare) benefits. An individual may deduct a portion of SE tax as an adjustment to income on Form 1040. The self-employed <u>must</u> pay SE tax and file Schedule SE (Form 1040) if either of the following applies:

- Net earnings from self-employment were $400 or more
- Had church employee income of $108.28 or more

In 2015, a tax rate of 15.3% applies to the first $118,500 of income from self-employment. A tax rate of 2.9% applies to the excess. For tax years beginning after December 31, 2012, a .9% *Additional Medicare Tax* applies when income exceeds one of the following threshold amounts (based on filing status).

- Married filing jointly—$250,000
- Married filing separately—$125,000
- Single, Head of household, or Qualifying widow(er)—$200,000

A taxpayer with both wages and self-employment income reduces the threshold amount for applying the Additional Medicare Tax on the self-employment income (but not below zero) by the amount of wages subject to Additional Medicare Tax.

Before applying the tax rates, a self-employed taxpayer reduces income from self-employment by the percentage of tax that employers normally pay for their employees

> Peter has $100,000 income from self-employment. If Peter were an employee, his employer would pay $7,650 (7.65%). He subtracts this portion from self-employment income to determine his net earnings from self-employment of $92,350. His SE tax is $ 14,129.55 ($92,350 x 15.3%).

Payroll Taxes

Employment taxes include Social Security, Medicare, federal income tax withholding, and *federal unemployment (FUTA)* tax. Generally, taxpayers do <u>not</u> pay or withhold tax on payments to independent contractors. The general rule is that an individual is an independent contractor if the person for whom the services are performed has the right to control or direct only the result of the work and <u>not</u> the means and methods of accomplishing the result.

- **Income tax** – Employers generally must withhold federal income tax from wages. They use Form W-4 to figure how much federal income tax to withhold from each wage payment.
- **FICA taxes** – Social Security and Medicare taxes pay for benefits that workers and their families receive under the *Federal Insurance Contributions Act (FICA)*. Social Security tax pays for benefits under the old age, survivors, and disability insurance part of FICA. Medicare tax pays for benefits under the hospital insurance part of FICA. Employers must withhold part of these taxes from their employee's wages and must pay a matching amount. The employee tax rate for social security is 6.2% in 2015. The employer tax rate for social security remains unchanged at 6.2%. The Medicare tax rate is 1.45% each (2.9% total) for employers and employees, and an additional Medicare tax of 0.9% applies to certain high-income employees. Employers are responsible for withholding the 0.9% Additional Medicare Tax on an individual's wages paid in excess of $200,000 in a calendar year, without regard to filing status. An employer is required to begin withholding Additional Medicare Tax in the pay period in which it pays wages in excess of $200,000 to an employee and continue to withhold it each pay period until the end of the calendar year. There is no employer match for Additional Medicare Tax. The social security wage base limit to which tax applies is $118,500 for 2015. There is no wage base limit for Medicare tax; all covered wages are subject to Medicare tax. Report these taxes on **Form 941**, Employer's Quarterly Federal Tax Return.

- **FUTA taxes** – This tax is part of the federal and state program under the *Federal Unemployment Tax Act (FUTA)* that pays unemployment compensation to workers who lose their jobs. Employers must report and pay FUTA tax separately from Social Security and Medicare taxes and withheld income tax. The employer must pay FUTA tax only from separate funds. Employees do not pay this tax or have it withheld from their pay. Employers must report federal unemployment tax on **Form 940**, Employer's Annual Federal Unemployment (FUTA) Tax Return.

Estimated Taxes

Generally, estimated tax payments are required to pay employment tax obligations.

- **Sole proprietors, partners, and S corporation shareholders** – When the owner(s) of such a business expect to owe $1,000 or more in taxes, those individuals generally make estimated tax payments. Individual taxpayers use Form 1040-ES to figure and pay estimated tax.

- **Corporations** – Generally, a corporation must make estimated tax payments (via EFTPS or Form 1120-W) if expecting to owe tax of $500 or more when filing a return.

- **When to pay estimated tax** – Installment payments are due by the 15th day of the 4th, 6th, 9th, and 12th months of the corporate tax year. The due date is different for individuals who must make payments by the 15th day of the 4th, 6th, 9th, and 1st month.

Electronic Deposit of Employment Taxes

All taxpayers must use electronic funds transfer to make all federal tax deposits (such as deposits of employment tax, excise tax, and corporate income tax). Generally, electronic funds transfers are made using the *Electronic Federal Tax Payment System (EFTPS)*. A taxpayer who does not want to use EFTPS can arrange for an authorized financial institution to make deposits on his behalf with **Form 941**. There are two deposit schedules—monthly and semi-weekly. Employers determine the required deposit schedule before the beginning of each calendar year by calculating prior employment tax liability within a look back period (begins July 1 and ends June 30).

- **Monthly deposit schedule** – tax liability during look back period was $50,000, or less.

- **Semi-weekly deposit schedule** – tax liability during look back period was more than $50,000.

Required Forms

Employers are required to collect Form I-9 and Form W-4 from employees.

- **Form I-9** – The employer must verify that each new employee is legally eligible to work in the United States. He must complete the U.S. Citizenship and Immigration Services *Form I-9, Employment Eligibility Verification* and maintain in records.

- **Form W-4** – Employers use the filing status and withholding allowances shown on this form to calculate the amount of income tax to withhold from the employee's wages.

Informational Returns

An information return is a tax document that businesses are required to file in order to report certain business transactions to the Internal Revenue Service. Any person, including a corporation, partnership, individual, estate, and trust, with reportable transactions during the calendar year must file information returns to report those transactions to the IRS. Persons required to file must also furnish statements to the recipients of the income. Filers who have 250 or more returns must file the returns electronically.

The recipient of an informational return does not send copies to the IRS unless required. A taxpayer must attach Form W-2 to the front of their Form 1040 series tax return. A taxpayer should also attach Forms W-2G and 1099-R, but only if federal income tax was withheld.

- **Form W-2, Wage and Tax Statement** – After the calendar year is over, each employer must furnish copies of Form W-2 to each employee who earned wages during the year. The employer must also send a copy to the Social Security Administration.

- **Form W-2G, Certain Gambling Winnings** – An organization conducting gaming activities must report certain gambling transactions to taxpayers and the IRS. Form W-2G reflects winnings and federal tax withholding. In general, the gambling organization must use Form W-2G if any tax is withheld or the taxpayer has winnings equivalent to the following:

    1) Bingo or Slot machine – $1,200 or more (not reduced by wager)

    2) Keno – $1,500 (reduced by wager)

    3) Poker – More than $5,000 (reduced by wager)

    4) All others – $600 or more and at least 300 times the amount of the wager.

- **Form 1098, Mortgage Interest Statement** – A person (or organization) engaged in a trade or business that receives at least $600 of mortgage interest (including certain points) on any one mortgage in the calendar year must report the mortgage interest on Form 1098 to the payor and the IRS. Report prepaid interest (other than points) only in the year in which it properly accrues. The form is not filed if the interest is received from a corporation, partnership, trust, estate, association, or company other than a sole proprietor.

- **Form 1098-E, Student Loan Interest Statement** – A person (including a financial institution, a governmental unit, and an educational institution) that receives interest payments of $600 or more during the year on one or more qualified student loans must furnish this statement to each student.

- **Form 1098-T, Tuition Statement** – An eligible educational institution must provide each enrolled student with reportable transactions on this form in order to report certain amounts billed or payments received by the institution for qualified tuition and related expenses. The institution also reports scholarships or grants using this form.

- **Form 1099-B, Proceeds from Broker and Barter Exchange Transactions** – In general, a securities broker must report and provide a Form 1099-B for each person for whom the broker has sold (including short sales) stocks, bonds, commodities, regulated futures contracts, foreign currency contracts, forward contracts, debt instruments, etc., for cash. Recent legislation now requires brokers to report cost basis in addition to proceeds from these transactions. Cost basis information makes the calculation of gains and losses easier for taxpayers.

- **Form 1099-C, Cancellation of Debt** – Certain entities must issue a Form 1099-C to each borrower for canceled debts in excess of $600 on secured property. Under certain circumstances, a borrower may recognize taxable income because of a debt that is canceled.

- **Form 1099-DIV,** – A corporation must generally send Forms 1099-DIV to the IRS with Form 1096 by February 28 of the year following the year of a distribution. Generally, a corporation must furnish Forms 1099-DIV to shareholders by January 31 of the year following the close of the calendar year during which the corporation made the distributions. It is necessary to file a *Form 1099-DIV* with the IRS for each person the corporation:

    1) Paid dividends (including capital gain dividends) and other distributions on stock of $10 or more,

2) Withheld and paid any foreign tax on dividends and other distributions on stock,

3) Withheld any federal income tax on dividends under the backup withholding rules, or

4) Paid $600 or more as part of a liquidation

- **Form 1099-G, Certain Government Payments** – This form reports certain payments that exceed $10, such as unemployment compensation and state or local income tax refunds.

- **Form 1099-INT, Interest Income** – Financial institutions that pay interest must report details regarding those payments in the following circumstances:

    1) The interest payments are at least $10. Certain types of interest, such as interest on delayed death benefits paid by a life insurance company or interest on a state or federal tax refund have a higher threshold of $600.

    2) If the institution withheld and paid any foreign tax on interest

    3) If the institution withheld (and did not refund) any federal income tax under the backup withholding rules regardless of the amount of the payment

- **Form 1099-MISC, Miscellaneous Income** – A business taxpayer uses Form 1099-MISC to report certain business payments. These payments include the following items:

    1) Payments of $600 or more for services performed for one's business by people <u>not treated as employees</u>, such as subcontractors, attorneys, accountants, or directors. Generally, payments to a corporation are excluded from this reporting requirement

    2) Rent payments of $600 or more, other than rents paid to real estate agents

    3) Prizes and awards of $600 or more (not for services), such as winnings on radio shows

    4) Royalty payments of $10 or more

    5) Payments to certain crew members by operators of fishing boats

- **Form 1099-OID** – Original issue discount (OID) is the difference between the purchase price of a debt instrument and its maturity value. Each year, a portion of the discount accrues as income to the recipient. A financial institution must report OID if it amounts to $10 or more.

- **Form 1099-R, Distributions from Pensions, Annuities, Retirement or Profit-Sharing Plans, IRAs, Insurance Contracts, etc.** – Form 1099-R communicates reportable distributions of $10 or more from retirement accounts, insurance contracts, and annuities. In addition to the amount distributed, a number or letter code in box 7 tells the taxpayer details about the type of distribution they received.

Backup Withholding

A business taxpayer reporting payments made to a U.S. person must withhold 28% (backup withholding rate) from a payment that is subject to Form 1099 reporting if one of the following conditions exists:

- The person does not provide its *taxpayer identification number (TIN)* in the manner required. Generally, a person provides a TIN on *Form W-9*,

- The IRS provides notification that the TIN furnished by the payee is incorrect.

- There has been a notified payee underreporting.

- There has been a payee certification failure.

Regular Gambling Withholding

Regular gambling withholding is 25% (33.33% for certain noncash payments) for 2015. Regular gambling withholding is applicable when gambling winnings exceed $5,000 for sweepstakes, wagering pools, or lotteries. Poker tournaments are "wagering pools" according to IRS Rev. Proc. 2007-57. For other wagering transactions (for example: blackjack, or similar table games), regular gambling withholding does not apply unless winnings are at least $600 <u>and</u> 300 times the amount wagered. If withholding applies, a taxpayer who does not provide a SSN or TIN is subject to backup withholding.

(Remainder of page intentionally left blank)

Table 10-1. Certain Informational Returns

Form	Title	What to Report	Amounts to Report	Due Date to IRS	Due Date to Recipient
1095-C	Employer-Provided Health Insurance Offer and Coverage	Offers of health coverage and enrollment in health coverage for employees.	See form instructions	February 28*	January 31
1098	Mortgage Interest Statement	Mortgage interest (including points) and certain mortgage insurance premiums you received in the course of your trade or business from individuals and reimbursements of overpaid interest.	$600 or more	February 28*	January 31
1098-E	Student Loan Interest Statement	Student loan interest received in the course of your trade or business.	$600 or more	February 28*	January 31
1098-T	Tuition Statement	Qualified tuition and related expenses, reimbursements or refunds, and scholarships or grants (optional).	See form instructions	February 28*	January 31
1099-B	Proceeds from Broker and Barter Exchange Transactions	Sales or redemptions of securities, futures transactions, commodities, and barter exchange transactions.	All amounts	February 28*	February 15
1099-C	Cancellation of Debt	Cancellation of a debt owed to the Federal Government or any organization having a significant trade or business of lending money.	$600 or more	February 28*	January 31
1099-DIV	Dividends and Distributions	Distributions, such as dividends, capital gain distributions, or nontaxable distributions, that were paid on stock and liquidation distributions.	$10 or more, except $600 or more for liquidations	February 28*	January 31
1099-G	Certain Government Payments	Unemployment compensation, state and local income tax refunds, agricultural payments, and taxable grants.	$10 or more for refunds and unemployment	February 28*	January 31
1099-INT	Interest Income	Interest income.	$10 or more ($600 or more in some cases)	February 28*	January 31
1099-MISC	Miscellaneous Income (Also for direct sales of $5,000 or more of consumer goods for resale.)	Rent or royalty payments; prizes and awards that are not for services, such as winnings on TV or radio shows.	$600 or more, except $10 or more for royalties	February 28*	January 31
1099-OID	Original Issue Discount	Original issue discount.	$10 or more	February 28*	January 31
1099-R	Distributions from Pensions, Annuities, Retirement or Profit-Sharing Plans, IRAs, Insurance Contracts, etc.	Distributions from retirement or profit-sharing plans, any IRA, insurance contracts, and IRA recharacterization.	$10 or more	February 28*	January 31
W-2G	Certain Gambling Winnings	Gambling winnings from horse racing, dog racing, jai alai, lotteries, keno, bingo, slot machines, sweepstakes, wagering pools, poker tournaments, etc.	Generally, $600 or more; $1,200 or more from bingo or slot machines; $1,500 or more from keno	February 28*	January 31
W-2	Wage and Tax Statement	Wages, value of healthcare benefits, tips, other compensation; social security, Medicare, and withheld income taxes. Include bonuses, vacation allowances, severance pay, certain moving expense payments, some kinds of travel allowances, and third-party payments of sick pay.	See form instructions	To SSA Last day of Feb*	January 31

*The due date is March 31 if filed electronically

Accounting Periods

Taxpayers must use a *tax year* to figure taxable income. A tax year is an annual accounting period for keeping records and reporting income and expenses. Taxpayers may use a calendar year or a fiscal year (including a 52-53-week tax year). All books, records, income, and expenses must reflect the same tax year. Unless a taxpayer has a *required tax year*, the taxpayer must adopt a tax year by filing the first income tax return using that tax year. A required tax year is a tax year required under the Internal Revenue Code or the Income Tax Regulations.

- A corporation establishes a tax year when filing the first income tax return.
- Partnerships, S corporations, or Personal Service Corporations (PSC) may adopt a fiscal year by filing:
    1) Form 1128 (2553 S corps). Must establish the business purpose for the election, or
    2) Form 8716, if they otherwise qualify to make a Section 444 election

Fiscal Year and Calendar Year

> A *fiscal year* is 12 consecutive months ending on the last day of any month except December 31. A calendar year is 12 consecutive months beginning on January 1 and ending on December 31.

If an individual adopts the calendar year, he must maintain books and records, and report income and expenses, from January 1 through December 31 of each year. If the taxpayer filed the first tax return using the calendar tax year, and later he starts a business as a sole proprietor, becomes a partner in a partnership, or becomes a shareholder in an S corporation, he must continue to use the calendar year on subsequent returns unless the IRS grants approval to change it. Generally, anyone can adopt the calendar year. However, the taxpayer must adopt the calendar year if:

- The taxpayer did not keep books or records,
- An annual accounting period does not exist,
- The tax year does not qualify as a fiscal year, or
- A provision in the Internal Revenue Code requires the taxpayer to use a calendar year.

52-53-week Tax Year

The taxpayer can elect to use a 52-53-week tax year if he keeps books and records and reports income and expenses on that basis. If the taxpayer adopts this method, the 52-53-week tax year must always end on the same day of the week. The 52-53-week tax year must always end on:

- Whatever date this same day of the week last occurs in a calendar month, or
- Whatever date this same day of the week occurs that is closest to the last day of the calendar month. For example, if the taxpayer elects a tax year that always ends on the last Monday in February, the 2015 taxable year will end on February 29, 2016.

Taxpayers elect a 52-53-week tax year by attaching a statement to tax return that includes the following:

- The month in which the new 52-53-week tax year ends
- The day of the week on which the tax year always ends
- The date on which the tax year ends

For purposes of depreciation or amortization, a 52-53-week tax year is considered 12 calendar months. The IRS may consent to a change in tax year, provided the business files Form 1128.

Accounting Methods

An accounting method is a set of rules that determines when and how taxpayers report income and expenses. A taxpayer should choose a method when filing his first tax return. The taxpayer must use the same accounting method from year to year. Once a taxpayer makes an election, he must seek IRS approval to change it. The IRS does not require a single accounting method for all taxpayers. The system must clearly reflect all income and expenses. Careful records must validate the information on the return. An accounting method clearly reflects income only if all items of gross income and expenses are treated the same from year to year. Permissible methods include the following:

- Cash method
- Accrual method
- Special methods of accounting for certain items of income and expenses
- Combination (hybrid) method using elements of two or more of the above

Combination (Hybrid) Method

Generally, a taxpayer can use any combination of cash, accrual, and special methods of accounting, as long as the combination clearly reflects income and is consistent. The following restrictions apply:

- If an inventory is necessary to account for income, the taxpayer must use an accrual method for purchases and sales. Generally, a taxpayer can use the cash method for other items.
- Taxpayers who use the cash method to report income must also use it for expenses.
- Taxpayers who use an accrual method for reporting expenses must also use it to figure income.
- Taxpayers must treat any combination that includes the cash method as the cash method.

Business and Personal Items

A taxpayer can account for business and personal items using different accounting methods. For example, an individual may determine business income and expenses under an accrual method, even if the individual uses the cash method to figure personal items.

Multiple Businesses

A taxpayer who operates multiple separate and distinct businesses may use a different accounting method for each. The taxpayer must maintain a complete and separate set of books and records for each business in order for those businesses to be considered truly separate and distinct.

Cash Method

Most individuals and many small businesses use the cash method of accounting. Generally, if an individual produces, purchases, or sells merchandise, he must keep an inventory and use an accrual method for sales and purchases of merchandise.

- Under the cash method, a taxpayer includes in gross income all items of income actually or *constructively* received during the tax year. Taxpayers must include in income the value of property or services received at fair market value (FMV).

Constructive receipt occurs when an amount is credited to an account or made available to the taxpayer without restriction. Possession is not a requirement. If an agent of the taxpayer receives income, the taxpayer is considered to receive it when the agent receives it. The taxpayer does not constructively receive income if control of its receipt is subject to substantial restrictions or limitations.

- The taxpayer deducts expenses in the tax year actually paid. However, a taxpayer can only deduct an expense paid in advance in the year to which it applies, unless the expense qualifies for the 12-month rule. Under the 12-month rule, a taxpayer is not required to capitalize amounts paid to create certain rights or benefits for the taxpayer that do not extend beyond the earlier of:
    1) Twelve months after the right or benefit begins, or
    2) The end of the tax year following the tax year in which payment occurred

The following entities cannot use the cash method, or any combination that includes it:

- A corporation (not SCORP or qualified PSC) with average annual gross receipts more than $5 million
- A partnership with a corporation (other than SCORP) as a partner, and with the partnership having average annual gross receipts exceeding $5 million
- A tax shelter

Accrual Method

A corporation (not a qualified PSC) must use the *accrual method* of accounting if average annual gross receipts exceed $5 million. A corporation engaged in farming also must use the accrual method. If the business requires inventory, the corporation generally must use the accrual method for sales and purchases of merchandise. Under the accrual method, an amount is includable in income when all events occur that fix the right to receive the income, which is the earliest of the date when:

- The required performance takes place
- Payment is due
- The corporation receives payment, and the amount can be determined with reasonable accuracy

Generally, an accrual basis taxpayer can deduct accrued expenses in the tax year when the following conditions exist:

- All events that determine the liability have occurred.
- The amount of the liability can be figured with reasonable accuracy.
- Economic performance takes place with respect to the expense.

A taxpayer reports an *advance payment* for services he will perform in a later tax year as income in the year he receives payment. The taxpayer can elect to postpone including the advance payment in income until the next tax year. However, recognition may not go beyond the next year.

Percentage of Completion Method

The taxpayer must account for long-term contracts (excluding certain real property construction contracts) by using the *percentage of completion* method described in IRC Sec. 460. Under this method, base gross income from the contract on the portion of completed work.

Inventory

An inventory is necessary to clearly show income when the production, purchase, or sale of merchandise is an income-producing factor. In order for a business to account for an inventory, the business must use the accrual method of accounting for purchases and sales. To figure taxable income, the inventory must be valued at the beginning and end of each tax year. The rules for valuing inventory are not the same for all businesses. The method used must conform to the generally accepted accounting principles for similar businesses and must clearly reflect income. The inventory practices must be consistent from year to year.

The following taxpayers can use the cash method of accounting even if they produce, purchase, or sell merchandise:

- A *qualifying taxpayer* with average annual gross receipts of $1 million or less, for each test period after December 17, 1998

- A *qualifying small business taxpayer* with average annual gross receipts of $10 million or less, for each test period ending on or after December 31, 2000

Each test period for gross receipts is three consecutive years. For example, the average of test period for year 2015 equals sum of gross receipts for (2013+2014+2015) divided by 3. Repeat this calculation for each year up to the present tax year. If the average receipts for any of the periods tested is more than the stated limit, the business may not use the cash method to value inventory.

What Constitutes Inventory

Inventory includes the following:

- Merchandise or stock in trade.

- Purchased merchandise if title has passed to an individual, even if the merchandise is in transit or the owner does not have physical possession for another reason.

- Goods under contract for sale that are not segregated and applied to the contract.

- Goods out on consignment.

- Goods held for sale in display rooms, merchandise mart rooms, or booths located away from the place of business.

- Raw materials, work in process, and finished product.

- Supplies that physically become a part of the item intended for sale.

- When selling merchandise by mail and receiving payment upon delivery (*COD*), the title passes when the buyer makes payment. Include the merchandise in closing inventory until the buyer pays for it

- Include containers (kegs, bottles, and cases) in inventory if the title has not passed to the buyer of the contents whether they are on hand or returnable. If the title has passed to the buyer, exclude the containers from inventory. Under certain circumstances, some containers can be depreciated.

Inventory does NOT include the following:

- Certain merchandise

    1) Goods sold, but only if the title has passed to the buyer

    2) Goods consigned to the person

    3) Goods ordered for future delivery if a person does not yet have the title

- Certain assets

    1) Land, buildings, and equipment used in business

    2) Notes, accounts receivable, and similar assets

    3) Real estate held for sale by a real estate dealer in the ordinary course of business

    4) Supplies that do not physically become part of the item intended for sale

Identifying Inventory Cost

An individual can use any of the following methods to identify the cost of items in inventory:

- **Specific identification method** – Use this method if the actual cost of items in inventory is identified and matched.

- **FIFO (first-in first-out) or LIFO (last-in first-out) method** – Use this method if specific identification is not possible, or the same type of goods are intermingled in the inventory and the individual cannot identify them with specific invoices.

    1) The **FIFO** method assumes the items purchased or produced first are the first items sold, consumed, or otherwise disposed of. Match the items in inventory at the end of the tax year with the costs of similar items most recently purchased or produced.

    2) The **LIFO** method assumes the items of inventory purchased or produced last are the first items sold. Items included in closing inventory are considered to be from the opening inventory in the order of acquisition and from those acquired during the tax year. Taxpayers must file Form 970 (or statement) with the tax return for the year in which the taxpayer first uses LIFO. The rules for this method are very complex. A brief explanation of two rules follows:

        A) **Dollar-value method** – Goods and products must be grouped into one or more pools (classes of items), depending on the kinds of goods or products in the inventories.

        B) **Simplified dollar-value method** – Multiple inventory pools are established in general categories from appropriate government price indexes. Use the related price index changes to estimate the change in price for inventory items.

            (a) An *eligible small business* (average annual gross receipts of $5 million or less for the three preceding tax years) can elect the simplified dollar-value LIFO method.

Inventory Valuation

The value of the inventory is a major factor in figuring taxable income. The valuation method for inventory is important. The following valuation methods are generally available for inventory:

- **Cost method** – To properly value inventory at cost, include all associated direct and indirect costs. The following rules apply:

    1) For merchandise on hand at the beginning of the tax year, cost means the ending inventory price of the goods.

    2) For merchandise purchased during the year, cost means the invoice price less appropriate discounts *plus* transportation or other charges incurred in acquiring the goods. It can also include other costs that the business must capitalize under the uniform capitalization rules.

    3) For merchandise produced during the year, cost means all direct and indirect costs that the business must capitalize under the uniform capitalization rules.

- **Lower of cost or market method** – Under the lower of cost or market method, compare the market value of each item on hand on the inventory date with its cost, and use the lower of the two as its inventory value.

    1) This method applies to the following:

        A) Goods purchased and on hand

        B) The basic elements of cost (direct materials, direct labor, and certain indirect costs) of goods being manufactured and finished goods on hand

2) This method does not apply to the following, which must be inventoried at cost:

   A) Goods on hand or being manufactured for delivery at a fixed price on a firm sales contract (that is, not legally subject to cancellation by either business or the buyer)

   B) Goods accounted for under the LIFO method

- **Retail method** – Under the retail method, reduce the total retail-selling price of goods on hand at the end of the tax year in each department or of each class of goods to approximate cost by using an average markup expressed as a percentage of the total retail-selling price.

  1) To figure the *average markup*, apply the following steps in order:

     A) Add the total of the retail prices of the goods in the opening inventory and the retail prices of the goods bought during the year (adjusted for all markups and markdowns).

     B) Subtract from the total in (A) the cost of goods included in the opening inventory plus the cost of goods bought during the year.

     C) The *average markup percentage* is the balance in (B) divided by the total in (A).

  2) Then determine the *approximate cost* in three steps:

     A) Subtract sales at retail from total retail-selling price to arrive at closing inventory at retail.

     B) Multiply the closing inventory at retail by the average markup percentage. The result is the markup in closing inventory.

     C) Subtract the markup in (B) from the closing inventory at retail. The result is the *approximate closing inventory at cost*.

Example – Calculate the cost of goods sold using the cost method. **Most likely to appear on exam. Jack Roston operates a small manufacturing business as a sole proprietorship. His business, Roston Rubber, manufactures industrial rubber seals and makes rubber bands used in packaging. He uses the accrual method of accounting. He incurred the following expenses during the year. What was his cost of goods sold? (Disregard uniform capitalization rules for this computation.)

Beginning inventory, raw materials	$14,000
Beginning inventory, work in process	$20,000
Beginning inventory, finished goods	$100,000
Ending inventory, raw materials	$15,000
Ending inventory, work in process	$12,000
Ending inventory, finished goods	$110,000
Purchases	$2,000,000
Salaries, factory	$200,000
Salaries, sales	$50,000
Chemicals used in manufacturing process	$10,000
Office supplies	$5,000
Freight-in on raw material purchases	$3,000

A. $2,210,000
B. $2,207,000
C. $2,268,000
D. $2,265,000

> **Answer** – If a business manufactures products or purchases them for resale, it generally must value inventory at the beginning and end of each tax year to determine the cost of goods sold. Deduct the cost of goods sold from gross receipts to figure gross profit for the year. Selling or administrative salaries and office supplies do not directly relate to the cost of the manufactured product and are not part of the cost of goods sold. The following are types of expenses that figure into the cost of goods sold:
>
> - The cost of products or raw materials, including freight
> - Storage
> - Direct labor (include contributions to retirement plans) for workers who produce the products
> - Factory overhead
>
> | | | |
> |---|---|---|
> | Beginning Inventory | $134,000 | ($100,000 + $20,000 + $14,000) |
> | + Purchases | $2,000,000 | |
> | + Factory Salaries | $200,000 | |
> | + Chemicals | $10,000 | |
> | + Freight | $3,000 | |
> | – Ending Inventory | $137,000 | ($110,000 + $12,000 + $15,000) |
> | **Cost of Goods Sold** | **$2,210,000** | |

Uniform Capitalization Rules

Under the ***uniform capitalization rules***, capitalize the direct costs and part of the indirect costs for production or resale activities. Include these costs in the basis of property produced or acquired for resale, rather than claiming them as a current deduction. Costs are recovered through depreciation, amortization, or cost of goods sold when property is used, sold, or disposed. An individual is subject to the uniform capitalization rules if he does any of the following:

- Acquires for resale or produces real or tangible personal property

    1) An individual produces property if he constructs, builds, installs, manufactures, develops, improves, creates, raises, or grows the property.

    2) Tangible personal property includes films, sound recordings, videotapes, books, artwork, photographs, or similar property containing words, ideas, concepts, images, or sounds.

The uniform capitalization rules do <u>not</u> apply to the following:

- Small resellers of personal property with average annual gross receipts of $10 million or less
- Property produced to use as personal or non-business property or for uses not connected with a trade or business or an activity conducted for profit
- Research and experimental expenditures deductible under Section 174
- Intangible drilling and development costs of oil, gas, or geothermal wells or any amortization deduction allowable under Section 59(e) for intangible drilling, development, or mining expenditures
- Property produced under a long-term contract, except for certain home construction contracts
- Timber and certain ornamental trees raised, harvested, or grown, and the underlying land
- Qualified creative expenses paid or incurred as a freelance (self-employed) writer, photographer, or artist that are otherwise deductible on the tax return

- Costs allocable to natural gas acquired for resale to the extent these costs would otherwise be allocable to cushion gas stored underground
- Property produced if substantial construction occurred before March 1, 1986
- Property provided to customers in connection with providing services (It must be *de minimis* in amount and not included in inventory in the hands of the service provider.)
- Loan origination
- Costs of producers using a simplified production method with indirect costs of $200,000 or less

Recordkeeping

A business should keep records for as long as needed for the administration of any provision of the Internal Revenue Code. Usually, the business must keep records that support items of income, deductions, or credits on the return for <u>three years</u> from the date the return is due or filed, whichever is later. Employers should keep all records of employment taxes for at least four years. The business should keep records that verify the business basis in property for as long as needed to figure the basis of the original or replacement property. The business should keep copies of all filed returns.

11 Business Taxation

Expenses and Deductions · Employee Compensation · General Business Credits
Net Operating Losses · Loss Limitations · Not-for-profit Activities · Affordable Care Act

This chapter summarizes IRS Publications 15-A, 15-B, 334, 535, 536, 463, and 547.

Expenses and Deductions

Business Start-up and Organizational Costs

Business start-up and organizational costs are generally capital expenditures. However, a taxpayer may elect (on the tax return) to deduct up to $5,000 of business start-up and $5,000 of organizational costs as an expense in the current year. For each category, reduce the deduction by the amount of costs that exceed $50,000. The taxpayer must amortize any remaining costs over a 180-month period, beginning with the initial month of operation.

A business using the cash method of accounting can deduct organizational costs only when paid by the end of the tax year. However, the business can deduct any cost the business could have deducted in an earlier tax year in the tax year of payment. A business that intends to amortize these costs must file Form 4562 in the initial year of operation.

- *Start-up costs* include any amounts paid or incurred in connection with creating or investigating the creation or acquisition of an active trade or business. Start-up costs do not include deductible interest, taxes, or research and experimental costs. Start-up costs include the following:

    1) Analysis or survey of potential markets, products, labor supply, transportation facilities, etc.

    2) Advertisements for business opening

    3) Salaries and wages for employees who are being trained and their instructors

    4) Travel and necessary costs for securing prospective distributors, suppliers, or customers

    5) Salaries and fees for executives and consultants, or for similar professional services

- *Organizational costs* include the costs of creating a corporation or partnership. These costs include temporary directors, organizational meetings, state incorporation, and legal services.

    1) The following items are capital expenses that cannot be amortized:

        A) Costs for issuing and selling stock, securities, or partnership interests, such as commissions, professional fees, and printing costs

        B) Costs associated with the transfer of assets to the business

Gifts

> A deduction is not available for business gifts made in excess of $25 to a person during the tax year. If a taxpayer gives a gift to a member of a customer's family, the gift is generally considered an indirect gift to the customer. This rule does not apply if taxpayer has a bona fide, independent business connection with that family member and the gift is not intended for the customer's eventual use.

If the taxpayer and the taxpayer's spouse both give gifts, the IRS treats them as one taxpayer. It does not matter whether they have separate businesses, are separately employed, or whether they each have an independent connection with the recipient. If a partnership gives gifts, the IRS treats the partnership and the partners as one taxpayer.

Rental Expenses

Rent is any amount paid for the use of property not owned by the individual. In general, a taxpayer may deduct rent as an expense only if the rent is for the use of property in the taxpayer's business. If the taxpayer has or will receive equity in or title to the property, the rent is not deductible. The taxpayer may not take a rental deduction for unreasonable rent. Ordinarily, the issue of reasonableness arises only if the taxpayer and the lessor are related. If an individual rents his home and uses part of it as a place of business, the individual may be able to deduct the rent paid for that part. The taxpayer must meet the requirements for business use of the home. Generally, rent paid because of one's business is deductible in the year paid or accrued. If the taxpayer makes a payment in advance, deduct only the amount that applies to use in the tax year. Deduct the remainder in the period to which it applies.

Expenses on Leased Property

The IRS treats lease payments, including taxes on leased property, as payments of rent. Amortize costs to acquire a lease over the remaining term of the lease. A taxpayer must depreciate permanent improvements to leased property, such as buildings, using the modified accelerated cost recovery system (MACRS) over an appropriate recovery period, not the remaining term of the lease.

Interest Expense

- **Deductible interest** – A taxpayer may generally deduct as a business expense all interest paid or accrued during the tax year on debts related to his business. Interest relates to business if the taxpayer uses the proceeds of the loan for a business expense. It does not matter what type of property secures the loan. A taxpayer may deduct interest on a debt only if all the following requirements are met:

    1) The taxpayer is legally liable for the debt. If liable for part of a business debt, the taxpayer may deduct his share of the total interest paid or accrued.

    2) Both the taxpayer and the lender intend that the taxpayer will repay the debt.

    3) The taxpayer and the lender have a true debtor-creditor relationship.

- **Capitalized interest** – Under the uniform capitalization rules, a taxpayer generally must capitalize interest on debt to produce (construct, build, demolish, install, manufacture, develop, improve, create, raise, or grow) real property or certain tangible personal property. Add the interest (and points) to the basis of the property. Designated property is any of the following:

    1) Real property

    2) Tangible personal property with a class life of 20 years or more

    3) Tangible personal property with an estimated production period of more than two years

    4) Tangible personal property with an estimated production period of more than one year if the estimated cost of production is more than $1 million

Insurance Premiums

A deduction may be available for certain premiums paid for insurance related to a business, which includes the following:

- Insurance that covers fire, storm, theft, accident, or similar losses.
- Credit insurance that covers losses from business bad debts.
- Group hospitalization and medical insurance for employees, including long-term care insurance:
    1) If a partnership pays accident and health insurance premiums for its partners, it generally may deduct them as guaranteed payments to partners.
    2) If an S corporation pays accident and health insurance premiums for its more-than-2% shareholder-employees, it generally may deduct them, but it must also include the amount in the shareholder's wages subject to federal income tax withholding.
- Liability insurance.
- Malpractice insurance that covers the taxpayer's personal liability for professional negligence resulting in injury or damage to patients or clients.
- Workers' compensation insurance set by state law that covers any claims for bodily injuries or job-related diseases suffered by employees in the taxpayer's business, regardless of fault:
    1) If a partnership pays workers' compensation premiums for its partners, it generally may deduct them as guaranteed payments to partners.
    2) Workers' compensation premiums paid by S corporation for its more-than-2% shareholder-employees, are generally deductible, but must be included in the shareholder's wages.
- Contributions to a state unemployment insurance fund are deductible as taxes if they are considered taxes under state law.
- Overhead insurance that pays for business overhead expenses incurred during long periods of disability caused by injury or sickness.
- Car and other vehicle insurance that covers vehicles used in business for liability, damages, and other losses. If taxpayer operates a vehicle partly for personal use, deduct only the part of the insurance premium applied to the business use of the vehicle. If using the standard mileage rate to figure car expenses, the taxpayer may not deduct any car insurance premiums.
- Life insurance covering officers and employees if the taxpayer is not a beneficiary under the contract.
- Business interruption insurance for lost profits if the business closes due to a fire or other cause.

A taxpayer may not deduct premiums on the following kinds of insurance:

- Self-insurance reserve funds.
- Premiums for a policy that pays for lost earnings due to sickness or disability.
- Certain life insurance and annuities.
- Insurance to secure a loan. If a taxpayer insures his life or the life of another person with a financial interest in the business to get or protect a business loan, the taxpayer may not deduct the premiums as a business expense. The taxpayer may not deduct the premiums as interest on business loans or as an expense of financing loans. In the event of death, the proceeds of the policy are generally not taxed as income even if the beneficiary uses them to liquidate the debt.

Self-employed Health Insurance Deduction

Premiums paid for medical and dental insurance and qualified long-term care insurance may be deductible provided they are for the taxpayer, his spouse, or his dependents, and the taxpayer is:

- A self-employed individual with a net profit reported on Schedule C Profit or Loss from Business, Schedule C-EZ Net Profit from Business, or Schedule F Profit or Loss from Farming, or

- A partner with net earnings from self-employment reported on Schedule K-1 (Form 1065), or

- A shareholder owning more than 2% of the outstanding stock of an S corporation with wages from the corporation reported on Form W-2, Wage and Tax Statement.

The taxpayer must establish the insurance plan under the taxpayer's business; however, the policy may be either in the name of the business or in the name of the individual.

- **A self-employed** individual filing a Schedule C, C-EZ, or F can have the policy in his name or under the business.

- **Partners** may pay the premiums themselves, or the partnership may pay the premiums and report the premium amounts on Schedule K-1 (Form 1065) as guaranteed payments to be included in the taxpayer's gross income. However, if the policy is in the taxpayer's name and the taxpayer pays the premiums, the partnership must reimburse the taxpayer and report the premium amounts on Schedule K-1 (Form 1065) as guaranteed payments to be included in gross income. Otherwise, the insurance plan is not considered established under the business.

- **More-than-2% shareholders** may pay their own premiums or the SCORP may pay them and report the premium amounts on Form W-2 as wages to be included in taxpayer's gross income. However, if the policy is in the taxpayer's name and he pays the premiums, the SCORP must reimburse the taxpayer and report the amount on Form W-2 as wages included in gross income. Otherwise, the insurance plan is not considered as established under the business.

Partners and more-than-2% shareholders may be able to amend prior year returns to claim self-employed health insurance deductions allowable under the rules explained above. Shareholders should write "Filed Pursuant to Notice 2008-1" at the top of any amended return.

Travel

An individual is traveling away from home if duties require him to be away from the general area of his tax home for a period substantially longer than an ordinary day's work, and he needs to get sleep or rest to meet the demands of work while away. Generally, a tax home is the entire city or general area where main place of business or work is located, regardless of where the individual maintains a family home.

A person lives with family in Florida but works in Boston where he stays in a hotel and eats in restaurants. He returns to Florida every weekend. The taxpayer may not deduct any of the travel, meals, or lodging in Boston because it is his tax home. The travel to the family home in Florida is not for work, so these expenses are also not deductible. If a person regularly works in more than one place, the person's tax home is the general area where main place of business or work is located.

Deductible travel expenses while away from home include the costs of the following:

- Travel by airplane, train, bus, or car between home and business destination

- Using personal car while at a business destination

- Fares for taxis or between the airport or train station and the hotel, the hotel and the work location, and from one customer to another, or from one place of business to another

- Meals and lodging
- Tips paid for services related to any of these expenses
- Dry cleaning and laundry
- Business calls while on a business trip. This includes business communications by fax machine or other communication devices.
- Other similar ordinary and necessary expenses related to business travel. These expenses might include transportation to and from a business meal, public stenographer's fees, computer rental fees, and operating and maintaining a house trailer.

In addition to the deductions described below, a taxpayer may deduct 50% of meals when traveling if he must stop for substantial sleep or rest to perform his duties properly while traveling away from home on business. The taxpayer may not deduct expenses for meals that are lavish or extravagant. An expense is not considered lavish or extravagant if it is reasonable based on the facts and circumstances.

- Travel in the United States
    1) Taxpayers may deduct all travel expenses if trip is entirely business related.
    2) If the trip is primarily for business and, while at the business destination, the taxpayer extends his stay for a vacation, makes a personal side trip, or has other personal activities, the taxpayer may deduct only business-related travel expenses.
    3) If the trip is primarily for personal reasons, such as a vacation, the entire cost of the trip is a nondeductible personal expense. However, a taxpayer may deduct any expenses he has while at a destination directly related to business.
- Travel outside the United States
    1) If a taxpayer travels outside the United States and spends the entire time on business activities, he may deduct all of the travel expenses:
        A) Even if he did not spend the entire time on business activities, the trip is considered entirely for business if the taxpayer meets any of the following exceptions:
            (a) Did not have substantial control over arranging the trip
            (b) The taxpayer is outside the United States for a week or less, combining business and non-business activities
            (c) The taxpayer spends less than 25% of the total time the taxpayer was outside the United States on non-business activities
            (d) The taxpayer can establish that a personal vacation is not a major consideration, even if the taxpayer has substantial control over arranging the trip
    2) If the trip is primarily for business but the taxpayer spends time on other activities, he generally may not deduct all of the travel expenses. Only the business portion of the cost of getting to and from the destination is deductible. Individuals must allocate costs between business and other activities to determine the deductible amount.
    3) If the trip is primarily for vacation or for investment purposes, the entire cost of the trip is a nondeductible personal expense. If a taxpayer spends time attending brief professional seminars or a continuing education program, the taxpayer may deduct registration fees and other expenses directly related to business.

Meals and Entertainment

A taxpayer may deduct business-related meals and entertainment expenses incurred for entertaining a client, customer, or employee. To deduct an entertainment-related meal, the taxpayer or the taxpayer's employees must be present when the food or beverages are provided. The deduction for entertainment expenses may be limited. Generally, a taxpayer may deduct 50% of unreimbursed entertainment expenses.

> Entertainment expenses are deductible only if they are both ordinary and necessary and meet one of the following tests:
>
> - **Directly-related test** – The taxpayer must show all of the following:
>   1) The main purpose of the combined business and entertainment is the active conduct of business. Business is generally not considered the main purpose when on hunting or fishing trips, or on yachts or other pleasure boats.
>   2) The taxpayer did engage in business with the person during the entertainment period.
>   3) There is more than a general expectation of getting income or some other specific business benefit at some future time.
>
> - **Associated test** – Even if the taxpayer's expenses do not meet the directly-related test, they may meet the associated test. The taxpayer must show that the entertainment is as follows:
>   1) Associated with the active conduct of the business, and
>   2) Directly before or after a substantial business discussion

A taxpayer may not deduct the following expenses:

- **Lavish or extravagant entertainment** – Expenses that are reasonable considering the facts and circumstances will not be disallowed just because they are more than a fixed dollar amount or take place at deluxe restaurants, hotels, nightclubs, or resorts.
- **If a taxpayer rents a private luxury box** for more than one event at the same sports arena, the taxpayer generally may not deduct more than the price of a non-luxury box seat ticket.
- **Membership dues** (including initiation fees) for any club organized for business, pleasure, recreation, or other social purpose.
- **Cost for the use of an entertainment facility** or any property he owns, rents, or uses for entertainment. Examples include a yacht, hunting lodge, fishing camp, swimming pool, tennis court, bowling alley, car, airplane, apartment, hotel suite, or home in a vacation resort.

Casualty and Theft

If a taxpayer has business or income-producing property, such as rental property, and it is stolen or completely destroyed, the decrease in FMV is not considered. The loss is the taxpayer's adjusted basis in the property minus the salvage value, insurance, and other re-imbursements. There are two methods to deduct a casualty or theft loss of inventory, including items held for sale to customers:

- Deduct the loss through the increase in the cost of goods sold by properly reporting opening and closing inventories. Taxpayers must not claim this loss again as a casualty or theft loss. If a taxpayer takes the loss through the increase in the cost of goods sold, the taxpayer should include any insurance or reimbursement in gross income.

- Deduct the loss separately. If deducted separately, a taxpayer must eliminate the affected inventory items from the cost of goods sold by making a downward adjustment to opening inventory or purchases. The taxpayer must reduce the loss by the reimbursement received and must not include the reimbursement in gross income. If the taxpayer does not receive reimbursement by the end of the year, the taxpayer may not claim a loss to the extent the taxpayer has a reasonable prospect of recovery.

> Losses on business property (other than employee property) and income-producing property are <u>not</u> subject to the 2% Misc Itemized Deduction and 10% of AGI limits like personal-use property. Taxpayers generally must deduct a casualty loss in the year it occurs. However, if there is a casualty loss from a federally declared disaster, a taxpayer may choose to deduct that loss on his return or amended return for the tax year immediately <u>preceding</u> the tax year of the disaster. If an individual makes this choice, treat the loss as having occurred in the preceding year. Claiming the loss on the previous year's return may result in a lower tax for that year, often producing or increasing a cash refund.

Bad Debts

If an individual owes a taxpayer money that the taxpayer is unable to collect, then the taxpayer has a bad debt. The taxpayer does not have to wait until a debt is due to determine whether it is worthless. A debt becomes worthless when there is no longer any chance the debtor will pay the amount owed. Generally, a ***business bad debt*** is one that comes from operating a business. A taxpayer may claim a bad debt deduction only if the amount owed to the taxpayer was previously included in gross income. This applies to amounts owed to the taxpayer from all sources of taxable income, including sales, services, rents, and interest. Business bad debts are mainly the result of ***credit sales*** to customers. In the books, record goods that have been sold, but not paid for, and services that have been performed, but not paid for, as either accounts receivable or notes receivable. After a reasonable period, if a taxpayer has tried to collect the amount due but is unable to do so, the uncollectible part becomes a business bad debt.

- A taxpayer who uses the accrual method of accounting should claim a bad debt deduction only if he previously included the entire uncollectible amount in income.

- If a taxpayer uses the cash method of accounting, the taxpayer may <u>not</u> claim a bad debt deduction for amounts owed to him because the amounts were never included in income.

- Taxpayers who claim a deduction for a bad debt and later recover (collect) all or part of it may have to include the recovery in gross income. The amount to include is limited to the amount actually deducted. However, taxpayers can exclude the amount deducted that did not reduce their tax. Report the recovery as "Other income" on the appropriate business form or schedule.

Taxes

The following taxes are deductible:

- **Employment taxes** – A deduction is allowed for FICA and FUTA taxes paid out of company funds as an employer. Deductible taxes also include payments made to a state unemployment compensation fund or to a state disability benefit fund.

- **Self-employment tax** – A self-employed taxpayer can deduct a portion of self-employment tax paid on his personal return.

- **Personal property tax** – Tax imposed by a state or local government on personal property used in a business. Registration fees for the right to use property within a state or local area are deductible.

- **Real estate taxes** – A deduction is allowed for real estate taxes paid on business property. Deductible real estate taxes are any state, local, or foreign taxes on real estate levied for the general public welfare.

The taxing authority must base the taxes on the assessed value of the real estate and charge them uniformly against all property under its jurisdiction. Add property assessments for improvements that increase the value of the property assessed to basis. Do not deduct these as taxes. Examples of assessments include roads, sidewalks, water connections, and extending utility service lines to the property.

- **Sales tax** – Sales tax paid on a service or on the purchase or use of property as part of the cost of the service or property. If the service or the cost or use of the property is a deductible business expense, the business can deduct the tax as part of that service or cost. If the property is merchandise bought for resale, the sales tax is part of the cost of the merchandise. If the property is depreciable, add the sales tax to the basis for depreciation.

- **Excise taxes** – A deduction is allowed for excise taxes that are ordinary and necessary expenses of carrying on a business. Taxpayers who owe excise taxes are required to file a quarterly Form 720 Federal Excise Tax Return. The person who receives payment for these items is responsible for collection and payment of the tax. Items subject to excise taxes include:

    1) Fuel taxes
    2) Environmental taxes
    3) Communications and air transportation taxes
    4) Manufacturers taxes
    5) Retail tax on heavy trucks, trailers, and tractors
    6) Ship passenger taxes
    7) Foreign insurance taxes
    8) Obligations not in registered form

- **Heavy highway use vehicle tax** – The tax applies to highway motor vehicles with a taxable gross weight of 55,000 pounds or more. Vans, pickup trucks, panel trucks, and similar trucks generally are not subject to this tax. The taxpayer who acquires the vehicle for use must report and pay the tax monthly on **Form 2290,** separate from the other excise taxes. A taxpayer may receive a credit or request the suspension of this tax if the vehicle is driven less than 5,000 miles (7,500 if agricultural vehicle) during a one-month tax period.

Miscellaneous Expenses

Business taxpayers may deduct certain expenses that relate directly to the conduct of business as Miscellaneous Expenses. These expenses include the following:

- Advertising
- Expenses for operation of vehicles used in business
- Credit card fees
- Franchise fees
- Internet-related expenses
- Legal and professional fees
- Tax preparation fees
- License and regulatory fees
- Costs of moving machinery

- Penalties paid for late performance or nonperformance of a contract
- Repairs
- Supplies and materials
- Utilities
- Telephone

Nondeductible Business Expenses

Not all business expenses are deductible. The following are examples of nondeductible expenses:

- Anticipated liabilities
- Bribes and kickbacks
- Charitable contributions (except for C corporation, all others claim on personal return)
- Lobbying expenses
- Political contributions
- Penalties or fines for violation of the law
- Demolition expenses
- Club dues and membership fees incurred for any club organized for business, pleasure, recreation, or any other social purpose. Certain exceptions are made for chambers of commerce, boards of trade, business leagues, professional associations, and trade associations.

Employee Compensation

Test for Deducting Pay

The employer may deduct employee pay that is an ordinary and necessary expense, provided it is both <u>reasonable</u> and for <u>services performed</u>. Wages subject to federal employment taxes generally include all pay to an employee for services performed. Payment may be in cash or in other forms. Wages include salaries, vacation pay, bonuses, commissions, and fringe benefits.

Employee Business Expense Reimbursements

A reimbursement or allowance arrangement is a system by which an employer pays the advances, reimbursements, and charges for employees' business expenses. How the employer reports a payment depends on whether the employer has an *accountable* or a *non-accountable plan*. If a single payment includes both wages and an expense reimbursement, the employer must specify the amount of the reimbursement. These rules apply to all ordinary and necessary employee business expenses that would otherwise qualify for a deduction by the employee.

- **Accountable plan** – Amounts paid under an *accountable plan* are <u>not wages</u> and are not subject to the withholding and payment of FICA, FUTA, and income taxes. An *accountable plan* reimbursement or allowance arrangement must meet <u>all</u> three of the following rules:

    1) The employee must pay or incur deductible expenses while performing services as an employee. The reimbursement or advance must be paid for the expense and must not be an amount that would have otherwise been paid by the employee.

    2) The employee must substantiate these expenses to the employer within a reasonable period.

    3) The employee must return any unsubstantiated expenses within a reasonable period.

Jade learns that she must attend a conference for her employer. She charges the cost of her hotel and airline tickets to her personal credit card. During her trip, she incurs various meals and expenses related to her job. When she returns, she submits her receipts to her employer who reimburses her for her business related costs. Her employer reimburses her for expenses on her next check but does not withhold or pay any taxes on the amount of the reimbursement.

- **Non-accountable plan** – Payments to an employee for travel and other necessary expenses of the business under a non-accountable plan are wages and are treated as supplemental wages and subject to the withholding and payment of FICA, FUTA, and income taxes. The payments are treated as paid under a non-accountable plan if:

    1) An employee is not required to, or does not, substantiate expenses to the employer with receipts or other documentation,

    2) The employer advances an amount to the employee for business expenses, and the employee is not required to, or does not, return in a timely manner any amount not used for business expenses,

    3) The employer advances or pays an amount to the employee regardless of whether the employer reasonably expects the employee to incur business expenses related to the business, or

    4) The employer pays a reimbursement that he would have otherwise paid as wages.

- **Per diem or other fixed allowance.** An employer may reimburse employees by travel days, miles, or other fixed allowance. In these cases, the employee is considered to have accounted to the employer if the reimbursement does not exceed rates established by the federal government. The standard mileage rate for 2015 is 57.5 cents per mile.

Wages Not Paid in Money

If in the course of business, an employer pays employees in a medium that is neither cash nor a readily negotiable instrument, such as a check, the employer has paid them "in kind." Payments in kind may be in the form of goods, lodging, food, clothing, or services. Generally, the FMV of such payments at the time that the employer provides them is subject to employment taxes and withholding. If the property is a capital asset, the difference between the FMV and the adjusted basis of the property is taxable income (capital gain) to the business.

Moving Expenses

Reimbursed and employer-paid qualified moving expenses (those that would otherwise be deductible by the employee) paid under an accountable plan are not includible in an employee's income unless the employer has knowledge that the employee deducted the expenses in a prior year. Reimbursed nonqualified moving expenses are includible in income and are subject to employment taxes and withholding. Deductible moving expenses include only the reasonable expenses of the following:

- Moving household goods and personal effects from the former home to the new home
- Traveling (including lodging) from the former home to the new home

Deductible moving expenses do not include any expenses for meals and must meet both the distance test and the time test. To meet the distance test, the new job location must be at least 50 miles farther from the employee's old home than the old job location was. To meet the time test, the employee must work at least 39 weeks during the first 12 months after arriving in the general area of the new job location.

De Minimis Meals

The employer may exclude from wages any meal or meal money provided to an employee if it has so little value (taking into account how frequently the employer provides meals to employees) that accounting for it would be unreasonable or administratively impracticable. The exclusion applies, for example, to the following items:

- Coffee, doughnuts, or soft drinks
- Occasional meals or meal money provided to enable an employee to work overtime (does not apply to meal money figured on the basis of hours worked)
- Occasional parties or picnics for employees and their guests

This exclusion also applies to meals provided at an employer-operated eating facility for employees if the annual revenue from the facility equals or exceeds the direct costs of the facility. If food or beverages furnished to employees qualify as a de minimis benefit, employers may deduct their full cost. The 50% limit on deductions does not apply to de minimis meals.

Meals on Business Premises

The value of meals provided by the employer, furnished on the business premises, for the employer's convenience are not taxable income and are not subject to income tax withholding, FICA, or FUTA taxes. This exclusion does not apply if employees may choose additional pay instead of meals.

- **Food service employees** – Meals furnished to a restaurant or other food service employee during, or immediately before or after, his shift are furnished for employer's convenience.
- **Employees available for emergency calls** – Meals furnished during working hours so an employee will be available for emergency calls during the meal period are furnished for employer's convenience. Employers must have a reasonable expectation for calls to occur.

Lodging on Business Premises

Employers may exclude the value of lodging from wages if it meets the following tests:

- It is furnished on employer's business premises
- It is furnished for employer's convenience
- The employee must accept it as a condition of employment

Different tests may apply to lodging furnished by educational institutions. The exclusion does not apply if employer allows the employee to choose to receive additional pay instead of lodging.

Health Insurance Plans

If the employer pays the cost of an accident or health insurance plan for company employees, including an employee's spouse and dependents, the payments are not wages and are not subject to FICA and FUTA taxes, or federal income tax withholding. Under the recently enacted *Affordable Care Act*, health coverage provided for children of employees who are under age 27 is now generally tax-free to the employee. Generally, this exclusion also applies to qualified long-term care insurance contracts. For income tax withholding, include the value of health insurance benefits in the wages of S corporation employees who own more than 2% of the S corporation (2% shareholders). For FICA and FUTA tax purposes, exclude the health insurance benefits from the wages only for employees and their dependents or for a class or classes of employees and their dependents.

Employer Retirement Plan Contributions

Eligible employer contributions to retirement plans are deductible by the employer and are not gross income for the employee.

Health Savings Accounts and Medical Savings Accounts

Employer contributions to an employee's Health Savings Account (HSA) or Archer medical savings account (MSA) are not subject to FICA or FUTA taxes, or federal income tax withholding if it is reasonable to believe at the time of the contributions that they will be excludable from the income of the employee. To the extent that it is not reasonable to believe that they will be excludable, the contributions are subject to these taxes. Employee contributions to HSAs or MSAs through a payroll deduction plan must be included in wages and are subject to FICA, FUTA, and income tax withholding. However, HSA contributions made under a salary reduction arrangement in a *Section 125-cafeteria plan* are not wages and are not subject to employment taxes or withholding.

Medical Care Reimbursements

Generally, medical care reimbursements paid for employees under an employer's self-insured reimbursement plan are not wages and are not subject to employment taxes or withholding.

Fringe Benefits

Employers generally must include fringe benefits in an employee's gross income. The benefits are subject to income tax withholding and employment taxes. Fringe benefits include employer-provided cars or aircraft flights, free or discounted commercial flights, vacations, discounts on property or services, memberships in country clubs or other social clubs, and tickets to entertainment or sporting events. In general, the amount that the employer must include is the amount by which the fair market value of the benefits is more than the sum of what the employee paid for it plus any amount that the law excludes.

Non-taxable Fringe Benefits

The following fringe benefits are not taxable (or are minimally taxable, as noted below):

- Services provided to employees at no additional cost to the employer
- Qualified employee discounts
- *Working condition fringes* of property or services that the employee could deduct as a business expense if the employee had paid for it. Examples include a company car for business use, subscriptions to business magazines, and the value of an employer-provided cell phone, provided primarily for noncompensatory business reasons.
- Certain *minimal value fringes* (including an occasional cab ride when an employee must work overtime, local transportation benefits provided because of unsafe conditions and unusual circumstances, and meals that the employer provides at eating places that the employer runs for the employees if the meals are not furnished at below cost)
- Qualified transportation subject to specified conditions and dollar limitations (including transportation in a commuter highway vehicle, any transit pass, qualified parking, and qualified bicycle commuting reimbursement)
- Qualified moving expense reimbursement
- The use of on-premises athletic facilities, if substantially all of the use is by employees, their spouses, and their dependent children
- A qualified tuition reduction an educational organization provides to employees for education

Awards

An employer may generally deduct amounts paid as awards, whether in cash or property.

- **Achievement awards** – Tangible personal property that meets all the following requirements:
   1) The employer gives the award to an employee for length of service or safety achievement.
   2) The employer gives the award as part of a meaningful presentation.
   3) The employer gives the award under conditions that do not create a significant likelihood of disguised pay.

- **Length-of-service award** – An award where either of the following applies:
   1) The employee receives the award after five years of employment.
   2) The employee did not receive another length-of-service award (other than one of very small value) during the same year or in any of the prior four years.

- **Safety achievement award** – An award for safety achievement will qualify <u>unless</u>:
   1) Given to a manager, administrator, clerical employee, or other professional employee
   2) During the tax year, more than 10% of employees, excluding those listed in (1), have already received a safety achievement award (other than one of very small value)

- The deduction for awards given to any one employee during the tax year is <u>limited</u> to:
   1) $400 for awards that are not qualified plan awards, or
   2) $1,600 for all awards, whether or not qualified plan awards

A qualified plan award is an achievement award given as part of an established written plan or program that does not favor highly compensated employees as to eligibility or benefits. A highly compensated employee for 2015 is an employee who meets <u>either</u> of the following tests:

- The employee was a 5% owner at any time during the year or the preceding year.
- The employee received more than $120,000 in pay for the preceding year.

General Business Credits

Taxpayers group most available business credits into a ***general business credit***, and report on ***Form 3800***. The general business credit for the year consists of any carry forward of business credits from prior years plus the total current year business credits. In addition, the general business credit for the current year may increase later by the carry-back of business credits from later years.

> The general business credit is not refundable. A taxpayer can only subtract the credit directly from tax liability. The general business credit cannot reduce tax liability <u>below</u> the *tentative minimum tax* <u>or</u> 25% of regular tax in excess of $25,000, whichever is greater. Any unused credit may be carried back one year <u>or</u> forward for up to 20 years. Under the ***Small Business Jobs Act of 2010***, an ***eligible small business*** (50 million or less average gross receipts over the past three years) may carry back 2010 general business credits five years and use the general business credit against their regular tax or AMT.

The following credits are part of the general business credit (**indicates common topic on past exams):

- **Alcohol and cellulosic biofuel fuels credit** – This credit consists of the alcohol mixture credit, alcohol credit, small ethanol producer credit, and cellulosic biofuel producer credit. The credit amount will vary based on the number of gallons and type(s) of fuels involved.

- **Alternative fuel vehicle refueling property** – This credit applies to the cost of any qualified fuel vehicle refueling property placed in service during the business's tax year.

- **Alternative motor vehicle credit **** – Unless otherwise indicated, the maximum tentative credit is based on year, make, model, and type of <u>new</u> qualifying alternative motor vehicle purchased, which may be a qualified fuel cell vehicle or a qualified plug-in electric drive motor vehicle.

- **Biodiesel and renewable diesel fuels credit** – This credit applies to certain fuels sold or used in a business. The amount of credit that the taxpayer can claim depends on the type of eligible fuels involved and how many gallons of each the taxpayer sold or used.

- **Carbon dioxide sequestration credit** – This credit is for carbon dioxide, which is captured at a qualified facility and disposed of in a secure geological storage or used in a qualified enhanced oil or natural gas recovery project.

- **Credit for employer Social Security and Medicare taxes paid on certain employee tips** – This credit is generally equal to the employer's portion of Social Security and Medicare taxes paid on tips received by employees of a food and beverage establishment where tipping is customary.

- **Credit for employer differential wage payments** – This credit provides certain small businesses with an incentive to continue to pay wages to an employee performing services on active duty in the uniformed services of the United States for a period of more than 30 days.

- **Credit for employer-provided childcare facilities and services **** – The credit is 25% of the qualified childcare facility expenditures *plus* 10% of the qualified childcare resource and referral expenditures paid or incurred during the tax year. The credit limit is $150,000 per year.

- **Credit for increasing research activities **** – This credit is designed to encourage businesses to increase the amounts they spend on research and experimental activities, including energy research. The regular credit is 20% of the <u>increase</u> in research activities.

- **Credit for small employer health insurance premiums** – The credit is generally 35% of premiums paid by the employer. The employer must have fewer than 25 full-time equivalent employees (FTEs) for the tax year and pay average annual wages for the tax year of less than $50,000 per FTE. The employer must be required under a qualifying arrangement to pay a uniform percentage (not less than 50%) of the premium cost for each enrolled employee's health insurance coverage.

- **Credit for small employer pension plan start-up costs **** – This credit applies to pension plan start-up costs of a new qualified defined benefit or defined contribution plan (including a 401(k) plan), SIMPLE plan, or simplified employee pension. The credit equals 50% of the cost to establish and administer the plan and educate employees about the plan, up to a maximum of $500 per year for each of the first three years of the plan. Taxpayers can choose to start claiming the credit in the tax year prior to the tax year in which the plan becomes effective.

- **Disabled access credit **** – This credit is for an eligible small business that pays or incurs expenses to provide access to persons who have disabilities. The credit is 50% of the first $10,000.

- **Distilled spirits credit** – This credit is available to distillers and importers of distilled spirits and eligible wholesalers of distilled spirits.

- **Empowerment zone and renewal community employment credit** – This credit is for employers who have employees in and engage in business in an empowerment zone or renewal community for which the credit is available. For tax years that include December 31, 2015, the credit is 20% of the employer's qualified wages (up to $15,000) paid or incurred during calendar year 2015 on behalf of qualified empowerment zone employees.

- **Energy efficient home credit** – This credit is available for eligible contractors of certain homes sold for use as a residence. The allowable credit is $2,000 for each home meeting the 50% energy efficient standard, and for those that meet the 30% energy efficient standard, the allowable credit is $1,000. The credit expires after 2016.
- **Indian employment credit** – This credit applies to qualified wages and health insurance costs paid or incurred for qualified (American Indian) employees. Credit is up to 20% of expenses.
- **Investment credit **** – The investment credit is the total of the following credits:
    1) Rehabilitation credit (<u>10%</u> for pre-1936 building, or <u>20%</u> if a certified historic structure)
    2) Energy credit
    3) Qualifying advanced energy project credits
    4) Qualifying advanced coal project
    5) Qualifying gasification project
- **Low sulfur diesel fuel production credit** – This credit is for the production of low sulfur diesel by a qualified small business. The credit generally is 5 cents for every gallon of low sulfur diesel fuel produced by a qualified small business refiner during the tax year.
- **Low-income housing credit** – This credit generally applies to each new qualified low-income building placed in service after 1986. Generally, it is taken over a 10-year credit period.
- **Mine rescue team training credit** – This credit applies to training program costs paid or incurred for qualified mine rescue team employees for tax years beginning before January 1, 2016.
- **New markets credit** – This credit is for qualified equity investments made in qualified community development entities. The primary mission is serving, or providing investment capital, for low-income communities or persons.
- **Nonconventional source fuel credit** – This credit is allowed for qualified coke or coke gas produced and sold to an unrelated person during the tax year.
- **Orphan drug credit** – This credit applies to qualified expenses incurred in testing certain drugs for rare diseases and conditions. The credit is 50% of qualified clinical testing expenses paid or incurred during the tax year.
- **Qualified railroad track maintenance credit** – This credit applies to certain regional and switching railroads that may be able to claim a credit for expenses made to upgrade their railroad tracks (including roadbed, bridges, and related track structures).
- **Renewable electricity, refined coal, and Indian coal production credit** – This credit is for the sale of electricity, refined coal, or Indian coal produced in the United States or U.S. possessions from qualified energy resources at a qualified facility.
- **Work opportunity credit**** – This credit is for qualified first- or second-year wages paid to <u>targeted group</u> employees during the tax year. In general, the amount of wages cannot exceed $6,000; however, it may for certain targeted groups. These employees have a high unemployment rate or other special employment needs. The business does not have to be in an empowerment zone, renewal community, or rural renewal county to qualify for this credit. The credit is 25% of qualified first-year wages of employees working more than 120 but less than 400 hours in the year, *plus* 40% of qualified first-year wages for employees working more than 400 hours in the year, *plus* 50% of qualified second-year wages of employees certified as long-term family assistance recipients. The *Protecting Americans from Tax Hikes (PATH) Act of 2015* extends the Work Opportunity Tax Credit (WOTC) for hiring certain workers through 2019.

Net Operating Losses

A taxpayer with annual business deductions that exceed business income may have a *net operating loss (NOL)*. Some typical losses that may produce an NOL include losses incurred from the following:

- A trade or business
- Work as an employee (unreimbursed employee business expenses)
- A casualty or theft
- Moving expenses
- Rental property

A loss from operating a business is the most common reason for an NOL. Partnerships and S corporations generally cannot use an NOL. However, partners or shareholders can use their separate shares of partnership or S corporation business income and business deductions to figure their individual NOLs. Chapter 13 includes additional NOL rules that apply only to C corporations.

How to Figure NOL

There are rules that limit which deductions from income are allowed for NOL purposes. Calculate the NOL only on the income and expenses directly related to a trade or business. In general, the following items are not allowed when figuring an NOL:

- Any deduction for personal exemptions
- Capital losses in excess of capital gains
- The Section 1202 exclusion of the gain from the sale of qualified small business stock
- Non-business deductions in excess of non-business income
- Net operating loss deduction
- The domestic production activities deduction

A loss resulting from non-business deductions that are not connected to a trade or business or employment cannot contribute to the NOL. Examples of non-business deductions include:

- Alimony paid
- Deductions for contributions to an IRA or a self-employed retirement plan
- Health savings account deduction for a taxpayer, spouse, or dependents
- Most itemized deductions (except for casualty and theft losses, state income tax on business profits, and any employee business expenses)
- The standard deduction

Carry-back Period

The normal rule for treatment of an NOL is that a taxpayer must carry back the entire amount of the NOL to the two tax years before the year the NOL occurs, and then carry forward any unused NOL for up to 20 years after the NOL year. Taxpayers who choose to carry back the NOL must first carry the entire NOL to the earliest carry-back year. If the taxpayer does not use up the NOL, carry the rest to the next earliest carry-back year, and so on. If the taxpayer does not use up the NOL in the carry-back years, carry forward what remains of it to the 20 tax years following the NOL year. Continue to carry any unused part of the NOL forward until the taxpayer uses up the NOL or the 20-year carry forward period ends. A taxpayer may elect not to carry back the NOL and only carry it forward or waive the carry-back period by attaching a statement to his return.

Exceptions to Two-year Carry-back Rule

Eligible losses, farming losses, qualified disaster losses, qualified GO Zone losses, qualified recovery assistance losses, qualified disaster recovery assistance losses, eligible small business losses, and specified liability losses qualify for longer carry-back periods.

- **Three-year carry-back period** – The taxpayer can carry back three years only the eligible loss portion of the NOL. An eligible loss is any part of an NOL that:

    1) Is from a casualty or theft, or

    2) Is attributable to a <u>federally declared disaster</u> for a *qualified small business* (sole proprietorship or a partnership that has average annual gross receipts of $5 million or less during the three-year period ending with the tax year of the NOL)

- **Five-year carry-back period** – The NOL carry-back period is five years for any portion attributed to:

    1) A farming loss

    2) Certain qualified disaster losses

    3) A qualified GO Zone loss

- **Ten-year carry-back period** – Any portion of an NOL attributed to a *specified liability* arising from:

    1) Product liability, or

    2) For accrual taxpayers only, an act (or failure to act) that occurred at least three years before the beginning of the loss year and resulted in a liability under a federal or state law requiring:

        A) Reclamation of land

        B) Dismantling of a drilling platform

        C) Remediation of environmental contamination

        D) Payment under any workers' compensation act

Loss Limitations

A taxpayer who actively conducts a trade or business may generally deduct losses according to the net operating loss rules, described earlier.

> A taxpayer may <u>not</u> take a deduction against ordinary income for a loss if the amount is not *at risk* or if the loss is the result of a *passive activity*.

At-risk Limits

Generally, any loss from an activity subject to the at-risk rules is allowed <u>only</u> to the extent of the total amount at risk in the activity at the end of the tax year. Losses disallowed because of the at-risk limits are deductions from the <u>same</u> activity in the next tax year. A taxpayer is at risk in any activity for:

- The money and adjusted basis of property he contributes to the activity, and

- Amounts he borrows for use in the activity if:
  1) He is personally liable for repayment, or
  2) He pledges property (other than property used in the activity) as security for the loan.

> Jim contributes $50,000 to a partnership that limits his liability. He also personally guarantees a recourse loan of $25,000 made to the partnership to purchase equipment. He is "at risk" for $75,000.

Passive Activities

> Generally, losses from passive activities are not deductible unless income from other passive activities exists to offset them. Carry forward any excess *passive activity loss (PAL)* or credit to the next tax year and use to offset only passive income.

There are two kinds of passive activities:
- Business activities in which the taxpayer does not <u>materially</u> participate during the year
- Rental activities (even with material participation, unless the taxpayer is a real estate professional)

Material Participation

The IRS will consider participation to be material if the taxpayer can satisfy any of the following tests:

- The taxpayer participated in the activity for <u>more than 500</u> hours during the tax year.
- The taxpayer's participation was substantially <u>all of the participation</u> in the activity of all individuals for the tax year, including the participation of individuals who did not own any interest in the activity.
- The taxpayer participated in the activity for <u>more than 100</u> hours during the tax year, and at least as much as <u>any</u> other individual for the year.

Rental Real Estate Professional Exception

A loss from rental real estate may offset ordinary income if under one of the following exceptions:

- A *Real Estate Professional* may deduct losses against ordinary income, when:
  1) More than <u>half</u> of work is involved in real property trades or businesses in which the person *materially participates*, and
  2) More than **750 hours** of material participation is in real property trades or businesses.
- If rental losses are *less than $25,000* and the taxpayer or spouse actively participates in the rental activity, the passive activity limits may not apply. *Active participation* is a less stringent standard than material participation. Active participation includes management decisions such as approving tenants, deciding rental terms, approving expenditures, etc.
  1) If a taxpayer (S or MFJ) has *modified adjusted gross income (MAGI)* more than $100,000, the $25,000 special allowance is limited to 50% of the difference between $150,000 and MAGI. There is no allowance when MAGI is more than $150,000.

Not-for-profit Activities

If the intention of the business is not to make a profit, there is a limit on the deductions allowed. The taxpayer cannot use a loss from the activity to offset other income. Hobby, sport, or recreation activities fall under this limit. The limit on not-for-profit losses applies to individuals, partnerships, estates, trusts, and S corporations. It does not apply to corporations other than S corporations. An activity is presumed carried on for profit if it:

- Produced a profit in at least three of the last five tax years, including the current year, or
- Produced a profit in at least two of the last seven tax years, including the current year if the activities consist primarily of breeding, training, showing, or racing horses

Limit on Deductions

If the taxpayer does <u>not</u> carry on the activity for profit, deductions occur in the following order and only to the extent stated in the three categories.

- **Category 1** – Deductions for personal as well as for business activities are allowed in full. For individuals, all non-business deductions, such as those for home mortgage interest, taxes, and casualty losses (in excess of $100 and 10% of AGI) belong in this category.

- **Category 2** – Deductions that do not result in an adjustment to the basis of property are allowed next, but only to the extent that gross income from the activity is more than the deductions under the first category. Most business deductions, such as those for advertising, insurance premiums, interest, utilities, and wages, belong in this category.

- **Category 3** – Business deductions that decrease the basis of property are allowed to the extent the gross income from the activity exceeds the deductions under the first two categories. Deductions for depreciation, amortization, and the part of a casualty loss an individual could not deduct in category (1) belong in this category.

A taxpayer must itemize to claim the deductions. The amounts in categories (2) and (3) are miscellaneous deductions on Schedule A, subject to the 2%-of-adjusted-gross-income limit.

Employer Provisions in the Affordable Care Act

Important Terms

- **Applicable Large Employer (ALE)** – An ALE is, for a particular calendar year, any single employer, or group of employers treated as an Aggregated ALE Group, that employed an <u>average of at least 50 full-time employees</u> (including full-time equivalent employees) on business days during the preceding calendar year. All types of employers can be ALEs, including tax-exempt organizations and government entities.

- **Full-time Employee** – An employee who is employed an average of at least <u>30 hours</u> of service per week with the employer for a calendar month. For this purpose, 130 service hours in a calendar month is treated as the monthly equivalent of at least 30 hours per week.

- **Full-time employee equivalent (FTE)** – Add up the total hours of service for which the employer pays wages to employees during the year (but not more than 2,080 hours for any employee), and divide that amount by 2,080. If the result is not a whole number, round to the next lowest whole number. (If the result is less than one, however, round up to one FTE.)

Employer Shared Responsibility Provision

Under the Affordable Care Act's employer shared responsibility provisions, certain employers (called applicable large employers or ALEs) must either offer minimum essential coverage that is "affordable" and that provides "minimum value" to their full-time employees (and their dependents), or potentially make an employer shared responsibility payment to the IRS. The employer shared responsibility provisions are sometimes referred to as "the employer mandate" or "the pay or play provisions."

> The vast majority of employers fall below the ALE threshold of 50 full-time employees and are not subject to the employer shared responsibility provisions.

An ALE member may choose either to offer affordable minimum essential coverage that provides minimum value to its full-time employees (and their dependents) or potentially owe an employer shared responsibility payment to the IRS. Depending on its decisions about offering minimum essential coverage to its full-time employees and their dependents, an ALE member may be subject to one of two potential employer shared responsibility payments, but not both, and the two types of payments are calculated differently:

- ALE <u>does not</u> offer minimum essential coverage to at least 95 percent of its full-time employees (and their dependents) – On an annual basis, this payment is equal to $2,000 (indexed for future years) for each full-time employee, with the first 30 employees excluded from the calculation. This calculation is based on all full-time employees (minus 30), including full-time employees who have minimum essential coverage under the employer's plan or from another source.

- ALE <u>does</u> offer minimum essential coverage to at least 95 percent of its full-time employees (and their dependents) – On an annual basis, this payment is equal to $3,000 (indexed for future years) but only for each full-time employee who receives the premium tax credit. The total payment in this instance cannot exceed the amount the employer would have owed had the employer not offered minimum essential coverage to at least 95 percent of its full-time employees (and their dependents).

For either type of employer shared responsibility payment to apply to an ALE member, at least one full-time employee must receive the premium tax credit for purchasing coverage through the Marketplace.

Annual Reporting Requirement

ALEs must report to the IRS information about the health care coverage, if any, they offered to full-time employees. ALEs also must furnish to employees a statement that includes the same information provided to the IRS. Employees may use this information to determine whether, for each month of the calendar year, they may claim the premium tax credit on their individual income tax returns.

- **Form 1095-C, Employer-Provided Health Insurance Offer and Coverage** – Form 1095-C is filed and furnished to any employee of an ALE member who is a full-time employee for one or more months of the calendar. ALE Members must report that information for all twelve months of the calendar year for each employee.

Generally, you must file Forms 1094-C and 1095-C by February 28 if filing on paper (or March 31 if filing electronically) of the year following the calendar year to which the return relates.

Anyone required to file 250 or more information returns, must file them electronically. This requirement applies separately for each type of return and separately to each type of corrected return.

12 Business Property

Property Types · Depreciation · Section 179 · Basis of Property · Like-kind Exchanges

This chapter summarizes data from IRS Publications 17, 523, 527, 537, 544, 550, 551, and 946.

Property Types

Generally, a sale or trade of an asset results in a ***capital gain*** or loss. A sale or trade of a non-capital asset results in ***ordinary gain*** or loss. In some situations, part of the gain or loss may be a capital gain or loss and part may be an ordinary gain or loss.

Capital Assets

Rather than defining capital assets, the law provides a list of properties that are not capital assets:

- **A**ccounts or notes receivable acquired in the ordinary course of a trade or business for services rendered or from the sale of property held mainly for sale to customers
- **C**opyright, literary, musical, or artistic composition when created by the efforts of the taxpayer.
- **I**nventory or property held mainly for sale to customers or property that will physically become a part of the merchandise that is for sale to customers
- **D**epreciable property and real property (real estate) used in the taxpayer's trade or business
- **S**upplies regularly used or consumed in the ordinary course of a taxpayer's trade or business

In general, ordinary income tax rates apply when selling assets other than capital assets. Capital assets receive preferential tax treatment. Taxpayers generally hold capital assets for business or investment purposes (for example, stocks or copyrights acquired for investment).

Section 1231 Property

Some property held more than one year receives special treatment when sold. Net §1231 gains are ordinary gains up to the amount of non-recaptured §1231 losses from the five prior years; the rest is long-term capital gain. A loss from §1231 property is an ordinary loss.

Section 1231 property includes:

- Depreciable or amortizable property (personal or real) used in a business
- Leasehold interests
- Timber, coal, or iron ore
- Livestock or un-harvested crops

- Goodwill and other Section 197 intangibles
- Copyrights if acquired for investment

Section 1245 Recapture

Any property (other than depreciable real property) that is or has been subject to an allowance for depreciation or amortization is subject to *Section 1245 recapture* rules. The taxpayer recaptures a portion of the gain from the disposition of the property due to depreciation as ordinary income.

> Section 1245 property does not include buildings and structural components. The term "building" includes a house, barn, warehouse, or garage. The term "structural component" includes walls, floors, windows, doors, central air conditioning systems, light fixtures, etc.

Section 1250 Recapture

All real property that is subject to an allowance for depreciation and has never been Section 1245 property is subject to *Section 1250 recapture* rules. It includes leasehold of land or Section 1250 property subject to an allowance for depreciation. A fee simple interest in land is not included because it is not depreciable. A tax rate of 25% applies to depreciation up to the amount of straight-line depreciation. This portion is *unrecaptured Section 1250 gain*. Any amount of *additional depreciation* is taxed as ordinary income and is recaptured as Section 1250 gain. Additional depreciation is the actual depreciation that is more than the depreciation figured using the straight-line method. If a taxpayer holds Section 1250 property for one year or less, all the depreciation is additional depreciation.

> Christine is in the 35% tax bracket. She purchased a rental property several years ago for $100,000. She sells the property for $150,000. The depreciation taken under ACRS was $41,840, but if she had used the straight-line method, the depreciation would have been $37,970. Christine used a method of accelerated depreciation (ACRS) and has a Section 1250 gain. Section 1250 gain is $3,870, the difference between ACRS and the straight-line depreciation. Ordinary income tax rates apply to Section 1250 Gain. Unrecaptured Section 1250 gain is $37,970, the amount of straight-line depreciation taxed as a capital gain at a 25% rate. The remaining $50,000 gain is taxable as a long-term capital gain at a maximum rate of 20% in 2015.

Depreciation

There are two basic types of property:

- **Tangible property** – Is physical in nature. Includes land, structures, equipment, natural resources, etc. Tangible property is further divided into:
    1) **Real property** – Real estate including land, houses, buildings, etc.
    2) **Personal property** – Any tangible property other than real property
- **Intangible property** – Does not have a physical presence. Includes computer software, patents, goodwill, stocks, and bonds.

Expenditures that do not have a useful life beyond one year are *expenses*, which are generally deductible in the year incurred. Property acquired with a useful life greater than one year or *improvements* that increase the value of the property, lengthen its life, or adapt it to a different use are *capital expenditures*. A capital expenditure is *capitalized* (added to capital), and the cost is systematically *recovered* (written off) each year, in various ways, depending on type of property. Depreciation reduces basis for figuring gain or loss on a later sale or exchange.

The methods for recovering the cost of an asset over its useful life include the following:

- **Depreciation** – For tangible income producing property, other than natural resources
- **Depletion** – For assets that diminish over time, such as oil, gas, and other natural resources
- **Amortization** – For intangible assets, such as patents and goodwill

The taxpayer recovers the cost of tangible income-producing property through yearly tax deductions by depreciating the property, that is, by deducting some of the cost each year on the tax return. Three basic factors determine how much depreciation the taxpayer may deduct:

- The basis in the property
- The recovery period for the property
- The depreciation method used

Taxpayers cannot simply deduct mortgages or principal payments, or the cost of furniture, fixtures, or equipment as an expense. Deduct depreciation only on the part of property used for a business or income-producing activity. A taxpayer cannot depreciate personal-use property. Depreciation reduces basis for figuring gain or loss on a later sale or exchange.

What Property Can Be Depreciated

- Property may be depreciated if it meets all the following requirements:
    1) The taxpayer owns the property.
    2) The taxpayer uses the property in business or income-producing activity (e.g., rental property).
    3) The property has a determinable useful life.
    4) The taxpayer expects the property to last more than one year.

- Certain property cannot be depreciated:
    1) Land (land preparation costs, such as landscaping costs are depreciable)
    2) Property placed in service and disposed of in the same year
    3) Equipment used to build capital improvements
    4) *Section 197 intangibles* – The following assets are Section 197 intangibles and must be amortized over 180 months:
        A) Goodwill
        B) Going concern value
        C) Workforce in place
        D) Business books and records, operating systems, or any other information base, including lists or other information concerning current or prospective customers
        E) A patent, copyright, formula, process, design, pattern, know-how, format, or similar item

F) A customer-based intangible

G) A supplier-based intangible

H) Any item similar to items (C) through (G)

I) A license, permit, or other right granted by a governmental unit or agency

J) A covenant not to compete in connection with the acquisition of a business

K) Any franchise, trademark, or trade name,

L) A contract for the use of, or a term interest in, any item in this list

A taxpayer cannot amortize any of the intangibles listed in items (A) through (H) that he creates rather than acquires unless he creates them in acquiring assets that make up a trade or business or a substantial part of a trade or business.

A taxpayer cannot depreciate personal-use property. Deduct depreciation only on the part of property used for a business or income-producing activity.

Repairs and Improvements

If depreciable property is improved, the taxpayer must treat the improvement as separate depreciable property. Improvement means an addition to or partial replacement of property that adds to its value, appreciably lengthens its useful lifetime, or adapts it to a different use. Generally, a taxpayer deducts the cost of repairing business property in the same way as any other business expense. However, if a repair or replacement increases the value of the property, makes it more useful, or lengthens its life, it is an improvement and is added to capital and depreciated.

Depreciation Methods

- Generally, a taxpayer must use the *Modified Accelerated Cost Recovery System (MACRS)* to depreciate residential rental property placed in service after 1986. MACRS consists of two systems that determine how property may be depreciated:

    1) **General Depreciation System (GDS)** – Generally, taxpayers must use GDS for property used in most rental activities. Recovery periods generally are shorter than under ADS.

    2) **Alternative Depreciation System (ADS)** – ADS uses the straight-line method of depreciation. A taxpayer electing to use ADS may not change the election, which applies to all property in the same class that is placed in service during the tax year of the election. However, the election applies on a property-by-property basis for residential rental property and nonresidential real property.

- If rental property was in service before 1987, the taxpayer uses one of the following methods:

    1) *ACRS (Accelerated Cost Recovery System)* for property in service between 1980 and 1987

    2) *Straight-line* or *declining balance method* over the useful life of property placed in service before 1981

Taxpayers must continue to use the same depreciation method unless the IRS grants approval to change accounting methods. The methods under MACRS for depreciating property are as follows:

- **Straight-line depreciation** – Deduct equal amounts throughout the recovery period.

    1) A taxpayer must use the straight-line method and a mid-month convention for residential rental property. In the first year of claiming depreciation for residential rental property, take depreciation only for the number of months the property is in use.

> Saul purchases a $2,000 computer for his business that has a useful life of 5-years. He uses the computer exclusively for business. He can claim $400 in annual depreciation until he no longer has a basis in the computer. If he uses the half-year convention, he claims $200 in the first year.

- **200% or 150% declining balance** – Allows for greater depreciation percentages in early years. Use the straight-line method in place of accelerated depreciation in the first tax year it provides an equal or larger deduction than either the 200% or 150% declining balance method.

    1) Upon sale or other disposition, certain nonresidential real estate may be subject to recapture of excess depreciation *(un-recaptured Section 1250 gain)* if a method other than straight-line depreciation was used. The recaptured amount is the excess depreciation amount above what would have been claimed using the straight-line method.

Special Depreciation Allowance

> A business taxpayer may take an additional 50% *special depreciation allowance*, often referred to as "bonus depreciation" on certain qualified property. The special depreciation allowance applies only for the first year the property is in service (new property only). The allowance is an additional deduction taken after any **Section 179 expense deduction** and before the taxpayer figures regular depreciation under MACRS. Qualified property includes tangible property depreciated in 20 years or less under MACRS.

Recovery Periods

Under regular MACRS (GDS), depreciable property generally falls into one of the following classes:

- **Five-year property** – Computers and peripheral equipment, office machinery (typewriters, calculators, copiers, etc.), automobiles, light trucks, appliances, carpeting, furniture, etc., used in a residential rental real estate activity. Depreciation on automobiles and certain computers is limited. Taxpayers may use 200% or 150% DB.

- **Seven-year property** – Office furniture and equipment (desks, file cabinets, etc.). This class also includes any property that does not have a class life and that has not been designated by law as being in any other class. Taxpayers may use 200% or 150% DB.

- **Fifteen-year property** – Roads, fences, and shrubbery. Taxpayers may use 150% DB.

- **Twenty-year property** – Includes improvements such as utilities and sewers.

- **Residential rental property (27.5-year property)** – Real property that is a rental building or structure (including mobile homes) for which 80% or more of the gross rental income for the tax year is from dwelling units. It does not include a unit in a hotel, motel, inn, or other establishment where more than half of the units are used on a transient basis. Depreciate additions or improvements to the structure over the same period. In a case like this, the straight-line method is necessary along with a mid-month convention. For the first year, take depreciation only for the number of months the property was in use.

- **Non-residential rental property (39-year property)** – Commercial buildings and structures. Includes Section 1250 property. Must use straight-line method and mid-month convention.

Conventions

Depreciation begins when the taxpayer places the property in service for the production of income. Depreciation ends when either the taxpayer fully recovers the cost, or the property is retired from service, whichever happens first. Property is placed in service in a rental activity when it is ready and available for a specific use in that activity. Even if unused, it is in service when it is ready and available for its specific use. A *convention* is a method established under MACRS to set the beginning and end of the recovery period. The convention used determines the number of months that the taxpayer may claim as depreciation in the year the property was placed in service and in the year in which it was disposed. Use the mid-month convention for residential rental property and nonresidential real property. For all other property, use the half-year or mid-quarter convention, as appropriate.

- **Mid-month convention** – Use a mid-month convention for all residential rental property and nonresidential real property. Treat all property placed in service, or disposed of, during the month as placed in service, or disposed of, at the midpoint of that month.

- **Mid-quarter convention** – Use a mid-quarter convention if the mid-month convention does not apply and the total depreciable basis of MACRS property placed in service in the last three months of a tax year is more than 40% of the total basis of all such property placed into service during the year. For this convention, the MACRS property excludes nonresidential real property, residential rental property, and property placed in service and disposed of in the same year. Under this convention, treat all property placed in service, or disposed of, during any quarter of a tax year as placed in service, or disposed of, at the midpoint of the quarter.

- **Half-year convention** – Use the half-year convention if neither the mid-quarter convention nor the mid-month convention applies. Under this convention, treat all property placed into service, or disposed of, during a tax year as being placed into service, or disposed of, at the midpoint of that tax year. If this convention applies, the taxpayer may deduct a half year of depreciation for the first year and the last year that the taxpayer depreciates the property. The taxpayer may deduct a full year of depreciation for any other year during the recovery period.

> The half-year convention applies to most transactions. Under this convention all propery transactions are considered to occur at the midpoint of the year.

Section 179 Deduction

Use a Section 179 deduction to recover the cost of qualifying property used in a trade or business. Unlike bonus depreciation, section 179 applies to both new and used equipment. If a taxpayer buys qualifying property with cash and a trade-in, its cost for purposes of the section 179 deduction includes only the cash paid. This deduction is not allowed for property held for the production of income, such as rental property. Instead of depreciating property over time, a taxpayer may elect to claim as an expense up to $500,000 in 2015. Section 179 deduction limits apply to both the partnership and its partners. The partnership determines its Section 179 deduction subject to the limits. It then allocates the deduction among its partners. The same is true for an S corporation and a shareholder. The property must be placed in service during the tax year, and must be one of the following types of depreciable property:

- Tangible personal property
- Machinery and equipment
- Property contained in or attached to a building (not structural components), such as office equipment, refrigerators, grocery store counters, printing presses, testing equipment, and signs

- Gasoline storage tanks and pumps at retail service stations
- Livestock, including horses, cattle, hogs, sheep, goats, and mink and other furbearing animals
- Other tangible property (except buildings and their structural components) used as:
  1) An integral part of manufacturing, production, or extraction; or as an integral part of furnishing transportation, communications, electricity, gas, water, or sewage disposal services,
  2) A research facility used in connection with any of the activities in (1) above, or
  3) A facility used in any of the activities in (1) for the bulk storage of fungible commodities
- Single purpose agricultural (livestock) or horticultural structures
- Petroleum storage or distribution facilities (except buildings and their structural components)
- Off-the-shelf computer software

Reduced Section 179 Deduction

Under certain conditions, the amount of the Section 179 deduction may be reduced or eliminated:

- If the cost of the qualifying Section 179 property placed in service in a year is more than $2 million, the taxpayer generally must reduce the dollar limit (but not below zero) by the amount of cost more than $2 million. If the cost of Section 179 property placed in service during 2015 is $2.5 million or more, the taxpayer cannot take a Section 179 deduction.

- Married taxpayers who file separately in 2015 must combine all purchases as if they are filing jointly to determine the allowable Section 179 deduction; otherwise, the deduction is $250,000 each.

- The taxpayer must use the property more than 50% for business in the year placed in service. The Section 179 deduction is allowed only for the business use portion of property. If the property is also for personal use, that part cannot receive a deduction. If the business use falls below 50% in future years, the taxpayer must include a portion of the Section 179 deduction in income.

- **Sport Utility and Certain Other Vehicles** – Taxpayers cannot elect to expense more than $25,000 of the cost of any heavy sport utility vehicle (SUV) and certain other vehicles placed in service during the tax year. This rule applies to any four-wheeled vehicle primarily designed or used to carry less than nine passengers over public streets, roads, or highways, rated at more than 6,000 pounds gross vehicle weight and not more than 14,000 pounds gross vehicle weight. In addition to the Section 179 deduction, a taxpayer may claim a special depreciation allowance and MACRS depreciation.

- **Passenger Vehicles** – The total depreciation deduction under §280F (including the Section 179 expense deduction) a taxpayer can take for a passenger automobile (not a truck or a van) first placed in service in 2015 is $3,160 ($11,160 if the special depreciation allowance applies). The maximum deduction for a truck or van is $3,460 ($11,460 if the special depreciation allowance applies).

Basis of Property

Basis is the amount of a taxpayer's investment in a property for tax purposes. A gain or loss is determined by subtracting the adjusted basis from the proceeds of the sale, exchange, or other disposition of property. Use basis to figure deductions for depreciation, amortization, depletion, and casualty losses. If a taxpayer uses property for both business and investment purposes and for personal purposes, the taxpayer must properly allocate basis according to percentage of use. The taxpayer can depreciate only the basis allocated to the business or investment use of the property. The basis of property is usually its cost. The cost is the amount paid in cash, debt obligations, other property, or services. A taxpayer's cost basis also includes (but is not limited to) amounts paid for the following:

- Commissions
- Sales tax, freight, installation, and testing
- Legal and accounting fees (when they must be capitalized)
- Excise taxes, revenue stamps, recording fees, and real estate taxes (if assuming seller's liability)

Certain events may adjust (increase or decrease) an original basis in property:

- Improvements to a property will increase basis.
- Deductions for depreciation, casualty losses, or claiming certain credits will reduce basis.

Real Property

Real property, also called real estate, is land and generally anything built on, growing on, or attached to the land. Certain fees and other expenses are part of the cost basis in the property. If a taxpayer buys buildings and the land on which the buildings stand for a lump sum, allocate the cost basis among the land and the buildings. Allocate the cost basis according to the respective FMV of the land and buildings at the time of purchase. Calculate the basis of each asset by multiplying the lump sum by a fraction. The numerator is the FMV of that asset, and the denominator is the FMV of the whole property at the time of purchase. If the FMV of the land and buildings is unknown, a taxpayer can allocate the basis using the assessed values for real estate tax purposes. If a taxpayer buys property and assumes an existing mortgage on the property, the basis includes the amount paid for the property plus the amount outstanding on the mortgage. Adjust the basis by certain settlement costs as described below:

- A taxpayer's basis includes the **settlement fees** and **closing costs** paid for buying the property. A fee for buying property is a cost that the taxpayer must pay even if the taxpayer buys the property with cash. Do <u>not</u> include fees and costs for getting a loan on the property in the basis.

    1) Taxpayers <u>may</u> add the following settlement fees or closing costs to the basis:

        A) Abstract fees (abstract of title fees)

        B) Charges for installing utility services

        C) Legal fees (fees for the title search and preparation of the sales contract and deed)

        D) Recording fees

        E) Survey fees

        F) Transfer taxes

        G) Owner's title insurance

        H) Any amounts the buyer agrees to pay for the seller, such as back taxes or interest, recording or mortgage fees, cost of improvements or repairs, and sales commissions

    2) Taxpayers may <u>not</u> add the following settlement fees and closing costs to basis:

        A) Casualty insurance premiums

        B) Rent for occupancy of the property before closing

        C) Charges for utilities or other services related to the property before closing

        D) Charges connected with getting a loan, such as points (discount points, loan origination fees), mortgage insurance premiums, loan assumption fees, cost of a credit report, and fees for an appraisal required by a lender

E) Fees for refinancing a mortgage. If a taxpayer pays points to get a loan (including a mortgage, second mortgage, line of credit, or a home equity loan), the points may not be added to the basis of the related property. Generally, the points are deducted over the term of the loan.

F) Amounts placed in escrow for the future payment of taxes and insurance

Basis Allocation

If a taxpayer acquires a trade or business for a lump sum, allocate the consideration paid to the various assets acquired. Generally, the purchaser will reduce the amount paid by any cash and general deposit accounts (including checking and savings accounts) received. Allocate the remaining consideration to the other business assets received in proportion to (but not more than) their fair market value. Any amount remaining (not allocated to assets) is goodwill.

EXAMPLE: Setting Sun Partnership purchased a business, Family Dry Cleaners, for $750,000. Family Dry Cleaners assets consist of: $50,000 in cash, equipment with a fair market value of $200,000, and land and building with a fair market value of $450,000.

For real estate tax purposes, the city assessed the value of the land at $100,000 and the building at $200,000. The buyer and seller did not enter into an allocation agreement for this transaction. What basis must Setting Sun Partnership use for the land, building, and intangible asset "goodwill"?

A. Land $100,000, Building $200,000, and Goodwill $150,000
B. Land $150,000, Building $300,000, and Goodwill $0
C. Land $150,000, Building $300,000, and Goodwill $50,000
D. Land $100,000, Building $350,000, and Goodwill $50,000

ANSWER: C. Basis for cash is always the amount received. Allocate basis to the equipment up to the FMV of the equipment. If a person purchases a building and land in a single transaction, allocate the cost between each. Figure the basis of each asset by multiplying the lump sum by a fraction. The numerator is the FMV of that asset, and the denominator is the FMV of the whole property at the time of purchase. If you are not certain of the FMV of the land and buildings, you can allocate the basis using the assessed values for real estate tax purposes. The building's assessed value is two thirds of the total assessed value. Allocate two thirds of the current FMV of the combined real estate to the building. The remainder is goodwill.

Cash	$50,000	
Equipment	$200,000	
Property	$450,000	($300,000 Building, $150,000 Land)
Goodwill	$50,000	($750,000 purchase price - $700,000 FMV of assets received)
Total	**$750,000**	

Adjusted Basis

Before figuring the gain or loss on a sale, exchange, or other disposition of property or figuring the allowable depreciation, depletion, or amortization, a taxpayer must usually make certain adjustments (increases and decreases) to the cost of the property. The result is the adjusted basis.

- **Increase** the basis of any property by all items properly added to a capital account. These include (but are not limited to) the following items:

    1) **Capital improvements** – Costs of improvements having a useful life of more than one year, which increase the value of the property, lengthen its life, or adapt it to a different use.

2) **Assessments for local improvements** – Increase basis by property assessments for improvements that increase the value of the property. Do not deduct these as taxes. Examples of assessments are as follows:

   A) Roads

   B) Sidewalks

   C) Water connections

   D) Extending utility service lines to the property

- **Decrease** the basis of any property by all items that represent a return of capital for the period during which the taxpayer held the property. Items that decrease basis include (but are not limited to) the following:

    1) **Non-taxable corporate distributions** – Also known as non-dividend distributions. This amount reflects a return of capital and reduces basis.

    2) **Casualty and theft losses** – Decrease the basis in a taxpayer's property by any insurance proceeds or other reimbursement and by any deductible loss not covered by insurance. Increase the basis in the property by the amount spent on repairs that restore the property to its pre-casualty condition.

    3) **Depreciation and Section 179 deduction** – The basis of a taxpayer's qualifying business property will be decreased by any Section 179 deductions taken and the depreciation deducted, or could have been deducted (including any special depreciation allowance), on the taxpayer's returns under the chosen method of depreciation.

    4) **Easements** – The amount received for granting an easement is considered proceeds from the sale of an interest in real property. It reduces the basis of the affected part of the property.

    5) **Certain credits** – Basis may be reduced by the amount of credits received for the following:

        A) Alternative motor vehicle credit

        B) Alternative fuel vehicle refueling property credit

        C) Residential energy efficient property credit

Property Received for Services

If a taxpayer receives property for services rendered, its FMV must be included in income. The amount included in income becomes the basis. If the taxpayer performed the services for a price agreed on beforehand, it will be accepted as the FMV of the property if there is no evidence to the contrary. If the property is subject to certain restrictions, the basis in the property is its FMV when it substantially vests. However, this rule does not apply if the taxpayer makes an election to include in income the FMV of the property at the time it is transferred, less any amount the taxpayer paid for it. Property is substantially vested when it is transferable or when it is not subject to a substantial risk of forfeiture.

Bargain Purchases

A bargain purchase is the purchase of an item for less than its FMV. If a taxpayer buys goods or other property at less than FMV as compensation for services, include the difference between the purchase price and the property's FMV in income. The basis in the property is its FMV (the purchase price plus the amount included in income).

Involuntary Conversions

If a taxpayer receives replacement property because of an *involuntary conversion*, such as a casualty, theft, or condemnation, calculate the basis of the replacement property by using the basis of the converted property.

- **Similar or related property** – If a taxpayer receives replacement property similar or related in service or use to the converted property, the replacement property's basis is the same as the converted property's basis on the date of the conversion, with the following adjustments:

    1) Basis decreases by the following:

        A) Any loss recognized on the involuntary conversion, and

        B) Any money received that the taxpayer does not spend on similar property

    2) Basis increases by the following:

        A) Any gain recognized on the involuntary conversion, and

        B) Any cost of acquiring the replacement property

- **Money or property not similar or related** – If a taxpayer receives money or property not similar or related in use to the converted property, and he buys replacement property similar or related in use to the converted property, the basis of the replacement property is its cost decreased by the gain not recognized on the conversion.

Property Received as a Gift

To establish the basis of property received as a gift, a taxpayer must know the adjusted basis to the *donor* (source of gift), its fair market value (FMV) at the time of the gift, and any gift tax paid. The relationship between the FMV and the donor's basis determines the applicable rule. If a taxpayer receives a gift of property and the donor's adjusted basis determines the basis, the taxpayer's holding period begins the same day as the donor's holding period. If the FMV of the property determines the basis, the holding period starts on the day after the date of the gift.

- **FMV <u>less</u> than donor's adjusted basis** – Basis depends on whether a gain or a loss occurs when the property is disposed of. The following *dual basis rules* prevent taxpayers from shifting unrealized losses to other taxpayers:

    1) The basis for figuring gain is the same as the donor's adjusted basis, or

    2) The basis for figuring loss is its FMV when the taxpayer received the gift.

- **FMV <u>equal to or greater</u> than donor's adjusted basis** – Basis is the donor's adjusted basis at the time the taxpayer received the gift.

    1) If the donor paid gift tax on the transfer, basis increases by the part of the gift tax that is due to the net increase in value of the gift. The net increase in value of the gift is the FMV of the gift minus the donor's basis. Figure the increase by multiplying the gift tax paid by a fraction.

$$Gift\ Tax\ Paid \times \frac{FMV\ at\ time\ of\ gift - Donor's\ basis}{Amount\ of\ gift\ (after\ annual\ exclusion)}$$

Property Transferred from a Spouse

If a taxpayer receives property from a spouse, or the spouse transfers property in trust for the taxpayer's benefit, the taxpayer's basis and holding period is the same as the spouse's adjusted basis and holding period. The same rule applies to a transfer by a taxpayer's former spouse that is incident to divorce. A taxpayer will not recognize a gain or loss on property transferred to a spouse or former spouse incident to divorce. This is true even if receiving cash or other consideration.

Inherited Property

The basis of an inherited capital asset is generally the FMV of the property on the date of death or an alternate valuation date, if elected by the personal representative. A *step-up* in basis occurs when the FMV is greater than the decedent's basis. Gains on inherited property are <u>always</u> long-term.

Property Changed from Personal to Business or Rental Use

If a taxpayer holds property for personal use and then changes it to business use or uses it to produce rent, the taxpayer may begin to depreciate the property at the time of the change. To do so, calculate the property's basis for depreciation. An example of changing property held for personal use to business or rental use would be the renting out of a former personal residence. The basis for depreciation is the lesser of the following amounts:

- The FMV of the property on the date of the change
- The adjusted basis on the date of the change

If the taxpayer sells the property at a loss, the FMV on date of conversion (with adjustments) is the cost for purposes of the determining basis. If the taxpayer sells the property at a gain, the original basis (with adjustments) is used. This rule prevents a taxpayer from shifting nondeductible losses on personal property to deductible losses on business property.

Securities

The following rules apply to most investors. Day-traders and dealers in securities may utilize different methods to account for their transactions.

- **Stocks or bonds** – The basis of purchased stocks or bonds is generally the purchase price plus any costs of purchase, such as commissions and recording or transfer fees.

  1) **Nontaxable stock dividends or stock splits** – Total basis and percentage ownership do not change. Allocate the total adjusted basis of all shares *pro rata* to each share. Reduce the basis of existing shares by the amount of basis allocated to the new shares. This rule applies only when the additional stock received is identical to the stock held.

  2) **Return of capital** – Also known as non-dividend distributions. This amount reflects a return of capital and reduces basis.

Like-kind Exchanges

If a taxpayer trades <u>business or investment</u> property for other business or investment property of a *like kind*, the taxpayer does not pay tax on any gain or deduct any loss until he sells or disposes of the property received. Like-kind properties are properties of the same nature or character, even if they differ in grade or quality. The exchange of real estate for real estate and the exchange of personal property for similar personal property are exchanges of like-kind property. For example, the following transactions involve property of a like kind:

- Trade of land improved with an apartment house for land improved with a store building
- City property for farm property
- Improved property for unimproved property
- Real estate owned by a taxpayer for a real estate lease that runs 30 years

- A barge for a tugboat
- Office desk for an office file cabinet
- A panel truck for a pickup truck

An exchange of personal property for real property does not qualify as a like-kind exchange. The following transactions do not involve property of a like kind:

- Exchange of a piece of machinery for a store building
- Real property located in the United States and real property located outside the United States
- Exchange of livestock of different sexes

In a like-kind exchange, the taxpayer must hold both the property transferred and the property received for investment or productive use in a trade or business. Machinery, buildings, land, trucks, and rental houses are examples of property that may qualify.

The rules for like-kind exchanges do not apply to exchanges of the following property:

- Personal use property, such as a home and family car
- Stock-in-trade or other property held primarily for sale, such as inventories, raw materials, and real estate held by dealers
- Stocks, bonds, notes, or other securities or evidences of indebtedness, such as accounts receivable
- Partnership interests
- Certificates of trust or beneficial interest
- Choses in action (a right to sue)
- Certain tax-exempt use property subject to a lease

The replacement property must be identified within 45 days and received by the earliest of the 180th day after the date on which the property given up in the exchange transfers, or the due date of the tax return, including extensions, for the tax year in which the transfer of the property given up occurs.

Gain Recognition

The amount *realized* from a sale or trade of property is everything received for the property. This includes the money, the fair market value of any property or services, and debt or other liabilities assumed by the buyer. The difference between the *adjusted basis* and the amount realized in a sale is the *realized gain (or loss)* on the transaction. The amount of income or loss *recognized* is the amount a taxpayer includes in taxable income for the tax year.

Boot

Transactions such as *like-kind exchanges* may defer or partially defer recognition of gain. A taxpayer may have a *partially nontaxable* exchange and could realize a gain if he receives property that is not like kind, known as *boot*.

> Boot is the total amount of the following:
> - Any money received
> - Net liabilities assumed by other party (after subtracting the liabilities assumed by taxpayer)
> - The FMV of unlike property received

A taxpayer must recognize the gain up to the amount of boot received or the amount of realized gain, whichever is less. If the taxpayer realizes a loss on the exchange, no loss is recognized. A taxpayer may recognize a loss only on transfers of unlike property. The recognized (taxable) gain on the disposition of the like-kind property given up is the smaller of the following:

- The amount of gain realized
- The FMV of boot received *less* exchange expenses (closing costs) paid

Exchange Expenses

Exchange expenses are generally the closing costs paid by the taxpayer. They include such items as brokerage commissions, attorney fees, and deed preparation fees. Subtract exchange expenses from the total consideration received to figure the amount realized on the exchange. Exchange expenses increase the basis of the like-kind property received by the amount of exchange expenses incurred. Exchange expenses reduce boot before determining the recognized gain.

Assumption of Liabilities

> To determine the amount of realized gain, increase the amount realized by any liabilities assumed by the other party. Subtract liabilities of the other party assumed by the taxpayer from the amount realized. For purposes of figuring the limit of recognized gain, if the other party assumes a net liability, treat the taxpayer as if he received money for the liability. The taxpayer can decrease (but not below zero) the amount of money he is treated as receiving by the amount of the other party's liabilities he assumes, by any cash he pays or unlike property he gives up.

Basis of Property Received

If a taxpayer acquires property in a like-kind exchange, the basis of that property is generally the same as the basis of the property transferred, with the following adjustments:

- **Increase** basis by the total amount of:
    1) Additional money paid, including exchange expenses
    2) FMV of any non-like-kind property transferred to other party
    3) Net liabilities assumed by the taxpayer
    4) Any gain recognized on the exchange

- **Decrease** basis by the amount of:
    1) Boot received (money, FMV of non-like-kind property, net liabilities other party assumes)
    2) Any loss recognized on the exchange

Allocate basis first to non-like-kind property in an amount equivalent to its FMV at the date of the exchange. Allocate the remaining basis to the like-kind property. In situations where a taxpayer receives multiple like-kind replacement properties, the basis is allocated between the properties (other than money) received in proportion to its relative FMV on the date of the exchange.

A taxpayer exchanges real estate held for investment with an adjusted basis of $8,000 for other real estate he now holds for investment. The fair market value (FMV) of the real estate received is $14,000. The taxpayer also receives $1,000 in cash and pays $500 in exchange expenses. The property the taxpayer gave up was subject to a $3,000 mortgage for which he was personally liable. The other party in the trade agreed to pay off the mortgage. The property received is subject to a $4,000 mortgage that the taxpayer assumes.

FMV of like-kind property received	$14,000
Cash	+$1,000
Mortgage assumed by other party	+$3,000
Total received	$18,000
less: Exchange expenses	-$500
Amount realized	$17,500
less: Adjusted basis of property transferred	-$8,000
less: Mortgage taxpayer assumed	-$4,000
Realized gain	$5,500

The realized gain is <u>recognized</u> (taxable) gain only up to $500, figured as follows:

Money received (cash)	$1,000
Net liability other party assumes ($3,000 – $4,000 not below $0)	+$0
Total money and unlike property received	$1,000
less: Exchange expenses paid	-$500
Recognized gain	$500

The <u>basis</u> for the property received is increased by $1,000:

Basis of transferred property	$8,000
Net liability taxpayer assumes ($4,000 – $3,000)	+$1,000
Exchange expenses	+$500
Recognized gain	+$500
less: Boot received	-$1,000
Adjusted basis	$9,000

Related Party

If a taxpayer and a ***related party*** enter into a like-kind exchange and either disposes of the like property within <u>two years</u>, both parties must report any unrecognized gain or loss from the original trade on the return for the year the disposition occurs. A taxpayer may not deduct a <u>loss</u>, other than a distribution in complete liquidation of a corporation, if the transaction involves the following related parties:

- Family members. This includes <u>only</u> brothers and sisters, half-brothers and half-sisters, spouse, ancestors (parents, grandparents, etc.), and lineal descendants (children, grandchildren, etc.)
- A partnership or corporation with more than 50% directly or indirectly owned by taxpayer
- A tax-exempt charitable or educational organization controlled by the taxpayer or family member

13 Corporations

Businesses Taxed as Corporations · Property Exchanged for Stock · Filing and Paying Taxes · Income, Deductions, and Special Provisions · Earnings and Profits · Distribution and Recognition Requirements · Redemption of Stock · Special Deductions · Figuring Tax · S Corporations

Summary of rules in Form 1120S, 2553, Pub 535, 542, 544, 550, 583, IRC §302, §1366, §1367 and §1368.

Businesses Taxed as Corporations

The following businesses formed after 1996 are taxed as corporations:

- A business formed under a federal or state law that refers to it as a corporation, body corporate, body politic, joint-stock company, or joint-stock association
- An insurance company
- Certain banks
- A business wholly owned by a state or local government
- A business specifically required to be taxed as a corporation by the Internal Revenue Code (for example, certain publicly traded partnerships)
- Certain foreign businesses
- Any other business that elects taxation as a corporation (for example, an LLC) by filing Form 8832, Entity Classification Election

Personal Service Corporations

A corporation is a ***personal service corporation*** if it meets all of the following requirements:

- Its principal activity during the "testing period" (generally the prior tax year) is performing personal services in the fields of accounting, actuarial science, architecture, consulting, engineering, health (including veterinary services), law, and the performing arts
- Its employee-owners substantially perform the services
- Employee-owners own more than 10% of FMV of outstanding stock on the last day of testing period:
    1) A person is an employee-owner of a personal service corporation if he is an employee of the corporation or performs personal services for, or on behalf of, the corporation on any day of the testing period, and owns any stock in the corporation.
    2) Furthermore, the PSC may be a ***qualified personal service corporation*** if current (or retired) employees performing the personal services, their estates, or their beneficiaries own at least 95% of the corporation's stock, by value, directly or indirectly.

Closely Held Corporations

A corporation (other than a personal service corporation) is closely held if and at any time during the <u>last half</u> of the tax year, more than 50% of the value of its outstanding stock is, directly or indirectly, owned by or for <u>five or fewer</u> individuals, including certain trusts and private foundations.

Affiliated Group

An affiliated group is one or more chains of includible corporations connected through stock ownership with a common parent corporation. The parent corporation must directly own stock equal to at least <u>80%</u> of the total <u>voting power</u> of the stock of such corporation, with a value equal to at least <u>80%</u> of the total <u>value</u> of the stock of such corporation.

Property Exchanged for Stock

Many of the questions on the exam regarding corporate funding transactions test the concepts of basis on contributed property, gain recognition, and contribution of services in exchange for ownership.

IRC Section 351 Exchange

The transfer of property (or money and property) to a corporation in exchange for stock in that corporation (other than nonqualified preferred stock) is usually <u>not</u> taxable if immediately afterward the taxpayer is in **control** of the corporation.

This type of nontaxable *§351 exchange* applies both to individuals and to groups who transfer property to a corporation. Both the corporation and any person involved in a nontaxable exchange of property for stock must attach to their income tax returns a complete statement of all facts pertinent to the exchange. It is important to recognize when a taxpayer has control. Without control, treat a contribution of property like a purchase and sale. Sometimes this can result in a loss.

A shareholder that owns—directly or indirectly—more than 50% of the corporation's stock cannot deduct the loss. *See Related Persons, later.*

Control of Corporation – To be in control of a corporation the transferors must own <u>at least 80%</u> of the total combined voting power of all classes of stock, and at least 80% of the outstanding shares of each class of nonvoting stock, <u>immediately</u> after the exchange. This does not apply if the corporation is an investment company, in a bankruptcy or similar proceeding in exchange for stock used to pay creditors, or if the taxpayer receives the stock in exchange for the corporation's debt that accrued while the taxpayer held the debt.

- **Services rendered** – The term "property" does <u>not</u> include <u>services</u> rendered to the issuing corporation. The value of stock received for services is income to the recipient. The basis of stock received for services is the amount the shareholder includes in income. If a shareholder performs services in exchange for stock, the control requirement for §351 can be lost. Only the shares attributed to the exchange of "property" count toward the control requirement.

- **Money or property received** – A taxpayer may need to recognize a gain if money or property other than stock is received during the exchange. The taxpayer recognizes gain only up to the amount of money _plus_ the FMV of the other property received.
- **Liabilities** – If the corporation assumes taxpayer liabilities, the exchange generally is not treated as if the taxpayer received money or other property. There are two exceptions:
    1) If liabilities assumed are more than the taxpayer's adjusted basis in the property, the taxpayer recognizes gain up to the difference. However, if the liabilities assumed give rise to a deduction when paid, such as a trade account payable or interest, no gain is recognized.
    2) If there is no good business reason for the corporation to assume the liabilities, or if the main purpose in the exchange is to avoid federal income tax, treat the assumption as if the taxpayer receives money in the amount of the liabilities.

> Basis of stock or other property received by shareholder
> - The basis of the stock received is generally the adjusted basis of the property transferred.
>   1) Increase basis by any amount treated as a dividend and by any gain recognized.
>   2) Decrease basis by any cash received (other than payment for services), the FMV of any other property received, and any loss recognized on the exchange. Also, decrease basis by the amount of liability the corporation or another party to the exchange assumed, unless payment of the liability gives rise to a deduction when paid.
> - The basis of any other property received by the shareholder is its FMV on the date of the trade.

- **Paid-in-capital** – Contributions to the capital of a corporation, whether or not by shareholders, are paid-in-capital. These contributions are not taxable to the corporation. The corporation's basis of property contributed by a shareholder is the same as the basis the shareholder had in the property, increased by any gain the shareholder recognized on the exchange. The basis of property contributed to capital by a person other than a shareholder is $0.
- **Election to reduce basis** – In a Section 351 transaction, if the basis of the property transferred exceeds the property's FMV, the parties may irrevocably elect to treat the basis of the stock received by the shareholder as having a basis equal to the FMV of the property transferred.

Detailed Examples of Corporate Transactions

Two shareholders each contribute property to a corporation in exchange for stock with a fair market value (FMV) of $50,000. Each shareholder now owns 50% of the corporation.

Shareholder A – Contributes $30,000 cash and a trailer with $15,000 basis and $20,000 FMV.

Shareholder B – Contributes a tractor with $20,000 basis and $60,000 FMV. The corporation pays $10,000 to Shareholder B in the transaction.

When applying the principal of control consider all shares of the transferors even if they are not related parties. The combined ownership of these shareholders is more than 80% immediately after the transaction. They have control, and the transaction is a §351 exchange. The exchange is non-taxable unless the shareholder receives money, property, or a relief of liabilities.

Shareholder A – Does not receive any property or recognize gain. The basis of stock for this shareholder is $45,000, the adjusted basis of property and money transferred to the corporation.

Shareholder B – Must recognize a gain up to the amount of property received of $10,000. The basis of stock for this shareholder is $20,000. Basis is unchanged because it increases by the $10,000 gain recognized by the shareholder and decreases by the $10,000 payment to the shareholder.

Corporation – Contributions to the capital of a corporation, whether or not by shareholders, are paid-in-capital. These contributions are not taxable to the corporation. The corporation's basis of property contributed by a shareholder is the same as the basis the shareholder had in the property, increased by any gain the shareholder recognized on the exchange. The corporation has a $15,000 basis in the trailer and an adjusted basis of $30,000 in the tractor.

Alternate Scenario #1 – Shareholder A contributes $10,000 in services, $20,000 in cash, and a trailer with a basis of $15,000 and a FMV of $20,000. Shareholder A must recognize income of $10,000; the value of stock received for services. Shareholder A's stock basis is $45,000, the adjusted basis of property and money transferred to the corporation *plus* value of stock received for services. The corporation still has a $15,000 basis in the trailer as this nontaxable exchange qualifies under §351.

Alternate Scenario #2 – Shareholder A contributes $30,000 in services and a trailer with a basis of $15,000 and a FMV of $20,000. This is no longer a nontaxable exchange under §351. The combined stock exchanged for property is only 70%. Shareholder A must recognize income of $30,000 for services performed and $5,000 in gain on the trailer. Shareholder B must recognize the entire gain of $40,000 on the tractor. The corporation now has a basis of $20,000 in the trailer and a basis of $60,000 for the tractor. Each shareholder has a basis of $50,000 in the stock.

Filing and Paying Income Taxes

A corporation generally must make estimated tax payments as it earns or receives income during its tax year. After the end of the tax year, the corporation must file an income tax return.

Income Tax Return

Unless exempt under Section 501 of the Internal Revenue Code, all domestic corporations in existence for any part of a tax year (including corporations in bankruptcy) must file an income tax return whether or not they have taxable income. A corporation generally must file *Form 1120* to report its income, gains, losses, deductions, and credits and to figure its income tax liability.

- **When to file** – Generally, a corporation must file its income tax return by the 15th day of the third month after the end of its tax year (March 15 for calendar year corporations). A new corporation filing a short-period return must generally file by the 15th day of the 3rd month after the short period ends. A corporation that has dissolved must generally file by the 15th day of the third month after the date it dissolved.

- **Extension of time to file** – A corporation uses *Form 7004* to request an automatic six-month extension of time to file a corporation income tax return. The IRS will grant the extension if the form is completed properly, filed timely, and any tax due is paid by the due date for the return. Form 7004 does not extend the time for paying the tax due on the return.

- A corporation must pay tax in full no later than the 15th day of the third month after the end of its tax year.

- All deposits (including Social Security, Medicare, withheld income, excise, and corporate income taxes) must be made by electronic funds transfer. Generally, electronic fund transfers are made using the *Electronic Federal Tax Payment System (EFTPS)*.

Penalties

Without reasonable cause, for each month or part of month a corporation:

- Does not file its tax return by the due date, including extensions, it may be penalized **5%** of the unpaid tax, up to a maximum of **25%** of the unpaid tax. The minimum penalty for a return that is more than 60 days late is the smaller of the tax due or $135.

- Does not pay the tax when due, it may be penalized **one-half of 1%** of the unpaid tax, up to a maximum of **25%** of the unpaid tax.

Estimated Tax

Generally, a corporation must make installment payments if it expects tax for the year to be $500 or more. If the corporation does not pay the installments when they are due, it could be subject to an underpayment penalty. Installment payments are due by the 15th day of the fourth, sixth, ninth, and 12th months of the corporation's tax year. If any due date falls on a Saturday, Sunday, or legal holiday, the installment is due on the next business day. The corporation will generally use one of the following methods to figure each required installment:

- **Method 1** – Each required installment is 25% of the income tax the corporation will show on its return for the current year.

- **Method 2** – Each required installment is 25% of the income tax shown on the corporation's return for the previous year. To use this method:

    1) The corporation must have filed a return for the previous year.

    2) The return must have been for a full 12 months.

    3) The return must have shown a positive tax liability (not $0).

- **Other methods** – If a corporation's income is expected to vary during the year because, for example, its business is seasonal, it may be able to lower the amount of one or more required installments by using one or both of the following methods:

    1) The annualized income installment method

    2) The adjusted seasonal installment method

Quick refund of overpayments – A corporation that has overpaid its estimated tax for the tax year may be able to apply for a quick refund if the overpayment is at least 10% of its expected tax liability and at least $500. The corporation must file *Form 4466, Corporation Application for Quick Refund of Overpayment of Estimated Tax* before the 16th day of the third month after the end of the tax year, and before the corporation files its income tax return. Do not file Form 4466 before the end of the corporation's tax year. The IRS will act on the form within 45 days from the date filed.

Form 1120 Schedules

A corporation with total receipts for the tax year and total assets at the end of the tax year of less than $250,000 is not required to complete Schedules L, M-1, and M-2. All others must report the required information on the appropriate schedules. Please review examples in the back of the book.

- **Schedule L, Balance Sheet per Books** – The balance sheet should agree with the corporation's books and records. Schedule L is a statement of the assets, liabilities, and capital at the beginning and end of the tax year. Total assets should equal the sum of total liabilities and shareholders' equity.

- **Schedule M-1, Reconciliation of Income (Loss) per Books with Income per Return** – Rules of accounting are different for financial (book) and tax reporting purposes. A corporation may report income to shareholders that is different from what it reports to the IRS. A corporation uses Schedule

M-1 of Form 1120 to reconcile book income with the income it reports on its tax return. Book income includes certain items that are not deductions for tax purposes (e.g. nondeductible travel and entertainment expenses). To reconcile with income for tax reporting purposes, the corporation adds these nondeductible amounts to book income. Book income also includes certain items not recognized for tax purposes (e.g. tax-exempt interest). Subtract these items from book income to arrive at the corporation's income per return. A corporation with total assets of $10 million or more on the last day of the tax year must complete Schedule M-3 instead of Schedule M-1.

- **Schedule M-2** – Tracks the adjusted items of income (loss), deductions, and distributions. Schedule M-2 provides insight into the taxation of distributions to shareholders.

    1) Analysis of Unappropriated Retained Earnings per Books (C corporation) –This reflects the amount available for shareholders as dividends.

    2) Analysis of Accumulated Adjustments Account, Other Adjustments Account, and Shareholders' Undistributed Taxable Income Previously Taxed (S Corporation) – These accounts influence the taxation of distributions to shareholders.

Income, Deductions, and Special Provisions

Rules on income and deductions that apply to individuals also apply, for the most part, to corporations. However, the following special provisions apply <u>only</u> to corporations.

Related Persons

A corporation that uses an accrual method of accounting cannot deduct business expenses and interest owed to a related person who uses the cash method of accounting until the corporation makes the payment and the corresponding amount is <u>includible</u> in the related person's gross income. Determine the relationship, for this rule, as of the end of the tax year for which the expense or interest would otherwise be deductible. If the IRS denies a deduction, the rule will continue to apply even if the corporation's relationship with the person ends before the expense or interest is includible in the gross income of that person. These rules also <u>deny the deduction of losses on the sale or exchange</u> of property between related persons.

- **Related persons** – For purposes of this rule, the following persons are related to a corporation:

    1) Another corporation that is a member of the same controlled group (*see control, earlier*)

    2) An individual who owns, directly or indirectly, more than 50% of the value of the outstanding stock of the corporation

    3) A trust fiduciary when the trust or the grantor of the trust owns, directly or indirectly, more than 50% in value of the outstanding stock of the corporation

    4) An S corporation if the same persons own more than 50% in value of the outstanding stock of each corporation

    5) A partnership if the same persons own more than 50% in value of the outstanding stock of the corporation and more than 50% of the capital or profits interest in the partnership

    6) Any employee-owner if the corporation is a personal service corporation, regardless of the amount of stock owned by the employee-owner

- **Ownership of stock** – The following rules determine whether an individual directly or indirectly owns any of the outstanding stock of a corporation:

    1) Stock owned, directly or indirectly, by a corporation, partnership, estate, or trust is treated as being owned proportionately by or for its shareholders, partners, or beneficiaries.

2) Treat an individual as owning the stock owned, directly or indirectly, by or for the individual's family. Family includes only brothers and sisters (including half-brothers and half-sisters), a spouse, ancestors, and lineal descendants.

3) Any individual owning (other than by applying rule 2) any stock in a corporation is treated as owning the stock owned directly or indirectly by that individual's partner.

Capital Losses

A corporation can deduct capital losses only up to the amount of its capital gains. In other words, if a corporation has an excess capital loss, it cannot deduct the loss in the current tax year. Instead, it carries the loss to other tax years and deducts it from any net capital gains that occur in those years. The character of a net capital loss carried to another tax year is always short-term. A corporation may not carry a capital loss from, or to, a year for which it is an S corporation.

Carry a capital loss to other years in the following order:
- Three years prior to the loss year
- Two years prior to the loss year
- One year prior to the loss year
- Carry forward any remaining loss for five years

Net Operating Losses

A corporation generally figures and deducts a net operating loss (NOL) the same way an individual, estate, or trust does. The same two-year carry-back and up to 20-year carry-forward periods apply, and the same sequence applies when the corporation carries two or more NOLs to the same year.

- **Figuring the NOL** – If its deductions are more than its gross income, the corporation has an NOL. The following rules apply when calculating NOL:

    1) NOL cannot increase because of carry-backs or carry-overs from other years.

    2) A corporation cannot consider the domestic production activities deduction.

    3) A corporation can take the deduction for dividends received without regard to the aggregate limits (based on taxable income) that normally apply.

    4) A corporation can figure the deduction for dividends paid on certain preferred stock of public utilities without limiting it to its taxable income for the year.

- **Claiming the NOL Deduction** – Generally, a corporation must carry NOL back two years prior to the year the NOL is generated. If the NOL is not used in the prior two years, the remaining NOL can be carried forward for up to 20 years after the tax year in which the NOL was generated. A corporation may elect to waive the carry-back period and use only the carry-forward period.

Shareholder Earnings and Profits (E&P)

The *earnings and profits* of a corporation determine the character of distributions paid to shareholders. If a corporation's E&P for the year (figured as of the close of the year without reduction for any distributions made during the year) is more than the total amount of distributions made during the year, all distributions made during the year are treated as dividends (distributions of *current year E&P*). Shareholders of a corporation receive dividend tax treatment for a distribution of E&P regardless of whether the source of E&P is taxable or tax-free income. If the distributions exceed current year E&P, the distribution may still be a dividend, provided the corporation has accumulated E&P. If the corporation has no E&P, the distribution is not a dividend and may be a tax-free return of capital or a capital gain. E&P is taxable income, plus or minus certain adjustments. Items the corporation must add back to taxable income to calculate E&P include the following:

- Muni bond interest
- Excluded life insurance proceeds
- Federal income tax refunds
- Dividends received deduction

Accumulated E&P

If a corporation's current year E&P is less than the total distributions made during the year, treat part or all of each distribution as a distribution of *accumulated E&P*. Accumulated E&P is earnings and profits the corporation accumulated (did not distribute) in previous years.

- If the corporation has current year E&P, figure the use of E&P as follows:

    1) Divide the current year E&P by the total distributions made during the year.

    2) Multiply each distribution by the percentage to get the amount treated as a distribution of current year E&P.

    3) Start with the first distribution, and treat the part of each distribution greater than the allocated current year E&P figured in (2) as a distribution of accumulated E&P.

    4) If accumulated E&P is reduced to $0, the remaining part of each distribution is applied against, and reduces, the adjusted basis of the stock in the hands of the shareholders. To the extent that the balance is more than the adjusted basis of the stock, treat it as a gain from the sale or exchange of property.

Example 13-1 – You are the only shareholder of a corporation that uses the calendar year as its tax year. In January, you figure your corporation's current year earnings and profits for the previous year. At the beginning of the year, the corporation's accumulated earnings and profits balance was $20,000. During the year, the corporation made four $4,000 distributions to you ($4,000 × 4 = $16,000). At the end of the year (before subtracting distributions made during the year), the corporation had $10,000 of current year earnings and profits.

Since the corporation's current year earnings of $10,000 are less than distributions made during the year of $16,000, treat part of each distribution as a distribution of accumulated earnings and profits. Divide the $10,000 by $16,000 and the result is .625. Multiply each $4,000 distribution by .625 to get $2,500, which is the amount of each distribution treated as a distribution of current year earnings and profits. Treat the remaining $1,500 of each distribution as a distribution from accumulated earnings and profits. The corporation distributed $6,000 ($1,500 × 4) of accumulated earnings. The remaining $14,000 ($20,000 − $6,000) of accumulated earnings is available for use in the following year.

- If there is no current year E&P (a loss), figure the use of accumulated E&P as follows:

    1) Prorate the current year loss to the date of each distribution made during the year.

    2) Figure the available accumulated E&P balance on the date of each distribution by subtracting the prorated amount of current year E&P from the accumulated balance.

    3) Treat each distribution as a distribution of the adjusted accumulated E&P.

4) If adjusted accumulated E&P is reduced to $0, the remaining distributions are applied against, and reduce, the adjusted basis of the stock in the hands of the shareholders. Treat any balance that is more than the adjusted basis of the stock as a gain from the sale or exchange of property.

Example 13-2 – Same circumstances as prior example, except at the end of the year (before subtracting distributions made during the year), the corporation had a <u>negative</u> $10,000 current year earnings and profits balance. The distributions occur on March 31, June 30, September 30, and December 31.

Accumulated earnings and profits		$20,000
less: Prorated current year earnings and profits	$2,500	
Accumulated earnings and profits available		$17,500
less: Amount of Mar 31 distribution treated as a dividend	$4,000	
Accumulated earnings and profits		$13,500
less: Prorated current year earnings and profits	$2,500	
Accumulated earnings and profits available		$11,000
less: Amount of Jun 30 distribution treated as a dividend	$4,000	
Accumulated earnings and profits		$7,000
less: Prorated current year earnings and profits	$2,500	
Accumulated earnings and profits available		$4,500
less: Amount of Sep 30 distribution treated as a dividend	$4,000	
Accumulated earnings and profits		$500
less: Prorated current year earnings and profits	$2,500	
Accumulated earnings and profits available		($2,000)
Amount of Dec 31 distribution treated as a dividend	$0	
Dec 31 Nondividend amount (reduces basis)	$4,000	
Year-end accumulated earnings and profits		($2,000)

Since the corporation had no current year earnings and profits, treat all of the distributions as distributions of accumulated earnings and profits. Prorate the negative current year earnings and profits balance to the date of each distribution made during the year. Spread the negative $10,000 evenly by prorating a negative $2,500 to each distribution.

Distribution and Recognition Requirements

In general, treat corporate distributions to a shareholder as:

- **Dividends** – If the distribution is from current or accumulated E&P

- **Non-dividend distribution** – Any part of a distribution that is not from E&P is applied against and reduces the adjusted basis of the stock in the hands of the shareholder

- **Gain** – To the extent the distribution is more than the adjusted basis of the stock, the shareholder has a gain (usually a capital gain) from the sale or exchange of property

Most distributions are in money, but they may also be in stock or other property. If distributions of property occur, other than stock dividends or rights, the amount of the distribution is generally the amount of any money paid to the shareholder plus the FMV of the property, reduced by any liabilities assumed. The basis of the property to the shareholder is the FMV of the property. In general, distributions are <u>taxable as dividends</u> to the extent of E&P.

Gain from Property Distributions

A corporation will recognize a gain on the distribution of property to a shareholder if the FMV of the property is <u>more</u> than its adjusted basis. This treatment is similar to a sale of property by the corporation. If the property was depreciable or amortizable, the corporation may have to treat all or part of the gain as ordinary income from depreciation recapture. For this purpose, the FMV of the property is the <u>greater</u> of the following amounts:

- The actual FMV
- The amount of any liabilities a shareholder assumed connected to the distribution of property

Distributions of Stock or Stock Rights

Distributions by a corporation of its stock are stock dividends. Stock rights (stock options) are distributions by a corporation of rights to acquire its stock. Distributions of stock dividends and stock rights are generally tax free to shareholders. Treat the distribution of stock or stock rights the same as other property if any of the following apply:

- Any shareholder has the choice to receive cash or other property instead of stock or stock rights.
- The distribution gives cash or other property to some shareholders and an increase in the percentage interest in the corporation's assets or E&P to other shareholders.
- The distribution is in convertible preferred stock and has the same result as previous rule.
- The distribution gives preferred stock to some shareholders and common stock to others.
- The distribution is on preferred stock.

Deemed Distributions

The following events may be treated as a distribution to a shareholder:

- **Below-market loans** – If a corporation gives a shareholder a loan on which no interest is charged or on which interest is charged at a rate below the applicable federal rate, the interest not charged may be treated as a distribution to the shareholder.
- **Corporation cancels shareholder's debt** – If a corporation cancels a shareholder's debt without repayment by the shareholder, treat the amount canceled as a distribution.
- **Transfers of property to shareholders for less than FMV** – A sale or exchange of property by a corporation to a shareholder may be treated as a distribution to the shareholder. If a shareholder is not a corporation and the FMV of the property on the date of sale or exchange exceeds the price paid by the shareholder, the excess may be treated as a distribution.
- **Unreasonable rents** – If a corporation rents property from a shareholder at above market rates, the excessive part of the rent may be treated as a distribution to the shareholder.
- **Unreasonable salaries** – If a corporation pays an employee who is also a shareholder a salary that is unreasonably high considering the services actually performed by the shareholder-employee, the excessive part of the salary may be treated as a distribution.

Form 1099-DIV

The corporation must generally send Forms 1099-DIV to the IRS with Form 1096 <u>by February 28</u> (March 31 if filing electronically) of the year following the year of the distribution. Generally, a corporation must furnish Forms 1099-DIV to shareholders by <u>January 31</u> of the year following the close of the calendar year during which the corporation made the distributions. It is necessary to file a ***Form 1099-DIV*** with the IRS for each person the corporation:

- Paid dividends (including capital gain dividends) and other distributions on stock of $10 or more,
- Withheld and paid any foreign tax on dividends and other distributions on stock,
- Withheld any federal income tax on dividends under the backup withholding rules, or
- Paid $600 or more as part of a liquidation

Redemption of Stock

A stock redemption is the acquisition of corporate stock from a shareholder in exchange for money or property. Treat stock redemptions as a distribution, in part or full payment, in exchange for stock. The transaction is a sale or trade and subject to the capital gain or loss provisions unless considered a dividend or other distribution on stock.

> Treat the redemption as a sale or trade of stock if any of the following are true:
> - The redemption is not essentially equivalent to a dividend.
> - The redemption is substantially disproportionate and is a distribution in partial liquidation:
>   1) Immediately after the redemption, the shareholder owns less than 50% of the total combined voting power of all classes of stock entitled to vote, and
>   2) The ratio of ownership is less than 80% of the ratio of ownership prior to the redemption.
> - There is a complete redemption of all the stock of the corporation owned by the shareholder.

Whether the redemption is treated as a sale, trade, dividend, or other distribution depends on the circumstances in each case. Both direct and indirect ownership of stock is considered.

Liquidating Distributions

Liquidating distributions are distributions received during a partial or complete liquidation of a corporation. These distributions are, at least in part, one form of a return of capital. The corporation may pay them in one or more installments.

> A liquidating distribution is **not** taxable until the taxpayer recovers the basis of the stock. After the basis of the stock is reduced to $0, the liquidating distribution is a capital gain, either long-term or short-term depending on how long the taxpayer held the stock.

If the total liquidating distributions are less than the basis of the stock, the shareholder has a capital loss, reportable only after receipt of the final distribution in liquidation that results in the redemption or cancellation of the stock. The disallowance of losses from the sale or exchange of property between related persons does not apply to liquidating distributions.

Special Deductions

Dividends-received Deduction

A corporation can deduct a percentage of the dividends received, within certain limits, if the corporation receiving the dividend, based on voting power and value:

- Owns less than 20% of the distributing corporation's stock, it can deduct 70% of the dividends, or
- Owns 20% or more of the distributing corporation's stock, it can deduct 80% of the dividends.

Small business investment companies and *affiliated corporations* can deduct 100% of the dividends received from taxable domestic corporations. A corporation can make a one-time election to deduct 85% of the dividends received from a controlled foreign corporation. Corporations cannot take a deduction for dividends received from the following entities:

- A real estate investment trust (REIT)
- A corporation exempt from tax under Section 501 or 521 of the Internal Revenue Code either for the tax year of the distribution or the preceding tax year
- A corporation whose stock was held less than 46 days during the 91-day period, beginning 45 days before the stock became *ex-dividend* (when the holder has no rights to the dividend)
- A corporation whose preferred stock was held less than 91 days during the 181-day period, beginning 90 days before the stock became ex-dividend with respect to the dividend if the dividends received are for a period or periods totaling more than 360 days
- Any corporation, if taxpayer's corporation is under an obligation to make related payments with respect to positions in substantially similar or related property

Charitable Contributions

A corporation can claim a limited deduction for charitable contributions made in cash or other property. The contribution is deductible if made to, or for the use of, a qualified organization. The corporation cannot take a deduction if any of the net earnings of an organization receiving contributions benefit any private shareholder. A corporation cannot deduct charitable contributions that exceed 10% of its taxable income for the tax year. Figure taxable income for this purpose without the following:

- The deduction for charitable contributions
- The dividends-received deduction
- The deduction allowed under Section 249 of the Internal Revenue Code
- The domestic production activities deduction
- Any net operating loss or capital loss carry back to the tax year

A corporation may carry forward to each of the subsequent five years any charitable contributions made during the current year that exceed the 10% limit. For a contribution of property, the corporation must reduce the contribution by the sum of the following:

- The ordinary income and short-term capital gain that would result if the property is sold at FMV, and
- For certain contributions, the long-term capital gain that would have resulted if the property were sold at its FMV. The reduction for the long-term capital gain applies to the following:
    1) Contributions of tangible personal property for use by an exempt organization for a purpose or function unrelated to the basis for its exemption
    2) Contributions of any property to or for the use of certain private foundations (except for stock)
    3) Contributions of any patent, certain copyrights, trademark, trade name, trade secret, know-how, software (that is a Section 197 intangible), or similar property, or applications or registrations of such property

Figuring Tax

A corporation must determine taxable income and figure its tax using the following tax rate schedule. An exception to the schedule is a *qualified* personal service corporation, where a flat rate of 35% applies.

Table 13-1. 2015 Corporate Tax Rate Schedule

Tax Rate Schedule			
If taxable income (line 30, Form 1120, or line 26, Form 1120-A) is:			
Over—	But not over—	Tax is:	Of the amount over—
$0	$50,000	15%	$0
$50,000	$75,000	$7,500 + **25%**	$50,000
$75,000	$100,000	$13,750 + **34%**	$75,000
$100,000	$335,000	$22,250 + **39%**	$100,000
$335,000	$10,000,000	$113,900 + **34%**	$335,000
$10,000,000	$15,000,000	$3,400,000 + **35%**	$10,000,000
$15,000,000	$18,333,333	$5,150,000 + **38%**	$15,000,000
$18,333,333	No Limit	35%	$0

Alternative Minimum Tax (AMT)

The tax laws give special treatment to some types of income and allow special deductions and credits for some types of expenses. These laws enable some corporations with substantial economic income to reduce their regular tax significantly. The corporate alternative minimum tax (AMT) ensures that corporations pay at least a minimum amount of tax on economic income.

- The tentative minimum tax is 20% of Alternative Minimum Taxable Income (AMTI) that exceeds the exemption amount.

- The exemption amount is $40,000 reduced by 25% of the excess AMTI more than $150,000.

- A corporation (that is not an exempt small corporation) owes AMT if its tentative minimum tax is more than its regular tax.

   1) The tentative minimum tax of a small corporation is $0. A corporation is treated as a small corporation exempt from the AMT for its current tax year in the corporation's first tax year in existence (regardless of its gross receipts for the year) or:

   2) It was a small corporation exempt from the AMT for all prior tax years after 1997, and

   3) Its average annual gross receipts for the three-tax-year period ending before its current tax year did not exceed $7.5 million ($5 million if the corporation had only one prior tax year)

- A corporation with AMT liability in the current year may recapture that amount in future years in the form of a credit. This non-refundable credit can offset future tax liability only to the extent prior AMT tax paid was due to deferral items. The credit cannot reduce tax below the tentative minimum tax for the year. Any unused credit carries forward indefinitely.

Generally, a corporation must file Form 4626 if any of the following apply:

- The corporation is not a "small corporation" exempt from the AMT.

- The corporation's taxable income or (loss) before the net operating loss (NOL) deduction plus its adjustments and preferences total more than the $40,000 AMT exemption amount or, if smaller, its allowable exemption amount.

- The corporation claims any general business credit, any qualified electric vehicle passive activity credit from prior years, or the credit for prior year minimum tax.

Accumulated Earnings Tax

While corporations are not required to distribute income, the law discourages them from building an investment portfolio subject only to the corporate income tax. A corporation can accumulate its earnings for a possible expansion or other bona fide business reasons. Earnings accumulate beyond the reasonable needs of the business may be subject to an accumulated earnings tax of 20%. To determine if the corporation is subject to this tax, treat an accumulation of $250,000 ($150,000 for PSC) or less generally as within the reasonable needs of most businesses. Reasonable needs of the business include the following:

- Specific, definite, and feasible plans for use of the earnings accumulation in the business, or
- The amount necessary to redeem stock included in a deceased shareholder's gross estate.

Personal Holding Company Tax

A tax rate of 20% may apply to undistributed *personal holding company* (PHC) income. This tax discourages using closely held corporations to attempt to avoid personal income taxes on investment income. Generally, a corporation is a PHC if it meets both of the following requirements:

- **Stock ownership requirement** – At any time during the last half of the tax year, more than 50% in value of the corporation's stock is owned—directly or indirectly—by five or fewer individuals.
- **PHC income test** – At least 60% of the corporation's adjusted ordinary gross income for the tax year is PHC income. PHC income includes income from dividends, interest, rents, and certain royalties.

S Corporations

An eligible domestic corporation can avoid double taxation by electing treatment as an *S corporation (SCORP)*. Like a partnership, an SCORP is a flow through entity.

> Generally, an SCORP is exempt from federal income tax other than tax on certain capital gains and passive income. On their tax returns, the SCORP shareholders include their share of the corporation's separately stated items of income, deduction, loss, and credit, and their share of non-separately stated ordinary business income or loss reported to them on **Schedule K-1 (Form 1120s)**.

Separately Stated Items

Some of the items stated separately on *Schedule K-1 (Form 1120s)* include the following:

- Net rental real estate income (loss)
- Other net rental income (loss)
- Interest income (loss)
- Ordinary and qualified dividends
- Royalties
- Capital gains and losses (LTCG, STCG, 1250, and 1231)
- Collectibles (28%) gains (loss)
- Section 179 deduction
- Foreign transactions
- AMT items
- Items affecting shareholder basis (including drilling costs)

- Charitable contributions
- Credits

Taxes

The income tax filing deadline and extension rules are the same as they would be for a CCORP. In most cases, all items pass through to SCORP shareholders; however, there are circumstances where the SCORP may have income tax liability if the SCORP was <u>previously</u> a CCORP and has:

- **Built-in gains** – If SCORP has a net recognized built-in gain on assets held when it was a CCORP
- **Excess net passive income** – An SCORP with accumulated E&P that has passive investment income exceeding 25% of gross receipts must pay tax on excess net passive income
- **LIFO recapture tax** – If CCORP had LIFO inventory and changed (or transferred it) to an SCORP
- **Investment Credit Recapture** – The SCORP may need to recapture certain credits allowed for periods it was not an SCORP

S Corporation Filing Penalties

An S corporation that is without reasonable cause is subject to penalties for the following failures:

- **Late filing** – $195 for each month or part of a month (for a maximum of 12 months) the failure continues, multiplied by the total number of persons who were shareholders in the S corporation during any part of the S corporation's tax year for which the return is due.
- **Failure to furnish K-1 to shareholder** – $100 for each Schedule K-1 for which a failure occurs. If the requirement to report correct information is intentionally disregarded the penalty increases to $250 or, if greater, 10% of the amount required to be reported.

The "S" Election

To receive S corporation treatment, a domestic corporation or other domestic entity eligible to elect to be treated as a corporation (such as LLC) must make the election on *Form 2553*. The corporation must file Form 2553 no more than <u>two months and 15 days</u> after the beginning of the tax year the election is to take effect, or in the year prior.

> To be an S corporation, the entity must meet <u>all</u> the following tests:
>
> - It must be a small business corporation:
>   1) It has no more than <u>100</u> shareholders.
>   2) All shareholders are individuals, estates, exempt organizations, or certain trusts (<u>not partnerships or corporations</u>).
>   3) It has <u>no</u> nonresident alien shareholders.
>   4) It has <u>only</u> one class of stock.
> - It is <u>not</u> one of the following <u>ineligible</u> corporations:
>   1) A bank or thrift institution that uses the reserve method of accounting
>   2) An insurance company subject to tax
>   3) A corporation that has elected to be treated as a possessions corporation
>   4) A domestic international sales corporation (DISC) or former DISC

A parent S corporation can elect to treat an eligible wholly-owned subsidiary as a qualified subchapter S subsidiary. If the corporation makes this election, the subsidiary's assets, liabilities, and items of income, deduction, and credit generally are treated as those of the parent.

An entity intending to be classified as an S corporation that fails to make a timely "S" election may qualify for late election relief under Revenue Procedure 2013-30. There must be reasonable cause, and generally less than 3 years and 75 days have passed since the effective date of the election.

Termination of Election

Once the corporation makes the election it stays in effect until terminated. If the corporation terminates the election, the corporation (or a successor corporation) can make another election on Form 2553 only with IRS consent for any tax year before the fifth tax year after termination. An election terminates automatically in any of the following cases:

- The corporation is no longer a small business corporation.
- The corporation, for each of three consecutive tax years, has accumulated earnings and profits and derives more than 25% of its gross receipts from passive investment income.
- The election is revoked with the consent of shareholders who hold more than 50% of the number of issued and outstanding shares of stock (including non-voting stock).

Income and Expenses

Unlike a partnership, the shareholders of an SCORP receive a share of income (or loss) and separately stated items in proportion to the percentage ownership of each shareholder. Ownership is determined for each day of the year. A shareholder cannot deduct a loss that exceeds the basis of his stock increased by any loans the shareholder made to the SCORP. A shareholder may carry forward any disallowed loss indefinitely. The amount of a shareholder's stock and debt basis is very important. Unlike a C corporation, the stock and/or debt basis of an S corporation goes up and/or down each year based upon the S corporation's operations.

Distributions

The earnings and profits of an SCORP are taxable to its shareholders, whether distributed or not. The taxable amount of distribution is contingent on the shareholder's stock basis. It is not the corporation's responsibility to track a shareholder's stock and debt basis; rather it is the shareholder's responsibility. Treat a distribution to shareholders from an SCORP that does not have accumulated E&P as a return of capital up to the shareholders' basis, and as gain from the sale or exchange of property on the excess. Generally, the S corporation has accumulated E&P only if it has not distributed E&P accumulated in prior years when the S corporation was a C corporation. Treat the portion of a distribution attributed to accumulated E&P as a dividend. If the S corporation has AE&P it must maintain the following accounts to determine taxable dividends:

- **Accumulated Adjustments Account (AAA)** – The accumulated adjustments account (AAA) is an account of the S corporation that generally reflects the accumulated undistributed net income of the corporation after 1982.
- **Accumulated Earnings and Profits Account (AE&P)** – Generally, S corporation accumulated E&P is from undistributed E&P accumulated in prior years when the S corporation was a C corporation.
- **Other Adjustments Account (OAA)** – The OAA tracks tax-exempt income if the S corporation has AE&P. Tax-exempt income increases shareholder basis. Treat OAA as non-taxable distribution to the shareholder, reducing the shareholder's basis.

Ordering rules determine the taxation of distributions:

1) Accumulated Adjustments Account (AAA) . . . . Not Taxable
2) Accumulated Earnings and Profits (AE&P). . . . Taxable Dividend
3) Other Adjustments Account (OAA) . . . . Not Taxable
4) Stock Basis/Return of Capital . . . . Not Taxable
5) In Excess of Stock Basis . . . . Capital Gain

Accumulated Adjustments Account

S corporations with accumulated E&P must maintain the AAA to determine the tax effect of distributions. On the first day of the corporation's first tax year as an S corporation, the balance of the AAA is $0. At the end of the tax year, adjust the AAA for the items as explained below:

- Increase the AAA by net income (other than tax-exempt income).
- Decrease AAA (but not below $0) by property distributions (other than dividends from accumulated E&P).

With the consent of all its affected shareholders, an SCORP can make an election to distribute accumulated E&P before the AAA, or they can elect to distribute all or part of the accumulated E&P with a deemed dividend. Otherwise, apply property distributions (including cash) in the following order (to reduce accounts of the SCORP to figure the tax effect of distributions made to its shareholders):

- Reduce the AAA by the amount of the distribution, but not below $0. Distributions from this account are a return of capital and reduce the shareholders' basis.
- Reduce the *previously taxed income (PTI)* account by any remaining amount, but not below $0. This account is for income prior to 1983. It is reduced only if there is a balance. Like the AAA, distributions from this account are tax free to the extent of the shareholders' basis.
- Reduce accumulated E&P by any amount remaining, but not below $0. Treat distributions from accumulated E&P as dividends.
- The remaining distributions are return of capital, up to the shareholders' basis. If the shareholders' basis is reduced to $0, the remainder is a capital gain.

For simplification purposes, this guide does not show these rules in their entirety.

Distributions of appreciated property are valued at FMV. The SCORP will recognize a gain (but not a loss) on the property to the extent that FMV of the property exceeds its basis. The gain will pass through to the shareholders on the K-1.

Shareholder Stock Basis in SCORP

In computing stock basis, the shareholder starts with the initial capital contribution to the S corporation or the initial cost of the stock purchased (the same as a C corporation). That amount is then increased and/or decreased based on the flow-through amounts from the S corporation. An income item will increase stock basis, while a loss, deduction, or distribution will decrease stock basis.

The order in which stock basis is increased or decreased is important. Since both the taxability of a distribution and the deductibility of a loss are dependent on stock basis, there is an ordering rule in computing stock basis. Stock basis adjusts annually, as of the last day of the S corporation year, in the following order:

1) Increased for income items and excess depletion;

2) Decreased for distributions;

3) Decreased for non-deductible, non-capital expenses and depletion; and

4) Decreased for items of loss and deduction.

If a shareholder receives a non-dividend distribution from an S corporation, the distribution is tax-free to the extent it does not exceed the shareholder's stock basis. A shareholder treats a non-dividend distribution in excess of stock basis as a capital gain (usually LTCG) on the shareholder's personal return.

- Shareholder basis is <u>increased</u> by the total of:

    1) Separately stated Items of income (including tax-exempt)

    2) Non-separately computed income

    3) The excess of the deductions for depletion over the basis of the property

- Shareholder basis is <u>decreased</u> by:

    1) Distributions by the corporation not includible in the income of the shareholder

    2) Separately stated loss items

    3) Non-separately computed loss

    4) Any expense of the corporation not deductible in computing its taxable income and not properly chargeable to capital account

    5) The shareholder's deduction for depletion for any oil and gas property held by the SCORP

14 Partnerships

Forming · Partnership Return · Limitations · Unrealized Receivables and Inventory
Distributions to Partners · Transactions · Basis · Disposition of Interest

Information from IRS Form 1065 instructions, Pub. 538 and 541, and IRC §444, §704, and §706

Forming a Partnership

An unincorporated organization formed after 1996 with two or more members is generally classified as a partnership. This organization is formed to carry on a trade or business, with each person contributing money, property, labor, or skill, and each expecting to share in the profits and losses of the business, whether or not a formal partnership agreement is made. Certain organizations are not partnerships:

- An organization formed under a federal or state law that refers to it as incorporated or as a corporation, body corporate, or body politic
- An organization formed under a state law that refers to it as a joint-stock company or joint-stock association
- An insurance company
- Certain banks
- An organization wholly owned by a state or local government
- An organization specifically required to be taxed as a corporation by the IRS
- Certain foreign organizations
- A tax-exempt organization
- A real estate investment trust
- An organization classified as a trust
- Any other organization that elects classification as a corporation

Partnership Agreement

The partnership agreement includes the original agreement and any modifications. All partners must agree to any modifications, or the partnership must adopt any modifications in any other manner provided by the partnership agreement. The agreement or modifications can be oral or written. Partners can modify the partnership agreement for a particular tax year after the close of the year but not later than the date for filing the partnership return for that year. This filing date does not include any extension of time. If the partnership agreement or any modification is silent on any matter, treat the provisions of local law as part of the agreement.

Exclusion from Partnership Rules

Certain partnerships that do not actively conduct business can choose complete or partial exclusion from treatment as a partnership for federal income tax purposes. All partners must agree to make the choice, and the partners must be able to compute their own taxable income without computing the partnership's income. An eligible organization that desires exclusion from the partnership rules must make the election on *Form 1065* no later than the time for filing the partnership return for the first tax year for which the organization desires exclusion, including extensions.

Family Partnership

Members of a family can be partners. The IRS will only recognize family members (or any other persons) as partners if one of the following is true:

- If capital is a material income-producing factor, they acquired their capital interest in a bona fide transaction (including gift or purchase), and actually own and control the partnership interest. Capital is a material income-producing factor if a substantial part of the gross income of the business comes from the use of capital.

- If capital is not a material income-producing factor, they joined in good faith to conduct business. They agreed that contributions of each entitle them to a share in the profits, and some capital or service has been (or is) provided by each partner. Capital is not material income-producing factor if business income consists primarily of fees, commissions, or other compensation for personal services performed by members or employees of the partnership.

If a family member receives a gift of a capital interest in a partnership, in which capital is a material income-producing factor, the donee's distributive share of partnership income is subject to both of the following restrictions:

- It must be figured by reducing the partnership income by reasonable compensation for services the donor renders to the partnership.

- The donee's distributive share of partnership income attributable to donated capital must not be proportionately greater than the donor's share attributable to the donor's capital.

If spouses carry on a business together and share in the profits and losses, they may be partners whether or not they have a formal partnership agreement. A husband and wife can elect not to treat the joint venture as a partnership if they meet each of the following requirements:

- The only members of the joint venture are the husband and wife.
- The filing status of the husband and wife is married filing jointly.
- Both spouses materially participate in the trade or business.
- Both spouses elect this treatment.

If both spouses elect this treatment, all income, gains, losses, deductions, and credits are divided based on each spouse's interest in the joint venture, and both spouses are treated as sole proprietors for income and self-employment tax. If the spouses do not make this election, they should carry their respective shares of the partnership income or loss from Schedule K-1 to their joint or separate Form(s) 1040. Each spouse should include his respective share of self-employment income on a separate Schedule SE. This generally does not increase the total tax on the return, but it does give each spouse credit for Social Security earnings on which retirement benefits are based.

Limited Partnership

A limited partnership is formed under a state limited partnership law and composed of at least one general partner and one or more limited partners.

- A general partner is personally liable for partnership debts.
- A limited partner's liability for partnership debts is limited to the amount of money or other property that the partner contributed or is required to contribute to the partnership.

Limited Liability Company

A limited liability company (LLC) is an entity formed under state law by filing articles of organization as an LLC. LLC owners are called members. Unlike a partnership, LLC members are not personally liable for company debts. An LLC may be classified for federal income tax purposes as either a partnership, a corporation (including an S corporation), or for a single member LLC, an entity disregarded as an entity separate from its owner. By default, a multi-member LLC is taxed as a partnership. The LLC may elect treatment as a corporation by filing Form 8832 (Form 2553 for SCORP).

Terminating a Partnership

A partnership terminates when one of the following events takes place:

- All of its operations are discontinued, and no part of any business, financial operation, or venture is continued by any of its partners in a partnership.
- One or more of the partners sell or exchange at least 50% of the total interest in partnership capital and profits within a 12-month period. This includes a sale or exchange to other partners.

Unlike other partnerships, an *electing large partnership* does not terminate on the sale or exchange of 50% or more of the partnership interests within a 12-month period. The partnership's tax year ends on the date of termination. If a partnership terminates before the end of the tax year or changes tax years, the partnership must file Form 1065 for the *short period*, which is the period from the beginning of the tax year through the date of termination or change. The return is due the 15th day of the fourth month following the date of termination.

Partnership Return (Form 1065)

Form 1065 is an information return used to report income, gains, losses, deductions, credits, etc., from the operation of a partnership. The partnership does not pay taxes; instead, income or loss items "pass through" to its partners. *Schedule K-1* states each partner's *distributive share* of these items for partners to include on their own tax returns:

- Income (loss) items
    1) Ordinary business income (loss)
    2) Net rental real estate income (loss)
    3) Other net rental income (loss)
    4) Guaranteed payments
- Portfolio income
    1) Interest income
    2) Ordinary and qualified dividends
    3) Royalties

4) Net short-term and long-term capital gain (loss)

  5) Collectibles (28%) gain (loss)

  6) Unrecaptured Section 1250 gain

  7) Net Section 1231 gain (loss)

- Deductions

  1) Section 179 deduction

  2) Other deductions (charitable contributions, intangible drilling costs, pensions, etc.)

- Self-employment earnings (loss)
- Credits
- Foreign transactions
- Alternative Minimum Tax (AMT) items
- Tax-exempt income and nondeductible expenses
- Distributions

A partnership is not considered to engage in a trade or business, and is not required to file a *Form 1065*, for any tax year in which it neither receives income nor pays or incurs any expenses treated as deductions or credits for federal income tax purposes. A general partner must sign the return. If a limited liability company is treated as a partnership, it must file Form 1065 and one of its members must sign the return.

When to File

A domestic partnership must file Form 1065 by the 15th day of the fourth month following the date its tax year ended. Taxpayers who need more time to file a partnership return may file Form 7004 to request a five-month extension of time to file. A penalty is assessed against the partnership if it is required to file a partnership return and it fails to file the return by the due date or files a return that fails to show all the information required, unless such failure is due to reasonable cause.

Required Tax Year

A partnership is generally required to have one of the following tax years:

- The tax year of the majority (more than 50%) of its partners
- If there is no majority, the tax year common to all principal partners (5% or more interest)
- If there is neither a majority tax year nor a tax year common to all principal partners, then the tax year that results in the least aggregate deferral of income
- Some other tax year if any of the following apply:

  1) The partnership can establish a business purpose for a different tax year

  2) The partnership elects under Section 444 to have a tax year other than a required tax year

  3) The partnership elects to use a 52-53-week tax year that ends with reference to either its required tax year or a tax year elected under Section 444

Filing Penalties

A partnership that is without reasonable cause is subject to penalties for the following failures:

- **Late filing** – $195 for each month or part of a month (for a maximum of 12 months) the failure continues, multiplied by the total number of persons who were partners in the partnership during any part of the partnership's tax year for which the return is due.

- **Failure to furnish K-1 to partner** – $100 for each Schedule K-1 for which a failure occurs. If the requirement to report correct information is intentionally disregarded the penalty increases to $250 or, if greater, 10% of the amount required to be reported.

Limitations on Losses, Deductions, and Credits

There are three potential limitations on partnership losses. These limitations in the order in which they apply are the *basis rules*, the *at-risk limitations*, and the *passive activity limitations*.

Basis rules – Generally, a partner may not claim a share of a partnership loss greater than the adjusted basis of his partnership interest. A partner may carry forward disallowed losses and deductions due to the basis limit indefinitely and deduct them subject to the basis limit for that year.

At-risk limitations – The at-risk rules generally limit the amount of loss and other deductions that a partner can claim to the amount the partner could actually lose in the activity. These losses and deductions include a loss on the disposition of assets and the Section 179 expense deduction. Generally, a partner is not at risk for amounts such as the following:

- Nonrecourse loans that are not secured by the partner's own property

- Cash, property, or borrowed amounts used in the activity that are protected against loss by a guarantee, stop-loss agreement, or other similar arrangement (excluding casualty insurance and insurance against tort liability)

- Amounts borrowed for use in the activity from a person (or relative of that person) that has an interest in the activity, other than as a creditor

Passive activity limitations – A partner's deduction of passive activity losses and credits may be limited. Generally, passive activities include the following:

- Trade or business activities in which the partner did not materially participate

- Activities that meet the definition of rental activities

Unrealized Receivables and Inventory

The income or a portion of income generated from the use or sale of *unrealized receivables* and *inventory items* is generally taxed as ordinary income rather than capital gain. Therefore, contributions, distributions, or subsequent sales of these assets may receive special treatment.

Unrealized Receivables

The basis for any unrealized receivables includes all costs or expenses for the receivables that were paid or accrued but not previously taken into account under the partnership's method of accounting. Basis is $0 for partnerships that use the cash method of accounting. Unrealized receivables include any rights to payment not already included in income for the following items:

- Goods delivered if payment would be treated as received for property other than a capital asset
- Services rendered or to be rendered
- Other items of potential gain that would be ordinary income if the following partnership property were sold at its fair market value on the date of the payment:

  1) Mining property for which exploration expenses were deducted
  2) Stock in a Domestic International Sales Corporation (DISC)
  3) Certain farm land if costs for soil and water conservation or land clearing were deducted
  4) Franchises, trademarks, or trade names
  5) Oil or gas property for which intangible drilling and development costs were deducted
  6) Stock of certain controlled foreign corporations
  7) Market discount bonds and short-term obligations
  8) Property subject to recapture of depreciation under Sections 1245 and 1250

Inventory Items

Inventory items include the following property:

- Property that would properly be included in the partnership's inventory if on hand at the end of the tax year or that is held primarily for sale to customers
- Property that, if sold or exchanged by the partnership, would not be a capital asset or Section 1231 property
- Property held by the partnership that would be considered inventory if held by the partner selling the partnership interest or receiving the distribution

Inventory items are considered to have appreciated substantially if, at the time of the distribution, the FMV of the inventory is more than 120% of the partnership's adjusted basis for the property.

Partnership Distributions to Partners

A partner must pay taxes on the ***distributive share*** of partnership income allotted to his interest in the partnership, regardless of whether or not the income is distributed. A partner reports his share of income, regardless of distributions, and does not recognize income simply because a distribution occurs.

In general, a distribution is a tax-free return of capital to the partner, and neither the partner nor the partnership recognizes any gain or loss. A partner's adjusted basis in his partnership interest decreases (but not below zero) by the money and adjusted basis of property distributed.

Example 14-1 – The adjusted basis of Jo's partnership interest is $14,000. She receives a distribution of $8,000 cash and land that has a basis of $2,000 and a FMV of $3,000. Because the cash received does not exceed the basis of her partnership interest, Jo does not recognize any gain on the distribution. She will recognize any gain on the land when she sells or otherwise disposes of it. The distribution decreases the adjusted basis of Jo's partnership interest to $4,000 [$14,000 – ($8,000 + $2,000)].

When a Partner Recognizes a Gain

In general, a partner recognizes gain on a partnership distribution only to the extent any money included in the distribution exceeds the adjusted basis of the partner's interest in the partnership. If the partnership distributes property to a partner, that partner generally does not recognize any gain until the sale or other disposition of the property.

Treat any discharge of partnership liabilities as a distribution of money to the partner. A distribution of marketable securities to a partner receives the same treatment as a distribution of money in determining whether the partner will recognize a gain on the distribution. This treatment does not apply if that partner contributed the security to the partnership or an investment partnership made the distribution to an eligible partner.

In general, treat a recognized gain as a <u>capital gain</u> from the sale of the partnership interest on the date of the distribution. A distribution that alters a partner's share of <u>unrealized receivables</u> or <u>substantially appreciated inventory</u> receives <u>ordinary</u> income treatment.

Example 14-2 – The adjusted basis of Jesse's partnership interest is $10,000. He receives a distribution of $12,000 cash. Because the money received exceeds the basis of his partnership interest, Jesse will recognize a gain on the distribution. The distribution decreases the adjusted basis of Jesse's partnership interest to $0 [$10,000 – $12,000], as it cannot be less than zero. The remaining $2,000 is a capital gain.

Partner's Basis for Distributed Property

The basis of property distributed to the partner by a partnership is its adjusted basis to the partnership immediately before the distribution. However, the basis of the property to the partner <u>cannot be more</u> than the adjusted basis of his interest in the partnership, reduced by any money received in the same transaction. A partner's holding period for property distributed to the partner includes the period the partnership held the property. If a partner contributed the property to the partnership, then the period that partner held the property is also included.

Example 14-3 – The adjusted basis of Steve's partnership interest is $10,000. He receives a distribution of $4,000 cash and property that has an adjusted basis to the partnership of $8,000. His basis for the distributed property is limited to $6,000 ($10,000 – $4,000, the cash he receives).

Example 14-4 – The adjusted basis of Jason's partnership interest is $6,000. He receives a distribution of $7,000 cash and a laptop computer that has an adjusted basis of $2,000 and a FMV of $4,000. Because the cash received exceeds the basis of his partnership interest, Jason will recognize a capital gain on the excess money received of $1,000 [$7,000 − $6,000]. The distribution decreases the adjusted basis of Jason's partnership interest to $0 [$6,000 − ($7,000 + $2,000)], as it cannot be less than zero. Since Jason does not have a basis in his partnership interest, the basis of the laptop is $0. He will recognize any gain on the laptop when he sells or otherwise disposes of it.

Liquidating Distributions

A partner does not recognize loss on a distribution unless all the following requirements exist:

- The adjusted basis of the partner's interest in the partnership exceeds the distribution.
- The partner's entire interest in the partnership is liquidated.
- The distribution is in money, unrealized receivables, or inventory items. No loss is recognized if any other property is received.

The basis of property received in complete liquidation of a partner's interest is the adjusted basis of the partner's interest in the partnership, reduced by any money distributed to the partner in the same transaction. If the basis of property received is more than the basis of the partner's interest in the partnership (reduced by money received), it must be divided among the properties distributed to the partner. Allocate the basis using the following rules:

- Allocate the basis first to unrealized receivables and inventory items included in the distribution by assigning a basis to each item equal to the partnership's adjusted basis in the item immediately before the distribution. If the total assigned basis exceeds the allocable basis, decrease the assigned basis by the amount of the excess.
- Allocate any remaining basis to properties other than unrealized receivables and inventory items by assigning a basis to each property equal to the partnership's adjusted basis in the property. If the allocable basis exceeds the total assigned basis, increase the assigned basis by the amount of the excess. If the total assigned basis exceeds the allocable basis, decrease the assigned basis by the amount of the excess.

Example 14-5 – Eun's basis in her partnership interest is $55,000. In a distribution in liquidation of her entire interest, she receives properties A and B, neither of which is inventory or unrealized receivables. Property A has an adjusted basis to the partnership of $5,000 and a fair market value of $40,000. Property B has an adjusted basis to the partnership of $10,000 and a fair market value of $10,000. To figure her basis in each property, Eun first assigns basis of $5,000 to property A and $10,000 to property B (their adjusted basis to the partnership). This leaves a $40,000 basis increase (the $55,000 allocable basis minus the $15,000 total of the assigned basis). She first allocates $35,000 to property A (its unrealized appreciation). She allocates the remaining $5,000 between the properties based on their fair market values: $4,000 ($40,000/$50,000) to property A and $1,000 ($10,000/$50,000) to property B. Eun's basis in property A is $44,000 ($5,000 + $35,000 + $4,000), and her basis in property B is $11,000 ($10,000 + $1,000).

Example 14-6 – Armando's basis in his partnership interest is $20,000. In a distribution in liquidation of his entire interest, he receives properties C and D, neither of which is inventory or unrealized receivables. Property C has an adjusted basis to the partnership of $15,000 and a fair market value of $15,000. Property D has an adjusted basis to the partnership of $15,000 and a fair market value of $5,000. To figure his basis in each property, Armando first assigns $15,000 basis to property C and $15,000 to property D (their adjusted basis to the partnership). This leaves a $10,000 basis decrease (the $30,000 total of the basis assigned minus the $20,000 allocable basis). He allocates the entire $10,000 to property D (its unrealized depreciation). Armando's basis in property C is $15,000, and his basis in property D is $5,000 ($15,000 − $10,000).

Transactions between Partnership and Partners

For the situations listed below, treat a partner as <u>not</u> being a member of the partnership.

- Performing services for, or transferring property to, a partnership if:
    1) There is a related allocation and distribution to a partner.
    2) The entire transaction, when viewed together, is property characterized as occurring between the partnership and a partner not acting in the capacity of a partner.

- Transferring money or other property to a partnership if:
    1) There is a related transfer of money or other property by the partnership to the contributing partner or another partner.
    2) The transfers together are properly characterized as a sale or exchange of property.

Guaranteed Payments

Guaranteed payments are those made by a partnership to a partner determined <u>without regard</u> to the partnership's income.

A partnership treats guaranteed payments for services, or for the use of capital, as if the partnership had made them to a person who is not a partner. This treatment is for purposes of determining gross income and deductible business expenses only. For other tax purposes, treat guaranteed payments as a partner's distributive share of ordinary income. Guaranteed payments are included in income in the partner's tax year in which the partnership's tax year ends. Guaranteed payments are <u>not</u> subject to income tax withholding.

- The partnership generally deducts guaranteed payments as a business expense on Form 1065. However, the partnership capitalizes guaranteed payments made to partners for organizing the partnership or syndicating interests in the partnership.

- If a partner is to receive a minimum payment from the partnership, the guaranteed payment is the amount by which the minimum payment is more than the partner's distributive share of the partnership income.

- If guaranteed payments to a partner result in a partnership loss in which the partner shares, the partner must report the full amount of the guaranteed payments as ordinary income. The partner separately takes into account his distributive share of the partnership loss, to the extent of the adjusted basis of the partner's partnership interest.

- Treat premiums for health insurance paid by a partnership on behalf of a partner, for services as a partner, as guaranteed payments. The partnership can deduct the payments as a business expense, and the partner must include them in gross income. However, if the partnership accounts for insurance paid for a partner as a reduction in distributions to the partner, the partnership cannot deduct the premiums.

Sale or Exchange of Property

Losses are not allowed from the sale or exchange of property directly or indirectly between a partnership and a person whose direct or indirect interest in the capital or profits of the partnership is more than 50%. The basis of each partner's interest in the partnership is decreased (not below zero) by the partner's share of the disallowed loss.

Gain is ordinary income in a sale or exchange of property directly or indirectly between a person and a partnership, or between two partnerships, if both of the following tests hold true:

- More than 50% of the capital or profits interest in the partnership(s) is directly or indirectly owned by the same person.
- The property in the hands of the transferee immediately after the transfer is not a capital asset.
    1) Accounts receivables
    2) Inventory
    3) Stock-in-trade
    4) Depreciable or real property used in a trade or business

To determine if there is more than 50% ownership in capital or profits, the following rules apply:

- An interest directly or indirectly owned by, or for, a corporation, partnership, estate, or trust is considered to be owned by, or for its shareholders, partners, or beneficiaries.
- An individual is considered to own the interest directly or indirectly owned by, or for, the individual's family. For this rule, "family" includes only brothers, sisters, half-brothers, half-sisters, spouses, ancestors, and lineal descendants. **This information frequently appears on the test.

Individuals A and B and Trust T are equal partners in Partnership ABT. A's husband, AH, is the sole beneficiary of Trust T. Trust T's partnership interest will be attributed to AH only for further attributing the interest to A. As a result, A is a more-than-50% partner. This means that any deduction for losses on transactions between her and ABT will not be allowed, and gain from property that in the hands of the transferee is not a capital asset is treated as ordinary gain, rather than capital gain.

Contribution of Property

Neither the partner nor the partnership recognizes a gain or loss when a person contributes property to the partnership in exchange for a partnership interest.

A contribution of money or other property to the partnership followed by a distribution of different property from the partnership to the partner (disguised sale) is treated not as a contribution and distribution, but as a sale of property, if both of the following tests are true:

- The distribution would not have been made but for the contribution.
- The partner's right to the distribution does not depend on the success of the partnership operations.

The following rules apply to property contributions:

- If a partner contributes property to a partnership, the partnership's basis for determining depreciation, depletion, gain, or loss for the property is the <u>same</u> as the partner's adjusted basis for the property when the partner contributed the property, increased by any gain recognized by the partner at the time of contribution.

- If contributed property is subject to a debt or if the partnership assumes a partner's liabilities, the basis of that partner's interest is reduced by the liability assumed by the other partners. If the liabilities assumed exceed the partner's basis in the property, the partner must recognize a gain for the excess liabilities assumed.

- If a partner contributes property to a partnership and the partnership distributes the property to another partner within seven years of the contribution, the contributing partner must recognize gain or loss on the distribution.

Contribution of Services

A partner can acquire an interest in partnership capital or profits as compensation for services performed or to be performed.

- A *capital interest* is an interest that would give the holder a share of the proceeds if the partnership sold its assets at fair market value and the proceeds were distributed in a complete liquidation of the partnership. The fair market value of such an interest received by a partner as compensation for services <u>must</u> generally be included in the partner's gross income in the first tax year in which the partner can transfer the interest, or the interest is not subject to a substantial risk of forfeiture.

- A *profits interest* is a partnership interest other than a capital interest. If a person receives a profits interest for providing services to, or for the benefit of, a partnership in a partner capacity or in anticipation of being a partner, the receipt of such an interest is <u>not</u> a taxable event for the partner or the partnership. However, this does not apply in any of the following situations:

    1) The profits interest relates to a substantially certain and predictable stream of income from partnership assets, such as income from high-quality debt securities or a net lease.

    2) Within two years of receipt, the partner disposes of the profits interest.

    3) The profits interest is a limited partnership interest in a publicly traded partnership.

Basis in Partnership

The basis of a <u>partnership interest</u> is the money *plus* the adjusted basis of any property the partner contributed. If the partner must recognize gain because of the contribution, this gain is included in the basis of his interest.

> Basis of a partner's interest is also adjusted by certain items:
>
> - **Increases** – A partner's basis is increased by the following items:
>
>   1) Additional contributions to the partnership (includes assumption of partnership liabilities)
>
>   2) The partner's distributive share of taxable and nontaxable partnership income
>
>   3) The partner's distributive share of the excess of the deductions for depletion over the basis of the property, unless the property is oil or gas wells and the partnership allocates basis to partners

> - **Decreases** – The partner's basis is decreased (but never below zero) by the following items:
>   1) The money (including a decreased share of partnership liabilities or an assumption of the partner's individual liabilities by the partnership) and adjusted basis of property distributed to the partner by the partnership
>   2) The partner's distributive share of the partnership losses, including capital losses
>   3) The partner's share of nondeductible partnership expenses that are not capital expenditures
>   4) The partner's deduction for depletion for any partnership oil and gas wells, up to the proportionate share of the adjusted basis of the wells allocated to each partner

Effect of Partnership Liabilities

A partner's basis in a partnership includes his share of a partnership liability if the liability:

- Creates or increases the partnership's basis in any of its assets,
- Gives rise to a current deduction to the partnership, or
- Is a nondeductible, noncapital expense of the partnership

If a property transfer occurs between a partner and a partnership and the property is subject to a liability, treat the transferee as having assumed the liability to the extent it does not exceed the FMV of the property. Liabilities assumed by either party receive the same treatment as a transfer of money:

- If a partner's share of partnership liabilities <u>increases</u> or a partner's individual liabilities increase because said partner assumes partnership liabilities, treat this increase as a <u>contribution</u> of money by the partner to the partnership.
- If a partner's share of partnership liabilities <u>decreases</u> or a partner's individual liabilities decrease because said partnership assumes his individual liabilities, treat this decrease as a <u>distribution</u> of money to the partner by the partnership.

Consider a partner or *related person* to assume partnership liability only to the extent that:

- He is personally liable for it (i.e., recourse liability),
- The creditor knows that the liability was assumed by the partner or related person,
- The creditor can demand payment from the partner or related person, and
- No other partner or person related to another partner will bear the economic risk of loss on that liability immediately after the assumption.

Related Person

Related persons, for these purposes (<u>different for a corporation</u>), include all the following:

- An individual and:
  1) His spouse, ancestors, and lineal descendants (<u>not</u> brothers and sisters)
  2) A corporation if it directly or indirectly owns <u>80%</u> of the value of outstanding stock
  3) A tax-exempt educational or charitable organization controlled directly or indirectly by the person or by members of the person's family (<u>not</u> brothers and sisters)
- A fiduciary of a trust and:
  1) A grantor of any trust

2) A beneficiary of the same trust

3) A fiduciary of a separate trust if the same person is the grantor of both trusts

4) A corporation if the trust or the grantor of the trust directly or indirectly owns 80% of the value of outstanding stock

- A corporation and:

    1) A different corporation if members of the same controlled group (*see control, in Chapter 13*)

    2) A partnership if the same persons own <u>80%</u> or more in value of the outstanding stock and interest in the partnership

    3) An S corporation if the same persons own <u>80%</u> of the value of outstanding stock of each corporation

- An executor and a beneficiary of an estate

- A partnership and:

    1) A person owning, directly or indirectly, <u>80%</u> or more interest in the partnership, or

    2) Another partnership if the same persons, directly or indirectly, own <u>80%</u> interest

Recourse Liability

A partnership liability is a *recourse liability* to the extent that any partner or a related person, defined earlier, has an economic risk of loss for that liability. A partner's share of a recourse liability equals his *economic risk of loss* for that liability. A partner has an economic risk of loss if that partner or a related person would be obligated— whether by agreement or law— to make a net payment to the creditor or a contribution to the partnership with respect to the liability if the partnership were constructively liquidated. A partner who is the creditor for a liability that would otherwise be a nonrecourse liability of the partnership has an economic risk of loss in that liability.

Nonrecourse Liability

A partnership liability is a *nonrecourse liability* if no partner or related person has an economic risk of loss for that liability. If a partnership fails to repay a nonrecourse liability, the lender can foreclose on the property but cannot take collection action against the partners individually. A partner's share of nonrecourse liabilities is generally proportionate to his share of partnership profits.

Disposition of Partner's Interest

Sale, Exchange, or Other Transfer

The sale or exchange of a partner's interest in a partnership usually results in capital gain or loss. This gain or loss is the difference between the amount realized and the adjusted basis of the partner's interest in the partnership.

Payments to Partner for Unrealized Receivables and Inventory Items

If a partner receives money or property in exchange for any part of a partnership interest, the amount due to his share of partnership unrealized receivables or inventory items results in <u>ordinary</u> income or loss. Treat this amount as if the partner receives it for the sale or exchange of property that is not a capital asset. The income or loss realized by a partner is the amount allocable to the partner if the partnership had sold all of its property for cash at FMV—in a taxable transaction—immediately prior to the partner's transfer of interest in the partnership.

Example 14-7 – You are a partner in ABC Partnership. The adjusted basis of your partnership interest at the end of the current year is zero. Your share of potential ordinary income from partnership depreciable property is $5,000. The partnership has no other unrealized receivables or inventory items. You sell your interest in the partnership for $10,000 in cash, and you report the entire amount as a gain since your adjusted basis in the partnership is zero. You report as ordinary income your $5,000 share of potential ordinary income from the partnership's depreciable property. The remaining $5,000 gain is a capital gain.

Liquidation at Partner's Retirement or Death

Payments made by the partnership to a retiring partner or successor in interest of a deceased partner in return for the partner's entire interest in the partnership may be allocated between payments in liquidation of the partner's interest in partnership property and other payments. Treat payments that include an assumption of the partner's share of partnership liabilities as a distribution of money.

A payment made in liquidation of the interest of a retiring or deceased partner:

- In exchange for his interest in partnership property is a <u>distribution</u>, not a distributive share or guaranteed payment that could give rise to a deduction for the partnership.

- <u>Not</u> made in exchange for an interest in partnership property is a <u>distributive share</u> of partnership income or guaranteed payment.

Recognize a gain – Upon receipt of the distribution, the retiring partner or successor in interest of a deceased partner will recognize gain <u>only</u> to the extent that any money distributed is more than the partner's adjusted basis in the partnership.

Recognize a loss – The partner will recognize a loss only if the distribution is in money, unrealized receivables, and inventory items. The partner will recognize no loss if <u>any</u> other property is received.

For income tax purposes, treat a retiring partner or successor in interest of a deceased partner as a partner until the complete liquidation of his interest in the partnership.

15 Retirement Plans

SEP IRA · SIMPLE IRA · 403(b) Plans · Qualified Plans

This chapter summarizes information from IRS Publications 560 and 571.

Common Terms

- **Highly compensated employees** – For 2015, a highly compensated employee is one who:
    1) Owned <u>more than 5%</u> of the interest in the business at any time during the year or the preceding year, regardless of how much compensation that person earned or received, or
    2) For the preceding year, received compensation from the employer of more than $120,000, and if the employer so chooses, was in the top 20% of employees when ranked by compensation
- **Excludable employees** – Employers are not required to cover the following employees under a SIMPLE or SEP IRA plan:
    1) Employees who are covered by a union agreement and whose retirement benefits were bargained for in good faith by the employees' union and employer
    2) Nonresident alien employees who have received no U.S. source wages, salaries, or other personal services compensation from employer
- **Compensation** – Compensation for plan allocations is the pay a participant received from the employer for personal services for a year. Compensation includes all of the following payments:
    1) Wages and salaries
    2) Fees for professional services
    3) Other amounts received (cash or noncash) for personal services actually rendered by an employee, including, but not limited to commissions, tips, fringe benefits, and bonuses
- **Compensation for the self-employed** – A self-employed taxpayer must make a special computation to determine compensation for purposes of retirement plan contributions and deductions for his own account. Compensation is net earnings from self-employment, plus the following:
    1) The deduction for the employer-equivalent portion of self-employment tax
    2) The deduction for contributions on own behalf to the plan
- **Annual compensation limit** – The <u>maximum</u> amount of compensation the employer may consider when determining contributions and benefits for an employee is <u>$265,000</u> for 2015.
- **Catch-up contribution** – A plan can permit participants who are age 50 or older at the end of the calendar year to make catch-up contributions in addition to elective deferrals and SIMPLE plan salary reduction contributions.
    1) The catch-up contribution limitation for defined contribution plans <u>other than SIMPLE</u> plans is <u>$6,000</u> in 2015.

2) The catch-up contribution limitation for SIMPLE plans is $3,000 for 2015.

- **Loans** – Loans are not permitted from IRAs or from IRA-based plans such as SEPs, SARSEPs and SIMPLE IRA plans. Loans are only possible from qualified plans that satisfy the requirements of §401(a), from annuity plans that satisfy the requirements of §403(a) or 403(b), and from governmental plans. (Code §72(p)(4); Reg. § 1.72(p)-1, Q&A-2)

SEP IRA

Simplified Employee Pensions (SEP) provide a simplified method for employers to contribute to a retirement plan for themselves and employees. Under a SEP, the employer can contribute to a traditional individual retirement arrangement (called a SEP-IRA) set up by or for each eligible employee. A SEP cannot be a Roth IRA. A SEP-IRA is one that the employee owns and controls; the employer contributes to the financial institution that maintains the SEP-IRA.

Establishing a SEP Plan

Employers can establish a SEP for any year as late as the due date (including extensions) of the income tax return for that year. There are three basic steps in setting up a SEP:

- The employer must execute a formal written agreement to provide benefits to all eligible employees. The employer can satisfy the written agreement requirement by adopting an IRS model SEP using *Form 5305-SEP*.
- Each eligible employee must receive certain information about the SEP.
- A SEP-IRA must be set up by or for each eligible employee.

Eligible Employees

The employer will establish participation requirements for employees in the plan. At minimum, employees who satisfy the requirements must be included in the plan. The requirements may be less restrictive, but not more than the following:

- Employee is age 21 or older.
- Employee has worked for employer in at least three of the last five years.
- Employee has received at least $600 in compensation from employer in 2015.

How Contributions Are Made

Employees cannot contribute to a SEP IRA (other than SAR SEP, which was discontinued in 1997). Annual employer contributions are not mandatory. If contributing, the employer must base all contributions on a written allocation formula and must not discriminate in favor of highly compensated employees. When the employer contributes, the employer must contribute to the SEP-IRAs of all participants who actually performed personal services during the year for which the contributions are made, including employees who die or terminate employment before contributions are made. Contributions are made as a percentage of each employee's compensation. The percentage must be the same for all employees.

Annual Contribution Limit

The SEP rules permit an employer to contribute a limited amount of money each year to each employee's SEP-IRA. A self-employed taxpayer can contribute to a SEP-IRA established on his own behalf. Contributions must be in the form of money (cash, check, or money order), not property.

Contributions made by employer for 2015 to a common-law employee's SEP-IRA cannot exceed the lower of 25% of the employee's compensation or $53,000. Compensation generally does not include the employer's contributions to the SEP.

- **Compensation** – Compensation for plan allocations is the pay a participant received from the employer for personal services for a year. Compensation includes all of the following payments:

  1) Wages and salaries
  2) Fees for professional services
  3) Other amounts received (cash or noncash) for personal services actually rendered by an employee, including, but not limited to commissions, tips, fringe benefits, and bonuses

- **Compensation for the self-employed** – Those who are self-employed must make a special computation to determine contributions for their own accounts. The deduction for contributions to the SEP-IRA and net earnings depend on each other. For this reason, a self-employed individual determines the deduction for contributions to his SEP-IRA indirectly by reducing the contribution rate called for in the plan. When figuring the deduction made to one's own SEP-IRA, compensation is net earnings from self-employment, increased by the following:

  1) The deduction for self-employment tax, and
  2) The deduction for contributions to one's own SEP-IRA

Peter is a sole proprietor with $100,000 net income on his Schedule C. He took a deduction for self-employment tax on Form 1040 of $7,650. Net earnings from self-employment equal $92,350. The contribution rate for his SEP plan for employees is 25%. The formula to determine his contribution percentage is *rate*/(1+*rate*) or .25/1.25 =.20. His SEP contribution is $18,470 ($92,350 x 20%).

Employer/Employee Contribution Limits

An employer cannot consider the part of an employee's compensation above the *annual compensation limit* ($265,000) when figuring the contribution limit for an employee. However, $53,000 is the maximum contribution for an eligible employee under §415(c)(1)(A). Excess contributions are included in the employee's income for the year and are treated as contributions by the employee to his SEP-IRA. SEP contributions are not included on an employee's Form W-2 unless contributions were made under a salary reduction arrangement. Additionally, if the employer maintains another *defined contribution* plan for employees, the *annual additions* to an account are limited to the lesser of $53,000 or 100% of the participant's compensation. When figuring this limit, the employer must combine contributions to all defined contribution plans. Because a SEP is considered a defined contribution plan for this limit, employer contributions to a SEP must be added to employer contributions to other defined contribution plans. Contributions are 100% immediately vested to the employee.

SAR SEP

A *Salary Reduction Simplified Employee Pension (SAR SEP)* is a SEP set up before 1997 that includes a salary reduction arrangement. Under a SAR SEP, employees can choose to have the employer contribute part of their pay to their SEP-IRAs rather than receive it in cash. This contribution is an *elective deferral* because an employee chooses (elects) to contribute the money and tax is deferred until it is distributed.

SIMPLE IRA

Generally, an employer with 100 or fewer employees making at least $5,000 in compensation last year can set up a *Savings Incentive Match Plan for Employees (SIMPLE)*. The employer cannot maintain another qualified plan unless the other plan is for collective bargaining (union) employees. Under a SIMPLE plan, employees can choose to make salary reduction contributions rather than receiving these amounts as part of their regular pay. In addition, the employer will contribute either matching or non-elective contributions.

> In order to avoid additional tax, the participant must maintain a SIMPLE IRA for at least two years from the date of initial contribution. If a withdrawal, rollover distribution, or transfer from a SIMPLE IRA does not satisfy the 2-year rule, and is otherwise an early distribution, the additional tax imposed because of the early distribution increases from 10% to 25% of the amount distributed.

The two types of SIMPLE plans are the SIMPLE IRA plan and the SIMPLE 401(k) plan. A SIMPLE plan cannot be a Roth IRA. Contribution methods and limits of a SIMPLE IRA and SIMPLE 401(k) are the same. Unlike the IRA version, the SIMPLE 401(k) is a *qualified plan* and is subject to those rules (under certain conditions, a SIMPLE 401(k) plan is not subject to the nondiscrimination and top-heavy rules).

Establishing a SIMPLE Plan

An employer can set up a SIMPLE IRA plan effective on any date from January 1 through October 1 of a year, provided the employer did not previously maintain a SIMPLE IRA plan. A new employer that comes into existence after October 1 may set up a SIMPLE IRA plan as soon as administratively feasible after the business comes into existence. If the employer previously maintained a SIMPLE IRA plan, he can establish a SIMPLE IRA plan effective only on January 1 of a year.

- **Notification requirement** – The employer must notify each employee of the following information before the beginning of the election period:
    1) The employee's opportunity to make or change a salary reduction choice
    2) The employer's contribution method
    3) A summary description provided by the financial institution
    4) Written notice that the employee can transfer his balance without cost or penalty if he uses a designated financial institution

- **Election period** – The election period is generally the 60-day period immediately preceding January 1 of a calendar year (November 2 to December 31 of the preceding calendar year). However, the dates of this period are modified if the plan is established mid-year.

Employers must adopt a written plan to establish a SIMPLE 401(k) or SIMPLE IRA. For a SIMPLE IRA only, the employer may establish the plan and notify employees with a model plan document:

- **Form 5304-SIMPLE** – To allow each plan participant to choose his own financial institution, or
- **Form 5305-SIMPLE** – If the employer requires an initial designated financial institution

Eligible Employees

Any employee who received at least $5,000 in compensation during any two years preceding the current calendar year and who can reasonably expect to receive at least $5,000 during the current calendar year is eligible to participate. The term "employee" includes a self-employed individual who received earned income. Employers may use less restrictive eligibility requirements (but not more restrictive ones) by eliminating or reducing the prior year compensation requirements, the current year compensation requirements, or both.

Contribution Deadline

The employer must make the salary reduction contributions to the SIMPLE IRA within 30 days after the end of the month in which the amounts would otherwise have been payable to the employee in cash. Matching contributions or non-elective contributions are due by the due date (including extensions) for filing the employer's federal income tax return for the year. Certain plans subject to Department of Labor rules may have an earlier due date for salary reduction contributions.

Employer/Employee Contribution Limits

- **Salary reduction contributions** – Employees may contribute to the SIMPLE IRA through salary reductions up to $12,500 for 2015. These contributions must be expressed as a percentage of the employee's compensation unless the employer permits the employee to express them as a specific dollar amount. Employers cannot place restrictions on the contribution amount (such as limiting the contribution percentage), except to comply with the $12,500 limit. The maximum percentage an employee may contribute is 100% of his compensation up to the dollar limit.

- **Catch-up contribution** – Participants who are age 50 or older at the end of the year can make catch-up contributions in addition to elective deferrals and SIMPLE plan salary reduction contributions. The catch-up contribution limitation for SIMPLE plans is $3,000 for 2015.

- The employer must also contribute, using one of two methods:

    1) **Elective contributions** – The employer must match employee contributions, dollar for dollar, up to a maximum of 3% of compensation. If the matching contribution is less than 3%, the percentage must be at least 1%. The employer must notify the employees of the lower match within a reasonable period before the 60-day election period for the calendar year. Employers cannot choose a percentage less than 3% for more than two years during the five-year period that ends with (and includes) the year for which the choice is effective, or

    2) **Non-elective contributions** – The employer must make mandatory 2% contributions based on compensation for all eligible employees, regardless of whether or not the employee chooses to make salary reduction contributions.

An employer deducts contributions for employees on its tax return, and employees can exclude these contributions from their gross income. However, salary reduction contributions are subject to FICA and federal unemployment (FUTA) taxes. Matching and non-elective contributions are not subject to these taxes. Contributions are not subject to federal income tax withholding.

> A sole proprietor or partner cannot deduct contributions made to a retirement plan for himself as a business expense, only those made for his common-law employees. Sole proprietors and partners deduct contributions on Form 1040.

403(b) Plans

A 403(b) plan, often called a tax-sheltered annuity (TSA), is a retirement plan for certain employees of public schools, tax-exempt organizations, and certain ministers. A 403(b) has similar contribution limits and features of qualified plans, such as the ability to borrow against a balance; however, a 403(b) is not necessarily a qualified plan for ERISA purposes. Employees cannot set up their own 403(b) account. Only employers can set up 403(b) accounts.

Any eligible employee may participate. The following employees are able to participate:

- Employees of tax-exempt organizations established under Section 501(c)(3)
- Employees of public school systems who are involved in the daily operations of a school
- Employees of cooperative hospital service organizations
- Civilian faculty and staff of the Uniformed Services University of the Health Sciences (USUHS)
- Employees of public school systems organized by Indian tribal governments
- Certain ministers

Individual accounts in a 403(b) plan can be any of the following types:

- An annuity contract, which is a contract provided through an insurance company
- A custodial account, which is an account invested in mutual funds
- A retirement income account set up for church employees. Generally, retirement income accounts can invest in either annuities or mutual funds.

Generally, the maximum amount contributable (MAC) to a 403(b) account is limited to the lesser of:

- **The annual additions limit** – For 2015 the limit is $53,000 or 100% of compensation for the most recent year, whichever is less.
- **The elective deferral limit** – In general, an employee may not contribute more than $18,000 for 2015. There is a special rule for those with at least 15 years of service giving them the potential to contribute up to $3,000 more. Additionally, individuals older than 50 are eligible for a catch-up contribution of up to $6,000 for 2015.

If, for any year, elective deferrals are contributed to multiple retirement accounts for the same taxpayer (whether or not with the same employer), consider all contributions to determine whether the total is more than the limit for that year. The limit on elective deferrals applies to amounts contributed to:

- 401(k) plans, to the extent excluded from income
- Section 501(c)(18) plans, to the extent excluded from income
- SIMPLE plans
- SEP plans
- All 403(b) plans

As of January 1, 2008, a taxpayer may convert distributions from tax-qualified retirement plans and tax-sheltered annuities by making a rollover into a Roth IRA, subject to the restrictions that currently apply to rollovers from a traditional IRA into a Roth IRA.

Qualified Plans

A *qualified plan* is a retirement plan that offers a tax-favored way to save for retirement. Employers may deduct contributions made to the plan for employees. Earnings on these contributions are generally tax free until distributed at retirement. Profit sharing, money purchase, and defined benefit plans are qualified plans. A 401(k) plan is also a qualified plan. The qualified plan rules are more complex than the SEP plan and SIMPLE plan rules. However, there are advantages to qualified plans, such as increased flexibility in designing plans and increased contribution and deduction limits in some cases. There are two basic kinds of qualified plans, **defined contribution** plans and **defined benefit** plans, and different rules apply to each. An employer can have more than one qualified plan, but contributions to all plans must not total more than the overall limits.

Defined Contribution Plan

A defined contribution plan has an individual account for each participant in the plan. It provides benefits largely based on the amount contributed to that participant's account. Any income, expense, gain, loss, and forfeiture of other accounts that may be allocated to an account also affect benefits. A defined contribution plan can be either *a profit-sharing plan* or a *money purchase pension plan.*

- **Profit-sharing plan (PSP)** – Although it is called a profit-sharing plan, employers do not actually have to make a business profit for the year in order to contribute (except for the self-employed). A PSP can be set up to allow for discretionary employer contributions, meaning the amount contributed each year to the plan is not fixed. An employer may even not contribute to the plan for a given year. The plan must provide a definite formula for allocating the contribution among the participants and for distributing the accumulated funds to the employees after they reach a certain age, after a fixed number of years, or upon certain other occurrences. In general, the employer can be <u>more flexible</u> in contributing to a PSP than to a money purchase pension plan or a defined benefit plan.

- **Money purchase pension plan (MPPP)** – Contributions to a money purchase pension plan are fixed and are not based on business profits. For example, if the plan requires that contributions be 10% of the participants' compensation without regard to whether the employer has profits (or the self-employed person has earned income), the plan is a money purchase pension plan. This applies even though the compensation of a self-employed individual as a participant depends on earned income derived from business profits.

Defined Benefit Plan

A defined benefit plan is any plan that is not a defined contribution plan. Contributions to a defined benefit plan are based on what is needed to provide definitely determinable benefits to plan participants. Actuarial assumptions and computations are required to figure these contributions. Generally, continuing professional help is necessary to have a defined benefit plan.

Qualified Plan Rules

To qualify for the tax benefits available to qualified plans, a plan must meet certain requirements (qualification rules) of the tax law. Generally, unless an employer writes his own plan, the financial institution that provided the plan will take the continuing responsibility for meeting qualification rules that are later changed. Some of the important rules include the following:

- The employer must adopt a written plan.
- The employer must use plan assets only for the benefit of employees or their beneficiaries.
- The plan must, at a minimum, cover at least the lesser of the following:
    1) 50 employees, or
    2) The greater of:
        A) 40% of all employees, or
        B) Two employees. If there is only one employee, the plan must benefit that employee.
- Contributions or benefits must not discriminate in favor of highly compensated employees.
- The plan must meet minimum vesting standards.
- In general, an employee who meets both the following requirements must be allowed to participate:

1) Has reached age 21, and
2) Has at least one year of service (two years if the plan is not a 401(k) plan and provides that after not more than two years the employee has a non-forfeitable right to all accrued benefits).

Establishing a Plan

To take a deduction for contributions for a tax year, the plan must be set up (adopted) by the <u>last day of that year</u> (December 31 for calendar year employers).

Minimum Funding Requirement

In general, if the plan is an MPPP or a defined benefit plan, the employer must pay enough into the plan to satisfy the minimum funding standard each year. The amount depends on the plan formula using actuarial assumptions and formulas.

- **Quarterly installments of required contributions** – If the plan is a defined benefit plan subject to the minimum funding requirements, the employer must make quarterly payments of the required contributions.
- **Due dates** – Installments are due <u>15 days</u> after the end of each quarter.
- **Installment percentage** – Quarterly installments must be 25% of the required annual payment.
- **Extended period for making contributions** – The employer must make contributions required to satisfy the minimum funding requirement for a plan year by <u>8.5 months</u> after the end of that year.

Contributions

Employer contributions generally fund a qualified plan. However, employees participating in the plan may be permitted to contribute, and the employer may be permitted to contribute on its own behalf. The employer may make deductible contributions for a tax year up to the due date of its tax return (plus extensions) for that year.

Limits on Contributions and Benefits

The plan must provide that contributions or benefits cannot exceed certain limits. The limits differ depending on whether a plan is a defined contribution plan or a defined benefit plan.

> **Defined benefit plan** – For 2015, the annual benefit for a participant under §415(b)(1)(A) for a defined benefit plan cannot exceed the lesser of the following amounts:
>
> - 100% of the participant's average compensation for his highest three consecutive calendar years
> - $210,000
>
> **Defined contribution plan** – For 2015, under §415(c)(1)(A) a defined contribution plan's annual contributions and other additions (excluding earnings) to the account of a participant cannot exceed the lesser of the following amounts:
>
> - 100% of the participant's compensation
> - $53,000

Employer Deduction Limits

Employers can usually deduct, subject to limits, contributions made to a qualified plan, including those made for their own retirements. The contributions (and earnings and gains on them) are generally tax free until distributed by the plan. The deduction limit for employer contributions to a qualified plan depends on the kind of plan the employer has.

- **Defined contribution plans** – The deduction for contributions to a defined contribution plan (PSP or MPPP) cannot be more than 25% of the compensation paid (or accrued) during the year to eligible employees participating in the plan. The following rules apply:

    1) Elective deferrals (discussed later) are not subject to the limit.

    2) Compensation includes elective deferrals.

    3) The maximum compensation taken into account for each employee in 2015 is $265,000.

- **Defined benefit plans** – The deduction for contributions to a defined benefit plan is based on actuarial assumptions and computations. An actuary must figure the deduction limit.

401(k) Plan Elective Deferrals

A qualified plan can include a cash or deferred arrangement under which a participant can choose to have the employer contribute part of his before-tax compensation to the plan rather than receive the compensation in cash. A plan with this type of arrangement is a *401(k) plan*. This contribution is an *elective deferral* because participants choose (elect) to defer receipt of the money. In general, a qualified plan can include a cash or deferred arrangement only if the qualified plan is one of the following defined contribution plans:

- A profit-sharing plan
- A money purchase pension plan in existence on June 27, 1974, that included a salary reduction arrangement on that date

The plan cannot require, as a condition of participation, that an employee complete more than one year of service. There is a limit on the amount an employee can defer each year under these plans. The plan must provide that employees cannot defer more than the limit that applies for a particular year. For 2015, the basic limit of §402(g)(1) on elective deferrals is **$18,000**, plus the catch-up contribution amount if the employee is old than age 50. This limit applies to all salary reduction contributions and elective deferrals. If, considering the plan in conjunction with other plans, the employee has exceeded the deferral limit, include the difference in gross income.

Employer contributions to a 401(k) plan are generally deductible by the employer for the year the employer contributes to the plan. Matching or non-elective contributions made to the plan are also deductible by the employer in the year of contribution. The employees' elective deferrals other than designated Roth contributions are not taxed until distributed from the plan. Elective deferrals are included in wages for FICA and federal unemployment (FUTA) tax. Employers report the total amount of elective deferrals to employees on Form W-2.

Distributions

Generally, an employer cannot make distributions until one of the following occurs:

- The employee retires, dies, becomes disabled, or otherwise severs employment.
- The plan ends, and the employer does not establish or continue another defined contribution plan.
- In the case of a 401(k) plan that is part of a profit-sharing plan, the employee reaches age 59.5 or suffers financial hardship.
- The employee becomes eligible for a qualified reservist distribution.

Rollovers

Distributions from a qualified plan minus a prorated part of any cost basis are subject to income tax in the year they are distributed. Since most recipients have no cost basis, a distribution is taxable. An exception is a distribution that is properly rolled over. The recipient of an *eligible rollover distribution* from a qualified plan can defer the tax on it by rolling it over into a traditional IRA or another eligible retirement plan. An eligible rollover distribution is a distribution of all or any part of an employee's balance in a qualified retirement plan that is not any of the following:

- A required minimum distribution
- A series of substantially equal payments made at least once a year over any of the following periods:
    1) The employee's life or life expectancy
    2) The joint lives or life expectancies of the employee and beneficiary
    3) A period of 10 years or longer
- A hardship distribution
- The portion of a distribution that represents the return of an employee's nondeductible contributions to the plan
- Loans treated as distributions
- Dividends on employer securities
- The cost of any life insurance coverage provided under a qualified retirement plan

If, during a year, a qualified plan pays to a participant one or more eligible rollover distributions that are reasonably expected to total $200 or more, the payor must withhold 20% of each distribution for federal income tax. If the participant chooses to have the plan pay it directly to an IRA or another eligible retirement plan (a direct rollover), no withholding is required.

Tax on Early Distributions

If a distribution is made to an employee under the plan before he reaches age 59.5, the employee may have to pay a 10% additional tax on the distribution. This tax applies to the amount received that the employee must include in income. The 10% tax will not apply if distributions before age 59.5 are made in any of the following circumstances:

- Made to a beneficiary (or to the estate of the employee) on or after the death of the employee
- Made due to the employee having a qualifying disability
- Made as part of a *series of substantially equal periodic payments* (SOSEPP under IRS Rule 72t) beginning after separation from service and made at least annually for the life or life expectancy of the employee or the joint lives or life expectancies of the employee and his designated beneficiary. (Payments, except in the case of death or disability, must continue for at least five years or until the employee reaches age 59.5, whichever is longer.)
- Made to an employee after separation from service if the separation occurred during or after the calendar year in which the employee reached age 55
- Made to an alternate payee under a QDRO
- Made to an employee for medical care up to the amount allowable as a medical expense deduction (determined without regard to whether the employee itemizes deductions)
- Timely made to reduce excess contributions under a 401(k) plan

- Timely made to reduce excess employee or matching employer contributions
- Timely made to reduce excess elective deferrals
- Made because of an IRS levy on the plan
- Made as a qualified reservist distribution

Loans

A qualified plan may, but is not required to, provide for loans. If a plan provides for loans, the plan may limit the amount available as a loan. The maximum amount that a plan can permit as a loan is the greater of $10,000 or 50% of the vested account balance, but the loan may not exceed $50,000. For example, if a participant has an account balance of $40,000, the maximum amount that he or she can borrow from the account is $20,000.

A plan that provides for loans must specify the procedures for applying for a loan and the repayment terms for the loan. The employee must repay the loan within five years and make payments in substantially equal payments that include principal and interest and that are paid at least quarterly. Loan repayments are not plan contributions. A loan for purchasing the employee's principal residence may be paid back over a period of more than five years.

Loans are not taxable distributions unless they fail to satisfy the plan loan rules of the regulations with respect to amount, duration, and repayment terms. In addition, a loan that is not paid back according to the repayment terms is treated as a distribution from the plan and is taxable as such.

Prohibited Transactions

Prohibited transactions are transactions between the plan and a *disqualified person* that are prohibited by law. A disqualified person who takes part in a prohibited transaction must pay a tax. Prohibited transactions generally include the following transactions:

- A transfer or use of plan income or assets to, or for the benefit of, a disqualified person
- Any act of a fiduciary that deals with plan income or assets in his own interest
- The receipt of consideration by a fiduciary for his own account from any party dealing with the plan in a transaction that involves plan income or assets
- Any of the following acts between the plan and a disqualified person:
    1) Selling, exchanging, or leasing property
    2) Lending money or extending credit
    3) Furnishing goods, services, or facilities

Disqualified Person

A disqualified person is any of the following:

- A fiduciary of the plan
- A person providing services to the plan
- An employer, any of whose employees are covered by the plan
- An employee organization, any of whose members are covered by the plan
- Any direct or indirect owner of 50% or more of any of the following:
    1) The combined voting power of all classes of stock entitled to vote, or the total value of shares of all classes of stock of a corporation that is an employer or employee organization

2) A partnership that is an employer or employee organization described previously

3) The beneficial interest of a trust or unincorporated enterprise that is an employer or an employee organization described previously

- A member of the family of any individual described previously. A member of a family is the spouse, ancestor, lineal descendant, or any spouse of a lineal descendant

- A corporation, partnership, trust, or estate of which (or in which) any direct or indirect owner is a disqualified person and holds 50% or more of any of the following:

    1) The combined voting power of all classes of stock entitled to vote, or the total value of shares of all classes of stock of a corporation

    2) The capital interest or profits interest of a partnership

    3) The beneficial interest of a trust or estate

- An officer, director, a 10% or more shareholder, or highly compensated employee

- A 10% or more (in capital or profits) partner

Tax on Prohibited Transaction

The initial tax on a prohibited transaction is 15% of the amount involved for each year (or part of a year) in the taxable period. If the person does not correct the transaction within the taxable period, the IRS will impose an additional tax of 100% of the amount involved.

Reporting Requirements

An annual return form is due by the last day of the seventh month after the plan year-ends. Taxpayers who are required to file must use one of the following forms:

- **Form 5500-SF** – This new simplified form is filed if a plan meets all the following conditions:

    1) The plan is a small plan (less than 100 participants at the beginning of the plan year).

    2) The plan meets the conditions for being exempt from the requirements for an independent qualified public accountant audit of the plan's books and records.

    3) Plan assets are 100% invested in secure investments with a readily determinable fair value.

    4) The plan holds no employer securities.

    5) The plan is not a multiemployer plan.

- **Form 5500-EZ** – This form is for a one-participant plan only, as described below:

    1) The plan is a one-participant plan if either of the following is true:

    2) The plan covers only the business owner (or the owner and his spouse), and the owner (or his spouse) owns the entire business (whether incorporated or unincorporated).

    3) The plan covers only one or more partners in a business partnership.

    4) A one-participant plan may not file an annual return on Form 5500. Every one-participant plan required to file an annual return must file either Form 5500-EZ or, if eligible, Form 5500-SF.

    5) A one-participant plan (or plans) with total assets of $250,000 or less at the end of the plan year does not have to file Form 5500-EZ for that plan year. All plans should file a Form 5500-EZ for the final plan year to show that all plan assets have been distributed.

- **Form 5500** – All qualified plans that are not eligible for the forms above must prepare the annual report on Form 5500.

Table 15-1. Key Retirement Plan Rules for 2015

Type of Plan	Last Date for Contribution	Maximum Contribution	Maximum Deduction	When to Set Up Plan
SEP	Due date of employer's return (including extensions)	Smaller of $53,000 or 25% of participant's compensation	25% of all participants' compensation	Any time up to the due date of employer's return (including extensions)
SIMPLE IRA and SIMPLE 401(k)	**Salary reduction contributions:** 30 days after the end of the month for which the contributions are to be made **Matching or nonelective contributions:** Due date of employer's return (including extensions)	**Employee contribution:** Salary reduction contribution up to $12,500, $15,500 if age 50 or older **Employer contribution:** *Either* dollar-for-dollar matching contributions, up to 3% of employee's compensation, *or* fixed non-elective contributions of 2% of compensation	Same as maximum contribution	Any time between 1/1 and 10/1 of the calendar year For a new employer coming into existence after 10/1, as soon as administratively feasible
Qualified Plan: Defined Contribution Plan	**Elective deferral:** Due date of employee's return (including extensions) **Employer contribution:** <u>Money Purchase or Profit-Sharing:</u> Due date of employer's return (including extensions)	**Employee contribution:** Elective deferral up to $18,000, $24,000 if age 50 or older **Employer contribution:** <u>Money Purchase:</u> Smaller of $53,000 or 100% of participant's compensation <u>Profit-Sharing:</u> Smaller of $53,000 or 100% of participant's compensation.	25% of all participants' compensation, plus amount of elective deferrals made	By the end of the tax year
Qualified Plan: Defined Benefit Plan	Contributions must be paid in quarterly installments depending on the plan year, due 15 days after the end of each quarter.	Amount needed to provide an annual benefit no larger than the smaller of $210,000 or 100% of the participant's average compensation for his highest three consecutive calendar years	Based on actuarial assumptions and computations	By the end of the tax year

16 Specialized Returns

The Final Return · Estate Income Tax · Trusts · Farmers · Exempt Organizations

This chapter covers information in IRS Publications 501, 559, 225, and 557 and IRC §651, §652, §661, §1.652, and §1.265-1.

The Final Return

An income tax return must be filed for a ***decedent*** (person who died) if the decedent met the filing requirements at the time of his death. Should death occur during the filing season (i.e., Jan 1–April 15) and before filing a prior year return, the normal deadline for filing (usually April 15) applies to that return. The individual responsible for filing the return may be a surviving spouse, relative, executor, administrator, or legal representative. This is not the final return, as the decedent was alive for several months into a new tax year.

> The final income tax return is due at the same time the decedent's return would have been due had death not occurred. A final return for a decedent who was a calendar year taxpayer is generally due on April 15 following the year of death, regardless of when during that year death occurred.

If the decedent is married at the time of death, the decedent and surviving spouse are considered married for the whole year for filing status purposes.

- A surviving spouse who does <u>not</u> remarry before the end of the tax year in which the decedent died may file a joint return with the ***decedent***. If otherwise applicable, the return can include the full standard deduction based on filing status and an exemption for the decedent. If filing separately, the survivor cannot claim an exemption for the decedent on his own return.

- If the surviving spouse remarries during the year, he <u>must file apart</u> from the decedent. The decedent must file separately (MFS); however, the surviving spouse can file a joint return with the new spouse. A surviving spouse with no income can be claimed as an exemption on <u>both</u> the final separate return of the decedent and the return of the new spouse for that year.

- A court-appointed personal representative may revoke an election to file a joint return that the surviving spouse previously made alone. The representative does this by filing a separate return for the decedent within one year from the due date of the return (including any extensions). The joint return made by the surviving spouse will then be regarded as the separate return of that spouse by excluding the decedent's items and refiguring the tax liability.

Income to Include

The decedent's income includible on the final return is generally determined as if the person were still alive except that the taxable period is usually shorter because it ends on the date of death. The method of accounting used by the decedent also determines the income and expenses includible on the final return.

- **Cash method** – The final return includes items actually or <u>constructively received</u> before death.

1) The decedent constructively received interest from coupons on bonds if the coupons matured in the decedent's final tax year but had not been cashed. Include the interest in the final return.

2) Generally, the decedent constructively received a dividend if it was available for use by the decedent without restriction. If the corporation customarily mailed its dividend checks, the dividend was includible when received. If the individual died between the time the corporation declared the dividend and the time it arrived in the mail, the decedent did not constructively receive it before death. Do not include the dividend in the final return.

- **Accrual method** – Generally, under an accrual method of accounting, report income <u>when earned</u>. If the decedent used an accrual method, only the income items normally accrued before death are included in the final return.

Medical Expense Deductions

- Medical expenses paid <u>before death</u> by the decedent are deductible, subject to limits, on the final income tax return if deductions are itemized. This includes expenses for the decedent, as well as for the decedent's spouse and dependents.
- Medical expenses that were <u>not</u> paid before death are liabilities of the estate and appear on the federal estate tax return (Form 706). If the estate pays medical expenses for the decedent during the one-year period beginning with the day after death, the executor may elect to treat all or part of the expenses as paid by the decedent at the time the decedent incurred them. An executor making this election may claim all or part of the expenses on the decedent's income tax return as an itemized deduction, rather than on the federal estate tax return (Form 706).

Loss Deductions

A decedent's <u>net operating loss</u> deduction from a prior year and any capital losses (including <u>capital loss carryovers</u>) can be deducted only on the decedent's final income tax return. A net operating loss on the decedent's final income tax return can be carried back to prior years. An unused net operating loss or capital loss is not deductible on the estate's income tax return.

Credits

The individual filing a decedent's tax return may claim any tax credits that applied to the decedent before death on the decedent's final income tax return. Certain credits, like the EIC or the child tax credit, still apply even though the return covers a period of less than 12 months

Filing the Return

If the court has appointed a personal representative, that person must sign the return. If it is a joint return, the surviving spouse must also sign it. If the court has not appointed a personal representative, the surviving spouse (on a joint return) signs the return and writes in the signature area "Filing as surviving spouse." If the court has not appointed a personal representative and there is no surviving spouse, the person in charge of the decedent's property must file and sign the return as "personal representative." A surviving spouse filing jointly with the decedent may submit a claim for refund by filing the return.

Write the word "DECEASED," the decedent's name, and the date of death across the top of the tax return.

Estate Income Tax

An estate is a taxable entity separate from the decedent and comes into being with the death of the individual. It exists until the final distribution of its assets to the heirs and other beneficiaries. The estate must report income earned by the assets during this period on **Form 1041**. The tax generally is figured in the same manner and on the same basis as for individuals, with certain differences in the computation of deductions and credits.

- The estate reports its income, like an individual reports income, annually on either a calendar or a fiscal year basis. The estate's first tax year can be any period that ends on the last day of a month and does not exceed 12 months. The personal representative chooses the estate's accounting period and method to report income (cash, accrual, or other) when filing its first Form 1041. The tax year and accounting method generally cannot change without IRS approval.

> Every domestic estate with gross income of $600 or more during a tax year must file a Form 1041. If one of the beneficiaries of the domestic estate is a nonresident alien, the personal representative must file Form 1041, even if the gross income of the estate is less than $600.

Income in Respect of a Decedent

Certain types of property, such as capital assets, receive a step-up in basis when included in the decedent's estate and transferred to a beneficiary due to death. Other assets, for example traditional IRAs, are transferred in-kind to the beneficiary and do not receive a basis adjustment. Untaxed income and growth within these accounts is subject to tax upon receipt by the beneficiary. All income the decedent would have received had death not occurred that was not properly includible on the final return, discussed earlier, is *income in respect of a decedent (IRD)*. Income in respect of a decedent is included in the income of one of the following:

- The decedent's estate, if the estate receives it
- The beneficiary, if the right to income is passed directly to the beneficiary and he receives it
- Any person to whom the estate properly distributes the right to receive it

The character of the IRD is the same as it would be to the decedent if he were alive. If the income would have been a capital gain to the decedent, it will be a capital gain to the taxpayer. If an executor filed an estate tax return (Form 706) for the decedent, the taxpayer who must include IRD in his gross income may be able to claim a deduction for the estate tax paid on that income.

Personal Representative

A *personal representative* of an estate is an executor, administrator, or anyone who is in charge of the decedent's property. Generally, a decedent's will names an *executor* (or *executrix*) to administer the estate and distribute properties as the decedent has directed. The court usually appoints an *administrator* (or *administratrix*) if no will exists, if no executor was named in the will, or if the named executor cannot or will not serve. The personal representative has a fiduciary responsibility to the ultimate recipients of the income and the property of the estate.

Exemption and Deductions

In figuring taxable income, an estate is generally allowed the same deductions as an individual. Special rules, however, apply to some deductions for an estate. This section includes discussions of those deductions affected by the special rules.

- **Exemption deduction** – An estate is allowed an exemption deduction of $600 in figuring its taxable income. An estate cannot claim an exemption for dependents.
- **Charitable contributions** – An estate qualifies for a deduction for amounts of gross income paid or permanently set aside for qualified charitable organizations. The adjusted gross income limits for individuals do not apply. However, to make a contribution deductible by his estate, the decedent must specifically provide for that contribution in his will. If there is no will, or if the will makes no provision for the payment to a charitable organization, then a deduction will not be allowed even though all of the beneficiaries may agree to the gift.
    1) An estate cannot deduct any contribution from income not included in the estate's gross income. If the will specifically provides that the estate is to pay contributions out of its gross income, the contributions are fully deductible.
    2) An estate cannot deduct a qualified conservation easement granted after the date of death and before the due date of the estate tax return. A contribution deduction is allowed to the estate for estate tax purposes.
- **Losses** – Generally, an estate can claim a deduction for a loss it sustains on the sale of property. An estate and a beneficiary of that estate are generally treated as related persons for purposes of the disallowance of a loss on the sale of an asset between related persons.
- **Casualty and theft losses** – The estate can deduct losses incurred from casualties and thefts during the administration of the estate only if the estate has not claimed them on the federal estate tax return (Form 706). The personal representative must file a statement with the estate's income tax return waiving the deduction for estate tax purposes.
- **Net operating loss deduction** – An estate can claim a net operating loss deduction, figured in the same way as an individual's, except that it cannot deduct any distributions to beneficiaries or the deduction for charitable contributions in figuring the loss or the loss carryover.
    1) The estate <u>cannot</u> deduct carryover losses resulting from net operating losses or capital losses sustained by the decedent before death on the estate's income tax return.
- **Administration expenses** – Expenses of administering an estate can be deducted either from the gross estate in figuring the federal estate tax on Form 706 or from the estate's gross income in figuring the estate's income tax on Form 1041. However, the estate cannot claim these expenses for both estate tax and income tax purposes. The personal representative must file a statement with the estate's income tax return waiving the deduction for estate tax purposes.
- **Depreciation and depletion** – The executor must apportion the allowable deductions for depreciation and depletion that accrue after the decedent's death between the estate and the beneficiaries, depending on the income of the estate that is allocable to each.
- **Distribution deduction** – An estate is allowed a deduction for the tax year for any income that the estate must distribute currently and for other amounts that are properly paid, credited, or required to be distributed to beneficiaries. The deduction is limited to the distributable net income of the estate.

Due Date and Estimated Tax

The estate must pay its income tax liability in full when it files the return. Estates with tax years ending two or more years after the date of the decedent's death <u>must</u> pay estimated tax in the same manner as individuals. The due date for filing Form 1041 for estates that use a calendar year accounting period is generally April 15. An estate may choose either a calendar or a fiscal year to report income. If on a fiscal year, the Form 1041 is due by the 15th day of the fourth month after the end of the tax year. If the due date is a Saturday, Sunday, or legal holiday, the form must be filed by the next business day. The personal representative can request an automatic **five-month extension** of time to file Form 1041.

Distributions to Beneficiaries from an Estate

- The beneficiaries of an estate that must distribute all of its income currently must report their share of the distributable net income whether or not they actually received it.

- The beneficiaries of an estate that does not have to distribute all of its income currently must report all income that must be distributed to them (whether or not actually distributed) plus all other amounts paid, credited, or required to be distributed, up to their share of distributable net income.

Trusts

A trust is a legal arrangement whereby one party (the trustee) manages property for the benefit of another (beneficiary). Federal laws govern the income tax treatment of trusts; however, many of the legal aspects fall under the laws of the state in which the trust was executed. An *inter vivos trust*, more commonly referred to as a *living trust*, is a trust that takes effect during the lifetime of the grantor. A *testamentary trust* is created at death by instructions in the decedent's will and is funded with property from the probate estate. The primary parties to a trust are as follows:

- **Grantor** – The person who creates and usually contributes property to the trust. Also called a trustor or settlor. A *grantor trust* is a trust in which the grantor retains control and has an interest as beneficiary. Income from a grantor trust is taxed to the grantor as if no trust existed.

- **Beneficiary** – The individuals or entities named in the trust that benefit from trust property.

- **Trustee** – The fiduciary responsible for assets within the trust who assumes legal title to trust property and is accountable for administering the provisions of the trust on behalf of the beneficiaries. The trustee also is responsible for the payment of trust taxes and accounting for trust income, assets, and distributions.

The property owned by the trust is the *Corpus* (also called principal). The character of distributions from a trust may be either principal (corpus) or income, or both. For trust accounting purposes, such factors as income type, the trust document, and local law determine this classification. This classification is important because it can determine who is entitled to the income and the distribution amount. There are various types of trusts, all with different intents and purposes. All trusts fall into one of the following categories:

- **Simple trust** – A simple trust is one that is required to distribute all income currently. The trust may not use any amount of trust assets for charitable purposes. No distributions may occur in excess of the *fiduciary accounting income (FAI)*, as determined by applicable law.

- **Complex trust** – Any trust that does not meet the definition of a simple trust is a complex trust.

Allocating Expenses against Income

A distribution to a beneficiary is not always taxable income. To determine the appropriate character of a distribution, and the **distribution deduction** for the trust, the trustee must allocate a portion of trust expenses to its various sources of income. No deduction is available for direct or indirect expenses related to tax-exempt income. All deductible items directly attributable to one class of income must reduce that class. For example, fees to manage a municipal bond portfolio reduce tax-exempt income, while the expenses of managing a rental property reduce rental income. The trustee may allocate expenses not attributable to a specific class of income (such as trustee fees or legal expenses) to any item of income included in computing DNI. The calculation considers all expenses, including those charged to principal for trust accounting purposes. The trustee has some discretion on which class of income he will apply the indirect expenses against; however, if the trust has tax-exempt income, he must allocate a portion of the expenses against it. In general, indirect expenses reduce tax-exempt income according to the ratio of tax-exempt income to all other income included in DNI (not capital gains allocated to corpus). Calculate this ratio before deducting direct expenses. The trustee must utilize a method that will allocate a "reasonable proportion" of indirect expenses to tax-exempt income.

Example 1 —Trust A (simple trust) has $8,000 in taxable interest and $2,000 in tax-exempt interest. The trust paid $500 in trustee fees. What is the taxable amount of income to the beneficiary?

All expenses in this example are indirect costs. Reduce tax-exempt interest by a pro-rata share of expenses of $100 ($500 in fees multiplied by 20%, the ratio of tax-exempt income to total income). Net taxable income is gross taxable interest less $400 in allocable indirect expenses (80% pro-rata share).

Net taxable income of trust	$7,600
Net tax-exempt income of trust	+$1,900
DNI of trust	**$9,500**

Because this is a simple trust, all income must be distributed currently. DNI is composed of 80% taxable and 20% tax-exempt income. The beneficiary has $7,600 in taxable income. The trust may claim a distribution deduction for the taxable amount of the distribution to the beneficiary.

Example 2 —Trust B (simple trust) has $15,000 in tax-exempt interest and $5,000 in taxable interest. The trust paid $1,000 in commissions to purchase tax-free municipal bonds and $2,000 in attorney fees. What amount of income is tax free to the beneficiary?

First, allocate the $2,000 of indirect expenses to income. The tax-exempt portion of income is 75% of the total (gross) income included in DNI. Allocate $1,500 of the attorney fees to tax-exempt interest and $500 to taxable interest. The trustee must also decrease tax-exempt income by $1,000 of direct expenses. The total required distribution to the beneficiary is $17,000, of which $4,500 is taxable.

Net taxable income of trust	$4,500
Net tax-exempt income of trust	+$12,500
DNI of trust	**$17,000**

Distributable Net Income (DNI)

Trusts and estates must calculate DNI each year to determine the maximum amount of income distributions for which a distribution deduction is available. A trust may not deduct distributions in excess of the taxable amount of DNI. DNI with respect to any taxable year is the taxable income (before the distribution deduction) of the estate or trust computed with the following modifications:

- **Deduction for distributions** – No deduction for income distributions (paid, credited, or required)
- **Deduction for personal exemption** – The trust shall take no deduction for personal exemptions
- **Capital gains and losses** – The trust shall exclude gains from the sale or exchange of capital assets from DNI to the extent that the trust allocates such gains to *corpus* (trust principal) and does not pay them, credit them, or require that they be distributed to any beneficiary during the taxable year.
- **Extraordinary dividends and taxable stock dividends** – (For simple trusts only.) A fiduciary, acting in good faith, who determines such dividends are allocable to *corpus* under the terms of the governing

instrument and applicable local law, may exclude these items from DNI, provided the dividends are not paid or credited to any beneficiary.

- **Tax-exempt income** – Add net tax-exempt income to DNI. To arrive at *net tax-exempt income*, reduce the total amount of tax-exempt income by any expenses that relate directly to the tax-exempt income and a pro-rata share of expenses that are not attributable to a specific class of income (such as trustee fees).

Taxable Income

Income from an estate or trust (other than a grantor trust) is taxable to the estate/trust unless distributions are made (or required to be made) to beneficiaries. The estate/trust must pay tax on undistributed income, and the beneficiary will pay tax on actual (or required) distributions. The income distributed to the beneficiary retains the same character in the hands of the beneficiary as in the hands of the estate or trust. The formula to determine the taxable income of the estate/trust is as follows:

Gross Income received by the estate/trust from all taxable sources (includes capital gains or losses)

...*less* deductions and expenses (excluding expenses credited to tax-exempt income)

The result is the taxable income of the estate/trust **before** the distribution deduction.

...*less* the ***distribution deduction*** (limited to the taxable portion of DNI)

...*less* the exemption amount ($300 simple trust, $100 complex trust, and $600 estate)

The result is the <u>taxable income</u> of the trust or estate.

Example 3 — Trust C (a simple trust) receives long-term capital gains on stock sales of $15,000, dividends of $50,000, rents of $25,000, and tax-exempt interest of $25,000. The terms of the trust require the trustee to allocate all gains to principal and distribute all income equally between two beneficiaries. The trust expenses include taxes on the rental property of $5,000, and the trustee's commissions of $3,900 (the trustee allocates $1,300 to principal and $2,600 to income). Determine the amount of income taxable to each beneficiary and the amount taxable to the trust.

Dividends	$50,000	
Rents	$25,000	
Tax-exempt interest	+$25,000	
Total		$100,000
Deductions:		
Rental expenses	$5,000	
Trustee's commissions allocable to income	+$2,600	
		($7,600)
Fiduciary accounting income (FAI)		$92,400

Fiduciary accounting income (FAI) is the amount of income (after expenses allocable to income) the trustee will use to determine distributions for beneficiaries. A simple trust is required to distribute all FAI currently. For purposes of FAI, the trustee may allocate certain items of income or expense to either the principal or the income accounts, according to the trust document under state law. For this example, the trust allocates capital gains to corpus. As a result, gains are not part of FAI. The capital expenses are also not a deduction for FAI. FAI is a separate calculation from net taxable income or DNI. Just like with FAI,

DNI does not include gains allocated to principal. Before calculating the DNI of the trust, the trustee must apportion expenses that do not directly relate to a specific item of income between tax-exempt and taxable income sources. The total amount of expenses in this example is $3,900. The trustee did allocate a portion of the commissions to principal; however, that is only important for FAI. For DNI purposes, all indirect expenses are applicable. The trustee will allocate indirect expenses to tax-exempt according to its percentage of all income included in the calculation for DNI. In this example, $25,000 in tax-exempt income represents 25% of total gross income included in DNI. Capital gains are generally not income for DNI purposes because the trust allocates them to principal.

Dividends		$50,000
Rents		$25,000
Tax-exempt interest	$25,000	
less: Commissions (tax-exempt)	($975)	
		+$24,025
Total		$99,025
Deductions:		
Rental expenses	$5,000	
Trustee's commissions (on taxable)	+$2,925	
		($7,925)
Distributable Net Income (DNI)		$91,100

DNI determines the maximum distribution deduction a trust may use to reduce trust income. The trust cannot claim a deduction for distributions that exceed the taxable amount of DNI. The taxable amount of DNI is $67,075 ($75,000 taxable income – $7,925 deductions), which is 73.6% of DNI. Accordingly, the distributions in the hands of each beneficiary will retain the same character of taxable and tax-exempt income. The trust must consider all income from taxable sources in the calculation for net income. The trustee will not include income or expenses (either direct or indirect) that relate to tax-exempt income in the calculation of net income. For more information, see IRC §265, 26 CFR §1.652(b)-3, and §1.265-1.

Capital Gains		$15,000
Dividends		$50,000
Rents		+$25,000
Gross Income		$90,000
Deductions:		
Rental expenses	$5,000	
Trustee's commissions on taxable income	$2,925	
Distributions to beneficiaries	$67,075	
Personal exemption	+ $300	
		($75,300)
Trust Taxable Income		$14,700

Depreciation

Trust may not allocate depreciation to principal, unless the specific provisions in the trust permit the trustee to maintain a depreciation reserve. If a trust does not allocate depreciation to principal, the deduction for depreciation passes through to the income beneficiaries and does not affect the calculation of DNI or the net income of the trust. An estate or trust may not make an election under Section 179 to expense certain tangible property.

Requirements for Trust Tax Returns

Trusts, similar to estates, use Form 1041 to report income tax liability. Unlike an estate, a trust cannot use a fiscal year. The due date for filing Form 1041 for a trust is April 15. The IRS will grant an automatic **five-month extension** of time to file Form 1041 at the request of the trustee (Form 7004). Trusts must pay estimated tax in the same manner as individuals. A trust (also for an estate) may be subject to AMT. If applicable, the trust (or estate) files *Schedule I* along with Form 1041 to compute the following:

- Alternative minimum taxable income
- The income distribution deduction on a minimum tax basis, and
- AMT for the trust (or estate)

Farmers

Schedule F

Farmers use *schedule F* (Form 1040) to figure the net profit or loss from regular farming operations. This includes farm products raised for sale or products bought for resale. Income from farming includes amounts received from cultivating, operating, or managing a farm for gain or profit, as either owner or tenant.

> Schedule F includes income from operating a stock, dairy, poultry, fish, fruit, or truck (vegetable) farm and income from operating a plantation, ranch, range, or orchard. It also includes income from the sale of crop shares if the taxpayer materially participates in producing the crop. Income received from operating a nursery, which specializes in growing ornamental plants, is considered income from farming. Livestock held primarily for sale must be included in inventory. When a farmer sells farm products bought for resale, his profit or loss is the difference between the selling price and the basis in the item (usually the cost).

Income reported on Schedule F does not include gains or losses from sales or other dispositions of the following farm assets:

- Land
- Depreciable farm equipment (§1245 property)
- Buildings and structures (§1250 property)
- Livestock held for draft, breeding, sport, or dairy purposes (§1245 property)

Land and depreciable property (including not held for resale) used in farming are not capital assets. Farmers generally use Form 4797 to report these transactions as ordinary income or capital gain under the rules for §1231 transactions. A farmer who sells depreciable property (§1245 property or §1250 property) at a gain, may have to recognize all or part of the gain as ordinary income under the depreciation recapture rules. Any gain remaining after applying the depreciation recapture rules is a §1231 gain, which may be taxed as a capital gain. Net §1231 gains are ordinary gains up to the amount of non-recaptured §1231 losses from the five prior years; the rest is long-term capital gain. Losses from §1231 property are ordinary losses. If the property is not held for the required holding period (generally 12 months), the transaction is not subject to §1231 treatment, and any gain or loss is ordinary income reported in Part II of Form 4797.

Livestock Used in Business

If the taxpayer holds livestock primarily for draft, breeding, dairy, or sporting purposes, it is used in the farm business and must either be depreciated or included in inventory. Sales of livestock used in the business may result in ordinary or capital gains or losses, depending on the circumstances. In either case, farmers should always report these sales on **Form 4797**. Livestock that the taxpayer raises usually has no depreciable basis because the costs of raising them are deducted and not added to basis.

- Sale or exchange of this livestock may qualify as a **Section 1231** gain or loss.
- For Section 1231 transactions, livestock includes cattle, hogs, horses, mules, donkeys, sheep, goats, fur-bearing animals, and other mammals. Livestock does not include chickens, turkeys, pigeons, geese, emus, ostriches, rheas, or other birds, fish, frogs, reptiles, etc.

Gain on the sale of **raised livestock** is generally the gross sales price reduced by any expenses of the sale. Expenses of sale include sales commissions, freight or hauling, and other similar expenses. The basis of the animal sold is zero if the taxpayer deducted the costs of raising it during the years the taxpayer raised the animal. Gain on the sale of **purchased livestock** is generally the gross sales price minus the adjusted basis and any expenses.

Table 16-1. Where to Report Sales of Farm Product

Item Sold	Schedule F	Form 4797
Farm products raised for sale, including crops and livestock	X	
Farm products bought for resale, including crops and livestock	X	
Farm products not held primarily for sale, such as livestock held for draft, breeding, sport, or dairy purposes (bought or raised)		X

Sales Caused by Weather-related Conditions

If a farmer sells or exchanges more livestock, including poultry, than he normally would in a year because of a drought, flood, or other weather-related condition, he may be able to postpone reporting the gain from the additional animals until the next year.

The farmer must meet all of the following conditions to qualify:

- Their principal trade or business is farming.
- They use the cash method of accounting.
- They can show that, under their usual business practices, they would not have sold or exchanged the additional animals this year except for the weather-related condition.
- The weather-related condition caused the federal government to designate an area as eligible for assistance.

Crop Insurance and Crop Disaster Payments

Farmers must include in income any crop insurance proceeds they receive as the result of crop damage. The income is generally recognized in the year received. Farmers treat the crop disaster payments received from the federal government as crop insurance proceeds. The government provides crop disaster payments to a farmer as the result of destruction or damage to crops, or the inability to plant crops, due to drought, flood, or any other natural disaster. Farmers can postpone reporting crop insurance proceeds as income until the year following the year the damage occurred if they meet all the following conditions:

- They use the cash method of accounting.
- They receive the crop insurance proceeds in the same tax year the crops are damaged.
- Under normal business practices, they would have included income from the damaged crops in any tax year following the year the damage occurred.

A December 2015 cold spell in Florida froze the entire Florida Citrus temple orange crop, scheduled for February harvest. The entire 2015 crop was declared a disaster, and Florida Citrus received a crop disaster payment in December 2015. Florida Citrus uses the accrual method of accounting and–unlike other citrus farmers using the cash method–cannot postpone reporting the payment.

Income Averaging for Farmers

Taxpayers who are engaged in a farming business may be able to average all or some of their farm income by allocating it to the three prior years (base years).

Only a taxpayer engaged in a farming business as an individual, a partner in a partnership, or a shareholder in an S corporation may use income averaging. Corporations, partnerships, S corporations, estates, and trusts cannot use income averaging.

Estimated Taxes

A taxpayer with at least two-thirds of gross income from farming who pays the entire tax liability by March 1 following the tax year does not need to make estimated tax payments. Otherwise to avoid penalty, he must make one estimated tax payment by January 15 (following the tax year) equaling the lesser of 66 2/3% of the tax due, or 100% of the prior year tax liability.

Gross income from farming is the total of the following amounts from the tax return:

- Gross farm income from Schedule F (Form 1040)
- Gross farm rental income from Form 4835
- Gross farm income from Schedule E (Form 1040)
- Gains from the sale of livestock used for draft, breeding, sport, or dairy purposes (Form 4797)

Gross income from farming does not include wages as a farm employee, income from contract grain harvesting and hauling with workers and machines furnished by the taxpayer, gains from the sale of farmland and depreciable farm equipment.

Exempt Organizations

Certain organizations receive an exemption from federal income taxes. In general, these exempt organizations must apply for recognition of their tax-exempt status and submit annual informational returns to the IRS. Contributions to domestic tax-exempt organizations, except organizations testing for public safety, are deductible as charitable contributions on the donor's federal income tax return. An organization may qualify for exemption from federal income tax if it is organized and operated exclusively for one or more of the following purposes:

- Religious
- Charitable
- Scientific
- Testing for public safety
- Literary
- Educational (includes public daycare for children to enable parents to work)
- Fostering national or international amateur sports competition (but only if none of its activities involve providing athletic facilities or equipment)
- The prevention of cruelty to children or animals

To qualify, the organization must be a corporation, community chest, fund, foundation, or trust. An individual or a partnership will not qualify. Qualifying organizations include the following:

- Nonprofit old-age homes
- Parent-teacher associations
- Charitable hospitals or other charitable organizations
- Alumni associations
- Schools
- State schools, universities, or hospitals
- Chapters of the Red Cross or Salvation Army
- Boys' or Girls' Clubs
- Churches

Form 1023 – Recognition of Exemption

The IRS will not treat most tax-exempt organizations organized after October 9, 1969, as tax exempt unless the organization applies for recognition of exemption by filing **Form 1023.** The IRS will not treat these organizations as tax exempt for any period before they file Form 1023, unless the organization files the form within 15 months from the end of the month in which it was organized. If the organization files the application within this 15-month period, the IRS will recognize the organization's exemption retroactively to the date it was organized. Otherwise, the exemption is recognized only for the period after the IRS receives the application. Some organizations are not required to file Form 1023. The following organizations are exempt automatically if they meet the requirements of Sec. 501(c)(3):

- Churches, interchurch organizations of local units of a church, conventions or associations of churches, or integrated auxiliaries of a church, such as a men's or women's organization, religious school, mission society, or youth group.

- Any organization (other than a private foundation) normally having annual gross receipts of not more than $5,000.

    1) **Gross receipts test** – For purposes of the gross receipts test, an organization normally does not have more than $5,000 annually in gross receipts if:

        A) During its first tax year, the organization received gross receipts of $7,500 or less,

        B) During its first two years, it had a total of $12,000 or less in gross receipts, and

        C) If in existence for at least three years, the total gross receipts received by the organization during the immediately preceding two years, plus the current year, are $15,000 or less

An organization with gross receipts more than the amounts in the gross receipts test, unless otherwise exempt from filing Form 1023, must file a Form 1023 within 90 days after the end of the period in which the gross receipts exceeded the amounts in the test.

Form 990 Informational Returns

All private foundations exempt under Section 501(c)(3) must file *Form 990-PF*. Exempt organizations, other than private foundations, must file annual information returns on *Form 990* or *Form 990-EZ* (short version). Form 990-EZ is designed for use by small exempt organizations and nonexempt charitable trusts. An organization may file Form 990-EZ instead of Form 990, if it meets both of the following requirements:

- Gross receipts during the year were less than $200,000.
- Total assets at the end of the year were less than $500,000.

Most tax-exempt organizations whose gross annual receipts are normally $50,000 or less can file the e-Postcard (*Form 990-N*). These returns are due by the 15th day of the fifth month after the end of the organization's accounting period. Thus, for a calendar year taxpayer the informational return is due May 15 of the following year. A taxpayer may use *Form 8868* to request an automatic three-month extension and apply for an additional (not automatic) three-month extension if needed.

Form 990-T Unrelated Business Taxable Income (UBTI)

Even though an organization is recognized as tax exempt, it still may be liable for tax on its *unrelated business taxable income (UBTI)*. Unrelated business taxable income is income from a trade or business, regularly carried on, that does not substantially relate to the charitable, educational, or other purpose that is the basis for the organization's exemption. An exempt organization that has $1,000 or more of gross income from an unrelated business must file *Form 990-T* in addition to the obligation to file the annual information return, Form 990, 990-EZ, or 990-PF. Organizations must make quarterly payments of estimated tax on UBTI if expecting tax for year to be $500 or more.

Failure to File Form 990 Penalties

Generally, an exempt organization that, without reasonable cause, fails to file a required return must pay a penalty of $20 a day for each day the failure continues. The same penalty will apply if the organization does not give all the information required on the return or does not give the correct information. The maximum penalty for any one return is the smaller of $10,000 or 5% of the organization's gross receipts for the year. For an organization that has gross receipts of more than $1 million for the year, the penalty is $100 a day up to a maximum of $50,000.

Employment Tax Returns

Every employer, including an organization exempt from federal income tax, who pays wages to employees is responsible for withholding, depositing, paying, and reporting federal income tax, Social

Security and Medicare (FICA) taxes, and federal unemployment tax (FUTA), unless that employer is specifically exempted by law from those requirements or if the taxes clearly do not apply. Payments for services performed by a minister of a church in the exercise of the ministry, or a member of a religious order performing duties required by the order, are generally not subject to FICA or FUTA taxes. Churches and qualified church-controlled organizations can elect exemption from employer FICA taxes by filing Form 8274.

Table 16-2. Organization Quick-reference Chart

Description of organization	General nature of activities	App. Form No.	Annual Info. Return required
Corporations Organized under Act of Congress (including Federal Credit Unions)	Instrumentalities of the United States	N/A	None
Title Holding Corporation for Exempt Organization	Holding title to property of an exempt organization	1024	990 (or EZ)
Religious, Educational, Charitable, Scientific, Literary, Testing for Public Safety, to Foster National or International Amateur Sports Competition, or Prevention of Cruelty to Children or Animals Organizations	Activities of nature implied by description of class of organization	1023	990 (or EZ), or 990-PF
Civic Leagues, Social Welfare Organizations, and Local Associations of Employees	Promotion of community welfare, charitable, educational, or recreational	1024	990 (or EZ)
Labor, Agricultural, and Horticultural Organizations	Educational or instructive, the purpose being to improve conditions of work, and to improve products of efficiency	1024	990 (or EZ)
Business Leagues, Chambers of Commerce, Real Estate Boards, etc.	Improvement of business conditions of one or more lines of business	1024	990 (or EZ)
Social and Recreational Clubs	Pleasure, recreation, social activities	1024	990 (or EZ)
Fraternal Beneficiary Societies and Associations	Lodge providing for payment of life, sickness, accident, or other benefits to members	1024	990 (or EZ)
Voluntary Employees Beneficiary Associations	Providing for payment of life, sickness, accident, or other benefits to members	1024	990 (or EZ)
Domestic Fraternal Societies and Associations	Lodge devoting its net earnings to charitable, fraternal, and other specified purposes. No life, sickness, or accident benefits to members	1024	990 (or EZ)
Teachers' Retirement Fund Associations	Teachers' association for payment of retirement benefits	N/A	990 (or EZ)
Cemetery Companies	Burials and incidental activities	1024	990 (or EZ)
State-Chartered Credit Unions, Mutual Reserve Fd	Loans to members	N/A	990 (or EZ)
Mutual Insurance Companies or Associations	Providing insurance to members substantially at cost	1024	990 (or EZ)
Supplemental Unemployment Benefit Trusts	Provides for payment of supplemental unempl. compensation benefits	1024	990 (or EZ)
Employee Funded Pension Trust (created before June 25, 1959)	Payment of benefits under a pension plan funded by employees	N/A	990 (or EZ)
Post or Organization of Past or Present Members of the Armed Forces	Activities implied by nature of organization	1024	990 (or EZ)
Black Lung Benefit Trusts	Funded by coal mine operators to satisfy their liability for disability or death due to black lung diseases	N/A	990-BL
Veterans Organization (created before 1880)	To provide insurance and other benefits to veterans	N/A	990 (or EZ)
Title Holding Corporations or Trusts with Multiple Parents	Holding title and paying over income from property to 35 or fewer parents or beneficiaries	1024	990 (or EZ)
State-Sponsored Organization Providing Health Coverage for High-Risk Individuals	Provides health care coverage to high-risk individuals	N/A	990 (or EZ)
State-Sponsored Workers' Compensation Reinsurance Organization	Reimburses members for losses under workers' compensation acts	N/A	990 (or EZ)
Religious and Apostolic Associations	Regular business activities. Communal religious community	N/A	1065
Cooperative Hospital Service Organizations	Performs cooperative services for hospitals	1023	990 (or EZ)
Child Care Organizations	Provides care for children	1023	990 (or EZ)
Charitable Risk Pools	Pools certain insurance risks of 501(c)(3)	1023	990 (or EZ)
Credit Counseling Organization	Credit counseling services	1023	1023
Farmers' Cooperative Associations	Cooperative marketing and purchasing for agricultural procedures	1028	990-C
Political Organizations	A party, committee, fund, association, etc., that directly or indirectly accepts contributions or makes expenditures for political campaigns	8871	1120-POL 990 (or EZ)

SEE EXAM PART 3
REPRESENTATION, PRACTICES, AND PROCEDURES

17 Preparing Returns

Return Preparers · Penalties · Taxpayer Supporting Documentation · Applying to Become an Authorized E-File Provider · The E-File Process

This chapter covers certain requirements for return preparers. Much of the information within this chapter originates from Publications 552, 556, 3112, 4164, and 1345; Treasury Circular 230; TR §301.7701-15; and IRC §6107, §6109, §6694, §6695, and §7701.

Return Preparers

The term "tax return preparer" means any person who prepares for compensation, or who employs one or more persons to prepare for compensation, any return of tax or any claim for refund of tax. A person may be a preparer without regard to professional status, educational qualifications, nationality, residence, or business location. It is not necessary to prepare the entire return; a person is considered a preparer as long as he prepares a substantial portion of the return.

- A person shall not be a "tax return preparer" merely because such person:

    1) furnishes typing, reproducing, or other mechanical assistance,

    2) prepares a return for an employer (or of an officer or employee of the employer) by whom he is regularly and continuously employed,

    3) prepares as a fiduciary a return or claim for refund for any person, or

    4) prepares a claim for refund for a taxpayer in response to any notice of deficiency or in response to any waiver of restriction after the commencement of an audit.

Duties for Handling Returns

A tax return preparer must:

- Sign the return (if paid preparer) unless not required by instruction or code of law

- Indicate their identifying number on the return. New laws require all paid tax return preparers (including attorneys, CPAs, and enrolled agents) to apply for a Preparer Tax Identification Number (PTIN) – even if they already have one – before preparing any federal tax returns in 2015.

- Provide a copy of the return to taxpayer no later than the time the original return is presented for signature to the taxpayer

- Keep the following records for a period of three years after the close of the return period during which the return or claim for refund was presented for signature to the taxpayer:

    1) Retain a completed copy of the return, or

    2) Retain a record of taxpayer's tax ID, tax year, and name of preparer required to sign the return.

Penalties

Return preparers are responsible for taking a reasonable position on a tax return. To be reasonable, there must be *substantial authority* for the position, or in the case of a disclosed position, a *reasonable basis* for the treatment of such item on the return. The return cannot contain *frivolous positions*, which have no basis for validity in existing law or which have been deemed frivolous by the U.S. Tax Court or other federal court. The IRS may assess penalties within three years after the taxpayer files the return. No proceeding in court without assessment for the collection of such tax shall begin after the expiration of such period. There is no statute of limitations for fraudulent returns.

The substantial authority standard is an objective standard involving an analysis of the law and application of the law to relevant facts. It is less stringent than the *more likely than not* standard (the standard that is met when there is a greater than 50% likelihood of the position being upheld), but more stringent than the reasonable basis standard. There is substantial authority for the tax treatment of an item only if the weight of the authorities supporting the treatment is substantial in relation to the weight of authorities supporting contrary treatment. All authorities relevant to the tax treatment of an item, including the authorities contrary to the treatment, are taken into account in determining whether substantial authority exists. The weight of authorities is determined in light of the pertinent facts and circumstances.

Reasonable basis is a relatively high standard of tax reporting that is significantly higher than not frivolous or not patently improper. The reasonable basis standard is not satisfied by a return position that is merely arguable. If a return position is reasonably based on one or more of the authorities set forth in §1.6662–4(d)(3)(iii) (taking into account the relevance and persuasiveness of the authorities, and subsequent developments), the return position will generally satisfy the reasonable basis standard even though it may not satisfy the substantial authority standard.

A *tax shelter*, for purposes of the substantial understatement portion of the accuracy-related penalty, is a partnership or other entity, plan, or arrangement, with a significant purpose to avoid or evade federal income tax. Tax shelters have a higher standard and must have a confidence level of at least *more likely than not* (greater than 50% likelihood) that one or more significant tax issues would be resolved in the taxpayer's favor.

Taxpayers and tax return preparers who wish to avoid certain penalties can use Form 8275, Form 8275-R, or Rev. Proc. 2008-14 to disclose items or positions that are not otherwise adequately disclosed on a tax return (use Form 8275-R to disclose items or positions taken contrary to a regulation). The form is filed in order to avoid the portions of the accuracy-related penalty due to disregard of rules or to a substantial understatement of income tax for non-tax shelter items if the return position has a reasonable basis. It also is used for disclosures relating to preparer penalties for understatements due to unreasonable positions or disregard of rules.

The portion of the accuracy-related penalty attributable to the following types of misconduct cannot be avoided by disclosure on Form 8275:

- Negligence
- Disregard of regulations
- Any substantial understatement of income tax on a tax shelter item
- Any substantial valuation misstatement under chapter one of the Internal Revenue Code
- Any substantial overstatement of pension liabilities
- Any substantial estate or gift tax valuation understatements

Avoidance vs. Evasion

- Avoidance of tax is not a criminal offense. Taxpayers have the right to reduce, avoid, or minimize their taxes by legitimate means. One who avoids tax does not conceal or misrepresent, but shapes and preplans events to reduce or eliminate tax liability within the parameters of the law.
- Evasion involves some affirmative act to evade or defeat a tax, or payment of tax. Examples of affirmative acts are deceit, subterfuge, camouflage, concealment, attempts to color or obscure events, or make things seem other than they are. Common evasion schemes include:
    1) Intentional understatement or omission of income
    2) Claiming fictitious or improper deductions
    3) False allocation of income
    4) Improper claims, credits, or exemptions
    5) Concealment of assets

Indicators of Fraud

Affirmative acts of fraud are actions taken by the taxpayer, return preparer and/or promoter to deceive or defraud. Signs of fraud, known as first indicators (or badges) of fraud:

- **Income**
    1) Omitting specific items where similar items are included.
    2) Omitting entire sources of income.
    3) Failing to report or explain substantial amounts of income identified as received.
    4) Inability to explain substantial increases in net worth, especially over a period of years.
    5) Substantial personal expenditures exceeding reported resources.
    6) Inability to explain sources of bank deposits substantially exceeding reported income.
    7) Concealing bank accounts, brokerage accounts, and other property.
    8) Inadequately explaining dealings in large sums of currency, or the unexplained expenditure of currency.
    9) Consistent concealment of unexplained currency, especially in a business not routinely requiring large cash transactions.
    10) Failing to deposit receipts in a business account, contrary to established practices.
    11) Failing to file a tax return, especially for a period of several years, despite evidence of receipt of substantial amounts of taxable income.
    12) Cashing checks, representing income, at check cashing services and at banks where the taxpayer does not maintain an account.
    13) Concealing sources of receipts by false description of the source(s) of disclosed income, and/or nontaxable receipts.

- **Expenses or Deductions**
    1) Claiming fictitious or substantially overstated deductions.
    2) Claiming substantial business expense deductions for personal expenditures.

3) Claiming dependency exemptions for nonexistent, deceased, or self-supporting persons. Providing false or altered documents, such as birth certificates, lease documents, school/medical records, for the purpose of claiming the education credit, additional child tax credit, earned income tax credit (EITC), or other refundable credits.

4) Disguising trust fund loans as expenses or deductions.

- **Books and Records**

    1) Multiple sets of books or no records.

    2) Failure to keep adequate records, concealment of records, or refusal to make records available.

    3) False entries, or alterations made on the books and records; back-dated or post-dated documents; false invoices, false applications, false statements, or other false documents or applications.

    4) Invoices are irregularly numbered, unnumbered or altered.

    5) Checks made payable to third parties that are endorsed back to the taxpayer. Checks made payable to vendors and other business payees that are cashed by the taxpayer.

    6) Variances between treatment of questionable items as reflected on the tax return, and representations within the books.

    7) Intentional under- or over-footing of columns in journal or ledger.

    8) Amounts on tax return not in agreement with amounts in books.

    9) Amounts posted to ledger accounts not in agreement with source books or records.

    10) Journalizing questionable items out of correct account.

    11) Recording income items in suspense or asset accounts.

    12) False receipts to donors by exempt organizations.

- **Allocations of Income**

    1) Distribution of profits to fictitious partners.

    2) Inclusion of income or deductions in the tax return of a related taxpayer, when tax rate differences are a factor.

- **Conduct of Taxpayer**

    1) False statement about a material fact pertaining to the examination.

    2) Attempt to hinder or obstruct the examination. For example, failure to answer questions; repeated cancelled or rescheduled appointments; refusal to provide records; threatening potential witnesses, including the examiner; or assaulting the examiner.

    3) Failure to follow the advice of accountant, attorney or return preparer.

    4) Failure to make full disclosure of relevant facts to the accountant, attorney or return preparer.

    5) The taxpayer's knowledge of taxes and business practices where numerous questionable items appear on the tax returns.

    6) Testimony of employees concerning irregular business practices by the taxpayer.

    7) Destruction of books and records, especially if just after examination was started.

    8) Transfer of assets for purposes of concealment, or diversion of funds and/or assets by officials or trustees.

9) Pattern of consistent failure over several years to report income fully.

10) Proof that the tax return was incorrect to such an extent and in respect to items of such magnitude and character as to compel the conclusion that the falsity was known and deliberate.

11) Payment of improper expenses by or for officials or trustees.

12) Willful and intentional failure to execute pension plan amendments

13) Backdated applications and related documents.

14) False statements on Tax Exempt/Government Entity (TE/GE) determination letter applications.

15) Use of false social security numbers.

16) Submission of false Form W–4.

17) Submission of a false affidavit.

18) Attempt to bribe the examiner.

19) Submission of tax returns with false claims of withholding (Form 1099-OID, Form W-2) or refundable credits (Form 4136, Form 2439) resulting in a substantial refund.

20) Intentional submission of a bad check resulting in erroneous refunds and releases of liens.

21) Submission of false Form W-7 information to secure Individual Taxpayer Identification Number (ITIN) for self and dependents.

- **Methods of Concealment**

    1) Inadequacy of consideration.

    2) Insolvency of transferor.

    3) Asset ownership placed in other names.

    4) Transfer of all or nearly all of debtor's property.

    5) Close relationship between parties to the transfer.

    6) Transfer made in anticipation of a tax assessment or while the investigation of a deficiency is pending.

    7) Reservation of any interest in the property transferred.

    8) Transaction not in the usual course of business.

    9) Retention of possession or continued use of asset.

    10) Transactions surrounded by secrecy.

    11) False entries in books of transferor or transferee.

    12) Unusual disposition of the consideration received for the property.

    13) Use of secret bank accounts for income.

    14) Deposits into bank accounts under nominee names.

    15) Conduct of business transactions in false names.

Understatement of Liability §6694

Circular 230 §10.34 outlines standards with respect to tax returns and documents, affidavits and other papers. A practitioner must not sign a tax return or claim for refund that the practitioner knows or reasonably should know contains an unreasonable position. Preparer penalties under §6694 apply to the following circumstances:

- **Unreasonable positions** – A penalty of $1,000 or 50% of preparer's fee, whichever is greater.

    1) A position lacking substantial authority is unreasonable if the preparer knew (or should have known) of the position, and

        A) For undisclosed positions – The position does not have substantial authority.

        B) For disclosed positions – The position does not have a reasonable basis.

        C) For tax shelters – There was not a reasonable belief that the position would *more likely than not* be sustained on its merits.

    2) If a return preparer understates tax liability on a return, the IRS will not impose a penalty if the preparer shows that there is reasonable cause and the tax return preparer acted in good faith.

- **Willful or reckless conduct** – A penalty of $5,000 or 50% of preparer's fee, whichever is greater.

    1) Willful or reckless conduct is conduct by the tax return preparer that is a willful attempt in any manner to understate the liability for tax on the return or claim, or a reckless or intentional disregard of rules or regulations.

    2) The amount of any penalty payable for willful misconduct is reduced by any penalty for an unreasonable position.

Failures under §6695

Any tax return preparer who fails to take certain actions may be assessed other penalties with respect to the preparation of tax returns for other persons.

- Penalty of $50 for each occurrence up to a maximum of $25,000/year unless it is shown that such failure is due to reasonable cause and not willful neglect:

    1) **§6695(a) Failure to furnish copy of return to taxpayer** – The tax preparer must furnish a completed copy of the return or claim for refund to the taxpayer no later than the time it is presented for the taxpayer's signature.

    2) **§6695(b) Failure to sign return** – The tax preparer must sign a tax return or claim for refund if the tax preparer has primary responsibility for the overall substantive accuracy of the preparation of the tax return or claim for refund.

    3) **§6695(c) Failure to furnish identifying number** – A tax return preparer must obtain and exclusively use a PTIN, rather than a social security number (SSN), as the identifying number to be included with the tax return preparer's signature on a tax return or claim for refund.

    4) **§6695(d) Failure to retain copy or list** – A tax return preparer must keep a copy of the tax return, or retain, on a list, the name and taxpayer identification number of the taxpayer for whom the return was prepared. The records must be available for inspection for the 3-year period following the close of the return period during which the return or claim for refund was presented for signature to the taxpayer. A "return period" is the 12-month period beginning on July 1 of each year and ending on June 30.

    5) **§6695(e) Failure to file correct information returns** – Each person who employs (or engages) one or more income tax return preparers to prepare any return of tax is responsible for retaining a record of the name, taxpayer identification number, and principal place of work during the return period of each income tax return preparer employed (or engaged) by the person at any

time during that period. The record must be available for inspection upon request by the district director for the 3-year period following the close of the return period.

- **§6695(f) Negotiation of check** – Any tax return preparer who endorses or otherwise negotiates (directly or through an agent) a refund check (including an electronic version of a check) issued to a taxpayer (other than the preparer), shall pay a penalty of **$500** with respect to each check. The penalty does not vary based on how much compensation the preparer receives from the taxpayer, the amount of the refund check, or the direct deposit. The penalty applies to a tax return preparer who directs the IRS to deposit a taxpayer's refund into a bank account in the preparer's name or into a bank account under the preparer's control. The preparer may not endorse or negotiate a check for a taxpayer even though the preparer was designated as the taxpayer's representative on a Form 2848, Power of Attorney.

A tax return preparer will not be considered to have endorsed or otherwise negotiated a check as a result of having affixed the taxpayer's name to a refund check for the purpose of depositing the check into an account in the name of the taxpayer or in the joint names of the taxpayer and one or more other persons (excluding the tax return preparer). See Treas. Reg. 1.6695-1(f)(1).

Taxpayers sometimes request that their refunds be direct deposited into a bank account in the preparer's name or into a bank account under the preparer's control when taxpayers do not have their own bank account. Even if a taxpayer has requested the direct deposit to be made in this manner, the preparer is still subject to the IRC 6695(f) penalty for complying with the request.

- **§6695(g) Failure to be diligent in determining eligibility for earned income credit** – Any return preparer who fails to comply with due diligence requirements imposed to determine eligibility for, or the amount of, the credit allowable shall pay a penalty of **$500** for each failure. Those who prepare Earned Income Tax Credit (EITC) claims must not only ask all the questions required on *Form 8867*, Paid Preparers' Earned Income Credit Checklist, but must also ask additional questions when information seems incorrect, inconsistent or incomplete. In addition, the preparer must verify identity, prepare an EIC computational checklist (Form 8867 or equivalent), and meet a recordkeeping requirement (keep form 8867 and the EIC worksheet (or equivalents) for 3 years after the June 30th following the date the return or claim was presented for signature).

Safeguarding Taxpayer Information

Tax return preparers must obtain consent to use tax return information before tax return information is used and before returns are provided to the taxpayer for signature. Internal Revenue Code §7216 is a criminal provision enacted by the U.S. Congress in 1971 that prohibits preparers of tax returns from knowingly or recklessly disclosing or using tax return information. A convicted preparer may be fined not more than $1,000 or imprisoned not more than one year or both, for each violation.

Internal Revenue Code §6713 imposes a civil penalty of $250 on any person who is engaged in the business of preparing, or providing services in connection with the preparation of returns of tax, or any person who for compensation prepares a return for another person, and who:

- Discloses any information furnished to him for, or in connection with, the preparation of any such return, or

- Uses any such information for any purpose other than to prepare, or assist in preparing, any such return. Imposition of the penalty under Internal Revenue Code §6713 does not require that the disclosure be knowing or reckless as it does under Internal Revenue Code §7216.

Generally, unless otherwise specified, a written consent is effective for a period of one year from the date the taxpayer signs the consent. Disclosing tax return information to another tax preparer within the United States that is assisting in the preparation of the return generally does not require the consent of the taxpayer.

Payment

The tax preparer has 30 days to pay the penalty upon receipt of a demand for payment from the IRS. The preparer may elect to pay at least 15% of the amount of the penalty and file a claim for refund. If the claim for refund is denied (or six months have passed), the preparer has 30 more days to begin a proceeding in the appropriate U.S. district court for determination of liability.

Taxpayer Supporting Documentation

A taxpayer must keep records as long as needed for the administration of any provision of the Internal Revenue Code. Generally, this means keeping records that support items shown on the return until the *period of limitations* for that return expires. The period of limitations is the period of time in which the taxpayer can amend a return to claim a credit or refund, or the Internal Revenue Service can assess additional tax. This is generally the later of **three years** from the due date of the return or the date the taxpayer filed the return. It is good practice for taxpayers to maintain records, both basic and specific.

Table 17-1. Period of Limitations

	IF you...	THEN the period is...
1	Owe additional tax and (2), (3), and (4) do not apply	3 years
2	Do not report income and it is more than 25% of the gross income shown on return	6 years
3	File a fraudulent return	No limit
4	Do not file a return	No limit
5	File a claim for credit or refund after filing return	Later of 3 years or 2 years after tax was paid
6	File a claim for a loss from worthless securities	7 years

It is good practice for taxpayers to maintain records, both basic and specific. Records do not need to be required to be of benefit. For example, a taxpayer who receives a Form W-2 should keep a copy until he begins receiving Social Security benefits. This will help protect his benefits in case there is a question about his work record or earnings in a particular year. The IRS does not require taxpayers to maintain records in a particular way. If using a computerized system, individuals must be able to produce legible records of the information needed to determine the correct tax liability and in addition, must keep proof of payment, receipts, and other documents to prove the amount shown.

Applying to Become an Authorized E-File Provider

An *Authorized IRS E-File Provider* is a business or organization authorized by the IRS to participate in *IRS e-file*. It may be a sole proprietorship, partnership, corporation, or other entity. The firm submits an e-file application, meets the eligibility criteria, and must pass a suitability check before the IRS assigns an

Electronic Filing Identification Number (EFIN). To register for e-file, the preparer must first register for e-services.

- **Step 1: Choose provider options** – Applicants determine the type of provider they are:
    1) **Electronic Return Originator (ERO)** – originates the electronic submission of tax returns
    2) **Intermediate service provider** – assists with processing between ERO and transmitter
    3) **Transmitter** – sends the electronic return data directly to the IRS
    4) **Online provider** – allows taxpayers to self-prepare returns by entering return data directly on commercially available software
    5) **Software developer**
    6) **Reporting agent** – originates the electronic submission of certain returns for its clients and/or transmits the returns to the IRS. A Reporting Agent must be an accounting service, franchiser, bank, or other approved entity.
- **Step 2: Complete and submit the IRS E-File Application** – The IRS E-File Application is available on the IRS Web site. Each individual who is a principal or responsible official must register for e-services on the IRS Web site, if not already registered, prior to submitting the IRS E-File Application to the IRS. Principals and responsible officials must submit either fingerprint cards or evidence of professional status as an attorney, certified public accountant, enrolled agent, officer of a publicly held corporation, or banking official.
- **Step 3: Pass a suitability check** – The IRS conducts a suitability check on the applicant, and on all principals and responsible officials listed on e-file applications, to determine the applicant's suitability to be an Authorized IRS E-File Provider. The IRS does not complete suitability checks on applicants applying only as a software developer.

Denial to Participate in IRS E-File

The IRS notifies the applicant of denial to participate in IRS e-file and the date on which the applicant may re-apply. In most circumstances, the denied applicant may appeal the decision through an Administrative Review. If the denial expires or reverses, the applicant may reapply to participate in IRS e-file. The IRS reviews each firm or organization, Principal, and Responsible Official listed on the IRS E-File Application. The IRS may deny an applicant participation in IRS e-file for a variety of reasons that include but are not limited to the following:

- An indictment or conviction of any criminal offense under the laws of the United States or of a state or other political subdivision, or an active IRS criminal investigation
- Failure to file timely and accurate federal, state, or local tax returns
- Failure to timely pay any federal, state, or local tax liability
- Assessment of penalties
- Suspension/disbarment from practice before the IRS or before a state or local tax agency
- Disreputable conduct or other facts that may adversely impact IRS e-file
- Misrepresentation on an IRS E-File Application
- Unethical practices in return preparation
- Assessment against the applicant of the earned income credit due diligence penalty under §6695(g)
- Stockpiling returns prior to official acceptance to participate in IRS e-file

- Knowingly and directly or indirectly employing or accepting assistance from any firm, organization, or individual denied participation in IRS e-file, or suspended or expelled from participating in IRS e-file
- Subject of a court injunction or prohibited from filing returns by any federal or state legal action that prohibits them from participation

Acceptance

After an applicant passes the suitability check and the IRS completes processing the application, the IRS notifies the applicant of acceptance to participate in IRS e-file. Transmitters and software developers must complete testing before acceptance. The IRS assigns Electronic Identification Filing Numbers (EFIN) to all providers and assigns Electronic Identification Transmission Numbers (ETIN) to transmitters. A provider must update his application information within 30 days of the date of any changes to the information on his current application.

The E-File Process

Tax preparers may file returns electronically through a system known as *IRS e-file* through *electronic return originators* who are authorized e-file providers.

- Modernized E-File (MeF) accepts tax returns for the current year and two prior years. The IRS accepts an electronic version of Form 4868 for the current tax year.
- In prior years, a taxpayer could not e-file an individual income tax return after October 15, even if the IRS granted an extension to file beyond that date. MeF now accepts electronic returns year round.
- All prescribed due dates for filing of returns apply to e-file returns. An electronically filed return is not considered filed until the IRS acknowledges acceptance of the electronic portion of the tax return for processing. The IRS accepts individual income tax returns electronically only if the taxpayer signs the return using a Personal Identification Number (PIN).
- The receipt of an electronic postmark provides taxpayers with confidence that they have filed their returns timely. The date of the postmark is considered the date of filing when the date of electronic postmark is on or before the prescribed due date even if the return is received by the IRS after the prescribed due date for filing. All requirements for signing the return and completing a paper declaration, if required, as well as for timely resubmitting of a rejected timely filed return must be adhered to for the electronic postmark to be considered the date of filing.

E-File Mandate

> Paid preparers—or the preparer's firm in the aggregate—who prepare and expect to file 11 or more 2015 income tax returns for individuals, trusts, and estates are required to file these returns electronically.

Electronic Return Originator (ERO)

An Electronic Return Originator (ERO) originates the electronic submission of returns for taxpayers who want to e-file their returns. An ERO originates the electronic submission of a return after the taxpayer authorizes (Form 8879) the filing of the return via IRS e-file. The ERO must have either prepared the return or collected it from a taxpayer. Duties of the ERO include the following:

- **Safeguarding IRS *e-file* from fraud and abuse** – An ERO who is also the paid preparer should exercise due diligence in the preparation of returns involving the Earned Income Tax Credit (EITC) because it is a popular target for fraud and abuse. EROs must not electronically file individual income tax returns prior to receiving Forms W-2, W-2G or 1099-R.

- **Verifying Taxpayer Identification Numbers (TIN)** – Confirm identities on the return.
- **Be aware of non-standard information documents** – Look for suspicious or altered documents.
- **Be careful with addresses** – Verify the taxpayer's address has not changed.
- **Avoiding refund delays** – Recommend taxpayers supply current information, and check their return.

Returns Not Eligible for IRS E-File

Taxpayers may file both state and federal returns using the IRS e-file system. However, e-file is not available for the following individual income tax returns and related conditions:

- Tax returns with fiscal year tax periods
- Amended tax returns
- Returns with tax years ending prior to December 31, 2013.
- Returns containing forms or schedules that cannot be processed by IRS e-file other than those forms and schedules that are required to be submitted with Form 8453
- Tax returns with a Taxpayer Identification Number (TIN) beginning with 9. This does not apply to certain Adopted Taxpayer Identification Numbers (ATIN) and Individual Taxpayer Identification Numbers (ITIN).
- The IRS cannot electronically process tax returns with rare or unusual processing conditions or that exceed the specifications for returns allowable in IRS e-file.

Form 8453

IRS e-file returns must contain all of the same information as paper returns. Not all forms are eligible to transmit electronically. In such cases, the ERO must submit to the IRS all paper documents required to complete the filing of returns by attaching them to the *Form 8453* and sending them to the IRS.

Length of Time to Keep Records

The ERO must retain the following material until the end of the calendar year at the business address from which it originated the return or at a location that allows the ERO access the material because it must be available at the time of IRS request. An ERO may retain the required records at the business address of the responsible official or at a location that allows the responsible official to access the material during any period of time the office is closed because it must be available at the time of IRS request through the end of the calendar year. The ERO must maintain the following records:

- A copy of *Form 8453, U.S. Individual Income Tax Transmittal for an IRS e-file Return*, and supporting documents that are not included in the electronic records submitted to the IRS
- Copies of Forms W-2, W-2G, and 1099-R
- A copy of signed IRS *e-file* consent to disclosure forms
- A complete copy of the electronic portion of the return that can be readily and accurately converted into an electronic transmission that the IRS can process
- The acknowledgement file for IRS accepted returns

> IRS e-file Signature Authorization Forms 8879 and 8878 <u>must</u> be available to the IRS for three years from the due date of the return or the IRS received date, whichever is later.

EROs may electronically image and store all paper records they are required to retain for IRS e-file. This includes Forms 8453 and paper copies of Forms W-2, W-2G, and 1099-R, as well as any supporting documents not included in the electronic record and Forms 8879 and 8878. In brief, the electronic storage system must ensure an accurate and complete transfer of the hard copy to the electronic storage media. The ERO must be able to reproduce all records with a high degree of legibility and readability (including the taxpayers' signatures).

Providing Information to the Taxpayer

The ERO must provide a complete copy of the return to the taxpayer. EROs may provide this copy in any media, including electronic, that is acceptable to both the taxpayer and the ERO. A complete copy of a taxpayer's return includes Form 8453 and other documents that the ERO cannot electronically transmit, when applicable, as well as the electronic portion of the return. The ERO should also advise taxpayers that, if needed, they must file an amended return as a paper return and mail it to the processing center that would handle the taxpayer's paper return.

Rules for Returning Records

In general, at the request of a client, a practitioner must promptly return all records of the client that are necessary for the client to comply with his federal tax obligations. The practitioner may retain copies of the records returned to a client. The existence of a dispute over fees generally does not relieve the practitioner of his responsibility under this section. Nevertheless, if applicable state law allows or permits the retention of a client's records in the case of a dispute over fees for services rendered, the practitioner need only return those records that must be attached to the taxpayer's return. The practitioner must provide the client with reasonable access to review and copy any additional records of the client retained by the practitioner that are necessary for the client to comply with his federal tax obligations.

Electronic Signature Requirements

> As with an income tax return submitted to the IRS on paper, the taxpayer <u>and</u> paid preparer must sign an electronic income tax return. Electronic signatures are required for returns using e-file.

Taxpayers must sign and date the Declaration of Taxpayer to authorize the origination of the electronic submission of the return to the IRS prior to the transmission of the return to the IRS. The Declaration of Taxpayer includes the taxpayer's declaration under penalties of perjury that the return is true, correct and complete, as well as the taxpayer's Consent to Disclosure. The Consent to Disclosure authorizes the IRS to disclose information to the taxpayer's providers. Taxpayers authorize Intermediate Service Providers, Transmitters and EROs to receive from the IRS an acknowledgement of receipt or reason for rejection of the electronic return, an indication of any refund offset, and the reason for any delay in processing the return or refund and the date of the refund.

There are currently two methods for signing individual income tax returns electronically. Both methods allow taxpayers to use a Personal Identification Number (PIN) to sign the return and the *Declaration of Taxpayer*. The Declaration of Taxpayer includes the taxpayer's declaration under penalties of perjury that the return is true, correct and complete, as well as the taxpayer's Consent to Disclosure, authorizing the IRS to disclose information to the taxpayer's providers.

- The **Self-select PIN** method <u>requires</u> a taxpayer to provide his prior year Adjusted Gross Income (AGI) amount or prior year PIN for use by the IRS to authenticate the taxpayer. This method <u>may</u> be completely paperless if taxpayers enter their own PIN directly into the electronic return record using key strokes after reviewing the completed return. Taxpayers may also authorize the ERO to enter the PIN on their behalf, in which case the taxpayers must review and sign a completed signature authorization form (Form 8879) after reviewing the return.

- The **Practitioner PIN** method does not require the taxpayer to provide their prior year AGI amount or prior year PIN. When using the Practitioner PIN method, a taxpayer must always appropriately sign a completed signature authorization form (Form 8879). A taxpayer, who uses the Practitioner PIN method and enters his own PIN in the electronic return record using keystrokes after reviewing the completed return, must still appropriately sign the signature authorization form. Regardless of the method of electronic signature used, a taxpayer may enter his own PIN; the ERO may select and enter the taxpayer's PIN; or the software may generate the taxpayer's PIN in the electronic return.

IRS E-File Signature Authorization

When a taxpayer is <u>unable to enter his PIN directly</u> in the electronic return, a taxpayer may authorize the ERO to enter his PIN in the electronic return record by signing the appropriate completed IRS e-file signature authorization form. *Form 8879, IRS E-File Signature Authorization,* authorizes an ERO to enter the taxpayer's PIN on Individual Income Tax Returns, and *Form 8878, IRS E-File Authorization for Application of Extension of Time to File,* authorizes an ERO to enter the taxpayer's PIN on Forms 4868 and 2350.

> The ERO may enter the taxpayer's PIN in the electronic return record before the taxpayer signs Form 8879 or 8878, but the taxpayer must sign and date the appropriate form <u>before</u> the ERO originates the electronic submission of the return. The taxpayer must sign and date Form 8879 or Form 8878 after reviewing the return and ensuring the tax return information on the form matches the information on the return. The ERO may sign Forms 8879 and 8878 by rubber stamp, mechanical device (such as signature pen), or computer software program. This does not alter the requirement that taxpayers must sign Form 8879 and Form 8878 by handwritten signature.

Electronic Signatures for EROs

The ERO must also sign with a PIN. The ERO should use the same PIN for the entire tax year. The ERO may manually input his PIN, or the software can generate the PIN in the electronic record in the location designated for the ERO Electronic Filing Identification Number (EFIN)/PIN. By entering a PIN in the ERO EFIN/PIN field, the ERO is attesting to the ERO Declaration. For returns prepared by the ERO firm, return preparers are declaring under the penalties of perjury that they reviewed the returns and they are true, correct, and complete. An ERO may authorize members of the firm or designated employees to sign for them, but the ERO is still responsible.

Rejected Returns and Resolution

The IRS electronically acknowledges the receipt of all transmissions. Returns in each transmission are either accepted or rejected for specific reasons. Accepted returns meet the processing criteria and IRS considers them "filed" as soon as the return is signed electronically or through the receipt by the IRS of a paper signature. Rejected returns fail to meet processing criteria and the IRS considers them "not filed."

> If the IRS rejects the electronic portion of a taxpayer's individual income tax return for processing, and the ERO cannot rectify the reason for the rejection, the ERO must take reasonable steps to inform the taxpayer of the rejection **within 24 hours**.

> The ERO may resubmit, without additional signatures, a return where the amounts do not differ by more than $50 to *Total Income* or *AGI*, <u>or</u> $14 to *Total Tax*, *Federal Income Tax Withheld*, or *Amount You Owe*.

When the ERO advises the taxpayer of an unfiled return, the ERO must provide the taxpayer with the reject code(s) accompanied by an explanation. If the taxpayer chooses not to have the electronic portion of the return corrected and transmitted to the IRS, or if the IRS cannot accept the return for processing, the taxpayer must file a paper return. In order to timely file the return, the taxpayer must file the paper return by the later of the due date of the return or <u>10</u> calendar days after the date the IRS gives notification that it rejected the electronic portion of the return or that the return cannot be accepted for processing. A taxpayer should include an explanation in the paper return as to why he is filing the return after the due date.

Payments

Taxpayers who owe additional tax must pay their balances due by the original due date of the return or be subject to interest and penalties. An extension of time to file may be filed electronically by the original return due date, but it is an extension of time to file the return, not an extension of time to pay a balance due. Taxpayers can e-file and, at the same time, authorize an electronic fund withdrawal (EFW). Taxpayers who choose this option must provide account numbers and routing transit numbers for qualified savings, checking, or share draft accounts. In addition, taxpayers may make payments through the Electronic Federal Tax Payment System (EFTPS), by check, electronically using a credit or debit card, or by filing an installment agreement request.

Refunds

> A provider must never charge a separate fee for direct deposit and must accept any direct deposit election by a taxpayer to any eligible financial institution designated by the taxpayer.

The taxpayer may designate refunds for direct deposit to qualified accounts in the taxpayer's name. Qualified accounts include savings, checking, share draft, or consumer asset accounts (for example, IRA or money market accounts). Providers should caution taxpayers that some financial institutions do not permit the deposit of joint income tax refunds into individual accounts. The IRS is not responsible if the financial institution refuses direct deposits for this reason. The provider must advise taxpayers that they cannot rescind a direct deposit election and they cannot make changes to routing transit numbers of financial institutions or to their account numbers after the IRS has accepted the return.

Advertising Standards

IRS e-file is a brand name. Firms accepted for participation in IRS e-file as EROs are "Authorized IRS E-File Providers." All providers must abide by the following advertising standards:

- A provider must comply with the advertising and solicitation provisions of Treasury Department Circular No. 230. This circular prohibits the use or participation in the use of any form of public communication containing a false, fraudulent, misleading, deceptive, unduly influencing, coercive, or unfair statement of claim.

- The provider must not use improper or misleading advertising in relation to IRS e-file.

- A provider must not use the IRS name, "Internal Revenue Service," or "IRS" within a firm's name. However, once accepted to participate in IRS e-file, a firm may represent itself as an "Authorized IRS E-File Provider." If promotional materials or logos provided by the IRS are used, the provider must comply with all IRS instructions pertaining to their use. Advertising materials must not carry the FMS, IRS, or other Treasury Seals.

- If a provider uses radio, television, Internet, signage, or other methods of communication to advertise IRS e-file, the provider must keep a copy of the text or, if prerecorded, the recorded advertisement. The provider must retain copies until the end of the calendar year following the last transmission or use. The records must be made available to the IRS upon request.

- If a provider uses direct mail, e-mail, fax communications, or other distribution methods to advertise, the provider must retain a copy, as well as a list or other description of the firms, organizations, or individuals to whom the provider sent the communication. The provider must retain the records until the end of the calendar year following the date sent.

- A provider must not advertise that individual income tax returns may be electronically filed prior to the receipt of Forms W-2, W-2G, and 1099-R.

Identity Theft

Tax preparers play a critical role in assisting clients, both individuals and businesses, who are victims of tax-related identity theft. The IRS is working hard to prevent and detect identity theft as well as reduce the time it takes to resolve these cases. Tax-related identity theft occurs when someone uses a stolen social security number to file a tax return claiming a fraudulent refund. Thieves may also use a stolen EIN from a business client to create false Forms W-2 to support refund fraud schemes.

> The IRS doesn't initiate contact with taxpayers by email to request personal or financial information. This includes any type of electronic communication, such as text messages and social media channels. The IRS does not call taxpayers with threats of lawsuits or arrests.

Signs of Tax-Related Identity Theft

- More than one tax return was filed using your client's SSN,
- Your client has a balance due, refund offset or a collection action taken for a year in which your client did not file a tax return,
- IRS records indicate your client received wages from an unknown employer,
- A business client may receive an IRS letter about an amended tax return, fictitious employees or about a defunct, closed or dormant business.

What to Do if Your Identity is Stolen

The Federal Trade Commission (FTC), lead federal agency on general identity theft issues, has recommended steps identity theft victims should take to protect their credit. See identitytheft.gov for general recommendations for your clients. The FTC recommends these steps for victims of identity theft:

- File a complaint with the FTC at identitytheft.gov.
- Contact financial institutions, and close any financial or credit accounts opened without permission or tampered with by identity thieves.

Contact one of the three major credit bureaus to place a fraud alert on your credit records:

Equifax www.Equifax.com, 1-800-766-0008
Experian www.Experian.com, 1-888-397-3742
TransUnion TransUnion.com, 1-800-680-7289

If your client's SSN has been compromised, whether from a data breach, computer hack or stolen wallet, and they have reason to believe they are at risk for tax-related identity theft, you should take these steps:

- If your client received an IRS notice, respond immediately to the telephone number provided.
- Complete Form 14039, Identity Theft Affidavit. Fax or mail to the IRS according to the instructions.
- To inquire about specific client's return information, you must have a power of attorney on file, and you must authenticate your identity with the IRS customer service representative.

A victim of identity theft or a person authorized to obtain the identity theft victim's tax information may request a redacted copy (one with some information blacked-out) of a fraudulent return that was filed and accepted by the IRS using the identity theft victim's name and SSN. Due to federal privacy laws, the victim's name and SSN must be listed as either the primary or secondary taxpayer on the fraudulent return; otherwise the IRS cannot disclose the return information. For this reason, the IRS cannot disclose return information to any person listed only as a dependent. Visit irs.gov for more information on how to make this request.

Business Identity Theft

Business identity theft happens when someone creates, uses, or attempts to use, the identifying information of a business, without authority, to obtain tax benefits. Business identity thieves file fraudulent business returns to receive refundable business credits or to perpetuate individual identity theft.

Sometimes the identity theft incident is related to tax administration and sometimes it's not. The incident may surface in different ways.

Business identity theft is more complex than individual identity theft. Many of the same indicators that signify simple filing or processing errors also hint at business identity theft. While on the surface these occurrences may appear to indicate business identity theft, they may also stem from something as simple as transposed numbers.

Signs of identity theft <u>related</u> to tax administration:

- Your client receives IRS notices about fictitious employees.
- Your client notices activity related to or receives IRS notices regarding a defunct, closed or dormant business after all account balances have been paid.
- Your client's return is accepted as an amended return, but the taxpayer has not filed a return for that year.

If these things occur, the IRS and the taxpayer will need to do some research before determining the incident is a result of identity theft. Identity theft not related to tax administration should be reported to the Federal Trade Commission.

Signs of identity theft <u>not related</u> to tax administration:

- Receive bills for business lines of credit or credit cards they do not have.
- Notice that a credit report indicates credit or other open accounts they did not authorize.

- See unexplained bank account withdrawals.
- Don't get their bills or other mail.
- Find unfamiliar accounts or charges on their credit report.
- Get a notice that information was compromised by a data breach at a company where they do business or have an account.

Protective actions to take if business information is compromised

Respond immediately to any notices from the IRS. If there is reason to believe someone fraudulently used the business Employer Identification Number, notify the IRS immediately using the contact information on the notice or letter.

- File a police report with the local police department.
- Carefully review and reconcile account statements as soon as they receive them.
- Regularly review business registration information online (for all active and closed businesses).
- Monitor credit reports for suspicious activity every 12 months.
- Close any accounts that have been tampered with or opened without their permission.
- File a complaint with the Federal Trade Commission.
- Update virus, malware, and other security software programs on their computers.
- Remain vigilant and be alert for suspicious or unusual activity.

Place a fraud alert on credit reports by contacting any one of the four nationwide credit reporting companies:

Dun & Bradstreet www.smallbusiness.dnb.com 800-234-3867
Equifax www.equifax.com 800-525-6285
Experian www.experian.com 888-397-3742
Trans Union www.transunion.com 800-916-8800

18 Practice Before the IRS

Director of the Office of Professional Responsibility · Practice before the IRS · Enrollment Duties and Restrictions · Sanctions and Penalties · Disciplinary Proceedings

This chapter relates to *Practice before the IRS* as explained in IRS Circular 230 and Publication 947.

Practice Before the IRS

Director of the Office of Professional Responsibility

The duties of the Director of the *Office of Professional Responsibility* (**OPR**) include the following:

- Acting on applications for enrollment to practice before the IRS
- Inquiries on matters under the Director's jurisdiction
- Institutes' disciplinary proceedings related to practitioners

IRS Return Preparer Office

The IRS *Return Preparer Office* (**RPO**) is responsible for implementing the new requirements and oversight of the IRS return preparer program. It will work in partnership with the Office of Professional Responsibility, which is responsible for the enforcement of Circular 230 conduct issues.

Definition of Practice before the IRS

Practice before the IRS comprehends all matters connected with a presentation to the IRS relating to a taxpayer's rights, privileges, or liabilities under laws or regulations administered by the IRS. Such presentations include but are not limited to the following:

- Preparing documents (this does NOT include preparing a tax return)
- Filing documents
- Corresponding and communicating with the IRS
- Representing a taxpayer at conferences, hearings, or meetings with the IRS
- Rendering written advice with respect to any entity, transaction, plan, or arrangement

> Certain tasks, which anyone may perform, do not constitute practice before the IRS. These tasks include appearing as a witness for a taxpayer before the IRS, or furnishing information at the request of the IRS.

Who May Practice

Any of the following individuals may practice before the IRS, with the assumption that they are not currently under suspension or disbarred:

- **Attorneys** – Any attorney who is a member in good standing of the bar of the highest court of any state, possession, territory, commonwealth, or the District of Columbia

- **Certified public accountants (CPAs)** – Any CPA who is duly qualified to practice as a CPA in any state, possession, territory, commonwealth, or the District of Columbia

- **Enrolled agents** – Any enrolled agent in active status

- **Enrolled retirement plan agents** – Any enrolled retirement plan agent in active status

- **Enrolled actuaries** – Any individual enrolled as an actuary by the Joint Board for the Enrollment of Actuaries

- **IRS Annual Filing Season Program (AFSP)** – A non-credentialed preparer that has a record of completion for the IRS Annual Filing Season Program has *limited representation rights*. Representation is limited to examinations of the taxable period covered by the tax return he prepared and signed.

Practice for *enrolled retirement plan agents* and *enrolled actuaries* is limited to certain Internal Revenue Code sections that relate to their area of expertise, principally those governing retirement plans.

Individuals placed in inactive status and individuals ineligible to practice before the Internal Revenue Service may not state or imply that they are eligible to practice before the Internal Revenue Service, or use the terms enrolled agent, enrolled retirement plan agent, the designation "EA" or other form of reference to eligibility to practice before the IRS.

Preparer Considerations

Preparer Tax Identification Number

All paid tax return preparers (including attorneys, CPAs, and enrolled agents) must have a ***Preparer Tax Identification Number (PTIN)*** before preparing any federal tax returns. A PTIN is a number issued by the IRS to paid tax return preparers. It is the tax preparer's identification number and, when applicable, must be placed in the paid preparer section of a tax return. Any individual who, for compensation, prepares all or substantially all of a tax return or claim for refund—including making determinations that affect tax liability—needs a PTIN.

Unenrolled Tax Return Preparer

An unenrolled return preparer is an individual other than an attorney, CPA, enrolled agent, or enrolled actuary who prepares and signs a taxpayer's return as the preparer, or who prepares a return but is not required (by the instructions to the return or regulations) to sign the return. The unenrolled return preparer designation includes individuals who passed the IRS registered tax return preparer competency test that was offered between November 2011 and January 2013. Unenrolled return preparers may only represent taxpayers before revenue agents, customer service representatives, or similar officers and employees of the Internal Revenue Service. Unenrolled return preparers cannot represent taxpayers, regardless of the circumstances requiring representation, before appeals officers, revenue officers, attorneys from the Office of Chief Counsel, or similar officers or employees of the Internal Revenue Service or the Department of Treasury. Unenrolled return preparers cannot execute closing agreements, extend the statutory period for tax assessments or collection of tax, execute waivers, execute claims for refund, or sign any document on behalf of a taxpayer.

- An unenrolled return preparer may not sign documents for a taxpayer and may only represent taxpayers in limited situations. An unenrolled return preparer **may not**:

    1) Represent a taxpayer before other offices of the IRS, such as Collection or Appeals

    2) Execute closing agreements

    3) Extend the statutory period for tax assessments or collection of tax

    4) Execute waivers

    5) Execute claims for refund

    6) Receive refund checks

Other Unenrolled Individuals

Because of their special relationship with a taxpayer, the following unenrolled individuals may represent the specified taxpayers before the IRS, provided they present satisfactory identification and proof of authority to represent the taxpayer:

- *Individuals* may represent themselves and members of their immediate family. Immediate family means a spouse, child, parent, brother, or sister of the individual.

- An *officer* of a corporation may represent the corporation.

- A *general partner* may represent the partnership before the IRS.

- A regular full-time *employee* may represent his employer.

- A *fiduciary* (trustee, executor, administrator, receiver, or guardian) stands in the position of a taxpayer and acts as the taxpayer, not as a representative.

- Any individual may represent an individual or entity, located outside the United States, before personnel of the IRS when such representation takes place outside the United States.

Those Who May Not Practice

In general, individuals who are not eligible or who have lost the privilege may not practice before the IRS. Corporations, associations, partnerships, and other non-individuals are not eligible to practice before the IRS.

A valid PTIN does not provide any representation rights. The IRS will **not** grant limited representation rights to an unenrolled preparer without an AFSP Record of Completion for the tax year of any tax return he prepares and signs after December 31, 2015. Attorneys, CPAs, and enrolled agents will continue to have unlimited representation rights and can represent clients before any office of the IRS.

Enrollment

The Enrollment Process

The Office of Professional Responsibility (OPR) may grant enrollment to practice before the IRS to an applicant who demonstrates special competence in tax matters by passing a written examination administered by the IRS. In addition, applicants may qualify because of past service and technical experience in the IRS. In either case, the applicant must file certain forms.

- Applicants apply to take the *special enrollment examination* by filing **Form 2587**.
- Individuals, who have passed the examination or are applying based on past service and technical experience with the IRS, may apply for enrollment by filing **Form 23**, *Application for Enrollment to Practice before the Internal Revenue Service*. This can be done online at pay.gov.
    1) The application must include a check or money order.
    2) If an application is denied, the OPR must inform the applicant of the reason in a notice of denial, which may be appealed within 30 days of receipt.

> Once enrolled, practitioners must renew enrollment as required under a **three-year enrollment cycle.** The year of renewal depends on the last digit of the SSN or EIN a practitioner uses to enroll, regardless of whether or not the practitioner was enrolled for a full three years. The IRS <u>only</u> processes applications for renewal between November 1 and January 31. Renewed enrollments are effective as of April 1 following the period of application.

Continuing Professional Education

All tax return preparers must annually renew their preparer tax identification number (PTIN). Certain requirements are necessary in order to continue registration. These include, but are not limited to, ongoing professional education and the avoidance of actions that can subject a practitioner to censure, suspension, or disbarment.

> An Enrolled Agent must complete a minimum of **72 hours** of continuing education during the three-year enrollment cycle and at least 16 hours for each respective year. These 16 hours must include at least two hours of ethics or professional conduct education. The continuing education requirements are pro-rated if enrollment occurs in the middle of an enrollment cycle, at a rate of two hours required education for each month or part of a month enrolled. ** Frequently appears on the exam.

To qualify for continuing education credit, a course of learning must be a qualifying continuing education program designed to enhance professional knowledge in Federal taxation or Federal tax related matters (programs comprised of current subject matter in Federal taxation or Federal tax related matters, including accounting, tax return preparation software, taxation, or ethics); and be a qualifying continuing education program consistent with the Internal Revenue Code and effective tax administration.

- All continuing education programs are measured in terms of **contact hours**. A contact hour is 50 minutes of continuous participation in a program. The IRS only grants credit for a full contact hour, i.e., 50 minutes or multiples thereof.
- Qualifying CPE programs must meet certain standards. A qualified sponsor must run all CPE programs. They must require attendance and issue a certificate of attendance. The instructor's background, experience, education, and training should be appropriate for the subject matter. The course must provide a written outline, textbook, or suitable electronic educational materials. Self-study courses (including online, correspondence, and taped program courses) meet this standard if they require registration by the participant, provide a means of measuring completion such as a written test, provide a certification of successful completion of said test, and provide a written outline, textbook, or acceptable electronic substitutes.
- Keep records of completed CPE for <u>**four years**</u> following the date of renewal of enrollment

Duties and Restrictions

Duties

Practitioners must promptly submit records or information requested by officers or employees of the IRS. When the Office of Professional Responsibility requests information concerning possible violations of the regulations by other parties, the practitioner must provide the information and be prepared to testify in disbarment or suspension proceedings. The IRS may exempt a practitioner from these rules if the information requested is privileged or the request is of doubtful legality. When making this determination, the practitioner must be acting in good faith and on reasonable grounds.

Competence

A practitioner must possess the necessary competence to engage in practice before the Internal Revenue Service. Competent practice requires the appropriate level of knowledge, skill, thoroughness, and preparation necessary for the matter for which the practitioner is engaged. A practitioner may become competent for the matter for which the practitioner has been engaged through various methods, such as consulting with experts in the relevant area or studying the relevant law.

Contingent Fees

A fee that is based on whether or not a position on a tax return avoids challenge by the IRS is known as a contingent fee. A practitioner may not charge a contingent fee for services in connection with any matter before the IRS, except:

- Services related to an IRS examination or challenge of:
  1) An original tax return, or
  2) An amended tax return filed within 120 days of a taxpayer receiving a notice of examination
- For services rendered in connection with a claim for credit or refund filed solely in connection with the determination of statutory interest or penalties assessed by the IRS.
- Services connected to a judicial proceeding

Confidentiality Privilege

The confidentiality protection of certain communications between a taxpayer and an attorney (privileged communications) applies to similar communications between a taxpayer and any federally authorized tax practitioner.

- One may not invoke this confidentiality privilege in any administrative proceeding with an agency other than the IRS.
- The protection of this privilege applies only to tax advice given to the taxpayer by any individual who is a federally authorized tax practitioner. The confidentiality protection applies to communications that would be considered privileged if they were between the taxpayer and an attorney and that relate to:
  1) Noncriminal tax matters before the IRS, or
  2) Noncriminal tax proceedings brought in federal court by or against the United States.
- This protection does not apply to any written communications between a federally authorized tax practitioner and certain representatives or employees of a corporation nor does it apply if the communication promotes a tax shelter to a corporation.

Client Omissions – Duty to Advise

A practitioner generally may rely in good faith on information furnished by the client. The practitioner may not, however, ignore the implications of information furnished and must make reasonable inquiries if it appears to be incorrect or inconsistent. A practitioner who is aware the client has not complied with the rules and regulations of the IRS, or knows of any error or omission, must promptly <u>advise</u> the <u>client</u> concerning the existence of the error or omission and of the consequences of allowing them to remain uncorrected. If not corrected, the practitioner <u>cannot</u> sign the return. A practitioner may not advise a client to take a frivolous position on a return.

Advertising and Solicitation

The practitioner may advertise using any method(s) he chooses. A practitioner may not make any advertising statement that is in any way false, fraudulent, coercive, misleading, or deceptive or that violates any state, federal, or other applicable rule. A practitioner may <u>not</u> use the word "certified" or otherwise imply an employment relationship with the IRS. If the practitioner publishes a schedule of fees, he must adhere to the schedule for at least 30 days from the last date of publication. Such a schedule must include fixed fees for specific routine services, hourly rates, range of fees for particular services and any fees charged for an initial consultation.

> Examples of acceptable descriptions for enrolled agents are "enrolled to practice before the IRS," "admitted to practice before the IRS" or "enrolled to represent taxpayers before the IRS."

Diligence as to Accuracy

A practitioner must exercise due diligence in preparing, approving, and filing tax returns and all other documents, as well as any oral statements relating to IRS or Treasury Department matters. The practitioner must use the same diligence in determining the correctness of oral or written statements made to clients with reference to any matter administered by the Internal Revenue Service. A practitioner will be presumed to have exercised due diligence if the practitioner relies on the work product of another person and the practitioner used reasonable care in engaging, supervising, training, and evaluating the person.

Conflict of Interest

A conflict of interest exists if the representation of one client is directly adverse to another client or if there is a significant risk that the representation of one or more clients will be materially limited by the practitioner's responsibilities to another client, to a former client or a third person, or by a personal interest of the practitioner. Practitioners may not represent a client if such representation causes or appears to cause a conflict of interest unless:

- The practitioner reasonably believes that he will be able to provide competent and diligent representation to each affected client,
- The representation is not prohibited by law, and
- Each affected client waives the conflict of interest <u>in writing</u> at the time the practitioner knows of the existence of the conflict of interest. The confirmation may be made within a reasonable period of time, but in no event later than 30 days after the practitioner becomes aware of the conflict.

Refund Check Negotiation

A practitioner may <u>not</u> endorse or otherwise negotiate any check (including directing or accepting payment by any means, electronic or otherwise, into an account owned or controlled by the practitioner or any firm or other entity with whom the practitioner is associated) issued to a client by the government in respect of a Federal tax liability.

Performance as a Notary

A practitioner who is a notary public and has an interest in a matter before the IRS may <u>not</u> engage in any notary activities related to that matter.

Requirements for Written Advice

A Federal tax matter is any matter concerning the application or interpretation of at least one of the following:

- A revenue provision as defined in section 6110(i)(1)(B) of the Internal Revenue Code,
- Any provision of law impacting a person's obligations under the internal revenue laws and regulations, including but not limited to the person's liability to pay tax or obligation to file returns, or
- Any other law or regulation administered by the Internal Revenue Service.

A practitioner providing a written advice concerning Federal tax matters must follow certain requirements. The practitioner must:

- Base the written advice on reasonable factual and legal assumptions (including assumptions as to future events),
- Reasonably consider all relevant facts and circumstances that the practitioner knows or reasonably should know,
- Use reasonable efforts to identify and ascertain the facts relevant to written advice on each Federal tax matter,
- Not rely upon representations, statements, findings, or agreements (including projections, financial forecasts, or appraisals) of the taxpayer or any other person if reliance on them would be unreasonable
- Relate applicable law and authorities to facts, and
- Not take into account the possibility that a tax return will not be audited or that a matter will not be raised on audit.

> In evaluating whether a practitioner giving written advice concerning one or more Federal tax matters complied with the requirements, the Commissioner, or delegate, will apply a reasonable practitioner standard, considering all facts and circumstances, including, but not limited to, the scope of the engagement and the type and specificity of the advice sought by the client.

Reliance on representations, statements, findings, or agreements is unreasonable if the practitioner knows or reasonably should know that one or more representations or assumptions on which any representation is based are incorrect, incomplete, or inconsistent. A practitioner may only rely on the advice of another person if the advice was reasonable and the reliance is in good faith considering all the facts and circumstances. Reliance is not reasonable when—

- The practitioner knows or reasonably should know that the opinion of the other person should not be relied on,

- The practitioner knows or reasonably should know that the other person is not competent or lacks the necessary qualifications to provide the advice, or

- The practitioner knows or reasonably should know that the other person has a conflict of interest in violation of the rules described in this part.

Continuing education presentations provided to an audience solely for the purpose of enhancing practitioners' professional knowledge on Federal tax matters are not considered written advice on a Federal tax matter.

Practice of Law

Nothing in the regulations in this part may be construed as authorizing those who are not members of the bar to practice law.

Best Practices for Tax Advisors

Practitioners should provide clients with the highest quality representation concerning federal tax issues by adhering to best practices in providing advice and in preparing or assisting in the preparation of a submission to the Internal Revenue Service. Best practices include the following:

- Communicating clearly with the client regarding the terms of the engagement

- Establishing the facts, determining which facts are relevant, evaluating the reasonableness of any assumptions or representations, relating the applicable law to the relevant facts, and arriving at a conclusion supported by the law and the facts. The practitioner generally may rely in good faith without verification upon information furnished by the client. The practitioner may not, however, ignore the implications of information furnished to, or actually known by, the practitioner, and must make reasonable inquiries if the information as furnished appears to be incorrect, inconsistent with an important fact or another factual assumption, or incomplete.

- Advising the client regarding the import of the conclusions reached, including, for example, whether a taxpayer may avoid accuracy-related penalties under the Internal Revenue Code if a taxpayer acts in reliance on the advice

- Acting fairly and with integrity in practice before the Internal Revenue Service

Recordkeeping

In general, practitioners must keep records for a period of three years. They must:

- Keep records of completed CPE for <u>four years</u> following the date of renewal of enrollment

- Keep written consents due to conflicts of interest for at least 36 months from the date of the conclusion of the representation of the affected clients

- Maintain copies of any direct mail, Internet, or radio/television advertising for at least 36 months from date of last publication or transmission

- The preparer must either retain a copy of the return, or as an alternative, a list showing the name, taxpayer identification number, type of return, and tax year for each return prepared. The records must indicate the name of the preparer required to sign the return and be available for inspection for three years following the close of the return period in which the return is presented to the taxpayer for signature (or the date the return becomes due for an extended return). A "return period" is the 12-month period beginning on July 1 of each year.

Sanctions and Penalties

The Secretary of the Treasury, or delegate, after notice and an opportunity for a proceeding, may censure, suspend, or disbar any practitioner from practice before the Internal Revenue Service if the practitioner is shown to be incompetent or disreputable, fails to comply with the prohibited conduct standards of §10.52 (not best practices), or with intent to defraud, willfully and knowingly misleads or threatens a client or prospective client. Censure is a public reprimand.

> A practitioner may face a monetary penalty if engaging in conduct subject to sanction. The amount of the penalty shall not exceed the gross income derived (or to be derived) from the conduct giving rise to the penalty. The Secretary of the Treasury, or delegate, may impose a monetary penalty on an employer, firm, or entity if it knew, or reasonably should have known of such conduct of a preparer acting on its behalf. Any monetary penalty imposed on an employer, firm or other entity may be in addition to or in lieu of penalties imposed on the practitioner.

Incompetence and Disreputable Conduct

Incompetence and disreputable conduct for which the IRS may sanction a practitioner includes, but is not limited, to the following:

- Conviction of any criminal offense under the Federal tax laws

- Conviction of any criminal offense involving dishonesty or breach of trust

- Conviction of any felony under federal or state law for which the conduct involved renders the practitioner unfit to practice before the Internal Revenue Service

- Giving false or misleading information, or participating in any way in the giving of false or misleading information to the Department of the Treasury or any officer or employee thereof, or to any tribunal authorized to pass upon federal tax matters in connection with any matter pending or likely to be pending before them

- Solicitation of employment as prohibited under §10.30, the use of false or misleading representations with intent to deceive a client or prospective client in order to procure employment, or intimating that the practitioner is able to improperly obtain special consideration or action from the IRS or any officer or employee thereof

- Willfully failing to make a federal tax return in violation of the federal tax laws, or willfully evading, attempting to evade, or participating in any way in evading or attempting to evade any assessment or payment of any federal tax

- Willfully assisting, counseling, or encouraging a client or prospective client in violating, or suggesting to a client or prospective client to violate, any Federal tax law, or knowingly counseling or suggesting to a client or prospective client an illegal plan to evade federal taxes

- Misappropriation of, or failure to properly or promptly remit funds received from a client for the purpose of payment of taxes or other obligations due the United States

- Directly or indirectly attempting to influence, or offering or agreeing to attempt to influence, the official action of any officer or employee of the IRS by the use of threats, false accusations, duress, or coercion by the offer of any special inducement or promise of an advantage or by the bestowing of any gift, favor, or item of value

- Disbarment or suspension from practice as an attorney, certified public accountant, public accountant, or actuary by any duly constituted authority of any state, territory, or possession of the United States, including a commonwealth, the District of Columbia, any federal court of record, or any federal agency, body, or board

- Knowingly aiding and abetting another person to practice before the Internal Revenue Service during a period of suspension, disbarment, or ineligibility of such other person

- Contemptuous conduct in connection with practice before the IRS, including the use of abusive language, making false accusations or statements, knowing them to be false, or circulating or publishing malicious or libelous matter

- Giving a false opinion, knowingly, recklessly, or through gross incompetence, including an opinion that is intentionally or recklessly misleading, or engaging in a pattern of providing incompetent opinions on questions arising under the federal tax laws

- Willfully failing to sign a tax return prepared by the practitioner when federal tax laws require the signature, unless the failure is due to reasonable cause and not due to willful neglect

- Willfully disclosing or otherwise using a tax return or tax return information in a manner not authorized by the Internal Revenue Code, contrary to the order of a court of competent jurisdiction, or contrary to the order of an administrative law judge in a proceeding instituted under the Circular 230 instructions for sanction proceedings

Violations Subject to Sanction

The IRS may sanction a practitioner if the practitioner willfully violates any of the regulations (not best practices), recklessly or through gross incompetence violates Circular 230 directives relating to: standards with respect to tax returns and documents, affidavits and other papers, requirements for covered opinions, procedures to ensure compliance, and requirements for other written advice.

Disciplinary Proceedings

Whenever the <u>Director of the OPR</u> determines a practitioner violated any provision of the laws governing practice before the IRS, that official may ***reprimand*** the practitioner <u>or</u> ***institute a proceeding*** for a sanction. An official institutes a proceeding by filing a complaint. Except in certain unusual circumstances, the director will not institute a proceeding for censure, suspension, or disbarment against a practitioner until the facts (or conduct) that may warrant such action have been given in writing to that practitioner, and the practitioner has been given the opportunity to demonstrate or achieve compliance with the rules.

Conferences

The Director of the OPR may confer with a practitioner concerning allegations of misconduct irrespective of whether a proceeding has been instituted. If the conference results in a stipulation in connection with an ongoing proceeding in which the practitioner is the respondent, either party may enter the stipulation in the record to the proceeding. In lieu of a proceeding being instituted or continued, a practitioner may offer consent to be sanctioned.

Contents of Complaint

- There are three required components of a complaint:

1) **Charges** – A complaint must <u>name</u> the respondent, provide a clear and concise <u>description of the facts and law</u> that constitute the basis for the proceeding, <u>and be signed by</u> the Director of the OPR or a person representing that official.

2) **Specification of sanction** – The complaint must specify the sanction sought by the Director of the OPR against the practitioner or appraiser.

3) **Demand for answer** – The Director of the OPR must notify the respondent of the following:

   A) The time for answering the complaint (which may not be less than 30 days from the date of service of the complaint)

   B) The name and address of the Administrative Law Judge with whom the answer must be filed

   C) The name and address of the person representing the Director of the OPR to whom a copy of the answer must be served

   D) That a decision by default may be rendered against the respondent in the event an answer is not filed as required

- The complaint must be properly served by either hand delivery, dropping off at the respondent's place of business, or by certified or first class mail to the respondent's last known address.

Time to Answer, Default

The respondent must file an answer with the Administrative Law Judge and serve it on the Director of the OPR within the time specified in the complaint.

- The answer must be written and contain a statement of facts that constitute the respondent's grounds of defense. General denials are not permitted. The respondent must specifically admit or deny each allegation set forth in the complaint, except that the respondent may state that the respondent is without sufficient information to admit or deny a specific allegation.

- Every allegation in the complaint that is not denied in the answer is deemed admitted and will be considered proved; no further evidence for such allegation need be adduced at a hearing.

- Failure to file an answer within the time prescribed constitutes an admission of guilt to the allegations of the complainant and a waiver of hearing, and the Administrative Law Judge may make the decision by default without a hearing or further procedure.

Supplemental Charges

The Director of the OPR may amend the complaint with the permission of the Administrative Law Judge in order to file supplemental charges against the respondent if it appears that the respondent:

- In the answer, falsely and in bad faith, denies a material allegation of fact in the complaint or states that the respondent has insufficient knowledge to form a belief, when the respondent possesses such information, or

- Has knowingly introduced false testimony during proceedings against the respondent

Reply to Answer

The Director of the OPR may file a reply to the respondent's answer, but unless otherwise ordered by the Administrative Law Judge, no reply to the respondent's answer is required. If the director does not file a reply, any new matter in the answer is deemed denied.

Proof

In the case of a difference between the charges and the evidence provided, the Administrative Law Judge, at any time before decision, may authorize amendment of the pleadings to conform to the evidence. The Administrative Law Judge must give the party to whom the amendment would adversely affect a reasonable opportunity to address the allegations as amended, and the Administrative Law Judge must make findings on any issue presented by the pleadings as amended.

Motions and Requests

At any time after the filing of the complaint, any party may file a motion with the Administrative Law Judge. A motion must concisely specify its grounds and the relief sought and, if appropriate, must contain a memorandum of facts and law in support. The Administrative Law Judge should issue written orders disposing of any motion or request and any response thereto.

Administrative Law Judge

An Administrative Law Judge (ALJ) conducts proceedings on complaints for the sanction of a practitioner, employer, firm or other entity, or appraiser. The ALJ has the authority, in connection with any proceeding above assigned or referred, to do the following:

- Administer oaths and affirmations
- Make rulings on motions and requests, which rulings may not be appealed prior to the close of a hearing except in extraordinary circumstances and at the discretion of the ALJ
- Determine the time and place of hearing and regulate its course and conduct
- Adopt or modify rules of procedure as needed for the orderly disposition of proceedings
- Rule on offers of proof, receive relevant evidence, and examine witnesses
- Take or authorize the taking of depositions or answers to requests for admission
- Receive and consider oral or written argument on facts or law
- Hold or provide for the holding of conferences for the settlement or simplification of the issues with the consent of the parties
- Perform such acts and take such measures as are necessary or appropriate to the efficient conduct of any proceeding
- Make decisions

Discovery

The ALJ may permit discovery, at his discretion, only upon written motion demonstrating the relevance, materiality, and reasonableness of the requested discovery. Within 10 days of receipt of the answer, the ALJ will notify the parties of the right to request discovery and the timeframe for filing a request. In response to a request for discovery, the ALJ may order depositions upon oral examination, or answers to requests for admission.

Hearings

An ALJ will preside at all hearings for the sanction of a practitioner. The hearing must occur within 180 days of the date for filing the answer, unless the ALJ determines that a later date better serves the interests of justice.

Representation

A respondent may appear in person, be represented by a practitioner, or be represented by an attorney. A practitioner, the attorney, or the proposed respondent may sign the answer or any other document required to be filed in the proceeding on behalf of the respondent.

Evidence

The rules of evidence common in courts of law are not controlling in hearings or proceedings conducted under this part. The ALJ may exclude evidence that is irrelevant, immaterial, or unduly repetitious. Any depositions taken as noted above are allowable as evidence as is any matter requested under the discovery process above. Any statements made are applicable to the hearing in process only and may not be used in any other proceeding. Official documents, records, and papers in the possession of the IRS or the OPR are always admissible as evidence.

Transcript

Transcripts of the proceedings, as well as copies of any presented evidence such as documents or affidavits, must be made available to the respondent upon request. The costs, if any, are based upon the nature of the items sought.

Proposed Filings and Conclusions

Except in cases where the respondent has failed to answer the complaint or where a party has failed to appear at the hearing, the parties must have a reasonable opportunity to submit proposed findings and conclusions and their supporting reasons to the ALJ.

Decisions of the Administrative Law Judge

- **Hearings** – Within 180 days after the conclusion of a hearing, the ALJ should enter a decision in the case. The decision must include a statement of findings and conclusions, as well as the reasons or basis for making such findings and conclusions, and an order of censure, suspension, disbarment, monetary penalty, disqualification, or dismissal of the complaint.

- **Summary adjudication** – In the event that a party files a motion for summary adjudication, the ALJ should rule on the motion for summary adjudication within 60 days after the party in opposition files a written response or, if no written response is filed, within 90 days after the party files a motion for summary adjudication.

- **Returns and return information** – In the decision, the Administrative Law Judge should redact any information that could identify third parties and replace it with a code, provide a key to the code to the IRS and the involved practitioner, and remind all parties of the penalties for disclosure of such information to uninvolved third parties.

- **Standard of proof** – If the sanction is censure or suspension of less than six months' duration the ALJ, in rendering findings and conclusions, will consider an allegation of fact to be proven if it is established by the party who is alleging the fact by a preponderance of the evidence in the record. If the sanction is a monetary penalty, disbarment, or a suspension of six months or longer duration, the party alleging a fact that is necessary for a finding against the practitioner must prove the allegation by clear and convincing evidence in the record.

- **Copy of decision** – The ALJ will provide the decision to the Director of the OPR, with copies to the director's authorized representative and to the respondent or the respondent's authorized representative.

- **When final** – In the absence of an appeal to the Secretary of the Treasury or delegate, the decision of the ALJ will become the decision of the agency 30 days after the date of the ALJ's decision without further proceedings.

Appeals

Any party to such a proceeding may file an appeal of the decision of the ALJ with the Secretary of the Treasury, or delegate. The appeal must include a brief that states exceptions to the decision of the ALJ and supporting reasons for such exceptions. The practitioner must file the appeal and brief, in duplicate, with the **Director of the OPR within 30 days** of the date that the decision of the ALJ is served on the parties. The Director of the OPR will immediately furnish a copy of the appeal to the Secretary of the Treasury or delegate who decides appeals.

Decision to Review

On appeal from or review of the decision of the Administrative Law Judge, the Secretary of the Treasury or associated delegate will make the agency decision. The Secretary of the Treasury or associated delegate should make the agency decision within 180 days after receipt of the appeal.

Disbarment, Suspension, Censure

The Secretary of the Treasury, after notice and an opportunity for a proceeding, may censure, suspend, or disbar any practitioner from practice before the IRS if the practitioner is shown to be incompetent or disreputable, fails to comply with any regulation in Circular 230, or with intent to defraud, willfully and knowingly misleads or threatens a client or prospective client.

Notice

On the issuance of a final order censuring, suspending, or disbarring a practitioner or a final order disqualifying an appraiser, the Director of the OPR may give notice of the censure, suspension, disbarment, or disqualification to appropriate officers and employees of the Internal Revenue Service and to interested departments and agencies of the federal government. The Director of the OPR may determine the manner of giving notice to the proper authorities of the state that licensed the censured, suspended, or disbarred person to practice.

Petition for Reinstatement

The Director of the OPR may entertain a petition for reinstatement from any person disbarred from practice before the Internal Revenue Service or any disqualified appraiser after the expiration of **five years** following such disbarment or disqualification. Reinstatement will not be granted unless the Internal Revenue Service is satisfied that the petitioner is not likely to engage thereafter in conduct contrary to the regulations in this part, and that granting such reinstatement would not be contrary to the public interest.

Expedited Suspension

The Director of the OPR may expedite a proceeding to suspend the practitioner from practice before the IRS, when the practitioner has:

- Had a license to practice as an attorney, certified public accountant, or actuary suspended or revoked for cause
- Been convicted of a tax-related crime, any crime involving dishonesty or breach of trust, or any felony, which renders the practitioner unfit to practice before the IRS
- Violated conditions imposed on the practitioner pursuant items covered in the section on disbarment, suspension, and censure above

- Been sanctioned by a court of competent jurisdiction, whether in a civil or criminal proceeding (including suits for injunctive relief), relating to any taxpayer's tax liability or relating to the practitioner's own tax liability, for:

    1) Instituting or maintaining proceedings primarily for delay,

    2) Advancing frivolous or groundless arguments, or

    3) Failing to pursue available administrative remedies

A proceeding under this section is instituted by a complaint, which must give a plain and concise description of the allegations that constitute the basis for the proceeding. The complaint must notify the respondent of the following information:

- The place and due date for filing an answer
- That a decision by default may be rendered if the respondent fails to file an answer as required
- That the respondent may request a conference with the Director of the OPR to address the merits of the complaint and that any such request must be made in the answer
- That the respondent may be suspended either immediately following the expiration of the period within which an answer must be filed or, if a conference is requested, immediately following the conference

The respondent must file an answer to a complaint described in this section no later than 30 calendar days following the date the complaint is served, unless the Director of the OPR extends the time for filing. If the respondent does not make a request for a conference in the answer or does not timely file the answer, the respondent will be deemed to have waived his right to a conference, and the Director of the OPR may suspend such respondent at any time following the date on which the answer was due. If a conference is held, it will be held at a place and time selected by the Director of the OPR, but no sooner than 14 calendar days after the date by which the answer must be filed with the Director of the OPR, unless the respondent agrees to an earlier date.

19 Representation before the IRS

Power of Attorney · Audits and Examinations · Duties and Restrictions · Sanctions and Penalties · Disciplinary Proceedings

This chapter covers certain requirements for representing taxpayers before the IRS. Much of the information within this chapter originates from Publications 1, 216, 556, 594, 947, 1345, 3112, and 3498, Treasury Circular 230, and Tax Topic 205.

Power of Attorney

Individuals may represent themselves before the IRS or grant another the legal authority to represent them with a **power of attorney**. The representative must be a person eligible to practice before the IRS. A power of attorney authorizes an individual to act in place of a taxpayer in tax matters. If the authorization is not limited, the individual may generally perform the following acts:

- Represent a taxpayer before any office of the IRS
- Record the interview
- Sign an offer or a waiver of restriction on assessment or collection of a tax deficiency, or a waiver of notice of disallowance of claim for credit or refund
- Sign consent to extend the statutory period for assessment or collection of a tax
- Sign a closing agreement
- Receive, but not endorse or cash, a refund check drawn on the U.S. Treasury

A power of attorney is most often required when authorizing another individual to perform at least one of the following acts on behalf of a taxpayer:

- Represent a taxpayer at a conference with the IRS
- Prepare and file a written response to the IRS

A newly filed power of attorney concerning the same matter will revoke a previously filed power of attorney.

Signature Authority

The representative named under a power of attorney may not sign a tax return on behalf of a taxpayer unless the Internal Revenue Code (IRC) permits the signature and the power of attorney specifically authorizes it. The IRC permits this in situations where the person liable for the return is unable to make it due to disease, injury, or prolonged absence from the United States for a period of at least 60 days prior to the due date of the return.

Form 2848 Power of Attorney and Declaration of Representative

Form 2848 appoints a representative admitted to practice before the IRS to act on a taxpayer's behalf. Specific authorization on the form is necessary to authorize:

- A *durable power of attorney*; otherwise, the powers terminate if a taxpayer becomes incapacitated or incompetent.

- Signing the return for a taxpayer, if permitted.

- Endorsing or cashing a refund check. If a representative is to receive a refund check on a taxpayer's behalf, it must specifically authorize this in the power of attorney. However, those permitted to practice before the IRS may <u>not</u> endorse or otherwise cash a refund check.

- Substitution or delegation of authority under the power of attorney to another recognized representative.

    1) Under a substitution, the IRS recognizes only the newly recognized representative as the taxpayer's representative.

    2) Under a delegation, the IRS recognizes both representatives as authorized to represent the taxpayer.

- Disclosure of returns to a third party. A representative may not execute consents that will allow the IRS to disclose tax return or return information to a third party unless this authority is specifically delegated to the representative.

The IRS will accept a **non-IRS power of attorney**, other than Form 2848. To be valid, the practitioner must sign a *Declaration of Representative*, and the taxpayer must provide the following information:

- Name and mailing address
- Social Security number and/or employer identification number
- Employee plan number, if applicable
- The name and mailing address of the representative
- The types of tax involved
- The federal tax form number
- The specific year(s) or period(s) involved
- For estate tax matters, the decedent's date of death
- A clear expression of intention concerning the scope of authority granted to a representative
- Signature and date

A newly filed power of attorney concerning the <u>same</u> matter will revoke a previously filed power of attorney. A copy of the previously executed power of attorney sent to the IRS with the word "REVOKE" written across the top will serve to revoke an existing power of attorney. If a representative wants to withdraw from representation, he may perform the same action.

Central Authorization File

The IRS has a centralized computer database system called the *centralized authorization file* (CAF) system. It contains information on the authority of taxpayer representatives and those with *Tax Information Authorization (TIA)*. The TIA allows a third party to receive or inspect written and/or oral tax account information, subject to limitations. Individuals may represent themselves before the IRS or grant another the legal authority to represent them with a power of attorney. Entry of *Form 2848, Power of Attorney and Declaration of Representative* on the CAF system enables IRS personnel who do not have a copy of the power of attorney to verify the authority of a representative by accessing the CAF. It also enables automatic mailing of notices and other IRS communications to the representative.

Third Party Designee

The IRS does not honor Form 2848 for any purpose other than representation before the IRS. A taxpayer can authorize the IRS to discuss his tax return with a preparer, a friend, family member, or any other person through a "checkbox authorization" indicating the *Third party designee* directly on the tax return and providing the information required. In doing so, the taxpayer authorizes the following:

- The IRS to call the designee to answer any questions that arise during the processing of the return
- The designee to:
    1) Give information that is missing from the return to the IRS
    2) Call the IRS about the processing of the return or the status of a refund or payments
    3) Receive copies of notices or transcripts related to the return, upon request
    4) Respond to certain IRS notices about math errors, offsets, and return preparation

The authorization automatically ends no later than the due date (without any extensions) for filing the tax return for the following year. The CAF does not record information about third party designees.

Tax Information Authorization, Form 8821

A power of attorney is not necessary to authorize the IRS to discuss and provide specific confidential tax return information to anyone designated with a Tax Information Authorization (TIA). There are two methods to grant the authorization–*Form 8821* or *Oral Tax Information Authorization* (verbal equivalent of Form 8821). However, the TIA is strictly a disclosure authorization. A taxpayer may not use this form to designate an individual as a representative. The authorization remains in effect until a taxpayer revokes or the appointee withdraws. Form 8821 does not revoke existing authority under a power of attorney, as Forms 2848 and Form 8821 do not affect each other in any way.

When Is a Power of Attorney Not Required?

A power of attorney is not always required when dealing with the IRS. The following situations do not require a power of attorney:

- Providing information to the IRS
- Authorizing the disclosure of tax return information through Form 8821
- Allowing the IRS to discuss return information with a third-party designee
- Allowing a tax matters partner or person (TMP) to perform acts for the partnership
- Allowing the IRS to discuss return information with a fiduciary
- The IRS may discuss tax return or return information with a third-party designee after receiving non-written (oral) consent. Under this temporary regulation, the IRS may disclose information to any person accompanying a taxpayer at a meeting, interview, or participating with them in a telephone conversation with the IRS.

Audits/Examinations

Statute of Limitations

> In most cases, the IRS has three years from the due date of the return or the date actually filed (whichever is later) to assess any additional taxes. The IRS generally has 10 years from the date of assessment to collect a timely assessed tax liability. There is no statute of limitations for fraud.

IRS Authority to Investigate

The Commissioner of the IRS, designated officers, and employees have the authority to examine any books, papers, records, or memoranda bearing upon the matters required to be included in the returns, to summon persons liable for tax and take testimony, and to administer oaths.

TEFRA Status

TEFRA (Tax Equity and Fiscal Responsibility Act of 1982) status determines the procedures the IRS must follow during an audit. TEFRA applies to partnerships and limited liability companies (LLCs) that file as partnerships. In a small partnership, the IRS conducts audits for partners independently and treatment of partnership items for one partner can be different for any other partner. In a TEFRA partnership, the audit occurs at the entity (partnership) level, and not at the partner level. A TEFRA partnership has a *tax matters partner* who deals with the IRS on behalf of the partnership.

Generally, a partnership with 11 or more partners at any one time during the partnership's tax year is a TEFRA partnership. A partnership containing fewer than 11 partners, commonly referred to as a *small partnership*, will qualify as a TEFRA partnership if it has as a partner that is any one of the following:

- Partnership
- Limited liability Company (LLC) which files a Form 1065 or is treated as a disregarded entity (see Revenue Ruling 2004-88) for federal tax purposes
- Trust (any type, including Grantor Trusts and grantor type trusts, even if the Schedule K-1 contains the SSN of the grantor)
- Nominee
- Nonresident alien individual
- S corporation

Taxpayer Rights

Among other rights, a taxpayer has the right to do the following:

- Disagree with his tax bill
- Meet with an IRS manager if there is a disagreement with the IRS employee who handles his tax case
- Appeal most IRS collection actions
- Transfer his case to a different IRS office if a valid reason exists (e.g., the taxpayer moves)
- Be represented by someone when dealing with IRS matters
- Receive a receipt for any payment made

Taxpayer Advocate Service

The Taxpayer Advocate Service (TAS) is an independent organization within the IRS whose goal is to help taxpayers resolve problems. If a taxpayer has an ongoing issue with the IRS that has not been resolved through normal processes, or if a taxpayer has suffered or is about to suffer a significant hardship because of the administration of the tax laws, he should contact the TAS for assistance.

Contact of Third Party by IRS

The IRS must give reasonable notice in advance that, in examining or collecting a tax liability, it may contact third parties such as neighbors, banks, employers, or employees. The IRS must also give notice of specific contacts by providing the affected taxpayer with a record of persons contacted on both a periodic basis and upon request. This provision does not apply:

- To any pending criminal investigation,
- When providing notice would jeopardize collection of any tax liability,
- Where providing notice may result in reprisal against any person, or
- When the taxpayer authorized the contact.

Examination of Returns

The IRS examines (audits) returns for a variety of reasons, and examinations occur in one of several ways. An **IRS Examination Officer** may conduct correspondence examinations. Do not confuse *examination officers* with *revenue officers*, who are highly skilled employees of the IRS Collection Division. A field examination is one conducted by an **Internal Revenue Agent**, usually at the taxpayer's place of business. Generally, these audits are the most comprehensive.

- A computer program assigns a numeric score to returns after they have been processed. If a return is selected because of a high score, the potential is high that an examination of that return will result in a change to that taxpayer's income tax liability.
- A return may also be selected for examination because of information from third-party documentation, such as Forms 1099 and W-2, that does not match the return.
- A return may be selected to address both the questionable treatment of an item and to study the behavior of similar taxpayers (a market segment) in handling a tax issue.
- In addition, a return may be selected because of information received from other sources on potential noncompliance with the tax laws or inaccurate filing. This information can come from a number of sources, including newspapers, public records, and individuals.

The IRS may close the case without change, or the taxpayer may receive a refund. The IRS can conduct an examination of a taxpayer's return through the mail (correspondence audit) or in person.

Examinations by Mail

Sometimes a taxpayer receives a 1099 or other tax form in the mail after filing his return. Usually the sophisticated IRS computer system catches these errors. If information the taxpayer reported to the IRS does not match what his employers, banks, and other payers reported, the IRS sends **Form CP 2000** to inform the recipient of changes the IRS is proposing to the tax return. The IRS sends a CP 2000 to provide detailed information about those differences, the changes proposed, and what to do if the taxpayer agrees or disagrees with the proposal. The CP 2000 reflects any corrections the IRS made to the original return and considers those changes in a recalculation of the tax due. It is possible that these changes result in a decrease in tax due, but usually an increase is the result.

An individual may receive the following documents along with the CP 2000:

- Notice 609, Privacy Act Notice
- Publication 5, Your Appeal Rights and How to Prepare a Protest if You Don't Agree
- Publication 1, Your Rights as a Taxpayer
- Publication 594, What You Should Know About The IRS Collection Process

The CP 2000 is only a proposal that offers the taxpayer an opportunity to disagree, partially agree, or agree with the proposed changes. The IRS has not charged any additional tax at this point. It is important to respond to the CP 2000 by the due date shown on the notice. If not, the IRS assumes the proposed changes are correct and will continue processing the proposal ultimately to an assessment. If the taxpayer is unable to respond by the due date on the notice because more time is necessary to research records, the taxpayer can call the IRS to request an extension. Generally, the IRS will allow an extension 30 days beyond the response date shown on the notice. It is important to remember that additional interest and any applicable penalties will accrue on the account during the period of the extension if the tax increase is correct.

The IRS conducts some examinations entirely by mail. If the IRS conducts the examination by mail, the taxpayer will receive a letter from the IRS asking for additional information about certain items shown on his return, such as income, expenses, and itemized deductions. If the IRS conducts the examination by mail, the taxpayer may:

- Respond directly. In the case of a jointly filed return, either spouse may respond or both spouses may send a joint response.

- Have someone represent him in correspondence with the IRS. This person must be an attorney, accountant, enrolled agent, an enrolled actuary, or the person who prepared the return and signed it as the preparer. If a taxpayer wishes to have representation, he must furnish the IRS with written authorization on Form 2848, Power of Attorney and Declaration of Representative.

Examinations in Person

Internal Revenue Agents conduct field examinations, which officially begin when the IRS notifies a taxpayer that his return is selected for review. The IRS will tell the taxpayer what information to have available for the examination. Field examinations can take place in the taxpayer's home, place of business, an IRS office, or the office of the taxpayer's attorney, accountant, or enrolled agent. The examiner will try to schedule a time and place convenient for the taxpayer (or representative) that is reasonable under the circumstances considering both the convenience of the taxpayer and the requirements of sound and efficient tax administration. During an opening conference, the revenue agent explains the audit plan and the reason the taxpayer has been selected for examination. During a field examination, a taxpayer may:

- Act on his own behalf. In the case of a jointly filed return, either spouse or both may attend the interview. Each of them may leave to consult with his or her representative.

- Have someone accompany him to support his position or as witness to the proceedings.

- Accompany someone who will represent the taxpayer. This person must be an attorney, accountant, enrolled agent, enrolled actuary, or the person who prepared the return and signed it as the preparer.

- Have his representative act for him and not be present at the audit personally. When a taxpayer chooses to have someone represent him in his absence, he must furnish written authorization to the IRS. He must make this authorization on Form 2848.

The IRS generally conducts a field examination where the books and records are located. The IRS will consider a written request to transfer an audit to another location, including an IRS office, on a case-by-case basis. Treasury Regulation 301.7605-1(e) indicates the IRS will take into account the location of the taxpayer's current residence or principal place of business, and other factors that indicate that conducting the examination at a particular location could pose undue inconvenience to the taxpayer. The IRS also considers the most efficient location for the examination, and the IRS resources available at the location to which the taxpayer has requested a transfer.

Results of the Examination

A field examination typically concludes with a closing conference. If the IRS accepts the return as filed, the taxpayer will receive a letter stating that the examiner proposed no changes to his return. The taxpayer should keep this letter with the other tax records for that year. If the IRS does not accept the return as filed, the IRS will explain any proposed changes. After the examination, if any changes to the tax are proposed, the taxpayer may either agree with those changes and pay any additional tax owed, or disagree with the changes and appeal the decision.

Fast Track Mediation

Most cases that are not docketed in any court qualify for fast track mediation. Mediation can take place at a conference the taxpayer requests with a supervisor, or later. The process involves an *Appeals Officer* with training in mediation. The IRS offers fast track mediation services to help taxpayers resolve many disputes resulting from the following:

- Examinations (audits)
- Offers in compromise
- Trust fund recovery penalties
- Other collection actions

30-Day Letter

A few weeks after a closing conference with the examiner, a taxpayer will receive a package containing the following:

- A notice of the right to appeal the proposed changes within 30 days (known as a **30-day letter**)
- A copy of the examination report explaining the examiner's proposed changes
- An agreement or waiver form
- A copy of Publication 5, Your Appeal Rights and How to Prepare a Protest If You Don't Agree

A taxpayer has 30 days from the date of the 30-day letter to tell the IRS if he will accept or appeal the proposed changes. The letter explains what steps will be taken, depending on the course of action.

Appeals Conference

Upon receipt of the *30-day letter*, the taxpayer may elect to appeal at a <u>conference with the IRS</u>. The parties can settle most differences within this system without expensive and time-consuming court trials. A taxpayer's reason for disagreeing must come within the scope of the tax laws. For example, a taxpayer cannot appeal a case based only on moral, religious, political, constitutional, conscientious, or similar grounds. The Appeals Office is the only level of appeal within the IRS. In most instances, a taxpayer is eligible to take the case to court if unable to come to an agreement at the appeals conference, or if he does not want to appeal his case to the IRS Office of Appeals. When requesting an appeals conference, the taxpayer may also need to file a formal written protest or a small case request.

- **Written protest** – Taxpayers need to file a written protest in the following cases:

    1) All employee plan and exempt organization cases without regard to the amount at issue

    2) All partnership and S corporation cases without regard to the dollar amount at issue

    3) All other cases, unless the taxpayer qualifies for the small case request procedure or other special appeal procedures such as requesting appeals consideration of liens, levies, seizures, or installment agreements

- **Small case request** – If the total amount for any tax period is not more than $25,000, the taxpayer may make a small case request instead of filing a formal written protest. This is different from the *small tax case procedure* for tax court cases of $50,000 or less. In figuring the total amount, include a proposed increase or decrease in tax (including penalties) or claimed refund. If making an offer in compromise, include total unpaid tax, penalty, and interest. For a small case request, the taxpayer must send a letter:

    1) Requesting appeals consideration,

    2) Indicating the changes the taxpayer does not agree with, and

    3) Indicating the reasons why the taxpayer does not agree

90-Day Letter

If the IRS does not receive a response to the 30-day letter, or if the taxpayer and an Appeals Officer cannot reach an agreement, the IRS will send a 90-day letter, also known as a ***notice of deficiency***. The taxpayer will have 90 days (150 days if addressed outside the United States) from the date of this notice to file a petition with the Tax Court. The taxpayer may not file a claim with the Tax Court prior to receipt of the notice of deficiency.

Penalties and Interest

If the taxpayer does not file a return and pay the tax by the due date, he may have to pay a penalty. Substantially understated tax, understated reportable transactions, erroneous claims for refund or credit, frivolous tax submissions, or failure to supply a Social Security number or individual taxpayer identification number may also result in the IRS assessing a penalty. The IRS may assess a civil fraud penalty if the taxpayer provides fraudulent information on a return.

- **Filing late or *(failure-to-file)*** – If the taxpayer does not file a return by the due date (including extensions) the IRS may assess a failure-to-file penalty. The penalty is usually **5% for each month** or part of a month that a return is late, but **not more than 25%**. The penalty is based on the tax not paid by the due date (without regard to extensions).

    1) *Fraud* – If the failure to file is due to fraud, the penalty is 15% for each month or part of a month that the return is late, up to a maximum of 75%.

    2) *Return more than 60 days late* – If the return is filed more than 60 days after the due date or extended due date, the minimum penalty is the smaller of $135 or 100% of the unpaid tax.

- **Paying tax late or *(failure-to-pay)*** – A taxpayer who does not pay all taxes by the due date is subject to the failure-to-pay penalty of **one-half of 1% (.50%)** of the unpaid taxes for each month, or part of a month, the tax is not paid. This penalty does not apply during the automatic six-month extension of time to file period if the taxpayer paid at least 90% of the actual tax liability on or before the due date of the return and paid the balance when he filed the return.

    1) The monthly rate of the failure-to-pay penalty is half the usual rate (.25% instead of .50%) if an installment agreement is in effect for that month. The taxpayer must file the return by the due date (including extensions) to qualify for this reduced penalty.

    2) If the IRS issues a notice of intent to levy, the rate will increase to 1% at the start of the first month beginning at least 10 days after the day the IRS issues the notice. If the IRS issues a notice and demand for immediate payment, the rate will increase to 1% at the start of the first month beginning after the day that the IRS issues the notice and demand.

    3) This penalty cannot be more than 25% of the unpaid tax.

- **Combined penalties** – If both the *failure-to-file penalty* and the *failure-to-pay* penalty apply in any month, the 5% (or 15%) failure-to-file penalty is reduced by the failure-to-pay penalty. However, if the return is filed more than 60 days after the due date or extended due date, the minimum penalty is the smaller of $135 or 100% of the unpaid tax.

- **Accuracy-related penalty** – A penalty of 20% of unpaid tax may be due if the tax is underpaid due to:

  1) Negligence or disregard of the rules or regulations, or

  2) Substantial understatement of income tax. The understatement is substantial if it is more than the largest of 10% of the correct tax or $5,000.

- **Frivolous tax submission** – A penalty of $5,000 may be due if frivolous tax returns or other frivolous submissions are made. A frivolous tax return is one that does not include enough information to figure the correct tax or that contains information clearly showing that the tax reported is substantially incorrect.

- **Fraud** – If there is any underpayment of tax on a return due to fraud, the IRS will add a penalty of 75% of the underpayment due to fraud to the tax owed.

- **Failure to supply Social Security number** – If a taxpayer omits a SSN where required on a return, statement, or other document, the taxpayer will be subject to a penalty of $50 for each failure.

How to Stop Interest from Accruing

If the taxpayer owes additional tax at the end of the examination, he can stop further accrual of interest by sending money to the IRS to cover all or part of the amount still owed. Interest on part or all of any amount still owed will stop accruing on the date the IRS receives this money.

Suspension of Interest and Penalties

Generally, the IRS has three years from the date the return was filed (or the date the return was due, if later) to assess any additional tax. However, if the return was filed timely (including extensions), interest and certain penalties will be suspended if the IRS does not mail a notice stating liability and the basis for that liability, within a 36-month period beginning on the later of:

- The date on which the tax return was filed

- The due date (without extensions) of the tax return

If the IRS mails a notice after the 36-month period, interest and certain penalties applicable to the suspension period will be suspended. The suspension period begins the day after the close of the 36-month period and ends 21 days after the IRS mails a notice to the taxpayer stating liability and the basis for that liability. In addition, the suspension period applies separately to each notice received stating liability and the basis for that liability. The suspension does not apply to the following:

- Failure-to-pay penalty

- Fraudulent tax return

- Penalty, interest, addition to tax, or additional amount with respect to any tax liability shown on the return or with respect to any gross misstatement

- Penalty, interest, addition to tax, or additional amount with respect to any reportable transaction that is not adequately disclosed or any listed transaction

- Criminal penalty

Seeking Relief from Improperly Assessed Interest

A taxpayer may seek relief if the IRS assesses interest for periods during which interest should have been suspended because the IRS did not mail a notice in a timely manner. If the taxpayer believes that the IRS assessed interest with respect to a period during which interest should have been suspended, submit *Form 843*, writing *"Section 6404(g) Notification"* at the top of the form, with the IRS Service Center where the return was filed. The IRS will review the Form 843 and notify the taxpayer whether or not interest will be abated. If the IRS does not abate interest, the taxpayer may pay the disputed interest assessment and file a claim for refund. If that claim is denied or not acted upon within six months from the date filed, the taxpayer may file a suit for a refund in U.S. District Court or in the U.S. Court of Federal Claims.

Abatement of Interest

The IRS may abate (reduce) the amount of interest owed if the interest is due to an unreasonable error or delay by an IRS officer or employee in performing a:

- **Ministerial act** – This is a procedural or mechanical act, not involving the exercise of judgment or discretion, during the processing of a case after all prerequisites (for example, conferences and review by supervisors) have taken place. A decision concerning the proper application of federal tax law (or other federal or state law) is not a ministerial act.

- **Managerial act** – This is an administrative act during the processing of a case that involves the loss of records or the exercise of judgment or discretion concerning the management of personnel. A decision concerning the proper application of law is not a managerial act.

Only the amount of interest on income, estate, gift, generation skipping, and certain excise taxes may be reduced. The amount of interest will not be reduced if the taxpayer or anyone related to the taxpayer contributed significantly to the error or delay. The interest is reduced only if the error or delay happened after the IRS contacted the taxpayer in writing about the deficiency or payment on which the interest is based. An audit notification letter is such a contact.

Reasonable Cause

Under certain situations, a taxpayer may appeal penalties assessed against him by the IRS for non-compliance with the tax laws. These involve the use of the reasonable cause criteria. Reasonable cause involves situations that are beyond one's control after exercising normal care and prudence. Most of the time, they involve death, serious illness, unavoidable absences, absence of needed records, and reliance on written advice from the IRS or tax professional. Similar to interest abatement, a taxpayer may use form 843 to claim a refund or request an abatement of certain taxes, penalties, and additions to tax.

- **Death** – This is the death (usually sudden) of a spouse, children, parents, grandparents, or siblings. This may include the tax preparer (or a member of the immediate family) or any individual on whom the taxpayer relies for data needed to prepare the return.

- **Serious illness** – Major and (usually) unexpected illness of the individuals listed directly above. This rarely applies to sources of return information.

- **Unavoidable absences** – This is related to absences of the taxpayer (or spouse), is very rarely related to the taxpayer's preparer, and is never related to sources of information. Situations include items such as incarceration, natural disasters, military deployment, and emergency hospitalization.

- **Inability to obtain needed records** – The provider of information crucial to the preparation of the return did not provide it by the date required by law, and the taxpayer has sufficient records to support unsuccessful attempts to secure the information in order to file in a timely manner. The taxpayer must also have attempted to obtain the records from any alternative sources without success;

for example, if the taxpayer did not receive a W-2, he could prepare a substitute W-2 from the year-end pay stub.

- **Reliance on advice** – If the actions taken as a direct result of, and in compliance with, written instruction from the IRS (or the oral or written advice of a tax professional) leads to the late filing and/or late payment of taxes, there are grounds for relief from the resulting penalties.

Table 19-1. Criminal Considerations

Title and Section	Definition
Title 26 USC § 7201 Attempt to evade or defeat tax	Any person who willfully attempts to evade or defeat any tax imposed by this title or the payment thereof shall, in addition to other penalties provided by law, be guilty of a felony and, upon conviction thereof: • Shall be imprisoned not more than five years • Or fined not more than $250,000 for individuals ($500,000 for corporations) • Or both, together with the costs of prosecution
Title 26 USC § 7202 Willful failure to collect or pay over tax	Any person required under this title to collect, account for, and pay over any tax imposed by this title who willfully fails to collect or truthfully account for and pay over such tax shall, in addition to penalties provided by the law, be guilty of a felony and: • Shall be imprisoned not more than five years • Or fined not more than $250,000 for individuals ($500,000 for corporations) • Or both, together with the costs of prosecution
Title 26 USC § 7203 Willful failure to file return, supply information, or pay tax	Any person required under this title to pay any estimated tax or tax, or required by this title or by regulations made under authority thereof to make a return, keep any records, or supply any information, who willfully fails to pay such estimated tax or tax, make such return, keep such records, or supply such information, at the time or times required by law or regulations, shall, in addition to other penalties provided by law, be guilty of a misdemeanor and, upon conviction thereof: • Shall be imprisoned not more than one year • Or fined not more than $100,000 for individuals ($200,000 for corporations) • Or both, together with cost of prosecution
Title 26 USC § 7206(1) Fraud and false statements	Any Person who ... (1) Declaration under penalties of perjury – Willfully makes and subscribes any return, statement, or other document, which contains or is verified by a written declaration that is made under the penalties of perjury, and which he does not believe to be true and correct as to every material matter; shall be guilty of a felony and, upon conviction thereof; • Shall be imprisoned not more than three years • Or fined not more than $250,000 for individuals ($500,000 for corporations) • Or both, together with cost of prosecution
Title 26 USC § 7206(2) Fraud and false statements	Any person who ...(2) Aid or assistance – Willfully aids or assists in, or procures, counsels, or advises the preparation or presentation under, or in connection with any matter arising under, the Internal Revenue laws, of a return, affidavit, claim, or other document, which is fraudulent or is false as to any material matter, whether or not such falsity or fraud is with the knowledge or consent of the person authorized or required to present such return, affidavit, claim, or document; shall be guilty of a felony and, upon conviction thereof: • Shall be imprisoned not more than three years • Or fined not more than $250,000 for individuals ($500,000 for corporations) • Or both, together with cost of prosecution
Title 26 USC § 7212(A) Attempts to interfere with administration of Internal Revenue laws	Whoever corruptly or by force endeavors to intimidate or impede any officer or employee of the United States acting in an official capacity under this title, or in any other way corruptly or by force obstructs or impedes, or endeavors to obstruct or impede, the due administration of this title, upon conviction: • Shall be imprisoned not more than three years • Or fined not more than $250,000 for individuals ($500,000 for corporations) • Or both
Title 18 USC § 371 Conspiracy to commit offense or to defraud the United States	If two or more persons conspire either to commit any offense against the United States, or to defraud the United States, or any agency thereof in any manner or for any purpose, and one or more of such persons do any act to effect the object of the conspiracy, each: • Shall be imprisoned not more than five years • Or fined not more than $250,000 for individuals ($500,000 for corporations) • Or both

Collection Process

An **Internal Revenue Officer** is a highly skilled employee of the IRS Collection Division whose role is to collect delinquent unpaid taxes and to secure tax returns that are overdue from taxpayers. A revenue officer generally conducts face-to-face interviews with taxpayers (and/or their representatives) at the taxpayer's place of business or residence. The Revenue Officer can consider alternative means of resolving tax debt issues when the taxpayer cannot pay the debt in full such as:

- Setting up payment agreements that allow the taxpayer to pay the bill over time
- When appropriate, granting relief from penalties imposed when the tax bill is overdue
- Suspending collection of accounts due to financial hardship

Injured Spouse Relief

> Sometimes a liability belongs only to one spouse. A taxpayer is an *"injured spouse"* if he files a joint return and all or part of his share of the refund was, or will be, applied against the separate past-due federal tax, state tax, child support, or federal non-tax debt (such as a student loan) of his spouse with whom he filed the joint return. An injured spouse may be entitled to recoup their share of the refund.

The injured spouse files *Form 8379* with a jointly filed tax return when the joint overpayment was—or is expected to be—applied to a past-due obligation of the other spouse. By filing Form 8379, the injured spouse may be able to get back his or her share of the joint refund. The taxpayer may file form 8379 with a joint return, with an amended return, or by itself at a later time.

Relief from Joint Liability

Relief from joint and several liabilities, such as *innocent spouse relief*, is different from an *injured spouse claim*. In some cases, a spouse can get relief from joint and several liabilities.

> Married taxpayers are jointly and severally liable for the tax and any additions to tax, interest, or penalties that arise because of the joint return, even if they later divorce. Joint and several liability means that each taxpayer is legally responsible for the entire liability. One spouse may be held responsible for all the tax due, even if the other spouse earned all the income or claimed improper deductions or credits.

There are three types of relief are available to married persons who filed joint returns.

- **Innocent spouse relief** – A taxpayer may be relieved of responsibility for paying tax, interest, and penalties because a spouse or former spouse failed to report income, reported income improperly, or claimed improper deductions or credits. A taxpayer will use *Form 8857* to request relief, provided he meets all of the following conditions to qualify:

    1) The spouses must have filed a joint return with an understatement of tax directly related to the spouse's erroneous items.

    2) The taxpayer seeking relief can establish that at the time he signed the joint return, he did not know, and had no reason to know, that there was an understatement of tax.

    3) Taking into account all the facts and circumstances, it would be unfair to hold taxpayer liable for the understatement of tax.

- **Separation of liability relief** – For those who are no longer married, widowed, or legally separated and have not been members of the same household for a 12-month period. The understated tax (plus interest and penalties) on the joint return is allocated between spouses (or former spouse). The tax allocated is generally the amount the taxpayer is responsible to pay. This type of relief is available only for unpaid liabilities resulting from the understated tax. Refunds are not allowed.

- **Equitable relief** – For properly stated, but underpaid tax. If taxpayer does not qualify for other forms of relief, the taxpayer may still be relieved of responsibility for tax, interest, and penalties.

Notice of Tax Due and Demand for Payment

If the taxpayer has not paid all that he owes, the IRS will send a bill called a *Notice of Tax Due and Demand for Payment*. The bill includes the taxes plus interest and penalties. A taxpayer may use a credit card, electronic funds transfer, check, money order, or cash to pay any taxes owed.

Extension of Time to Pay

An extension of time to pay does not extend the due date of the tax payment; it is simply a delay in taking the collection actions that the IRS is otherwise legally entitled to take and is usually based on financial distress. If the IRS determines that a taxpayer cannot pay any of the tax debt, the IRS may temporarily delay collection until the taxpayer's financial condition improves. If the IRS does delay collecting from a taxpayer, the debt will increase because of penalties and interest until the full amount is paid. During a temporary delay, the IRS may continue to review a taxpayer's ability to pay. The IRS may also file a Notice of Federal Tax Lien, discussed in detail below.

IRS Collection Information Statement

Form 433 is the IRS *collection information statement*, which is a statement of a taxpayer's financial condition. It includes an overview of income, expenses, assets and liabilities. The IRS uses the information to determine how a taxpayer can satisfy an outstanding tax liability. Form 433 is a requirement to prove economic hardship. A taxpayer must file a collection information statement with an OIC request related to *doubt as to collectability* or to *promote effective tax administration*.

- **Form 433-A** – Collection Information Statement for Wage Earners and Self-Employed Individuals
- **Form 433-B** – Collection Information Statement for Businesses
- **Form 433-D** – Installment Agreement
- **Form 433-F** – Collection Information Statement (short form)

Installments

A taxpayer may request a monthly installment plan if he is unable to pay the full amount of tax owed.

> Installment agreements generally provide up to **72 months** to pay the tax. In certain circumstances, the payment period could be longer or the amount agreed to could be less than the amount of tax owed. Before applying for any payment agreement, a taxpayer must file all required tax returns. An installment plan is not valid unless accepted by the IRS.

The IRS must accept the request if a taxpayer owes $10,000 or less and meets the following requirements:

- During the past five tax years, the taxpayer (and spouse if MFJ) has timely filed all income tax returns and paid any tax due, and has not entered into an installment agreement for payment of income tax.
- The IRS determines that the taxpayer cannot pay the tax owed in full when it is due and the taxpayer gives the IRS any information needed to make that determination.
- The taxpayer agrees to pay the full amount within three years and to comply with the tax laws while the agreement is in effect.

An *installment agreement* generally requires equal monthly payments, and the taxpayer must fully pay all of the tax owed within the time left in the 10-year period during which the IRS can collect the tax. If a taxpayer cannot pay in full by the end of the collection period, but can pay some of the tax owed, he may qualify for a partial payment installment agreement. To request an installment agreement a taxpayer can attach *Form 9465 Installment Agreement Request* to the front of his tax return, or–in cases where the return is already filed–mail it directly to the IRS.

> If the balance due is not more than $50,000, the taxpayer can apply online for a payment agreement instead of filing Form 9465. To do that, go to IRS.gov and enter *Online Payment Agreement* in the search box.

If the IRS approves a request, they send a notice detailing the terms of the agreement and request a fee of $120 ($52 if payments are by electronic funds withdrawal). Lower income taxpayers may qualify to pay a reduced fee of $43. Once approved, a taxpayer may submit a request to modify or terminate the installment agreement. This request will not suspend the statute of limitations on collection. While the IRS considers a request to modify or terminate the installment agreement, the taxpayer must comply with the existing agreement.

If a taxpayer is able to pay the full amount owed within 120 days, he should not request an installment agreement on Form 9465. Instead, he can call or apply online to establish a request to pay in full. A taxpayer who can pay within the 120-day period can avoid paying the fee to set up the agreement.

> A taxpayer with outstanding tax liability (including penalties and interest) of $50,000 or less may file Form 9465, or 9465-FS. This is known as a **streamlined installment agreement** because the IRS does not require a financial statement (Form 433-A, Form 433-B, Form 433-D, or Form 433-F) or substantial disclosure of financial information. A liability greater than $50,000 can be considered if the taxpayer pays down the liability to $50,000 or less prior to the agreement being granted. Generally, a taxpayer must pay off the balance due on a streamlined IA within a 72-month period.

If the total amount the taxpayer owes is greater than $25,000 but not more than $50,000, the taxpayer may use a slightly expanded *Form 9465-FS Installment Agreement Request.* This form has an extra page (Part II) with additional information to complete. A taxpayer using Form 9465-FS must agree to a Direct Debit Installment Agreement (DDIA) to qualify for an IA without completing a financial statement (Form 433-F, Collection Information Statement).

The IRS generally may not levy against property:

- While a request for an installment agreement is being considered,
- While an installment agreement is in effect,
- For 30 days after a request for an agreement has been rejected,
- For 30 days after termination of an installment agreement (due to taxpayer default), or
- While the IRS Office of Appeals is evaluating an appeal of the rejection or termination.

However, the IRS may file a Notice of Federal Tax Lien to secure the government's interest against other creditors. Termination of an installment agreement may cause the filing of a Notice of Federal Tax Lien and/or an IRS levy action.

Offer in Compromise

The IRS may accept an Offer in Compromise (OIC) to settle unpaid tax accounts for less than the full amount of the balance due. The OIC program is an option for those taxpayers who are unable to pay their tax accounts in a lump sum or through an installment agreement. Requests must include a $150 application fee. The IRS may legally compromise a tax liability for any of the following reasons:

- **Doubt as to liability** – There is doubt as to whether or not the assessed tax is correct.
- **Doubt as to collectability** – There is doubt that the taxpayer could ever pay the full tax debt. In these cases, the total amount owed must be greater than the sum of the taxpayer's assets and future income.
- **Promote effective tax administration** – There is no doubt that the assessed tax is correct and no doubt that the amount owed could be collected, but the taxpayer has an economic hardship or other special circumstances that may allow the IRS to accept less than the total balance due.

The IRS and the taxpayer may agree to one of the following three types of OIC payment terms:

- **Lump sum cash** – must be paid within five or fewer installments from notice of acceptance
- **Short-term periodic payment** – must be paid within 24 months from when the IRS receives the OIC
- **Deferred periodic payment** – must be paid within 25 months or longer, but within the time remaining on the 10-year period for collection

Lien

- A *lien* gives the IRS a legal claim to a taxpayer's property as security for payment of a tax debt. The federal tax lien arises when:
    1) The IRS assesses the liability,
    2) The IRS sends a client a **Notice and Demand for Payment**, and
    3) The taxpayer neglects or refuses to pay the debt within 10 days after notification. The IRS then may file a **Notice of Federal Tax Lien** in the public records. The Notice of Federal Tax Lien tells a taxpayer's creditors that the IRS has a claim against all the taxpayer's property, including property acquired after the IRS filed the lien. The lien attaches to all property (such as homes and cars) and to all rights to property (such as the accounts receivable of a business).
- Appealing the filing of a Notice of Federal Tax Lien
    1) The IRS is required by law to give written notice of the taxpayer's right to a **Collection Due Process (CDP) hearing** not more than five business days after the first filing of a Notice of Federal Tax Lien for each tax liability.
    2) At the conclusion of the CDP hearing, the IRS Office of Appeals will issue a determination. The taxpayer will have 30 days after the date of the determination to seek review of the determination in the U.S. Tax Court.
- Usually 10 years after a tax is assessed, a lien releases automatically if the IRS has not filed it again or issued a Certificate of Release of Federal Tax Lien. The IRS will issue a Certificate of Release of the Federal Tax Lien within:
    1) 30 days after it is determined that the tax due (including accrued interest and penalties and other additions) is satisfied by paying the debt or by having it adjusted, or
    2) 30 days after the IRS accepts a taxpayers' posted bond guaranteeing payment of the debt.

Levies

- A *levy* is a legal seizure of a taxpayer's property to satisfy a tax debt. Levies are different from liens. A lien is a claim used as security for the tax debt, while a levy actually takes the property to satisfy the tax debt. The levy will be continuous until the tax debt is paid in full, other arrangements are made to satisfy the debt, or in most instances, the time-period (usually 10 years) for collecting the tax expires. If a taxpayer does not pay taxes (or arrange a settlement):

1) The IRS can seize and sell property (such as a taxpayer's car, boat, or home), or

2) The IRS can levy property that is the taxpayer's but is held by someone else (such as wages, retirement accounts, dividends, bank accounts, rental income, accounts receivables, the cash value of life insurance, or commissions).

- The IRS usually issues a levy only when the following three conditions have occurred:

    1) The IRS assessed the tax and sent the taxpayer a Notice and Demand for Payment.

    2) The taxpayer neglected or refused to pay the tax.

    3) The IRS sent the taxpayer a "Final Notice of Intent to Levy and Notice of Your Right to a Hearing" (levy notice) at least 30 days before the levy.

- The IRS may sell seized property. The following conditions apply:

    1) The IRS must give a notice of pending sale and wait at least 10 days.

    2) If the proceeds of the sale are less than the total of the tax bill and the expenses of levy and sale, the taxpayer will still have to pay the unpaid tax.

    3) If the proceeds of the sale are more than the total of the tax bill and the expenses of the levy and sale, the taxpayer may ask for a refund.

    4) If the IRS sells real estate, the taxpayer has the right to buy it back within 180 days of the sale for the amount paid plus 20% annual interest.

- The following property cannot be levied:

    1) School books and certain clothing

    2) Fuel, provisions, furniture, and personal effects for a household (limited)

    3) Books and tools used in the taxpayer's trade, business, or profession (limited)

    4) Unemployment benefits and certain public assistance payments

    5) Certain annuity and pension benefits

    6) Certain service-connected disability payments and workers' compensation

    7) Salary, wages, or income included in a judgment for court-ordered child support payments

    8) A minimum weekly exemption for wages, salary, and other income

- **Appealing a levy** – A taxpayer may request a CDP hearing with the Office of Appeals by sending a request for a CDP hearing to the address shown on the notice. The taxpayer must file the request within 30 days of the date on the notice. At the conclusion of the CDP hearing, the IRS Office of Appeals will issue a determination. The taxpayer will have 30 days after the date of the determination to seek review of the determination in the U.S. Tax Court.

- **Filing a wrongful levy claim** – A taxpayer may be entitled to the return of the wrongfully levied property if they were not liable for the tax. For example, a taxpayer may file an administrative wrongful levy claim for the return of wrongly levied property if the taxpayer is a non-liable spouse and the IRS levees a state income tax refund or a bank account belonging to the taxpayer or spouse.

- **Releasing a levy** – In general, the IRS must release a levy if a taxpayer pays the tax along with penalties and interest. In addition, the IRS must release the levy if:

    1) The IRS did not follow proper procedures,

2) An automatic stay during bankruptcy is in effect,

3) The levy is on property that the IRS is not allowed to levy,

4) The levy occurred after accepting (or while the IRS considers) an OIC or installment request, or

5) The levy occurred while the IRS Office of Appeals considers certain appeals or requests for innocent spouse relief or during review by the Tax Court (unless court permits).

20 Tax Law

The Court System · Burden of Proof · Legal Authority and Reference

This chapter is a summary of the legal system pertaining to tax regulation in the United States. Some of the information appears in Publication 556, irs.gov, and ustreas.gov.

The Court System

If a taxpayer and the IRS still disagree after the appeals conference, the taxpayer may be entitled to take his case to the ***U.S. Tax Court***, the ***U.S. Court of Federal Claims***, or the ***U.S. District Court***. These courts are independent of the IRS. If a taxpayer unreasonably misuses the IRS' appeals system, or if the intent of the taxpayer in filing the case is primarily to cause a delay or the taxpayer's position is frivolous or groundless, the Tax Court may impose a penalty of up to $25,000.

U.S. Tax Court

The U.S. Tax Court has federal jurisdiction and only hears cases related to tax. A taxpayer cannot take a case to the Tax Court before the IRS sends a notice of deficiency (90-Day Letter). The taxpayer can only appeal a case if he files a petition within 90 days from the date the IRS mails the notice (150 days if the mailing address is outside the United States). Taxpayers represented by counsel must file all documents electronically. Generally, the Tax Court hears cases <u>before</u> any tax has been assessed and paid. A taxpayer can take his case to the U.S. Tax Court if he disagrees with the IRS over any of the following:

- Income tax
- Estate tax
- Gift tax
- Certain excise taxes of private foundations, public charities, qualified pension and other retirement plans, or real estate investment trusts

If the amount of the case is $50,000 or less for any one tax year or period, the taxpayer can request that the Tax Court handle the case under the ***small tax case procedure***. If the Tax Court approves, the taxpayer can present his case to the Tax Court for a decision that is final (cannot appeal).

U.S. District Courts and U.S. Court of Federal Claims

Generally, the *District Court* and the *Court of Federal Claims* hear tax cases only <u>after</u> the taxpayer paid the tax and filed a claim for a credit or refund. The taxpayer can file a claim with the IRS for a credit or refund if he believes the tax paid is incorrect or excessive. If the IRS disallows the claim, the taxpayer should receive a notice of claim disallowance. If the IRS does not act on the claim within six months from the date filed, the taxpayer can then file suit for a refund. In general, the taxpayer must file suit for a credit or refund no later than two years after the IRS informs him that it has rejected his claim. The taxpayer may file a suit for a credit or refund in *U.S. District Court* or in the *U.S. Court of Federal Claims*. However, he cannot appeal to the *U.S. Court of Federal Claims* if the claim is for credit or refund of a penalty that relates to promoting an abusive tax shelter or to aiding and abetting the understatement of tax liability on someone else's return.

Appellate Courts

A taxpayer may appeal trial court decisions to a court of appeals, dependent upon what court handled the trial. A taxpayer may appeal a case heard in *U.S. Tax Court* or *U.S. District Court* to the **U.S. Court of Appeals** in the circuit where the taxpayer resides at the time of appeal. A taxpayer who brought his case to the *U.S. Court of Federal Claims* can appeal to the **Court of Appeals for the Federal Circuit.** In all cases, the non-prevailing party in the appeal may request that the **U.S. Supreme Court** hear the case. However, it is doubtful a tax case will go before the *U.S. Supreme Court* unless it is one of great significance.

Burden of Proof

The IRS has the burden of initially producing evidence in court proceedings with respect to the liability of any individual taxpayer for any penalty, addition to tax, or additional amount imposed by the tax laws. In the case of an individual, the IRS has the burden of proof in court proceedings based on any IRS reconstruction of income solely using statistical information on unrelated taxpayers.

For other court proceedings, the IRS generally has the burden of proof for any factual issue if the taxpayer has met the following requirements:

- Introduced credible evidence relating to the issue
- Complied with all substantiation requirements of the Internal Revenue Code
- Maintained all records required by the Internal Revenue Code
- Cooperated with all reasonable requests by the IRS for information regarding the preparation and related tax treatment of any item reported on the tax return
- Had a net worth of $7 million or less and not more than 500 employees at the time the tax liability is contested in any court if the tax return is for a corporation, partnership, or trust

Tax Law and Regulations

Tax laws are not always clear and may not provide a definitive answer or guidance to all issues. The code is further interpreted administratively by **Treasury Regulations**, **Revenue Rulings**, and **Revenue Procedures**. Many consider these interpretations and decisions to be "tax law."

The IRS must follow their rulings; however, a taxpayer may contest them in tax court. If laws are in dispute or need clarification, the tax court may hear the case to clarify the intent of the code. Both **judicial** (court) and **administrative** interpretations of the code may be cited as **precedent** for future arguments in similar cases.

Internal Revenue Code

Federal tax law begins with the **Internal Revenue Code (IRC)**, enacted by Congress in **Title 26** of the U.S. Code (26 USC.) The *Internal Revenue Code* is the basis for all tax law. Changes to tax law are proposed in the form of a "tax bill" and voted on in the U.S. Congress and Senate. If the legislature approves the tax bill and the president signs it into law, the code is amended to include the new law. Sections of the code are often referenced when citing tax laws. Sections are often referenced by "Sec." or the "§" symbol prior to the section number such as Sec. 1031 or §6695.

Treasury Regulations

In its role in administering the tax laws enacted by the U.S. Congress, the IRS must take the specifics of these laws and translate them into detailed regulations, rules, and procedures. ***Treasury regulations (26 CFR)***—commonly referred to as federal tax regulations—pick up where the *Internal Revenue Code* leaves off by providing the official interpretation of the IRC by the U.S. Department of the Treasury. A regulation is issued to provide guidance for new legislation or to address issues that arise with respect to existing Internal Revenue Code sections. Regulations interpret and give directions on complying with the law. Regulations are published in the ***Federal Register***. Generally, regulations are first published in *proposed* form. After considering public input, a ***final regulation*** or a ***temporary regulation*** is published as a ***Treasury Decision (TD)***, again, in the *Federal Register*.

Revenue Rulings

A revenue ruling is an official interpretation by the IRS of the Internal Revenue Code, related statutes, tax treaties, and regulations. Rulings indicate how the law applies to a specific set of facts. The IRS publishes rulings in the *Internal Revenue Bulletin* as guidance to taxpayers, IRS personnel, and tax professionals. For example, a ruling may hold that taxpayers can deduct certain automobile expenses.

Revenue Procedures

A revenue procedure is an official statement of a procedure that affects the rights or duties of taxpayers or other members of the public under the Internal Revenue Code, related statutes, tax treaties, and regulations and that should be a matter of public knowledge. The IRS also publishes revenue procedures in the *Internal Revenue Bulletin*. While a revenue ruling generally states an IRS position, a revenue procedure provides return filing or other instructions concerning an IRS position. For example, a revenue procedure might specify how those entitled to deduct certain automobile expenses should compute them by applying a certain mileage rate in lieu of calculating actual operating expenses.

Case Law

Case law is born out of the decisions of the courts interpreting the law. Once a court arrives at a decision, a justice (or several justices) will write an opinion. This ***judicial decision*** may be cited as precedent, and any court lower in the pecking order must follow the decision as law. Lawyers and taxpayers often use these decisions to argue a position. The IRS, which is an agency within the U.S. Department of the Treasury, may disagree with a tax court determination when a ruling is against their position. IRS policy is to announce their ***acquiescence*** (acceptance) to follow a court ruling in future matters of an equivalent issue. The intention of the IRS to follow (or not) a court decision is published in the ***Internal Revenue Bulletin (IRB)*** and listed as *acq.* or *nonacq.* in the court citation. A decision of the U.S. Supreme court carries the same authority as the Internal Revenue Code.

Legal Reference

Only rules of law may be cited as precedent for the purposes of defending a tax position or action. However, many other resources offer guidance as to how the IRS may treat a certain position.

IRS Notices

A notice is a public pronouncement that may contain guidance involving substantive interpretations of the Internal Revenue Code or other provisions of the law. For example, notices are used to relate what regulations will say in situations where the regulations may not be published in the immediate future.

Private Letter Rulings

The IRS Office of Chief Counsel may issue a *private letter ruling (PLR)* to a taxpayer, which is a written statement that interprets and applies tax laws to the taxpayer's specific set of facts. The IRS issues a PLR to establish with certainty the federal tax consequences of a particular transaction before the transaction is consummated or before the taxpayer files a return. A PLR issues in response to a written request submitted by a taxpayer and binds the IRS if the taxpayer fully and accurately described the proposed transaction in the request and carries out the transaction as described. Other taxpayers or IRS personnel may not rely on a PLR as precedent. PLRs are generally made public after all information has been removed that could identify the taxpayer to whom it was issued.

Technical Advice Memorandum

A technical advice memorandum, or TAM, is guidance furnished by the *Office of Chief Counsel* upon the request of an IRS director or an area director for appeals, in response to technical or procedural questions that develop during a proceeding. A request for a TAM generally stems from an examination of a taxpayer's return, a consideration of a taxpayer's claim for a refund or credit, or any other matter involving a specific taxpayer under the jurisdiction of the territory manager or the area director for appeals. A TAM issues only on closed transactions and provides the interpretation of proper application of tax laws, tax treaties, regulations, revenue rulings, or other precedents. The advice rendered represents a final determination of the position of the IRS but only with respect to the specific issue in the specific case in which the advice is issued. A TAM is generally made public after all information has been removed that could identify the taxpayer whose circumstances triggered a specific memorandum.

IRS Form Instructions and Publications

Forms instructions or IRS publications offer instructions in plain English to assist taxpayers with the preparation of returns. These informational documents do not supersede the rule of law.

Treasury Department Circular 230

Circular 230 contains the rules indicated in *31 CFR, Subtitle A, Part 10*. Circular 230 contains regulations governing the practice of attorneys, certified public accountants, enrolled agents, enrolled actuaries, enrolled retirement plan agents, and appraisers before the Internal Revenue Service. In order to practice before the IRS, a tax practitioner must understand the rules contained within Circular 230, many of which were covered in prior chapters within this guide.

Internal Revenue Bulletin

The *Internal Revenue Bulletin (IRB)* is the authoritative instrument for announcing official rulings and procedures of the IRS and for publishing Treasury Decisions, Executive Orders, Tax Conventions, legislation, court decisions, and other items of general interest.

Internal Revenue Manual

The *Internal Revenue Manual (IRM)* is the single official source for IRS policies, directives, guidelines, procedures, and delegations of authority in the IRS.

Glossary

50% limit organizations – Organizations where the deduction to a taxpayer for a charitable contribution is limited to 50% of adjusted gross income. These include churches and conventions or associations of churches, educational organizations with a regular faculty and curriculum that normally have a regularly enrolled student body attending classes on site, hospitals and certain medical research organizations associated with these hospitals, and publicly supported charities.

15-year property – One of the six classes of depreciable property, items such as roads, fences and shrubbery are depreciated over a 15-year period.

2010 Tax Relief Act – Officially named the Tax Relief, Unemployment Insurance Reauthorization, and Job Creation Act of 2010, this Act provides a two-year extension of the provisions of the Economic Growth and Tax Relief Reconciliation Act of 2001 (EGTRRA) and the Jobs and Growth Tax Relief Reconciliation Act of 2003 (JGTRRA). It revives the estate tax for those dying after 2009.

20-year property – One of the six classes of depreciable property, 20-year property includes improvements such as utilities and sewers the cost of which is depreciated over a 20-year period.

30% limit organizations – Organizations subject to a 30% of AGI limit for deduction of charitable contributions. 30% limit organizations include veterans' organizations, fraternal societies, nonprofit cemeteries, and certain private non-operating foundations.

403(b) Plan – Often called a tax-sheltered annuity (TSA), this is a retirement plan for certain employees of public schools, tax-exempt organizations, and certain ministers.

529 program – A qualified tuition program set up to allow the taxpayer to either prepay or contribute to an account established for paying a student's qualified higher education expenses at an eligible educational institution.

5-year property – One of the six classes of depreciable property, 5-year property includes computers and peripheral equipment, office machinery, automobiles, light trucks, appliances, carpeting, furniture, etc., used in a residential rental real estate activity.

7-year property – One of the six classes of depreciable property, 7-year property not only includes office furniture and equipment (desks, file cabinets, etc.), but also includes any property that does not have a class life and that has not been designated by law as being in any other class.

Abatement – To reduce the amount, typically interest, owed if the interest is due to an unreasonable error or delay by an IRS officer or employee in performing a ministerial act or managerial act.

Accelerated death benefits – Benefits available under a life insurance contract or viatical settlement before the insured's death, usually due to chronic or terminal illness.

Accountable plan – An employee reimbursement plan which requires the employee to account for reimbursable expenses. Amounts paid are not wages and are not subject to withholding and payment of FICA, FUTA, and income taxes. Employees must have paid or incurred deductible expenses while performing services as employees, substantiate these expenses to the employer within a reasonable period, and return any unsubstantiated expenses within a reasonable period.

Accounting method – Set of rules that determines when and how taxpayers report income and expenses.

Accounting period – A tax year for figuring taxable income.

Accrual Method – A method of accounting which requires the taxpayer to report interest income when earned, whether or not it has been received by the taxpayer.

Acquiescence – The IRS's acceptance to follow a court ruling in future matters of an equivalent issue.

Active participation – A standard of participation used in connection with passive activities that describes a level of involvement with daily activities including management decisions such as approving tenants, deciding rental terms, approving expenditures, etc.

Additional child credit – A credit available in the event the Child Tax Credit is greater than the amount of income tax owed. The additional child tax credit is refundable.

Adjusted Basis – The result of certain adjustments to the cost of property prior to figuring the gain or loss on a sale, exchange, or other disposition or property or figuring the allowable depreciation, depletion, or amortization.

Adjustments – Any change made to gross income. Adjustment items appear on the front of form 1040.

Administrative Law Judge (ALJ) – Conducts proceedings on complaints for the sanction of a practitioner, employer, firm or other entity, or appraiser.

Adoption Taxpayer Identification Number (ATIN) – Issued by the IRS as a temporary taxpayer identification number for the child in a domestic adoption where the adopting taxpayers do not have and/or are unable to obtain the child's Social Security Number (SSN). The ATIN is to be used by the adopting taxpayers on their Federal Income Tax return to identify the child while final domestic adoption is pending.

Advance rent – An amount designated as rent that the owner receives before the period that it covers.

Affiliated group – A parent corporation and one or more subsidiary corporations.

Alimony – A payment to (or for) a spouse or former spouse under a divorce or separation instrument. Alimony is included in the gross income of the recipient and can be taken as a deduction by the payor.

Alternate valuation date – For estate valuation purposes, a date that is six months from the date of death.

Amortization – A plan that provides for the gradual payment of a debt in regular installments over a period of time.

Annuities – An insurance product commonly used as part of a retirement strategy. There are many different types of annuities. An annuity may provide for immediate or deferred payments of a fixed or variable amount.

Annuitization – Process of converting an annuity into a series of periodic payments.

Appeal – A party's right to challenge the decision of an ALJ with the Secretary of the Treasury or delegate. An appeal must include a brief that states exceptions to the decision and supporting reasons.

Applicable federal rate – The rate used by the IRS to calculate assigned interest charges. The rate fluctuates and the current rate is published monthly.

Assessed value – The value of a property according to a jurisdictional tax assessment.

Assessment – Assessment is the statutorily required recording of tax liability.

Back pay – Amounts paid to taxpayer, commonly as an award of a settlement or judgment, which may include, owed wages, payments made to a person for damages, unpaid life insurance premiums, and unpaid health insurance premiums.

Backup withholding – A specified percentage rate (currently 28%) withheld by a payor in connection with certain 1099 transactions.

Bargain purchases – The purchase of an item for less than its fair market value.

Barter income – Taxable income that is generated as a result of an exchange of property for goods and/or services.

Basis – The amount of a taxpayer's investment in a property for tax purposes, adjusted for certain items.

Beneficiary – The person designated to be the recipient of the money or property.

Boot – Cash or property received in a like kind exchange that does not qualify as like kind property for purposes of the specific transaction. The fair market value of boot is taxable, limited to the amount of gain on the exchange.

Calendar year – The 12-month period from January 1 through December 31.

Call option – The right to buy from the writer of the option, at any time before a designated future date, a specified amount of property a certain price.

Capital assets – Tangible property, commonly held for investment purposes.

Capital gain – The positive result of a sale or trade of a capital asset.

Capital gain distributions – Distributions paid to shareholders out of the capital gains from the sale of company property.

Capital gains rates – Tax rate that applies to net capital gain; typically, lower than tax rates that apply to other income.

Capital improvements – Costs of improvements having a useful life of more than one year, which increases the value of a property, lengthen its life, or adapt it to a different use.

Capital interest – A capital interest in a partnership is an interest in its assets.

Capital loss – The negative result of a sale or trade of a capital asset.

Carry back period – When referring to Net Operating Loss, carryback period is generally the two-year period immediately prior to the year the NOL occurred and for which the taxpayer can claim the loss for tax purposes.

Cash Method – A method of accounting that requires the taxpayer to report income in the year of constructive receipt.

Casualty loss – The damage, destruction, or loss of property resulting from an identifiable event that is sudden, unexpected, or unusual.

Catch-up contribution – Extra amount retirement plan participants who are age 50 or older at the end of the calendar year may make in addition to regular contributions.

Censure – An official public reprimand.

Child support – Court-ordered payments, typically made by a noncustodial divorced parent, to support a minor child or children. Child support does not qualify as income or deduction items.

Clergy – Ministers, members of a religious order, and Christian Science practitioners.

Closing costs – Fees paid in addition to the contract price of the property when buying a home.

Closing transaction – Final transaction or series of transactions that satisfies the terms of a contract.

Commissions – A fee paid for transacting business or performing a service.

Community Property – A classification of ownership of property that establishes a fifty percent interest in all community property by each spouse. The community property system has been adopted by nine states: Arizona, California, Idaho, Louisiana, New Mexico, Nevada, Texas, Washington and Wisconsin. The U.S. Territory of Puerto Rico is also a community property jurisdiction.

Compensatory damages – Compensation awarded for actual physical injury, physical sickness, or emotional distress.

Condemned – Deemed unsuitable for use or consumption.

Confidentiality privilege – Protection of certain communications, commonly between a taxpayer and an attorney; also applies between a taxpayer and any federally authorized tax practitioner.

Conflict of interest – Exists if the representation of one client is directly adverse to another client or if there is a significant risk that the representation of one or more clients will be materially limited by the practitioner's responsibilities to another client, to a former client or a third person, or by a personal interest of the practitioner.

Constructive receipt – When the income is available for a taxpayer's unrestricted withdrawal.

Contingent fees – A fee contingent upon whether or not a position taken on a return avoids challenge by the IRS.

Continuing professional education – Education required to maintain a professional designation or certification.

Conventions – A method that determines the number of months a taxpayer can claim depreciation in the year the property is placed in service or disposed.

Conversion – A distribution from a qualified retirement plan or IRA into a Roth IRA.

Corpus – A capital sum within a trust or estate; also called principal.

Cost Method – A method of inventory valuation that takes into account all associated direct and indirect costs.

Cost-of-living adjustment (COLA) – Periodic change in salary based on cost-of-living index.

Covered opinion – Written advice by a practitioner concerning federal tax matters (certain limitations apply).

Credits – A credit reduces the amount of tax. Certain credits are refundable if greater than total tax.

De minimis benefits – Employer provided benefits, the cost of which is so small that it would be unreasonable for the employer to account for them. The value of the benefit is not included in income. Examples include coffee, doughnuts, etc.

Decedent – A deceased person.

Declaration of representative – A signed statement authorizing a person to represent a taxpayer before the IRS.

Deduction – Certain items that reduce the amount of income subject to tax.

Default – A selection made, usually automatically or without active consideration, due to a failure to file an answer within the time prescribed; typically constitutes an admission of guilt.

Deferral – The postponement of taxation or benefits.

Dependent – A person supported by a taxpayer. Often a dependent is a member of the taxpayer's immediate family, or an individual who lives with the taxpayer for the entire year.

Depletion – Method used to recover the cost of assets that diminish over time, such as oil, gas, and other natural resources.

Depreciation – Method used to recover the cost of tangible income-producing property, other than natural resources.

Descendant – A person who is a lineal family member of a particular ancestor.

Diligence – The practitioner's reasonable care in the preparation, approval, and filing of tax returns and all other documents, as well as any oral statements relating to IRS or Treasury Department matters, as it pertains to accuracy and completion.

Direct skip – The transfer of property to, or for the benefit of, persons more than one generation younger than the taxpayer.

Disbarment – To expel any practitioner from practice before the IRS if the practitioner is shown to be incompetent or disreputable, fails to comply with any regulation in Circular 230, or with intent to defraud, willfully and knowingly misleads or threatens a client or prospective client. A practitioner may petition for reinstatement after 5 years.

Discharge – To relieve an obligation or debt.

Discovery – The disclosure of pertinent facts or documents by one or both parties to a legal action or proceeding.

Disposition – The final settlement of a matter, particularly the giving up of property by way of transfer to the care or possession of another.

Disregarded entity – A business entity that is not separate from its owner for tax purposes.

Distributive share – The allocation of income, loss, deduction, or credit from a business to a partner.

Dividend – The most common type of distribution from a corporation, paid out of its earnings and profits.

Domestic – Within the United States.

Double taxation – Two or more taxes levied upon the same income, assets, or financial transaction.

Durable power of attorney – A power to act in place of a person that continues during periods of incapacity.

Earned income – Earned income includes all the taxable income and wages you get from working or from certain disability payments. For EITC purposes, a taxpayer may elect to include nontaxable combat pay in earned income.

Easements – A privilege granted by a property for the use of a specified piece of land.

Elective deferrals – Voluntary contribution of wages, which otherwise would be taxable, to an employer-sponsored retirement plan.

Employer Identification Number (EIN) – A federal identification number required for businesses that have one or more employees, file returns for employment or excise taxes, maintain a qualified retirement plan, or operate as a corporation, partnership, nonprofit, estate, or trust.

Enrolled actuary – Any individual enrolled as an actuary by the Joint Board for the Enrollment of Actuaries.

Enrolled agent – An enrolled agent is a person who has earned the privilege of representing taxpayers before the Internal Revenue Service by either passing a three-part comprehensive IRS test, or through equivalent experience as a former IRS employee. Enrolled agent status is the highest credential the IRS awards. Enrolled agents, like attorneys and certified public accountants (CPAs), have unlimited practice rights. This means they are unrestricted as to which taxpayers they can represent, what types of tax matters they can handle, and which IRS offices they may practice before.

Enrolled retirement plan agent – An individual authorized to represent employers before the IRS on retirement plan matters.

Equitable relief – A refund granted pursuant to the innocent spouse rules with regard to understated or underpaid tax. The taxpayer may seek a refund for payments he or she made directly. The taxpayer may not receive a refund of payments made with the joint return, joint payments, or payments made by a spouse (or former spouse).

Estate – All property owned by a taxpayer.

Estate Tax – A tax on the right to transfer property at death.

Estimated tax – The method used to determine and pay tax on income that is not subject to withholding.

Examinations – An IRS a review/examination of accounts and financial information to ensure information is being reported correctly, according to the tax laws, to verify the amount of tax reported is accurate.

Excess contributions – Contributions to retirement accounts that are above the established annual limitations.

Exchange – The act or process of substituting one thing for another. Certain exchanges may defer payment of tax.

Excise tax – An indirect tax paid on the purchase of specific goods, such as gasoline.

Exclusion – The option to remove an item from consideration for federal income tax purposes.

Executor – An individual named in a decedent's will to administer the estate and distribute properties as the decedent directed.

Exempt organizations – Certain organizations that receive an exemption from federal income taxes.

Exemption – To deduct or exclude from taxable income.

Exemption portability – Allows the executor of a deceased spouse's estate to transfer any unused exemption to the surviving spouse.

Exercise – To implement the terms of an agreement.

Extension – An increase of time to file an income tax return. An automatic extension to file is available lasting 6 months for forms 1040, 1120, and 1120S. An extension for form 1065 is 5 months.

Fair Market Value (FMV) – The price that a property would sell for in an open market assuming a willing buyer and seller would likely agree upon the price when acting freely, carefully, and with complete knowledge.

Fiduciary accounting income (FAI) – The amount of income (after expenses allocable to income) the trustee will use to determine distributions for beneficiaries.

Filing Status – A classification for income tax purposes that determines threshold amounts for standard deduction, applicable tax rates, and eligibility for benefits and credits.

Final return – The last income tax return that is filed for a decedent that meets the filing requirements at the time of death. The final income tax return is due at the same time the decedent's return would have been due had death not occurred. A final return for a decedent who was a calendar year taxpayer is generally due on April 15 following the year of death, regardless of when during that year death occurred.

Fiscal year – A tax year election consisting of twelve consecutive months ending on the last day of any month except December.

Foster child – A child other than a natural or adopted child who is placed with a taxpayer by an authorized placement agency or by judgment, decree, or other order of any court of competent jurisdiction.

Fraud – A deception by misrepresentation of material facts, or silence when good faith requires expression, resulting in material damage to one who relies on it and has the right to rely on it. Simply stated, it is obtaining something of value from someone else through deceit.

Fringe benefits – Items of monetary value provided to an employee in connection with performance of services and in addition to the employee's salary.

Frivolous position – A position taken on a tax return without basis for validity in existing law, or that is deemed frivolous by the United States Tax Court or other federal court.

Gift – To give property (including money), or the use of (or income from) property, without expecting to receive something of equal value or more in return. A gift is not complete until the transferor relinquishes all rights.

Grantor – The person who creates and usually contributes property to a trust. Also called a trustor or settlor.

Grantor trust – A trust in which the grantor retains control over the property in the trust. Often called a living trust or a revocable trust.

Gross income – The total of earned and unearned income subject to tax.

Gross income threshold – The sum of the standard deduction and personal exemption amounts for each filing status; also determines whether a taxpayer must file a return.

Guaranteed payments – Payments made by a partnership to a partner determined without regard to the partnership's income.

Hearing – A legal proceeding before a court, usually less formal than a trial.

Holding period – Length of time an asset is held. For investment property, the holding period begins the day after the day the property is acquired (trade date) or receipt of title and includes the date of disposition, transfer, or sale.

Home acquisition debt – A loan taken against the value of a home to buy, build, or substantially improve a qualified home (main or second home).

Home equity debt – Debt secured by a primary residence or second home to the extent of the excess of fair market value over acquisition debt.

Improvements – An addition that adds to the value of property, prolongs its useful life, or adapts it to new uses.

Incompetence – The inability to act with legal effectiveness, especially within the context of Circular 230.

Independent contractor – Individuals who follow an independent trade, business, or profession in which they offer their services to the public and are typically not employees.

Individual Taxpayer Identification Number (ITIN) – A tax processing number issued by the IRS to individuals who are required to have a U.S. taxpayer identification number but who do not have, and are not eligible to obtain, a Social Security Number (SSN) from the Social Security Administration (SSA).

Injured spouse – A taxpayer who files a joint return and all or part of his share of the refund was, or will be, applied against the separate past-due federal tax, state tax, child support, or federal non-tax debt (such as a student loan) of his spouse with whom he filed the joint return. An injured spouse may be entitled to recoup their share of the refund.

Innocent spouse – A taxpayer who may be relieved of responsibility for paying tax, interest, and penalties because a spouse or former spouse failed to report income, reported income improperly, or claimed improper deductions or credits.

Insolvency – When liabilities exceed the FMV of assets.

Installment – Debt payments made at specified intervals over a period of time.

Intangible property – A commercially transferable interest in property that does not have a physical presence. Examples include computer software, patents, goodwill, government license, franchises, trademarks, etc.

Interest – A charge for borrowed money that is generally a percentage of the amount borrowed or an excess above what is due or expected.

Internal Revenue Code (IRC) – The basis for all tax law. Federal tax law begins with the Internal Revenue Code (IRC), enacted by Congress in Title 26 of the U.S. Code (26 USC.)

Inventory – Merchandise or goods used or held for sale.

Investment – The outlay of money or property with the expectation of income or profit.

Involuntary conversions – Occurs when property is destroyed, stolen, condemned, or disposed of under the threat of condemnation.

Itemized deductions – Allowable deductions from income that are individually identified. A taxpayer will itemize deductions instead of claiming a standard deduction of a lesser amount.

Levy – A levy is an administrative means of collecting taxes by seizure and sale of property to satisfy delinquent taxes. It enables the government to collect outstanding taxes without first going to court. An exception is the seizure of a principal residence, which requires court approval.

Liability – A legal debt or obligation for which a taxpayer is responsible.

Lien – The government's legal claim against a taxpayer's property resulting from an unpaid tax debt.

Life expectancy – The average period that a person may expect to live.

Like-kind exchange – The trade of business or investment property for other business or investment property of a similar (like) kind.

Long-term – A period longer than one year.

Loss – The negative result of a sale or trade.

Lump sum – A monetary distribution made in its entirety.

Main home – The home in which the taxpayer lives most of the time; in addition to a house, a main home may also be a condominium, cooperative apartment, houseboat, or mobile home.

Marketed opinion – Written advice that is used or referred to by a person other than the practitioner in promoting, marketing, or recommending a partnership or other entity, investment plan, or arrangement to one or more taxpayer(s).

Material participation – A taxpayer materially participates in an activity if he or she works on a regular, continuous and substantial basis in operations (IRC § 469(h)(1)). If a taxpayer does not materially participate, losses are passive, which means they generally are not deductible in the absence of passive income. Material participation is time sensitive. A taxpayer materially participates in an activity only if he or she meets any one of the seven material participation tests in Reg. § 1.469-5T(a).

Member of household – A person that lives with the taxpayer all year as a member of the household. Does not include domestic employees such as babysitters or maids.

Net operating loss (NOL) – A loss that occurs when annual deductions exceed income.

Non-accountable plan – An employee expense reimbursement plan under which employees are not required to substantiate expenses.

Nonrecourse liability – A liability for which there is no economic risk of loss to the individual.

Nonresident alien – Any individual who is not a U.S. citizen or U.S. national that does not meet the green card test or the substantial presence test.

Notary – A state licensed clerk who performs acts in legal affairs, such as witnessing signatures to documents.

Office of Professional Responsibility (OPR) – The Internal Revenue Service office that establishes and enforces consistent standards of competence, integrity and conduct for tax professionals.

Omission – Failure to include information or data known.

Ordinary – Common and accepted in the taxpayer's trade, business, or profession.

Original Issue Discount (OID) – A form of interest that is the difference between the stated redemption price at maturity and the issue price.

Passive activities – Activities that generate income from certain businesses where no material participation occurs.

Pension – A fund that is established for the payment of taxpayer's retirement benefits; generally paid in part by the employer.

Per diem – A daily allowance for certain travel related expenses.

Points – Prepaid interest, which may be deductible as home mortgage interest when itemizing deductions on Form 1040, Schedule A.

Principal residence – The home where the taxpayer typically lives most of the time. There can only be one principal residence at any specific time.

Private activity bond – A bond where the amount of the proceeds to finance loans to persons other than government units is more than 5% of the proceeds or $5 million, whichever is less. Private activity bonds are often used to build a sports facility or industrial park, airport, or for-profit hospital.

Private letter ruling (PLR) – A written statement that interprets and applies tax laws to a stated set of facts for a specified taxpayer.

Progressive tax – Tax rates increase as taxable income increases; e.g., U.S. income tax.

Punitive damages – Monetary compensation awarded to an injured party as punishment to the defendant.

Put option – The right to sell a stated number of shares at a specified price to the writer (seller) at any time before a specified future date.

Real property – A type of tangible property that includes land, houses, buildings, etc.

Realized amount – The entire amount received from a sale or trade of property.

Recapture – The process of adding back an amount that a taxpayer had previously deducted from income.

Recognized – The amount a taxpayer includes in taxable income as a result of a sale or trade of property.

Recourse liability – A liability that has an economic risk of loss.

Recovery periods – The designated amount of time that property depreciates.

Redemption – To gain or regain possession of in exchange for payment, or to clear a debt.

Repairs – Costs that keep property in a good operating condition, but do not add value to the property or substantially prolong its life.

Representation – To act on behalf of a person, group, or entity. Commonly before the Internal Revenue Service.

Reprimand – A disciplinary act either given in private or public in regards to one's actions or performance.

Required minimum distributions – A minimum amount a taxpayer is annually required to distribute from a qualified plan or IRA.

Resident alien – A lawful permanent resident of the United States who has not yet gained citizenship.

Refund Anticipation Loans (RAL) – Money borrowed by a taxpayer from a lender based on the taxpayer's anticipated income tax refund.

Reversionary interest – A transferor's right to have property returned after the termination of an intervening estate or interest.

Revocable – Capable of being cancelled.

Rollover – To transfer a withdrawal from one qualified plan or IRA into another within 60 days of initial withdrawal.

S corporation – A small business corporation for which an election under section 1362(a) is in effect for such year. S corporations are corporations that elect to pass corporate income, losses, deductions and credit through to their shareholders for federal tax purposes. Shareholders of S corporations report the flow-through of income and losses on their personal tax returns and are assessed tax at their individual income tax rates. This allows S corporations to avoid double taxation on the corporate income. S corporations are responsible for tax on certain built-in gains and passive income.

Sanctions – Punishment that may include private reprimand, public censure, suspension or disbarment from practice before the IRS, and imposition of a monetary penalty.

Securities – An investment term used to describe stocks, stock rights, bonds, etc.

Security deposits – Money paid by a tenant to the taxpayer (property owner) to ensure the lease's obligation.

Settlement fees – A fee paid by the taxpayer in connection with the purchase of property.

Severance pay – Supplemental wages made upon or after termination of employment for an employment relationship that has terminated.

Standard deduction – A flat dollar amount determined by filing status that reduces taxable income.

Start-up costs – Any amounts paid or incurred in connection with creating or investigating the creation or acquisition of an active trade or business.

Statute of limitations – The period of time during which legal proceedings can be initiated.

Statutory employee – An employee who is not considered a common law employee but is considered an employee by statute for Social Security, Medicare, and FUTA tax purposes.

Statutory nonemployee – Those who are treated generally as self-employed for all federal tax purposes; includes direct sellers, qualified real estate agents, and some companion sitters.

Suspension – To temporarily remove the right to practice for a specified period, typically less than 5 years.

Tangible property – Property that is physical in nature.

Tax home – The entire city or general area where the main place of business or work is located, regardless of where the individual maintains a family home.

Tax shelter – Any entity, plan, or arrangement, with the purpose of avoiding or evading federal income tax.

Tax withholding – The tax that an employer withholds from the employee's pay; it is deposited to the IRS in the name of the employee; also includes pensions, bonuses, commissions, and gambling winnings.

Tax year – An annual accounting period for keeping records and reporting income and expenses.

Taxable estate – The gross estate minus allowable deductions.

Taxable income – The taxpayer's gross income minus all adjustments and deductions.

Tax-exempt income – Income received on which income tax is not required to be paid.

Taxpayer – Any individual who must pay or is responsible for income tax.

Tenants by the entirety – Allows spouses to own property together as a single legal entity.

Tenants with rights of survivorship – Allows the successor of a decedent to acquire the property of the decedent.

Tentative minimum tax – A minimum amount of tax that an individual or corporation must pay. The amount is a percentage of alternative minimum taxable income (AMTI). Tentative minimum tax must be calculated to determine the alternative minimum tax liability.

Trustee – The fiduciary responsible for assets within the trust who assumes legal title to trust property and is accountable for administering the provisions of the trust on behalf of the beneficiaries.

Tuition – The cost or payment to an educational institute in return for education.

Uncollected rent – An estimate in rent that has not yet been collected; cannot be deducted because it has not been considered income.

Unearned income – Payments classified as income that are not considered earned, including unemployment compensation, taxable Social Security benefits, taxable pensions, annuity income, canceled debt, unearned income from a trust, taxable interest, dividends, and capital gains.

Unemployment benefits – Payment made to an unemployed person by the government or union.

Uniform Lifetime Table – The life expectancy table used to calculate required minimum distributions from individual retirement arrangements.

Unrealized receivables – Rights to payment for goods or services not previously included in income.

Viatical settlement – The sale or assignment of any part of the death benefit under a life insurance contract to a viatical settlement provider in the business of buying insurance contracts on the lives of insured individuals who are terminally or chronically ill.

Wages – Money that is paid for work or services.

Withholding – The income tax that is taken from an employee's pay and deposited to the IRS.

Workers' compensation – Payments for occupational sickness or injury under the workers' compensation act.

Appendix

Form 1120 (2010) Page **5**

Schedule L — Balance Sheets per Books

	Assets	Beginning of tax year		End of tax year	
		(a)	(b)	(c)	(d)
1	Cash				
2a	Trade notes and accounts receivable				
b	Less allowance for bad debts	( )		( )	
3	Inventories				
4	U.S. government obligations				
5	Tax-exempt securities (see instructions)				
6	Other current assets (attach schedule)				
7	Loans to shareholders				
8	Mortgage and real estate loans				
9	Other investments (attach schedule)				
10a	Buildings and other depreciable assets				
b	Less accumulated depreciation	( )		( )	
11a	Depletable assets				
b	Less accumulated depletion	( )		( )	
12	Land (net of any amortization)				
13a	Intangible assets (amortizable only)				
b	Less accumulated amortization	( )		( )	
14	Other assets (attach schedule)				
15	Total assets				

Liabilities and Shareholders' Equity

16	Accounts payable				
17	Mortgages, notes, bonds payable in less than 1 year				
18	Other current liabilities (attach schedule)				
19	Loans from shareholders				
20	Mortgages, notes, bonds payable in 1 year or more				
21	Other liabilities (attach schedule)				
22	Capital stock: a Preferred stock				
	b Common stock				
23	Additional paid-in capital				
24	Retained earnings—Appropriated (attach schedule)				
25	Retained earnings—Unappropriated				
26	Adjustments to shareholders' equity (attach schedule)				
27	Less cost of treasury stock		( )		( )
28	Total liabilities and shareholders' equity				

Schedule M-1 — Reconciliation of Income (Loss) per Books With Income per Return

Note: Schedule M-3 required instead of Schedule M-1 if total assets are $10 million or more—see instructions

1	Net income (loss) per books		7	Income recorded on books this year not included on this return (itemize): Tax-exempt interest $ _____
2	Federal income tax per books			
3	Excess of capital losses over capital gains			
4	Income subject to tax not recorded on books this year (itemize): _____			
			8	Deductions on this return not charged against book income this year (itemize):
5	Expenses recorded on books this year not deducted on this return (itemize):		a	Depreciation $ _____
a	Depreciation $ _____		b	Charitable contributions $ _____
b	Charitable contributions $ _____			
c	Travel and entertainment $ _____			
			9	Add lines 7 and 8
6	Add lines 1 through 5		10	Income (page 1, line 28)—line 6 less line 9

Schedule M-2 — Analysis of Unappropriated Retained Earnings per Books (Line 25, Schedule L)

1	Balance at beginning of year		5	Distributions: a Cash	
2	Net income (loss) per books			b Stock	
3	Other increases (itemize): _____			c Property	
			6	Other decreases (itemize): _____	
			7	Add lines 5 and 6	
4	Add lines 1, 2, and 3		8	Balance at end of year (line 4 less line 7)	

Form **1120** (2010)

Index

—A—

Abatement of interest, 296
Accelerated cost recovery system, 176
Accelerated death benefits, 64, 74
Accident plan. *See* Fringe benefits
Accountable plan, 64, 161
Accounting, 5, 24, 144
   accrual method, 6, 146, 236
   cash method, 5, 17, 145, 235
   fees, 46, 180
   methods, 145
   periods and methods, 5, 144, 176
Accumulated adjustments account, 194, 204
Accumulated earnings and profits, 196, 204
Accumulation phase, 41
Accuracy, 276
Accuracy-related penalty, 295
Acquiescence, 307
Active participation, 39, 170
Additional depreciation, 174
Adjusted basis, 48, 181, 185
Adjustments, 77, 89, 112, 204
   to gross income, 77
Administration expenses, 238
Administrative law judge, 280
Adoption, 68, 120
Advance commissions, 30
Advance payment, 146
Advance rent, 37
Advertising
   and solicitation, 276
   standards, 266
Affiliated group, 190
Age rules, 80
Age test, 26, 122
Alcohol and cellulosic biofuel fuels credit, 165
Alimony, 42, 88, 168
Allocating expenses against income, 239
Alternate valuation date, 129, 130
Alternative depreciation system, 176
Alternative fuel vehicle refueling property, 166
Alternative minimum tax, 112, 201
Alternative motor vehicle credit, 166
American Opportunity credit, 72, 118, 119
Amortization, 45, 144, 175

Amount
   eligible for the exclusion, 67
   excludable, 71
   realized, 54, 56, 185
   recognized, 55, 56
Annual contribution limit, 222
Annual exclusion, 128
Annuities, 40
Appeals, 3, 284, 301
   Conference, 293
Applicable federal rate, 55
Applying the unified credit to estate tax, 130
Archer MSA contributions. *See* Fringe benefits
Assessed value, 96
Assessments for local improvements, 48, 182
Associated test, 105, 158
Assumption of liabilities, 186
At risk, 39, 169, 211
Athletic facilities, 69, 246
Attorney, 284, *See* Circular 230 practitioner
   power of, 287
Audits, 289
Authority to investigate, 290
Authorized e-file provider, 260
Automatic six-month extension, 5, 294
Automobile expenses. *See Car expenses*
Average cost method, 52
Awards, 30, 43, 67, 165

—B—

Back pay, 30
Backup withholding, 141
Bad debts, 159
Balance sheet per books, 193
Bankruptcy, 42, 63
Bargain purchases, 49, 182
Basis, 45
   adjusted, 48, 181, 185
   allocation, 181
   cost, 46
   in partnership, 217
   of property, 46, 186
   rules, 211
Below-market loans, 198
Beneficiary, 239

Bequests, 127
Biodiesel and renewable diesel fuels credit, 166
Bona fide residence test, 75
Bonds, 51, 184
Bonuses, 30
Boot, 185, 186
Built-in gains, 203
Burden of proof, 306
Business
    bad debt, 102
    entities, 135
    liability insurance, 102
    property, 173
    start up, 153
    taxation, 153
    taxed as corporation, 189
    use, 66

—C—

Call option, 52
Canceled debt, 42
Capital assets, 57, 173
Capital expenditures, 45, 153, 175
Capital gain, 57
    distributions, 36
    gains and losses, 17, 240
    net long-term capital gain, 59
    net short-term capital gain, 59
    rates, 58
Capital improvements, 48, 181
Capital loss, 195
    carryover, 59
Capitalize, 45, 150, 175
Car expenses
    actual, 108
    employee, 107
    medical, 96
    moving, 87
Carbon dioxide sequestration credit, 166
Carry-back period, 168
Case law, 307
Cash method, 5, 145, 235
Casualty, 158
    insurance, 64
    losses, 48, 182, 238
Catch-up contribution, 221
Censure, 279, 284
Centralized authorization file (CAF), 288
Certified public accountants (CPA), 272
Charitable contributions, 98, 200, 238

Child and dependent care credit, 116
Child support, 89
Child tax credit, 125
Childcare
    credit, 166
    providers, 30
Clergy, 33, 63, 69
Client omissions, 276
Closely held corporations, 190
Closely related in place and time, 86
Closing costs, 47, 180
Closing transaction, 52
Collection process, 291, 299
Common-law employees, 137
Community property, 51
Compensation, 221
    employee, 161
    for sickness and injury, 74
    worker, 73
Compensatory damages, 43
Complex trust, 239
Condemned, 54
Conditions for exclusion, 70
Conferences, 280
Confidentiality privilege, 275
Conflict of interest, 276
Considered unmarried, 23
Constructive receipt, 5
Contact of third party, 290
Contents of complaint, 280
Contingent fees, 275
Continuing professional education, 274
Contribution, 225, 238
    Archer MSA, 68
    charitable, 98, 200
    deadline, 78, 225
    employer retirement plan, 164
    excess, 79
    IRA, 78
    nondeductible, 80, 98
    of property, 99
    qualified retirement plan, 69
    records, 100
Conventions, 101, 178
    half-year, 178
    mid-month, 178
    mid-quarter, 178
Conversion, 40
    involuntary, 183
Copy of decision, 283

Corporate transactions, 191
Corporation, 136, 139, 140, 189
   S corporation, 136
Corpus. *See* Principal
Cost basis, 46
Cost method, 148
Cost-of-living allowances and reimbursements, 30
Court awards and damages, 43
Court system, 305
Coverdell Educational Savings Account (ESA), 72
Credit, 111, 165, 211, 236
   adoption, 120
   alternative fuel vehicle refueling property credit, 166
   alternative motor vehicle, 49, 166
   American opportunity, 72
   biodiesel and renewable diesel fuels, 166
   carbon dioxide sequestration, 166
   child and dependent care, 116
   child tax, 125
   disabled access, 166
   distilled spirits, 166
   earned income, 121
   education, 117
   empowerment zone and renewal community employment, 166
   energy efficient home, 167
   first-time homebuyer, 123
   for elderly or the disabled, 124
   for employer differential wage payments, 166
   for employer Social Security, 166
   for employer-provided childcare, 166
   for increasing research activities, 166
   for Medicare taxes paid on employee tips, 166
   for prior year's minimum tax, 113
   for small employer pension plan start-up costs, 166
   for tax on prior transfers, 130
   foreign tax, 126
   general business, 165
   Indian employment, 167
   investment, 167, 203
   Lifetime Learning, 118
   limitations, 211
   low-income housing, 167
   mine rescue team training, 167
   new markets, 167
   nonconventional source fuel, 167
   orphan drug, 167
   qualified railroad track maintenance, 167
   renewable electricity, refined coal production, 167
   sales, 159
   savers, 126
   unified, 127
   when to claim, 121
   work opportunity, 167
Crop
   disaster payments, 244
   insurance, 244

—D—

Damages for breach of employment contract, 102
De minimis
   fringe benefits, 68
   meals, 163
   OID, 35
Decedent, 42, 50, 127, 237
Declaration of representative, 287
Declining balance method, 176
Decreases, 218
Deductible
   interest, 154
   medical expenses, 95
   moving expenses, 87
   part of self-employment taxes, 90
   taxes, 96
Deduction, 93, 211, 240
   dividends-received, 199
   for distributions, 240
   for personal exemption, 240
   limitations, 211
Deemed distributions, 198
Defined benefit plan, 227
Defined contribution plan, 223, 227
Dental expenses, 94
Dependent care
   assistance, 68
   credit, 116
Dependent taxpayer test, 25
Depletion, 45, 175, 238
Depreciation, 45, 174, 238, 243
   on computers, 103
   recapture, 54
Designated Roth accounts, 84
Determine gross profit, 54
Diligence, 276
Direct skips, 129
Directly related, 158
Director of the Office of Professional Responsibility, 271
Disability income, 31

Disbarment, 284
Discharge of debt due to bankruptcy or insolvency, 63
Discharge of qualified principal residence indebtedness, 67
Disciplinary proceedings, 280
Disposition
   of an installment obligation, 55
   of interest, 219
   of property, 53
Disqualified person, 231
Disregarded entity, 136
Disreputable conduct, 279
Distance test, 86
Distilled spirits credit, 166
Distributable Net Income (DNI), 240
Distributions, 204, 240
   capital gain, 36
   deductions, 238
   deemed, 198
   due to death, 42
   from a Roth IRA, 84
   from Coverdell ESA or 529 plan, 63
   gain from property, 198
   mandatory, 41
   non-dividend, 36
   of stock and stock rights, 36
   of stock or stock rights, 198
   phase, 41
   qualified, 41
   Roth IRAs, 42
   to beneficiaries from an estate, 239
   to partners, 212
Distributive share, 209
Dividends, 35, 199
   capital gain distributions, 36
   distributions of stock and stock rights, 36
   money market funds, 36
   non-dividend distributions, 36
   ordinary, 35
   qualified, 35
   used to buy more stock, 35
Dollar-value method, 148
Domestic production activities, 91
Donor, 50, 183
Double taxation, 136
Doubt as to collectability, 300
Dual basis rules, 183
Dual-status alien. *See* Nonresident
Dues, 103, 158
Durable power of attorney, 288

Duties, 275
   for handling returns, 253

—E—

Earned income, 6
   credit, 121
Earnings, 29, 195
Easements, 49, 182
Economic risk of loss, 218, 219
Education benefits
   529 program, 73
Education related
   adjustments, 89
   benefits, 70
   credits, 117
Education savings bond program, 71
Educational assistance, 68
Educational savings account (ESA), 72
Educator expenses, 89, 103
Effect of partnership liabilities, 218
E-file, 260
Electing large partnership, 209
Election period, 224
Election to reduce basis, 191
Elective
   contributions, 225
   deferral, 223
   deferrals, 69
   deferrals, 401(k) plan, 229
Electronic deposit of employment taxes, 139
Electronic federal tax payment system, 139
Electronic filing identification number, 261
Electronic return originator (ERO), 261
Electronic signature requirements, 264
Eligible
   educational institution, 71, 118
   educator, 103
   employee, 222, 224
   individual, 85
   small business, 148, 165
Employee
   achievement awards, 67
   business expense reimbursements, 161
   compensation, 161
   contribution limits, 223, 225
   discounts, 69
Employer
   contribution limits, 223, 225
   deduction limits, 228
   identification number, 115, 136

retirement plan contributions, 164
Employment tax, 159, 247
Empowerment zone and renewal community employment credit, 166
Endowment contract proceeds, 74
Energy efficient home credit, 167
Enrolled
   actuaries, 272
   agents, 272
   retirement plan agents, 272
Enrollment, 273
Entertainment, 105, 158
   expenses, 105
Equitable relief, 300
Establishing a plan, 228
Estate, 127, 237
   tax, 127, 129, 305
Estimated tax, 20, 139
   corporations, 193
   estates, 238
   farmers, 245
Examination, 289
   of returns, 291
Exceptions to reporting OID, 35
Excess net passive income, 203
Exchange, 41, 216
   expenses, 186
   of property, 216
Excise taxes, 160
Excludable employees, 221
Exclusion
   for chronic illness, 75
   for terminal illness, 75
   from gross income, 63
   from partnership rules, 208
Executor, 129
Exempt organizations, 246
Exemption, 237
   deduction, 238
   for dependents, 25
   portability, 128
Expedited suspension, 284
Expenses, 36, 153, 160, 186
   interest, 154
   on leased property, 154
   paid by tenant, 37
   rental, 37, 154
Extension of time to pay, 300
Extraordinary dividends, 240

—F—

Failure to file form, 247
Failure to supply Social Security number, 295
Fair market value (FMV), 42, 129, 185
Family partnership, 208
Farmers, 18, 243
Fast track mediation, 293
Federal Insurance Contributions Act (FICA), 138
Federal unemployment, 114, 138
   Federal Unemployment Tax Act (FUTA), 139
Fellowships, 63, 70
Fiduciary, 273
   fiduciary accounting income (FAI), 239
Fifteen-year property, 177
Figuring tax, 201
Filing
   a claim or refund, 3
   aliens, 13
   deadlines, 1
   dependents, 6
   extensions, 5
   individuals, 6
   information, 1
   penalties, 203, 211
   requirements, 6
   taxes, 192
Filing status, 23
Final return, 235
Fire and liability insurance, 37
First in, first out (FIFO), 51, 148
First-time homebuyer credit, 123
Fiscal year, 144
Five-year deferral, 81
Five-year property, 177
Foreign
   earned income exclusion, 64, 75
   employer, 33
   housing, 75
   income, 30, 96
   tax credit, 126
   transactions, 202
Form
   2555, 75
   2555-EZ, 75
   8606, 80
   8949, 17, 58
Forming a partnership, 207
Foster care, 64
Fraud, 295
Fringe benefits, 31, 63, 164

Frivolous positions, 254
Frivolous tax submission, 295
Future interests, 128

—G—

Gain, 197
   from property distributions, 198
   on sale of main home, 65
   recognition, 56, 185
Gambling winnings, 43
General business credit, 165
General depreciation system, 176
General limit on IRA contributions, 78
General partner, 273
Generation-skipping transfer tax, 127
Gift, 63, 154
   expenses, 104
   splitting, 128
   tax, 127
Grantor, 239
   trust, 239
Gross
   estate, 129
   income, 6, 29, 63, 77
   profit, 54
   receipts test, 247
Group term life insurance, 31
Guaranteed payments, 215

—H—

Head of household, 23
Health flexible spending arrangement, 68
Health insurance plans, 163
Health plan, 31, 67, *See* Fringe benefits
Health reimbursement arrangement, 68
Health savings account, 68, 85, 164
Hearings, 282
High deductible health plan, 85
Highly compensated employees, 221
Holding period, 56
Holiday gifts, 68
Home acquisition debt, 97
Home equity debt, 97
Home mortgage interest, 98
Home office, 103, 108
Housing, 33
   allowance, 33, 63, 69

—I—

Improvements, 38, 46, 175, 176
Income, 194, 235
   averaging for farmers, 245
   in respect of a decedent, 42, 237
   limits, 125
   tax, 138, 305
Incompetence, 279
Independent contractor, 137
Indian employment credit, 167
Individual retirement arrangement, 40, 77
Informational returns, 139, 247
Inherited IRAs, 81
Inherited property, 50, 184
Injured spouse relief, 299
Innocent spouse relief, 4, 299
Insolvency, 42
Installment, 300
   agreement, 2, 301
   method, 54
   sale, 54
Insurance premium, 155
Intangible property, 45
Inter vivos trust, 239
Interest, 294, 295
   expense, 97, 154
   income, 34, 141, 209
   on series EE and I savings bonds, 63
   suspension of, 295
Intermediate service provider, 261
Internal Revenue
   agent, 291
   bulletin, 308
   code, 306
   manual, 308
   officer, 299
Inventory, 146, 148, 173, 212
Investment
   credit, 167, 203
   interest, 98
   property, 58
Involuntary conversion, 49, 183
IRA (individual retirement arrangement), 77
IRS e-file signature authorization, *264*, 265
IRS Examination Officer, 291
IRS notices, 307
Itemized deductions, 93
Items excluded from gross income, 63

—J—

Job search expenses, 103
Joint liability, *4*, 299
Joint return test, 25, 117
Joint tenancy with rights of survivorship, 50
Judicial, 306
Jury duty pay, 43

—L—

Last in, first out (LIFO), 148
    recapture tax, 203
Legal fees, 103
Legal reference, 307
Levy, 302
Liabilities, 186
Licenses, 103
Lien, 302
Life expectancy, 81
Life insurance
    employer provided, 31
    proceeds, 74
Lifetime Learning credit, 72, 118
Like-kind exchanges, 56, 184
Limitations
    on charitable deductions, 99
    on contributions and benefits, 223, 228
    on credits, 125
    on deductions, 79
    on losses, 39
Limited liability company, 136, 209
Limited partnership, 209
Liquidating distributions, 199, 214
Liquidation, 220
Livestock used in business, 244
Living trust, 239
Loans, 231
Local benefit taxes, 38
Lodging, 95, 107, 163
Long-term
    care coverage, 67
    gains and losses, 59
Loss, 53, 101, 240
    deductions, 236
    limitations, 169
Low income housing credit, 167
Low sulfur diesel fuel production credit, 167
Lump sum, 81

—M—

Main home, 63
Managerial act, 296
Mandatory distributions, 41
Marginal tax rate, 111
Marital deduction, 128, 130
Market method, 148
Married filing jointly, 24
Married filing separately, 24
Material participation, 170
Maximum capital gain rates, 58
Maximum exclusion, 65
Meals, 68, 105, 158
Medical
    care reimbursements, 164
    expense deductions, 236
    insurance premiums, 95
    savings accounts, 164
Medicare, 111
Members of religious orders, 33
Mid-month convention, 178
Mid-quarter convention, 178
Military and government disability pensions, 63, 70
Military pay, 33
Military uniforms, 104
Mine rescue team training credit, 167
Minimum funding requirement, 228
Miscellaneous adjustments, 77
Miscellaneous deductions, 93, 102
Modified Accelerated Cost Recovery System (MACRS), 176
Modified adjusted gross income (MAGI), 39, 170
    education savings bonds, 72
Money, 183
    market funds, 36
    purchase pension plan, 227
Mortgage insurance premiums, 98
Moving expenses, 86
Multiple businesses, 145
Multiple support agreement, 26
Municipal bond interest, 63
Mutual funds, 52

—N—

Negotiation of check, 259
Net capital gain, 58
Net estate tax due, 131
Net gains and losses, 59
Net investment income, 98

Net operating loss, 168
   corporations, 195
   deduction for estate, 238
Net short-term capital gain, 59
Net tax-exempt income, 241
New markets credit, 167
Ninety-day letter, 294
No additional cost services, 69
Nominees, 34
Non-accountable plan, 162
Non-business bad debt, 53
Non-business casualty and theft losses, 101
Nonconventional source fuel credit, 167
Nondeductible
   business expenses, 161
   contributions, 80, 98
   expenses, 87, 109
   taxes, 96
Non-dividend distributions, 36
Non-elective contributions, 225
Non-qualified annuity, 40
Nonrecourse liability, 219
Non-refundable, 124, 125
Nonresident, 93
Non-statutory stock option, 32
Non-taxable corporate distributions, 48, 182
Non-taxable stock dividends, 51, 184
Not rented for profit, 38
Notary, 277
Not-for-profit activities, 171
Notice and demand for payment, 302
Notice of federal tax lien, 302
Notification requirement, 224
Nursing home, 95

—O—

Occupational taxes, 103
Offer in compromise, 301
Office of professional responsibility, 271
Officer, 137, 273
Online provider, 261
Options, 52
Ordering rules, 84
Ordinary
   dividends, 35
   gain, 57, 173
Organizational costs, 153
Original issue discount (OID), 34
Orphan drug credit, 167
Other adjustments account, 204

Other adjustments to income, 90
Other income, 42
Out-of-pocket expenses in giving services, 100
Overpayments, 193
Ownership of stock, 194
Ownership test, 65

—P—

Paid-in-capital, 191
Partially nontaxable, 185
Partnership, 135, 207
   agreement, 207
   and S corporation income, 29
   distributions to partners, 212
   family, 208
   limited, 209
   return, 209
   rules, 208
   terminating, 209
Passenger vehicles, 179
Passive activity, 39, 61, 169
   limitations, 211
Paying income taxes, 192
Payment, 260, 266
Payroll taxes, 138
Penalties, 193, 279, 294
   failure to file form 990, 247
   filing, 211
   on early withdrawal of savings, 91
   S corporation filing, 203
   suspension, 295
Pension, 33, 40, 70
Per diem, 162
Percentage of completion method, 146
Performance as a notary, 277
Period of limitations, 260
Periods of nonqualified use, 66
Personal
   exemptions and dependents, 25
   holding company, 202
   property, 45
   property tax, 159
   representative, 50, 237
   service corporation, 189
   use property, 36
Petition for reinstatement, 284
Physical presence test, 76
Power of attorney, 287
   durable, 288
Practice before the IRS, 271

Practice of law, 278
Practitioner PIN, 265
Preference items, 112
Preparer considerations, 272
Preparer tax identification number, 272
Preparing returns, 253
Previously taxed income, 205
Principal residence, 67
Private activity bond, 64
Private letter rulings, 308
Procedures, 251
Profits, 195, 204
    interest, 217
Profit-sharing plan, 141, 227
Progressive tax, 111
Prohibited transactions, 82, 231
Promote effective tax administration, 302
Property
    business, 173
    changed from personal to business use, 51
    changed to rental use, 38
    distributions, 198
    exchanged for stock, 190
    or services, 37
    personal use, 58
    received as a gift, 50, 183
    received for services, 49, 182
    settlements, 64
    transfers, 50, 183, 198
    types, 173
Public assistance, 64
Punitive damages, 43
Purchased livestock, 244
Put option, 52

—Q—

Qualified
    charitable distribution, 81
    disaster relief payments, 64
    distributions, 41, 82
    dividends, 35
    domestic trust, 130
    education expenses, 72, 118
    expenses, 71, 89, 103, 120
    farm indebtedness, 43
    home, 97
    joint interest, 50
    joint venture, 135
    mortgage insurance, 98
    organization, 98
    plan, 226
    principal residence indebtedness, 42, 67
    production activities deduction, 91
    railroad track maintenance credit, 167
    real property business indebtedness, 42
    retirement plan, 40, 69
    small business stock, 60
    student loan, 90
    tuition program, 72
    U.S. savings bonds, 71
Qualifying
    child, 23, 26
    person, 23, 116
    relative, 23
    small business taxpayer, 147
    taxpayer, 147
    widow(er) with dependent child, 24
    work-related education, 104
Qualifying person test, 116

—R—

Raised livestock, 244
Real estate professional, 39
Real estate taxes, 159
Real property, 45, 180
Realized, 54, 185
    gains, 56
Reasonable cause, 296
Recapture rule, 89
Reckless conduct, 258
Recognition of exemption, 246
Recognized, 56
Reconciliation, 193
Recordkeeping, 151, 278
Records for cash contributions, 100
Recourse liability, 219
Recovered, 175
Recovery periods, 177
Redemption of stock, 199
Reduction for certain benefits, 71
Refund, 193, 253, 266
Refund check negotiation, 277
Refundable, 120
Rejected returns, 265
Related
    expenses, 37
    party, 56, 187
    person, 55, 194, 218
    property, 49, 183
Relationship test

EITC, 122
  exemption for dependent, 26
Renewable electricity, refined coal, and Indian coal production credit, 167
Rental
  expenses, 37, 154
  income, 36
  of home, 66
  real estate professional exception, 170
Renting part of property, 38
Rents from personal property, 37
Repairs, 38, 46, 176
Repayment, 123
  of income aid payment, 104
Reporting, 114
  agent, 261
  gains and losses, 56
  requirements, 232
Representation, 251
  before the IRS, 287
Required beginning date, 41, 81
Required minimum distribution, 41, 81
Required tax year, 144
  partnerships, 210
Requirements for trust tax returns, 243
Requirements for written advice, 277
Research expenses, 104
Residency test, 26, 122
Residential rental property, 177
Restricted property, 31
  83(b) election, 31
Restrictions, 275
Retail method, 149
Retained life estate, 129
Retirement plans, 40
  for businesses, 221
Return of capital, 51, 184
Return preparers, 253
Returning records, 264
Returns, 283
Revenue
  procedures, 306
  rulings, 306
Reversionary interest, 129
Revocable, 129
Rollover, 40, 230
Roth IRAs, 42, 82
  conversions, 83
Royalties, 202, 209
Rules to figure gain or loss, 55

Rural mail carrier, 104

—S—

S corporation, 139, 202
Safeguarding taxpayer information, 259
Salary reduction simplified employee pension, 223
Sale of property, 53, 216
Sales caused by weather-related conditions, 244
Sales tax, 160
Sanctions, 279
Savers credit, 126
Savings incentive match plan for employees (SIMPLE), 224
Schedule
  A, 17, 94
  C, 17, 29, 37
  D, 17, 58
  E, 17, 36
  F, 18, 243
  H, 114
  R, 17
Scholarships, 63, 70
Section 1202 exclusion, 60
Section 121 exclusion, 65
Section 1244 small business stock, 60
Securities, 51, 184
Security deposits, 37
Self-employed, 114
  health insurance, 86, 156
Self-employment
  income, 29
  tax, 137, 159
Self-select PIN, 264
SEP IRA, 222
Separation of liability relief, 299
Series of substantially equal periodic payments, 230
Service-connected disability, 70
Services rendered, 190
Settlement fees, 47, 180
Seven-year property, 177
Severance pay, 30
Shareholder earnings and profits, 195
Short tax year, 93
Short-term, 56
  gains and losses, 59
Sick pay, 30
Signature authority, 287
Similar property, 49
Simple trust, 239
Simplified dollar-value method, 148

Simplified employee pensions (SEP), 222
Single, 23
Single life table, 81
Small business corporation, 60
Small partnership, 290
Small tax case procedure, 294
Social Security
    benefits, 40, 63
    taxes, 114
Software developer, 261
Sole proprietor, 17, 135
Solicitation, 276
Special deductions, 199
Special depreciation allowance, 177
Special provisions, 194
Special rules for certain employees
    clergy, 33
    foreign employer, 33
    members of religious orders, 33
    military pay, 33
Specialized returns, 235
Specific identification method, 148
Specific individuals, 98
Sport utility vehicle, 179
Spousal IRA limit, 78
Standard deductions, 93
Standard mileage rate, 108
Standard of proof, 283
Statute of limitations, 289
Statutory
    employees, 137
    stock option, 32
Step-up, 184
Stock, 51, 184
    non-statutory, 32
    options, 32
    ownership, 190, 202
    property exchanged for, 190
    redemption, 199
    statutory, 32
Stock options, 52
Straight-line depreciation method, 176
Streamlined installment agreement, 2, 301
Student loan, 42, 90
Subsequent transactions, 51
Substantial authority, 254
Substantiation requirements, 121
Summary adjudication, 283
Support test, 26
Supporting documentation, 260

Suspension, 284
Suspension of interest and penalties, 295

—T—

Tangible property, 45, 174
Tax
    advisors, 278
    brackets, 111
    calculations, 111
    credits, 111
    generation-skipping transfer, 127
    heavy highway vehicle, 160
    home, 75, 106
    information authorization, 288
    law, 305, 306
    matters partner, 290
    on early distributions, 230
    on excess contributions, 79
    on investment income of certain children, 113
    on prohibited transaction, 232
    preference items, 112
    preparation fees, 108
    regulations, 306
    shelter, 254
    withholding and estimated tax, 20
    withholding and reporting, 137
    year, 144
Taxable
    compensation, 77
    estate, 129
    income, 111, 241
    interest, 34
    stock dividends, 240
Taxes, 96, 103, 111, 138, 159, 192
Taxpayer
    advocate service, 290
    identification number, 141
    rights, 290
    supporting documentation, 260
Technical advice memorandum, 308
TEFRA status, 290
Temporary work location, 108
Tenants
    by the entirety, 50
    with rights of survivorship, 50
Tentative
    estate tax, 130
    tax base, 130
Terminating a partnership, 209
Termination of election, 204

Test for deducting pay, 161
Testamentary trust, 239
Theft, 48, 101, 158, 238
Third party designee, 289
Thirty-day letter, 293
Time test, 86
Tip income, 32
Tools used in work, 104
Total net gain or loss, 59
Total tax, 111
Traditional IRAs, 77
Transactions, 140, 191, 215
Transfers of property, 198
Transit pass, 69
Transmitter, 261
Transportation, 31, 69, 95
Travel expenses, 105
Treasury regulations, 306
Trust, 136, 239
Trustee, 239
Tuition and fees deduction, 90
Twenty-year property, 177
Two percent limit, 102

—U—

Uncollected rent, 38
Understatement of liability, 257
Unearned income, 6
Unemployment, 114
    benefits, 43
Unified credit, 127
Uniform capitalization rules, 150
Uniforms, 104
Union dues, 104
Unrealized receivables and inventory, 211
Unreasonable
    positions, 258
    rents, 198
    salaries, 198
Unreimbursed
    employee expenses, 102
    employee local transportation and lodging, 107
    employee meals, 105
    employee travel expenses, 105
    entertainment expenses, 105
Unrelated business taxable income, 247
Use test, 65

—V—

Vacant rental property, 38
Veterans (VA) benefits, 63
Viatical settlement, 75
Violations subject to sanction, 280

—W—

W-9, 141
Wages, 29
    not paid in money, 162
Wash sale, 52
Welfare, 64
Willful or reckless conduct, 258
Withholding, 20, 114, 137
Work clothes, 104
Work opportunity credit, 167
Workers' compensation, 63, 73
Work-related education, 104
Work-related expenses, 117
Worthless securities, 53
Written advice, 277
Written protest, 293

CPSIA information can be obtained
at www.ICGtesting.com
Printed in the USA
LVOW03s1033120316
478875LV00002B/2/P